Pierre Bourdieu and Literacy Education

Edited by
James Albright
National Institute of Education,
Singapore
and Allan Luke
Queensland University of
Technology, Australia

Routledge
Taylor & Francis Group

NEW YORK AND LONDON

First published 2008
by Routledge
270 Madison Ave, New York, NY 10016

Simultaneously published in the UK
by Routledge
2 Park Square, Milton Park, Abingdon, Oxon OX14 4RN

This edition first published in paperback in 2008

*Routledge is an imprint of the Taylor & Francis Group,
an informa business*

© 2008 Taylor & Francis

Typeset in Baskerville by
RefineCatch Limited, Bungay, Suffolk
Printed and bound in the United States of America on acid-free
paper by Edwards Brothers, Inc.

Library of Congress Cataloging-in-Publication Data
Pierre Bourdieu and literacy education / editors James Albright and
Allan Luke.
p. cm.
Includes bibliographical references and index.
ISBN 978-0-8058-5687-3 (hardback : alk. paper)—ISBN 978-0-203-93750-1
(e-book) 1. Literacy—Social aspects. 2. Bourdieu, Pierre,
1930-2002. I. Albright, James. II. Luke, Allan.
LC149.P54 2008
302.2′244—dc22
2007025261

ISBN10: 0-805-85687-0 (hbk)
ISBN10: 0-415-99589-2 (pbk)
ISBN10: 0-203-93750-3 (ebk)

ISBN13: 978-0-805-85687-3 (hbk)
ISBN13: 978-0-415-99589-4 (pbk)
ISBN13: 978-0-203-93750-1 (ebk)

Contents

Illustrations

Figures

Tables

Preface

James Albright and Allan Luke

This book is a generative set of theoretical, narrative, empirical, and practical applications of Bourdieusian concepts to and around the field of language and literacy education. It offers three major clusters of work: rethinkings of the doxa of the social fields of language and literacy education (Albright, Kramsch, Heller, Luke); explorations of alternative objectifications of educational fields forming around cultural and linguistic minorities, new media and technologies (Uhlmann, Dressman and Wilder, Hill, Wong and Grant); and studies on the formation of the literate habitus in homes and classrooms, curriculum and schooling (Pahl, Goldstein, Rowsell, Zacher, Curry, Bracewell and Witte). We conclude with three essays on future theoretical, policy and practical directions (Albright, Luke, Collins). The volume brings together scholars who have focused their work on Bourdieu and social theoretic approaches to literacy over a period of time with a current generation of critical scholars, teacher educators, and researchers who have turned to Bourdieu to address and redress what they perceive as systematic inequities that are generated by the schools, their affiliated language-in-education policies, and their everyday practices.

Our interest here is in new studies, new combinatory theoretical models that use Bourdieu as a departure or arrival point, and renewing the application of Bourdieu's ideas to the study of those students, communities, and systems that historically have been marginalized by mainstream schooling. The theme of how to alter and shift the flows of capital in the social fields of educational institutions runs across these authors' works. In commissioning and editing these pieces, we have avoided a systematic overview of Bourdieu's model and theories and how these might apply to language, literacy, and education. This has been done capably over the past two decades in accessible and cited work (e.g., Collins, 1993; Cook-Gumperz, 1986; Grenfell and James, 1998; Luke, 1996; Norton, 1996). That work has applied Bourdieu's sociology to the face-to-face formation of habitus, the operations of state and schooling as social fields, resultant differential formations of capital, and attendant reproductive effects upon particular communities and cultures.

There are several reading pathways through this collection. Those who are new to Bourdieu's work may wish to read across the chapters as a series of narratives and investigations of local sites, considering the relevance of each study and then returning to the primary texts. For those who have worked with Bourdieu previously, the theoretical reconsiderations in the first section will set the stage for the subsequent studies. For readers interested in pursuing the application of a specific Bourdieusian concept, we suggest that you work from the index back to the individual chapters. We have focused the index on key theoretical terms.

References

Collins, J. (1993) Determination and contradiction: an appreciation and critique of the work of Pierre Bourdieu on language and education. In C. Calhoun, E. LiPuma and M. Postone (eds), *Bourdieu: Critical Perspectives*. Chicago: University of Chicago Press, 116–38.

Cook-Gumperz, J. (ed.) (1986) *The Social Construction of Literacy*. Cambridge, UK: Cambridge University Press.

Grenfell, M. and James, D. (1988). *Bourdieu and Education*. London: Falmer Press.

Luke, A. (1996) Genres of power: literacy education and the production of capital. In R. Hasan and G. Williams (eds), *Literacy in Society*. London: Longman, 308–38.

Norton, B. (2000). *Identity and Language Learning*. London: Longman.

Acknowledgments

We would like to thank the authors and our colleagues for their unstinting support: Naomi Silverman, James Ladwig, Carmen Luke, Courtney Cazden, Phil Graham, and Janet Miller. This volume benefited from the expert editorial assistance of Lin Ai-Leen and Mary Sefranek. And thanks to our music teacher, Dr Axe.

Part I

Objectifying the field

Chapter 1

Introduction

Renewing the cultural politics of literacy education

James Albright and Allan Luke

Literacy education is indeed at a historical crossroads. If we are to take educational policymakers, politicians and the media at their word, it is the same old great debate replayed over and over again: declining standards, loss of the literary canon, troubled and unruly students, irresponsible parents and overly permissive teachers. These, we are told yet again, can be fixed by marketization of schools, increased testing, a return to the basics of reading and writing, better teachers, and a more disciplined approach to child-rearing, education and schooling. In this way, a neoliberal focus on tightened accountabilities and steering mechanisms blends seamlessly with a neoconservative educational fundamentalism: economic and bureaucratic rationalism in the delivery of the basics. This is the public policy doxa of literacy education.

Yet the social facts of the matter speak with a compeling and different simplicity: the continued and increased impacts of socioeconomic disparity, exclusion and marginalization of cultural and linguistic minorities, and the inability of these same systems to engage with and address the major social and cultural, technological and economic shifts in nations, communities and emergent transnational corporate spheres of influence. Further, we know that a decade of this particular policy approach has increased global and local disparities between children of rich and poor.

Bourdieu's trenchant vocabulary for talking about the systems of unequal and inequitable exchange in language and pedagogy, material and symbolic resources is more relevant than ever. From the French postwar system that he and Claire Kramsch (Ch. 3) experienced, to the worlds of inner-city students and migrants described here (Hill, Ch. 8; Grant and Wong, Ch. 9; Pahl, Ch. 10; Zacher, Ch. 13; Curry, Ch. 14), to Canadian workers described by Heller (Ch. 4), to those linguistic minorities subjugated by hegemonic monolingualism (Uhlmann, Ch. 6; Goldstein, Ch. 11)—the matter still is one of reproduction and counter-reproduction. As these chapters show, this is not a matter of an iron-cage structuralism of class, gender, and cultural reproduction. It is a complex system of generational and intergenerational exchanges of capital, the ongoing interplay of positions and position-taking in relation to the structuring fields of school, workplace, civic, and media cultures.

Concurrently, the digitalization of text production has altered what counts as literacy in many ways, and the use of online representational forms is supplanting, augmenting, and appropriating print per se, altering its author/reader relations of exchange (Pahl, Ch. 10; Rowsell, Ch. 12; Dressman and Wilder, Ch. 7). This is to say nothing of the impact of cinema, video, and online texts on emergent claims about what might influence and reconstitute the canonical elements of the quality children's literature, academic study, and class-based literary taste. That is, the developmental sequences and systems of exchange that are hallmarks of the old literacy are being disrupted by convergence and crossover with the new literacies, even as schools and systems offer bare-bones policy and curricular attempts to incorporate new modes of representation and forms of life.

We return to questions of habitus, capital, social field, and exchange not simply as sociologists and socialists seeking a golden lining to social theory, but rather as researchers and teacher educators seeking to know how Bourdieusian frames can enable us to do schools, pedagogy, curriculum, and all this affiliated work differently, in normative social directions that are committed to the egalitarianism and equity that Bourdieu professed in *Acts of Resistance* (1998).

Two decades on, researchers and teacher educators work from many stereotypes about Pierre Bourdieu's contributions to the field of education. One assumption is that Bourdieu's explanation of class reproduction in schooling is a structuralist determinism that takes the forces of primary socialization as given and thereby subjugates the human agency and potential of teachers and students. Such a view, further, does not map handily onto close analyses of discourse interactions and cultural dynamics of schools and classrooms that stress the fractures and gaps in classroom life, the idiosyncratic turns of discourse, and the very possibilities of the remaking of identity, capital, and social relations explored in this volume.

A second assumption is that Bourdieu's descriptivist science does not set the generative grounds or programmatic agendas for social movements and political actions. These beliefs are in part attributable to the expanse of Bourdieu's corpus, and indeed its limited systematic application to literacy education to date (for excellent applications to education more generally, see Ladwig, 1996, and recent editions of the *British Journal of Sociology of Education*, especially vol. 25, issue 4, 2004). If one's sole engagement were a graduate school encounter with *Reproduction in Education, Society and Culture* (Bourdieu and Passeron, 1990), such a claim about the primacy of class-based socialization and the "black box" model of reproduction might seem warranted. Yet Bourdieu built a body of work that can be taken as a set of generative sociological models and principles, loosely coupled and reiterated as he moved to and from the study of pre-modern to modern and postmodern cultures—from high art to popular culture, from the formation of science and the academy to mass media, from reflections on dialectical to idealist philosophies, from consideration of gender identities to class relations—landing squarely at a pitched engagement with contemporary social issues confronting the state. It is a rich, dense, and at times elusive, corpus that, interestingly, has stayed one step ahead of a secondary literature that has attempted to canonize, critique, and encapsulate it. We take it as something other than the classical unified theory of continental philosophy. Rather Bourdieu's writing unfolds—from the early anthropological work on the Kabyle to the analysis of postwar French society and academy, to the later critical commentaries on the neoliberal state—as a species of habitus itself: structured and structuring, durable, generative, and in progress. The matter now is not to consolidate it or find its "proper" applications around what he might have meant, but to generate a new wave of critical self-objectifications, expansions, disruptions, models, and reconstructions.

Following on from Jenny Cook-Gumperz's (1986) landmark, *The Social Construction of Literacy*, Bourdieu's work was incorporated into symbolic interactionist and interactional sociolinguistic work with a principal focus on the concept of literacy as cultural capital. This is not surprising, since Bourdieu's entrée to Anglo-American education through M. F. D. Young's *Knowledge and Control* (1971), the prototypical statement on the then "new" sociology of education. That volume brought together elements of symbolic interactionism, structural sociology and anthropology, and historical materialist theory, featuring remarkable work by Bourdieu, Basil Bernstein, Robin Horton, Ioan Davies, and others. In "Systems of education and systems of thought," first published in 1967, Bourdieu outlined his view of the relationship of pedagogy and linguistic habitus:

> all teaching practices implicitly furnish a model of the "right" mode of intellectual activity; for example, the very nature of the tests set (ranging from the composition, based on the technique of "development", which is the predominant form in most arts examination, to the "brief account" required in advanced science examinations, the type of rhetorical and linguistic qualities required and the value attached to these qualities, the relative importance given to written papers and oral examinations, and the qualities required in both instances, tend to encourage a certain attitude towards the use of language—sparing or prodigal, casual or ceremonious, complacent or restrained. In this way the canons governing school work proper, in composition or exposition, may continue to govern writings apparently freed from the disciplines of the school—newspaper articles, public lectures, summary reports and works of scholarship.
>
> (1971: 201)

Yet the subsequent uptake of his concept of cultural capital in the American literature often neglected Bourdieu's concepts of social and intellectual field, social class, and combinatory models of capital. This had the effect of focusing attention on the value of literacy in the general field of educational exchange without explicating the practices and institutional economies wherein that exchange occurred. This was remediated in part by a stronger emphasis in the 1990s on notions of habitus in an attempt to explain minority and lower patterns of socioeconomic underachievement. Though not explicitly drawing from Bourdieu, James Gee's (1991) arguments around the educational primacy of "primary discourses" of early cultural socialization refocused attention on the interaction of habitus with the social field of the school. It is extended in promising work that begins to track the longitudinal traverse of human subjects and capital across volatile social fields of education, through work, everyday life, civic participation, and consumption (e.g., Bullen and Kenway, 2005).

With the consolidation of neoliberal discourses and "third way" governance into a new corporatist model of education in recent years, Bourdieu's work has been selectively mined once again. The concept of social capital now sits centrally within mainstream educational and social policy, with ubiquitous calls for the rebuilding of social infrastructure, networks, institutions, and relations, many of which have been systematically dismantled by the state and the new corporate political economies. Hence, in the discourses of educational policy formation, the concept of symbolic capital—like that of cultural capital before—has been wrenched from a systematic sociological analysis of the complexities of the new political economies of education, corporation, and social life. The enlistment of Bourdieusian ideas in a corporatist agenda is, at the least, ironic.

A great deal has changed since 1968, since Bourdieu and his academic generation did their fieldwork in North Africa, since they made their political and intellectual choices in 1968, and since the rise and consolidation of the corporate, neoliberal state. The ongoing social and political conflict in France underlines the contradictions of opposition to the neofeudal agenda of multinational corporations (see Graham and Luke, 2005), while dealing with the fact that this self-same opposition may lend itself to the further economic and political disenfranchisement of migrant and minority populations in France, across the European Union, North America, Australasia, and elsewhere.

The clearest outline of Bourdieu's later politics can be found in an extended dialogue he had with the installation artist Hans Haacke (Bourdieu and Haacke, 1995). Haacke earned an international reputation for his art, which challenges the censorship of artists in the United States, corporate influence in art, the resurgent Right in North America and Europe, and political and social amnesia in general. In their dialogue, Haacke and Bourdieu make clear comparisons between their various projects over the years. They discuss the problems of defending artists, writers and scholars from corporate and governmental attacks to their relative autonomy. Further, they analyze the "increasingly subtle strategies of business to subordinate and seduce artists and scholars . . . with the extraordinary result that citizens still finance the arts and sciences through tax exemptions . . . an extremely perverse mechanism which operates in such a way that we contribute to our own mystification" (pp. 15, 16).

Bourdieu and Haacke develop a generalized political strategy based on an analysis of the symbolic strategies of other actors in the field of power. They suggest that the powerful and sophisticated symbolic weapons of the Right have unarmed those who oppose material and symbolic forms of domination. Bourdieu praises Haacke for the efficacy of his critical actions. Haacke describes his art as not only taking a position but also creating a productive provocation for his viewers (p. 21).

Bourdieu echoes Haacke's characterization of public forums as a battlefield that should not be abandoned: "We can and must intervene in the world of politics, but with our own means and ends. Paradoxically, it is the name of everything that assures the autonomy of their universe that artists, writers, or scholars can intervene in today's struggles" (p. 29). Haacke rejoins: "The evacuation of the political is tantamount to inviting whoever wants to occupy the vacuum that's left behind" (p. 39). What is needed is sociological explanation for how economic values are inscribed in symbolic ones under fast capitalism.

Bourdieu and Haacke analyze the Right's ascendancy through its politics of damnation (pp. 50–2). It has been able to name reality and, consequently, tell the story. Discourse violence has dominated the field of power by constructing an ideological climate (doxa) that requires considerable effort to combat. They trace the history of some "epistemic individuals and organizations" who have positioned themselves as representatives. They articulate an ethic for a counter politics. Haacke states: "A democratic society must promote critical thinking, including a constant critique of itself. Without it, democracy will not survive" (p. 54). Most troubling, they note, is the Right's positioning of itself as defender of the West and as upholder of absolute values against multiculturalism and relativism. Further, they observe that the Right is well networked in a "veritable international conservative movement, with its networks, its journals, its foundations and its associations" (p. 67).

Bourdieu and Haacke concur that "research activities in art as well as science need the state to exist" (p. 69). The first order of business is the defense of public spaces that can only be paradoxically guaranteed by the state. The threat to privatize must be resisted in order for artists, writers, and scholars to use against the state the freedom that the state assures them: "They must work simultaneously, without scruples or a guilty conscience, to increase the state's involvement as well as their vigilance in relation to the state's influence . . . A truly critical form of thought should begin with a critique of the more or less unconscious economic and social basis for critical thought in mind" (pp. 72, 73).

There is indeed a need to disrupt or denaturalize symbolic social relations. Complicated fields with relative autonomy and complex intersections with other fields create possible openings for political action for those with the knowledge and project "to take advantage of the 'game' that social structures always entail" (p. 82). This is the action of "bad subjects," who should work to identify and construct other bad subjects. Haacke argues that the attempts to suppress his work show that the Right recognizes that there is a "market" of those who are open to re-examining the social positions they hold. He argues that art institutions, such as schools, are places of education, "branches of the consciousness industry," and thus places of political contestation.

Haacke describes conservatives as having an advantage in resources and organization: "They use a language which has the air of the 'normal' " (p. 105). He charges the Left with "lacking a sense of the practical" and using "an esoteric language" (p. 105). Bourdieu counters that the aesthetic has a language that requires knowledge of art history and logic. Haacke agrees but states that he has created pieces to address his peers and others in a wider audience. They agree that what is needed is to produce messages at several levels. Haacke states: "If one pays attention to the forms and language that are accessible to an uninitiated public, one can discover things that could enrich the esoteric repertoire" (p. 107). He speculates that advertising provides lessons in techniques and strategies of communication that are open to subversion. Bourdieu suggests that collaborations of researchers, artists, dramatists, and communications specialists might be mobilized to confront conservative symbolic forces.

Making a pointed reference to Brecht (1964), Haacke insists that pleasure must be mobilized in this effort. Bourdieu and Haacke propose intellectual acts that are more concerned with *the moment of performance*, which would be more effective in reaching audiences who are able to take an active role in civic life, and who take pleasure in being taken seriously. Haacke paraphrases Brecht:

> In his 1935 essay about the "Five Difficulties in Writing the Truth" he offered a list of what it takes to write the truth: the courage to write it, the intelligence to recognize it, the art to use it as a weapon, the practical sense for the choice of those who could make use of it most effectively, and the cunning to spread it widely.
>
> (Bourdieu and Haacke, 1995: 110)

They conclude their conversation with an agreement for a *Realpolitik* that would not be stymied by the common fear in the Left regarding the co-option of its ideas: "The most profound effect in the end is total co-option" (p. 111).

In Anglo-American social sciences, appreciation of Bourdieu's sociology has been evolving over the last four decades. Part of the initial difficulty with appropriating his thought may have been a result of readings constrained by differences between French and Anglo-American academic worlds. These differences have led to particularist readings of Bourdieu's various studies; time has allowed for a more generative reading. The loss of continuity in his evolving social theory has been a result of the uneven translation of his work. The slotting of his philosophical stance has been confusing and oddly poignant, considering his goal to steer a middle course between dominant theoretical paradigms. Bourdieu's language is seen as an obstacle. Like other French social theorists read in Anglo-American academia, he has fought against the ideology of clarity through a strategic use of language to position and provoke his peers, disrupting classifications, distributions, and power relations.

Yet in his earlier theoretical work, he describes the struggle at hand:

> Each state of the social world is thus no more than a temporary equilibrium, a moment in the dynamics through which the adjustment between disruptive and incorporated or institutionalised classifications are constantly broken and restored. The struggle which is the very principle of the distributions is inextricably a struggle to appropriate rare goods and a struggle to impose the legitimate way of perceiving the power relations manifested by the distributions, a representation which, through its own efficacy, can help to perpetuate or subvert these social relations. Classification, and the very notion of social class, would not be such a decisive stake in the struggle (among the classes) if they did not contribute to the existence of the social classes, enhancing the efficacy of the objective mechanisms that determine the distribution and ensure their reproduction, by adding to them the consent of the minds which they structure.
>
> (Bourdieu and Wacquant, 1992: 141)

Given the recurrent patterns of failure of cultural and linguistic minorities in mainstream educational systems, there is an urgent need to explore and recover alternative models of literacy education. This is doubly the case in those policy and legislative environments that are busily de-legitimating sociological inquiry as a proper "science" of literacy and education. At the same time, this volume is an attempt to go beyond the claim that literacy is fundamentally an ideological act, an act of symbolic violence upon the working class or culturally different habitus. Across this volume, the crucial issues are about reforming literacy—and being clear and transparent about its objectification and ideological purposes, and about the preferred kinds of habitus, subjectivity, and action it is to entail. More than ever, we need a strong, defensible social science that names and explicates, that "re-objectifies" the systems of classification that are taken as natural and organic, scientific and logical in teachers' and students' everyday lives.

The chapters that follow reveal openings for rethinking and moving beyond binary accounts of agency and reproduction in education. They exemplify how his concepts can be productively used to rethink literacy education in all its various manifestations as a field of practice. Adopting a strongly theorized Bourdieusian stance within our field is a strategic move. It is a continuing challenge to researchers and teachers to objectify and reflexively question the relations of class, exploitation, and inequality. Importantly, Bourdieu's analytical framework, as suggested by his dialogue with Haacke and his more recent critiques of neoliberalism as the "new planetary vulgate" (Bourdieu and Wacquant, 2001), may provide and revive a cultural politics that would make a difference in the field of literacy education, which is being pushed by the organized forces he identified into a legislated and doxic allergy to theory, especially theory that sheds light once again on the principal role of state, school, and corporation in the destructive, unequal, and symbolically violent construction of literacy in the interests of dominant classes and the new corporate order.

References

Brecht, B. (1964) *Brecht on Theatre: The Development of an Aesthetic* (J. Willett, ed. and trans.). Stanford, CA: Stanford University Press.

Bourdieu, P. (1998) *Acts of Resistance* (R. Nice, trans.). Cambridge, UK: Polity Press.

Bourdieu, P. (1971) Systems of education and systems of thought. In M. F. D. Young (ed.), *Knowledge and Control*. London: Macmillan, 189–207.

Bourdieu, P. and Haacke, H. (1995). *Free Exchange*. Stanford, CA: Stanford University Press.

Bourdieu, P. and Passeron, J. C. (1990) *Reproduction in Education, Society and Culture* (2nd edn). Beverley Hills, CA: Sage.

Bourdieu, P. and Wacquant, L. (1992) *An Invitation to Reflexive Sociology*. Chicago: Chicago University Press.

Bourdieu, P. and Wacquant, L. (2001) Neoliberal newspeak: notes on the new planetary vulgate. *Radical Philosophy*, 108, 1–6.

Bullen, E. and Kenway, J. (2005) Bourdieu, subcultural capital and risky girlhood. *Theory and Research in Education*, 3, 47–61.

Cook-Gumperz, J. (ed.) (1986) *The Social Construction of Literacy*. Cambridge, UK: Cambridge University Press.

Gee, J. P. (1991). *Social Linguistics and Literacies*. London: Falmer Press.

Graham, P. and Luke, A. (2005) The language of neofeudal corporatism and the war on Iraq. *Language and Politics*, 4(1), 11–39.

Ladwig, J. (1996) *Academic Distinctions*. London: Routledge.

Young, M. F. D. (ed.) (1971) *Knowledge and Control*. London: Macmillan.

Chapter 2

Problematics and generative possibilities

James Albright

> Bourdieu's work is so central now because the real world has changed to a point at which it has come to agree with Bourdieu's world. And this cannot be said of the work of many other social theorists.
>
> (Lash, 1993: 132)

Presenting some of the varied readings of Pierre Bourdieu's work, I will try to show how the utility of Bourdieusian research and theorizing has not been fully appreciated. I outline and question critiques of Bourdieu's reflexive sociology, especially the assertion that it is ultimately a reproductionist stance, not able to account for agency and change. Within this survey I focus on the contribution his sociology has made to various fields of academic inquiry, including literacy education. I will attempt to make the case that Bourdieu's evolving research and theorizing is more generative than may have been allowed by some and within it there are productive opportunities to extend his work in literacy research and practice. Here I focus on theorizing and research with fully developed Bourdieusian frameworks. Many more have appropriated piecemeal, selected concepts; for example, taking up notions of capital and ignoring habitus and field. Tracing the trajectory of uses and critiques of Bourdieu's reflexive sociology may be helpful in appreciating the possibilities it brings to educational research and theorizing.

There is little question that Pierre Bourdieu occupies a significant position in sociology (Brown and Szeman, 2000; Calhoun et al., 1993; Harker et al., 1990; Lane, 2000; Shusterman, 1999; Swartz, 1997; Webb et al., 2002). Bourdieu assumed all social practices are political, enacting contested relations of power. His project attempted to overcome the bedeviling binarisms in social theorizing and research between subjectivism and objectivism, and voluntarism and determinism, uniting empirical research and social theory. Along with the theoretical tools of *habitus, capital,* and *field*, he is credited with contributing to the notion of *structuration*—social life as mutually constructed through interactions of structures, dispositions, and actions, such that actors shape and are shaped by social practice (Bourdieu, 1977: 77, 95).

It is generally acknowledged that Bourdieu's work over the past several decades contributed significantly to theorizing and practice in the social sciences. Bourdieu's reflexive sociology positions the research/researcher in academic fields, engaging in struggles for capital and working toward some articulated or, more often, unarticulated political project. Reflexivity is a condition of any social theory attempting to overcome the dualisms characteristic of modern social theory in order to better describe social patterns of inequality and domination. A sociology that does not help subjects to grasp the meaning of their practices is not worth the trouble. At the very least, Bourdieu may be read as an emancipatory project concerned with throwing light on social and cultural reproduction through processes of misrepresentation in the construction and transmission of knowledge, institutionalization of distinctions, and uses of symbolic violence.

Bourdieu's reception in American sociology

Bourdieu's difficult transition from Continental social science to American social research and theorizing is well documented. While Habermas, Lyotard, Derrida, Foucault, and Baudrillard were more readily translated and productively read, the uneven reception of Bourdieu in American academic fields has, until recently, limited his full potential for research and practice.

One difficulty of appropriating Bourdieusian social analysis is an effect of translation tearing his works "from their original intellectual contexts and insert[ing] them into new ones" (Postone et al., 1993: 7; Simeoni, 2000: 77). Yet others argue, "[I]t is only by understanding the specificity of field of French higher education in the 1960s, for example, we can decide on what conditions, at the price of what modifications, Bourdieu's conclusions regarding education, class and culture might be relevant to our own national experience and historical contexts" (Lane, 2000: 5). A related difficulty has been that the sequential development of his intellectual production was lost. His studies and interviews, as translations for American readers, became available in English as a jumble rather than as an ongoing conversation. Connected to these difficulties associated with the translation and ordering of Bourdieu's intellectual production is that his conscious positioning within Continental sociology is unappreciated. Much of his language is intentionally provocative, meant to create distinctions between other European scholars and his work.

Bourdieu was not unaware of this problem and attempted to clarify his work to American audiences (Bourdieu, 1993, 1999; Bourdieu and Wacquant, 1992). He contended that his "entire scientific enterprise [was] indeed based on the belief that the deepest logic of the social world can be grasped only if one plunges into the particularity of an empirical reality, historically located and dated, but with the objective of constructing it as a 'special case of what is possible,' as Bachelard puts it, that is, as an exemplary case in a finite world of possible configurations" (Bourdieu, 1998: 2). This put him in conflict with Levi-Straussian structuralist positions and Sartrian existentialist ones; his early training in empirical sociological methodologies in the United States placed him in conflict with the more functionalist perspective dominant in his own country. Interestingly, his adoption of language as social action theorizing and the vocabulary of economic maximization set him at odds with French social science. His connection to American theorizing has been generally overlooked. Again, Bourdieu wrote about "particularist" readings of his work:

> My work, and especially *Distinction*, is particularly exposed to such a reading. Its theoretical model is not embellished with all the marks by which one usually recognizes "grand theory," such as lack of any reference to some empirical reality. The notions of social space, symbolic space, or social class are never studied in and for themselves; rather, they are tested through research in which the theoretical and empirical are insepara- ble and which mobilizes methods of observation and measurement— quantitative and qualitative, statistical and case, macro-sociological and micro-sociological (all of which are meaningless oppositions)—for the purpose of studying an object well defined in space and time, that is French society in the 1970s. The report of this research does not appear in the language to which certain sociologists, especially Americans, have accustomed us and whose appearance of universality is due only to the imprecision of a vocabulary hardly distinguishable from everyday use.
>
> (Bourdieu, 1998: 1, 2)

Consequently, those sympathetic to Bourdieu insist American readers should attend to Bourdieu's theoretical side, without which "the critical moments of his empirical works should be lost" (Postone et al., 1993: 10).

Loic Wacquant notes that this "fragmentation of readings" is partially a result of how academic disciplines are policed in American universities. Bourdieu wrote in the wider field of French social science. In the American academy, separate works are read within the specific fields of the arts, socio- logy, cultural studies, and education and rarely as a set (Postone et al., 1993). Many Continental theorists entered American scholarship as more speculative and philosophical thinkers, enabling them to slip more easily over disciplinary borders. Bourdieu's "middle-theorizing," it can be argued, made his work more open to these "particularist readings." Further, American responses to Bourdieu's work often focused on determining his sociological antecedents and pinning him down to one particular school of theorizing. The result of this speculation linked and then dismissed Bourdieu's reflexive sociology with any number of conflicting philosophical positions. Webb and colleagues (2002) ascribe this response to Bourdieu's "eclecticism," discussing his connection to Marx, Wittgenstein, Nietzsche, and Pascal.

Dreyfus and Rabinow (1993) and LiPuma (1993) illustrate how Bourdieu can be read from opposite stances. The first critiques Bourdieu from a micro perspective; the second comes from a more macro stance to social analysis.

Each makes recommendations situating Bourdieu closer to their own perspective. In an analysis linking Bourdieu's work to the philosophical speculations of Heidegger, Wittgenstein, and Merleau-Ponty, Dreyfus and Rabinow praise it as being "one of the most analytically powerful and heuristically promising approaches to human reality on the current scene" (Dreyfus and Rabinow, 1993: 35). Bourdieu's "outstanding achievement," they claim, is in building on phenomenology, providing ontological descriptions of social space as it is worked out in locales and periods and can make sense of social practices including those of the social scientist (p. 39). But Dreyfus and Rabinow take issue with what they see as Bourdieu's desire to make claims about having "scientific knowledge" concerning human social action. This, they assert, leads to methodological problems avoided by a phenomenological appreciation that can only be understood as particular instances of human life at particular times and situations. They call this problematic an "empirical metaphysics" accounting for all practices beyond the local. Bourdieu's "science," specifically its assumption of meaning for human beings, is found in maximizing symbolic capital, staking out a position above the context from which he describes social relations, and is unsustainable.

Dreyfus and Rabinow's critique begins with their reading of Bourdieu's notion of misrepresentation. His theory, they contend, must account for "why the practitioners are deluded and why the social scientists are not" (p. 41). They argue that in constructing a social theory to account for misrepresentation and in describing the social scientist's work as one of demystification, Bourdieu builds arguments accounting for all situations. This tautological bind is tightened, they contend, by his encompassing notion of symbolic capital: "To say that whatever people do they do for social profit does not tell us anything if profit is defined as whatever people pursue in a given society" (p. 42). Yet, Dreyfus and Rabinow offer,

> if, however, in response to these methodological problems it raises, one gives up this universal claim [that there is an analog to human nature], as well as a science that makes it possible and that it is in turn supposed to justify, none of Bourdieu's objective descriptive contributions to our understanding of specific societies need be sacrificed.
>
> (p. 42)

They assert that privileging social, cultural, symbolic, and economic capitals must be abandoned. Setting aside any claim to scientific sociology even in the interest of promoting social justice, they argue, is analogous to Heidegger's realization that he could not speak from any "uniquely authentic position" (p. 44).

Alternatively, Edward LiPuma (1993) notes Bourdieu's repeated insistence that the writing of "scientific text" is a political act (p. 15). For Bourdieu, the possibility of change lies in the intersection of a social structure and the actions of agents mediated by habitus. As an anthropologist, LiPuma's critique takes on Bourdieu's analysis of culture. He agrees that changes in culture do follow changes in social relations as actors in fields take up positions and vie for, defend and enhance the capital available to them (pp. 17, 18). LiPuma notes two serious silences in Bourdieu's work: he does not offer a theory of the relationship of culture and capital, and he fails to account for social classification and agency. Yet, LiPuma asserts Bourdieu has a "genuine" critique of capitalism. But, he argues it is deficient in its inability to explain how capitalism constructs antithetical "forms of thought," enabling critiques of inequality. LiPuma claims that while Bourdieu has been able to reveal the dynamic of binary distinctions within the fields (male/female, individual/community), he cannot account for them. LiPuma offers a solution consistent with Bourdieu's thinking: individuals are able to "strategize" particular "modes of life" when culture and capitalism are linked. He argues that this would help historicize Bourdieu's analysis. "However," he writes, "for Bourdieu's theory to embrace culture and capital in this way would grant them a certain authority over social structure and the positioning of agents in it. Culture and capitalism would, in this respect, ground the analysis of the specific fields. Even more, this would suggest that the very notions of rationality and maximization are culturally and historically defined and need to be so specified" (p. 32).

LiPuma also makes what he feels is a more telling critique. He points out that, for Bourdieu, knowledge is always interested and always produced as a result of position taking within a field of practice. Learning is a matter of understanding the positionality of the producer of knowledge, the knowledge itself, and one's place as a learner within the field. LiPuma calls this a "positional epistemology" which assumes "there is never critical leverage to step outside the field of the field of producers" (pp. 22, 23). Consequently, LiPuma reads Bourdieu's sociology as somewhat static; there is no room for a non-positional epistemology, for habitus that are "relative," and for transcending social classifications. He points to Bourdieu's own rise from humble rural origins to elite intellectual as a key example for this critique. Building on this line of argument, LiPuma makes the case that "to account for a critical theory of culture, Bourdieu has to account for why the internalizations of objective probabilities is socially relative of how the internalizations processes are organized along gender, ethnic, racial and regional lines" (p. 23). Finally, LiPuma questions the generalizability of Bourdieu's concepts of field, capital, and habitus. He notes that Bourdieu is inconsistent, positing them at times as universal and at others as highly contextualized.

Dreyfus and Rabinow, and LiPuma are representative of American readings of Bourdieu's work. Depending on where critics situate themselves on the micro/macro divide, they either assert that Bourdieu cannot logically stake any space outside of relative social relations for a critical project, or Bourdieu's positional epistemology hinders his critical project. Interestingly, in a reading of Bourdieu similar to Dreyfus and Rabinow's, connecting Bourdieu to

Heidegger, Wittgenstein and Merleau-Ponty, Charles Taylor (1993) sees particular merit in Bourdieu's notion of habitus. Taylor argues that the concept of
habitus is an advance in thinking about our social experience, free from the
"distorting grip" of intellectualism in the social sciences. He asserts that historically, anthropology and other social sciences have theorized some notion of
rule. Taylor argues that the concept of habitus as embodied dispositions avoids
the pitfall of representation of human behavior as self-consciously rule-
governed decisions made by individuals to act. Taylor's reading appears closer
to Bourdieu's project of steering between phenomenology and structuralism.

Calhoun (1993), a sociologist and historian, provides an interesting interpretation of Bourdieu that can be read against LiPuma's. Calhoun begins,
like others, by noting Bourdieu's indebtedness to Continental philosophy. But
he goes on to show his connection to the early Frankfurt School of Adorno,
Horkheimer, and Marcuse, sharing with it the project of critiquing received
categories, theoretical practices, "and substantive analysis of social life in terms
of the possible, not just the actual" (p. 63). This similarity, Calhoun notes,
extends to a shared interest with Habermas in notions of praxis. He notes that
Bourdieu, unlike Habermas, is not interested in formal systemic theorizing.
This, he argues, is a consequence of Bourdieu's more poststructuralist understanding of power as always in use rather than something that is "systemic"
(p. 64). Echoing LiPuma, Calhoun notes:

> His [Bourdieu's] theory is weakened by inattention to this issue [differ-
> ence]: he offers an inadequate account of how to address the most basic
> categorical differences in how his analytic tools fit or work in historically or
> culturally distinct instances. Despite this, I will argue that Bourdieu's work
> gives us extremely useful tools and that it thereby contributes importantly
> to getting contemporary theoretical discourse out of the rut of post-
> modernist vs. modernist.
>
> (p. 64)

Unlike LiPuma, Calhoun connects Bourdieu to Marx's analysis of capital.
Calhoun argues that Bourdieu enlarges the kinds of labour-producing capital
and the forms of capital produced. Calhoun contends, like LiPuma, that
Bourdieu is less than clear about how capitals are exchanged—a theory of
capitalism. Yet, he sees Bourdieu's approach to capital as generative to improving our understanding about capitalism derived from Marxist analysis.

Calhoun reads Bourdieu as having focused his attention on the inner workings of the social system and less on its change. But he contends there is an
implied "dynamism" to Bourdieu at the level of the strategic actor whose
"interest" is, historically and implicitly, trans-historically constructed. Calhoun
recognizes that Bourdieu rejected the charge of being overtly reductionist in
his analysis. Bourdieu describes human action as constructed between "ranges
of possibilities durably inscribed" (p. 74) within the habitus of agents as well as

in the fields in which they find themselves. Bourdieu's theory of practice attempts to give an account of the limits of awareness involved in human action as a struggle over the possibilities of what can be named/known/acted upon within fields. Against those reading Bourdieu as only reproductive, Calhoun argues that the case is overstated.

> Bourdieu's emphasis on reproduction did not foreclose contrary action, though neither did it introduce any notion of systematic revolutionary pressures for such action. Bourdieu addressed the issue directly, although very briefly [see Bourdieu, 1977: 82, 83], and argued that they were imbricated within conjunctures and still crucially dependent on the same habitus which had hitherto organized reproduction. In other words, revolution did not break with the habitus but was based on it, even though it broke the pattern of stable reproduction.
>
> (p. 75)

Consequently, Calhoun's generative reading sees the gaps in Bourdieu not as closures but as doors to more productive study.

This retelling of the responses to Bourdieu's intellectual output as outlined above is not exhaustive but they are representative. It is important to remember Bourdieu's ongoing critical project began with a concern with the exploitative conditions of labor in colonial Algeria, and grew and developed into an ongoing critique of categories of knowledge construction and relations of domination in language in such fields as education, the academy, art, and other fields of cultural production. Ultimately, Bourdieu's research linked identity to strategies for the accumulation of cultural capital and structures of domination (Postone et al., 1993: 10–12). Along with difficulties of translation, ordering, and intellectual attribution, the cross-disciplinary breadth and political orientation of his project almost invites misapprehension and critique.

Issues of difference and agency in Bourdieu's theorizing

The inability to adequately account for both difference and human agency are two of the most persistent critiques against Bourdieu's theorizing. Bourdieu's initial writing in education (Bourdieu, 1967, 1973, 1974, 1977, 1979; Bourdieu and Passeron, 1977; Bourdieu and de Saint Martin, 1974) garnered critical responses from those American theorists allied to the New Sociology of Education. Henry Giroux's (1983) well-cited and reworked argument is exemplary (Aronowitz and Giroux, 1993; Giroux, 1997). Comparing Bourdieu to other "radical reproductionist" theorists (Anyon, 1980; Bowles and Gintis, 1977; Willis, 1977), Giroux (1983) acknowledges Bourdieu's invaluable contribution to understanding the nature of schooling in relation to dominant society. He particularly notes Bourdieu's theorizing of schools as relatively autonomous fields in relations to fields of power, his description of the often subtle and tacit nature of the hidden curriculum of schools, and the employment of symbolic violence in maintaining social inequalities. Giroux also admires Bourdieu's understanding of learning as embodied within the habitus and hexis of individuals. But Giroux objects to several theoretical flaws in Bourdieu's studies. He reads Bourdieu as being overly mechanistic in relating how power and dominant relations work in schools and society, and as being unable to account for difference. Bourdieu is pessimistic—a theme Giroux returns to in his essay, "Pedagogy of the depressed: beyond the new politics of cynicism" (2001). Giroux finds little opening for resistance and social transformation in Bourdieu's theories: class and capital are treated in a static manner. Consequently, Giroux and other allied theorists at this time found that Bourdieu's sociology "ultimately [failed] to provide the comprehensive theoretical elements for a radical pedagogy" (p. 274). In reproduction theories in general, the overemphasis on structure and underemphasis on agency, Giroux argues, cannot account for the logic of resistance implicated in the logic of reproduction, cultural production, and the autonomy of different sites and fields. Based on his reading of theorists such as Bourdieu, he sets out a project for resistance theorists to begin with conflict and agency in analysis, to incorporate case studies with neo-Marxist social theory, and to articulate emancipatory possibilities for social reconstruction.

Ten years later, James Collins (1993) and Aaron Cicoucel (1993) echo Giroux's analysis, but both argue for a generative stance toward Bourdieu's sociology. Collins takes up Bourdieu's intervening studies (1984, 1988; and Bourdieu and Wacquant, 1989) to review his positive contribution to the linguistic deficit debate in language and education, and later in what has been termed the "canon wars" in education. He notes a shift in Bourdieu's analysis in terms of addressing social contradictions, not simply in economic antagonisms but also in individuals and social interactions. Cicoucel notes that sociolinguistic studies generally at this time have not addressed issues of power and hegemony, and suffer from an overtly macro or micro perspective. He finds Bourdieu's work helpful in navigating between the objectivist and subjectivist poles found in the study of language, social structure and education, concluding that there is a correspondence between Bourdieu's and James Gee's work on discourse. Collins remains skeptical but open to Bourdieu's analysis. He asserts:

> We might agree that the configuration of capital, habitus, and field provide general constraints on the discursive or interactive, that it seems to account for objective social space and provide a systematic account of practice, but it also ultimately depends upon such a precise articulation that we are left genuinely puzzled, and troubled, by just how the dialectic of objective possibilities and subjective aspirations unfolds.
>
> (Collins, 1993: 134)

Circoucel observes that while Bourdieu's level of abstraction is problematic, his notions, like that of habitus,

> can provide a powerful conceptual tool for examining domination as everyday practice, but [these] must be cognitively and linguistically documented . . . An understanding of local circumstances of displays of power is essential for making inferences about more abstract conceptions of power in complex organizations and as institutionalized activities.
>
> (Circoucel, 1993: 111)

These readings illustrate the difficulty his work has faced in American sociology and education. The critiques made of Bourdieu's sociology, especially against its purportedly reproductionist stance, have seemingly modified over time. More focus is now placed on the contributions his sociology has made to various fields of academic inquiry. This has been, in part, a consequence of Bourdieu's willingness to engage with his American readers. For example, Miller and Branson (1987) conclude their review of Bourdieu's studies arguing:

> Those who see inflexibility in the concept of reproduction fail to grasp Bourdieu's meaning that it is "transformations within a mode". These transformations concern not the reproduction of specific values, roles or relationships, but a very general and variable style of behavior, a style capable of wide-ranging change and variation limited nevertheless by the broad structure that encompasses that mode or style.
>
> (Miller and Branson, 1987: 223, 224)

David Swartz (1997) makes the same point ten years later.

Loic Wacquant (1987, 1989, 1990, 1992, 1993a, 1993b, 1993c) wrote extensively over this time, explaining the generative possibilities of Bourdieu's reflexive sociology, arguing that Bourdieu's symbolic anthropology of power was read through the very theoretical stances his work attempted to overcome (Wacquant, 1989). Quoting Jean-Yves Caro (1980), Wacquant challenges critics of Bourdieu's "difficult" language. Bourdieu's epistemic reflexivity, theorizing intellectual practice as inherently interested and positioned within sets of relational constraints, makes purely rational engagement with his work problematic. Wacquant contends that "it throws us 'back in the game' and cuts through the mist of our enchanted relation with the social world, and in particular to our own condition of intellectuals—that is, bearers of cultural capital and thus wielders of a dominated form of domination that scarcely wants to recognize itself as such" (Wacquant, 1989: 247).

Bourdieu made similar claims, insisting that his work should be read as evolving over time, and that it has always had as a goal "to create a theory of practice as *practice*, that is to say, as an activity premised on cognitive operations involving a mode of knowledge that is not that of theory, logic, or concept, without for all that being (as is often claimed by those who feel its specificity) a kind of mystical communion or ineffable participation" (Bourdieu, 1989: 267). He analyzed his habitus as an outsider in the French intelligentsia as helping him to break the intellectual doxa, refuting the ideology of clarity in French writing, revealing the conservatism inherent in so-called liberating schools of thought, exposing the construction of particular oppositions within it, and rejecting populist stances take up by some intellectuals. Echoing Mills' socio-logical imagination, Bourdieu argued that his studies function to make con-scious the craft that becomes the social scientific disposition, enabling the habitus that defines the "sociological eye" (p. 271). He rejected claims that he was mechanical and reductive in his analysis. He agreed his studies of French education cannot be universalized to other societies or even to other times in French society, and asserted that, "At every moment and in every society we are faced with a set of social positions bound through a relation of homology to a set of activities and goods that can themselves be only characterized relationally" (p. 273).

Bourdieu also rejected the charge that he portrays human action as overtly rational. Action, he countered, is not so much a calculation of interest as a "practical sense" or "a sense of the game," an orientation to the field of action embodied in habitus. The construction of this "libido, the socially constituted and fashioned principle of every action" which Bourdieu described, is an opening to the construction of desire in human subjects, including us. He concluded, "It is not true to say that everything that people do or say is aimed at maximizing their social profit; but one may say they do it to perpetuate or to augment their social being" (p. 274).

Swartz (1997) reviews Bourdieu's own political practice from the 1950s to the present. He notes that over these years, Bourdieu has become more pro-minent in political engagements in France. Bourdieu's choice of research topics and his criticism of the role of social science and scientists are also part of his politics. The clearest outline of his evolving project can be found in an extended dialogue he had with the installation artist, Hans Haacke (Bourdieu and Haacke, 1995). This argument is repeated by later commentators (Brown and Szeman, 2000; Lane, 2000; Shusterman, 1999; Wacquant, 2005; and Webb et al., 2002).

Feminist researcher Krais, writing about a normative problem in the field of gender studies, provides a counter-reading to the argument that Bourdieu has difficulty in dealing with difference, and is illustrative of the utility of Bourdieu's theorizing. She notes that Bourdieu wrote on the topic of gender domination (Bourdieu, 1990a) and argues that the basis of female oppression and the "mechanisms" for reproduction of male domination have not been adequately answered (Krais, 1993: 158). Bourdieu extends this argument in *Masculine Domination* (2001). In Bourdieu's conceptual framework, Krais sees a "real logic of action" whereby the mutual objectification of habitus and institutions are sustained though the "revisions and transformations that are counterpoint and condition of reactivation" (Krais, 1993: 169). Positing social reproduction as production, she contends that restructuring habitus in particular sites and fields is possible. The division of labor between genders, as between class and class factions, is reproduced through symbolic violence and a doxa that is co-opting, subtle, seductive, and/or invisible. Krais argues that denaturalizing these social mechanisms is "a *conditio sine qua non* for the liberation of women" (p. 173). She concludes:

> The conditions of the possibility of this struggle have to be seen in the fact that mental structures are not perfectly adjusted to the complex social structure, with the social structure constantly producing problems and contradictions that cannot be solved on the basis of the dispositions of habitus. But, as a social scientist, I believe that *the necessity of this attack on cultural constructions* [italics added] can be theoretically understood only within the context of a theory that relates social structure and mental structure; so the theory of Pierre Bourdieu is of utmost relevance. Theories of the patriarchate or the exploitation of female labour fail to reach this essential point, as they give a much too restricted account of social practice.
>
> (p. 173)

Krais's endorsement of a Bourdieusian turn in gender studies exemplifies how some researchers productively take up his work. Like Krais, some raise the "problem of normativity" as a particular issue related to their field. Bridget Fowler (1997) contends that Bourdieu's theorizing provides a way around the "dilemmas of necessity and choice . . . But what marks out Bourdieu's work most clearly is his full conception of class and culture as a response to class experience" (p. 3). She argues that critics such as Calhoun (1993) overlook Bourdieu's writing on social contradictions and class antagonisms, more evident in his later studies. Fowler argues that his output has to be regarded as a whole, and as evolving in response to the wider conversation his work has engendered across the social sciences and the arts. She characterizes some readings of Bourdieu as "strange . . . that I don't think can be sustained by exhaustive assessment, especially of both early and very recent work. They gain their impact in part from the genuine difficulty of synthesizing all Bourdieu's different projects" (1997: 7). Fowler argues that Bourdieu's work is relevant to theories of culture and that he has "rescued" artists from reductionist positions within cultural production and exposed the contemporary ideologies circulating about creativity and reception. She hopes her study will promote further inquiry along Bourdieusian lines. In her conclusion, while stressing the generative aspects of his logic of practice, she sees areas that have not been fully articulated, which need further elaboration and study.

Some of Fowler's observations about the cultural production of art seem relevant to the Bourdieusian perspectives in literacy education adopted in this volume. Fowler suggests that Bourdieu can contribute to exposing the social relationships within the binarism of literature and popular culture; he provides an alternative to the charismatic quality of notions of creativity, regarding the author as subject to social determinants and the necessity to construct distinction. Such a position undermines the notion that some texts have only material and factional (class, race, gender, sexual orientation) interests and others have ethical objectives. Fowler notes that "the artist in his/her active practice [is] no longer merely the site for the play of discursive forces, in contrast with the Foucauldian version of authorship" (p. 177). She concludes her study by noting that Bourdieu conceded the over-determined nature of his earlier work. She argues that in Bourdieu's framing of material struggles as involving both material conditions and beliefs, artists have a role in:

> reflecting those beliefs and legitimating those struggles. . . . It is this concern with the suspension and production of belief which is the organizing principle of Bourdieu's sociology of culture. Subjects may come to understand reflexively the mechanisms that create the reproduction of the haute bourgeoisie, which he has himself exposed, and these determining forces will lose their effectiveness.
>
> (p. 180)

Bourdieu's reflexive sociology is used to broader effect by Carol Stabile (1995) to argue against what she describes as the "polarized framework of resistant banality or recuperative fatality which limits the range and scope of cultural studies" (p. 403). This framework, she contends, is a product of the dominance of the resistance model in the field of cultural studies. Stabile asserts that Bourdieu's sociology is a corrective to the Gramscian model of hegemony in which, she argues, consent is the privilege of those who can afford to consent. Her article reviews the analyses of the television sitcom *Roseanne*, found in both the popular media and in the academic field of cultural studies. Calling upon Bourdieu's *Field of Cultural Production* (1993), she finds little critical difference between the two areas of analysis, noting that both are governed by a similar logic of fields—the creation of capital through distinction. She observes that in cultural studies, "a textual analysis must either legitimize the text itself as distinct from other texts (as subversive or resistant) or its analytic approach as distinct from other such available approaches" (Stabile, 1995: 409). In summarizing her review of these sitcom studies and media articles, Stabile contends that the "resistance industry," as she calls it, "effectively overlooks the ways in which ideology secures the economic, not necessarily in terms of overcoming ideological contradictions in favour of tradition, but also in resolving or repressing ideological contradictions through a logic of progression," reproducing "the logic of capitalist democracies, wherein women now have the choice to parent and hold jobs, while the concept of recuperation—by highlighting the conservative and preservative elements of hegemony—disregards the fact that there can be no return to the traditional nuclear family *because it is no longer economically feasible* [her emphasis]." She argues that "contemporary struggles over the family and gender in the media actually illustrate the process whereby capitalist economies package their necessities in terms of woman's gains" (p. 415).

Stabile's argument is important. She draws upon Bourdieu's sociology, positing the resistance model in cultural studies as failing to account for the productive aspects of both the media and the academy. It allows the cultural critic to play the critical game while constructing new forms of resistance to display distinctions, within and as a part of the individual's position in the field. This academic production is both ideological and economic. Stabile goes on to note, "The mediations between the field of media production and the academic field (expressed partly through the anti-economism of intellectual practices) engender an illusion of autonomy from the larger economic and political context" (p. 417). This disables an effective pedagogy and politics. Textual analysis within the framework of resistance/recuperation is unreflexive, blinding the cultural critic from his/her intersection with the field of production and from his/her interest in resistance in the academic field. This is a challenge to intellectuals, the autonomy of field they so highly covet. In linking media rhetoric with the resistance model of academic production, Stabile makes the sobering conclusion that "Bourdieu's reflexive sociology forces us to theorize agency—be it our own or that attributed to consumers in the mass media—within the constraints exercised by structuring structures" (p. 418).

In a similar reflexive move, recent feminist interest in Bourdieu and other reproductionist theorists, quite often Bernstein, especially in the United Kingdom, can be seen in the work of Arnot (2002) and in contemporary feminist research on intersections of class and gender (Reay, 1997, 2000, 2004). Writing in the field of physical education, Gorely and colleagues (2002) argue that Bourdieu's concepts of habitus and capitals are useful in conceptualizing issues of embodiment and gender. In 2002, Manchester University held a widely influential conference entitled, "Feminists Evaluate Bourdieu: International Perspectives." In the United States, Dumais (2002) uses a Bourdieusian frame to study the role of capital and habitus in boys' and girls' differential educational outcomes, and Horvat (2003) argues that Bourdieu provides a "nuanced and complicated understanding of how race and class interact to shape lived experience . . . in urban settings" (p. 19).

The centrality of normativity in Bourdieusian theorizing and research

Bourdieusian reflexivity cuts through forms of misrecognition at the heart of fields to ignore how questions are typically asked and pursue lines of inquiry thought unthinkable in these fields. Questions of normativity are frequently raised to overcome theoretical and research impasses and re-open alternative ways of thinking about them (Luke and Freebody, 1997). For example, in a piece of particularly clever and delightfully recursive reasoning, Prosise and colleagues (1996) argue for the integration of Bourdieu's theory of social practice to overcome problems in establishing a normative foundation for argument studies. Earlier attempts to construct such failed because they were not dynamic. Defining discourse fields on an *a priori* basis could not account for the symbolic practices of agents and how the logical types used in analyzing these practices came to be invented and authorized. They see a Bourdieusian foundation as a way of avoiding the conflict of objectivist and subjectivist positions and as a means of taking up argument studies as a critical endeavor.

Citing Kevin Olson's (1985) assertion that Bourdieu's symbolic power, linking agency and social structure, is more generalizable for critical studies than Foucault's notions of power, Prosise and colleagues argue that Bourdieu's analysis of social fields as dynamic arenas of contestation has strong implications for individuals and groups. "Practical argumentative struggles for legitimacy can change the meanings and values in fields" (Prosise et al., 1996: 124, 125). Consequently:

> Armed with Bourdieu's insights, argumentation scholars will be better able to understand the practical process of social power in the celebration and exclusion of arguments. Furthermore, the dynamics of the change and stability of symbolic authority within fields is advanced through the notion of symbolic struggle. Rather than having clear defining boundaries fields can be conceptualized as overlapping and dynamic arenas, consisting of social agents who negotiate daily activities in relation to their own subjective perception of the objective social realities of particular fields. The study of symbolic struggles that renegotiate the fundamental assumptions of an argument community will allow scholars to understand how symbolic authority can shift over time, how fields influence one another. Additionally, the examination of how symbolic capital operates in particular fields can increase our understanding of how people and forms of knowledge and experience become included or excluded from social fields in general.
>
> (p. 125)

Prosise and colleagues' argument echoes that of Krais's in cultural studies. Denaturalizing discourses, constructing, maintaining, and mystifying dominant social relations would be "an important weapon for practical political resistance," distinguishing "zones of necessity and of freedom." Such a field, in taking a stance toward normativity as a subjective response to objective sets of possibilities, would be able to carve out spaces "open to moral action" (p. 126).

Similarly, Nahrwold (1996) employs Bourdieu's notions of habitus, capital and field to understand the differences between traditional and electronic academic publishing. She demonstrates how changes in the means of production of academic capital in publishing promote struggle and conflict within the field. She employs Bourdieusian sociology to normatively ground their defense of the e-publishing forum "The PreText Conversation: REINVW" (www.pre-text.com/ptlist/reinvw.html) as distinct from the online journal *Postmodern Culture*, and traditional print-bound journals, which she shows as being very much the same. She makes normative pedagogical appeals in support of her position to both the academic need to create capital through publishing and the need to induct others into the academy in an efficacious manner.

Min (1996) also studies the apparent incompatibility between cultural studies and political economy. Tracing misreadings of Bourdieu's theorizing and his problematic reception in American social sciences, Min speculates that these readings may have little to do with theory and method and much to do with the difference in culture between French and American societies. Brubaker (1993) makes a similar argument. Dominative normative discourses of exceptionalism and volunteerism may favor subjectivist perspectives in the social sciences.

Normativity and education

While Bourdieu's death in 2002 occasioned considerable press and scholastic re-evaluation, Bourdieusian-informed research and theorizing in education has been growing over the previous decade. Again, most of this work has been outside the United States. One early Bourdieusian study in education is Johannesson (1993), who researched the professionalization of teachers' work in the 1980s. Positing the professionalism of teaching as a social trajectory rather than a normative evaluation of teachers' work, he used Bourdieu's theory of social fields to analyze the struggle between what he termed "epistemic individuals" over the symbolic and material value of teachers' labor (p. 270). In particular, Johannesson traces the strategies employed by teachers in gaining the social capital and, in particular, in winning a margin of autonomy for teachers' labor, which goes with the social recognition of education as a professional field against other fields, especially in relation to the field of power. Johannesson's Bourdieusian analysis is able to tie into issues of class— professionalism grounded in middle-class culture and issues of difference—as the reformers he studied were often young, female, and from rural areas in Iceland. Johannesson's study is helpful because it highlights an account of a process of contestation and social change. In winning legitimacy, Icelandic reformers contested the normative discourses of their field, making appeals to social democracy and science. As a result, they created distinctions with pre-reform pedagogical practices and relations. Johannesson was able to discern factions within the reform, which vied over what discourses were to count in struggling with conservatives. He documented instances of technological versus progressive stances taken by reform agents, and academic versus curricular theory stances by others. These are clearly contests over whose capital counted in its field and in the reform. A connection can be made to Prosise and colleagues' (1996) study, which used Bourdieu's normative analysis as a framework for a field of argument studies. Johannesson made some interesting observations: Icelandic teachers were successful in "professionalizing" teacher knowledge into capital but, in the process, they masked their pre-reform pedagogy to critics, the public and themselves. Maintaining and enhancing their reform discourse, in a process Bourdieu (1990b) calls "officialization," resulted in teachers not clearly evaluating if their reform pedagogy was better for students. Further, reformed teachers failed to find equal social status with other professions. Thus, Johannesson pointed to some interesting conclusions about a politics of strategies for enacting education change.

Significant theorizing and research has recently been conducted in Britain, Australia, and New Zealand. Particularly noteworthy are two books, by Grenfell and James (1998) and Grenfell and Kelly (1999). These two edited volumes provide extensive overviews of research from scholars across the globe using Bourdieusian approaches in areas as diverse as primary education, educational policy, higher education, media studies, and assessment. Grenfell and James (1998: Chapters 8 and 9) synthesize a number of invaluable methodological applications for employing Bourdieusian analysis broadly in educational research. In Australia, Thompson (2000) used Bourdieusian field analysis to interrogate reforms in teacher education in order to question normative tropes implicit in the theory/practice binarism at the heart of educational policy, calling for a greater emphasis on "practice" in teacher education programs. And in New Zealand, Nash (2002a, 2002b, 2003a, 2003b) researched Bourdieu's central concern with education inequality and argues for extending and adapting his theoretical framework.

Literacy education

The trajectory of Bourdieusian-informed research in literacy education parallels its growth in education. As noted earlier, much of this work productively incorporates Bourdieusian concepts in isolation. A typical example is Rex (2002), who employed habitus to theorize research in high-school teaching of academic literacy and student–teacher identity relations. Lareau and Weininger (2003) used and assessed Bourdieu's theory of cultural capital in a study of the intersection of race and class differences in family–school relationships. In a fuller engagement with Bourdieu's framework, Goldstein (2003) investigated Asian immigrant high-school students' achievement in English language instruction, working with Bourdieu's concepts of social and cultural capitals and field. Collins' (2000b) comparison of Bernstein and Bourdieu provides informative commentary on theoretical and pragmatic limitations in New Literacy Studies.

Carrington and Luke (1997) argue for a more fully realized Bourdieusian approach to research and theorizing in literacy education. They posit that "literacy and literate persons are social constructions, formed within the context of dynamic fields and as the cumulative result of participation within a range of discourses and social relations . . . any number of literacies may coexist within social spaces" (pp. 98, 99). They contend that Bourdieusian-informed research and theorizing provides for a complex, contingent, and contextualized analysis of capitals, fields, and habitus. Carrington and Luke identify some of the contingencies that affect students' social trajectories—students' access to sufficient capitals, the capitals students can access relevant to systems of exchange within sites in education, and students' capitals valued by institutions and players in these sites. Beyond the school, the embodied competencies constructed within these sites may not be able to guarantee social access. Schools may have limited autonomy to other fields.

> Without prerequisite forms of other capital, the ability to demonstrate a particular literate practice may well be of limited value to the individual . . . that is schools and school systems cannot control completely the variability of conversion between what students learn (habitus, embodied capital), the visible textual and objective signs of that learning (objectified capital) and relevant credential (institutional capital).
>
> (pp. 107, 108)

These general constraints on literacy in schools lead Carrington and Luke to make a number of conclusions about literacy education, contending that Bourdieusian analysis offers a language to trace the many literacies important in students' lives.

This is necessary for any thorough study of curriculum and teaching practices. Literacy education is more than a set of classroom strategies and techniques. It makes commitments to what knowledge is valued, how knowledge is enacted, and who enacts knowledge and where. Bourdieu's sociology places subject formation as a central pedagogical issue. All pedagogies are interventions in the lives of people and in the multiple social fields they inhabit. Outlining Bourdieu's conceptual framework of social space and his method of field analysis, I elaborate on how position, distinction, and contest within sites in literacy education are constructive and allow for (re)production and change in pedagogical practice (Albright, 2006). Bourdieu's theorizing may be profitably read alongside such researchers, in particular, Kelly's (1997) study of the cost to identity or habitus in "the ongoing achievement of difference with the structure symbolic order . . . [as a] condition of entry into language" (p. 109) is an important extension of Bourdieu's thinking and a significant pedagogical observation. A reflexive stance may attend to the ways in which our pedagogies construct our students through intersections of power and pleasure in our literate practices (p. 132). Kelly's language of desire provides a constructive adaptation of Bourdieu's sociological notion of habitus and a caution against a project that would address the universalized dispositions of class members.

Bourdieusian theorizing and research does not enter literacy education unchallenged. See, for example, the contentious debate found in *Linguistics and Education* between Hasan (1999, 2000) and her critics: Chouliaraki and Fairclough (2000), Collins (2000a), Corson (2000), and Robbins (2000). But, in a growing appreciation of the dynamic in Bourdieu's theoretical framework, the works cited above reveal either openings in his work for theorizing change or actual mechanisms for accounting for agency and for social transformation. Several studies I have reviewed employ his sociology as a normative basis for rethinking their fields of inquiry, pointing to the efficacy of Bourdieu's sociology in denaturalizing literate practices, subject positions, and political stances within fields. For example, Fowler (1997) and Min (1996) address the production and consumption of literary and artistic texts, their relation to what is judged as non-literary or popular, and doxic notions closely connected to authorship and readership.

This is a necessarily selective reading of the history of reception and employment of Bourdieu's theories and research. In American social sciences, appreciation of Bourdieu's sociology has been evolving over the last four decades. Part of the initial difficulty with appropriating his thought may have been a result of readings constrained by differences between French and American academic worlds. These differences have led to what I have described above as particularist readings of Bourdieu's various studies; time has allowed for more generative readings. His framework is still more often poached for particular explanatory ideas than fully employed. The loss of continuity in his evolving social theory has been a result of the uneven translation of his work. The attempt to pigeonhole his intellectual production into a philosophical stance has been confusing and oddly poignant, considering his goal to steer a middle course between dominant theoretical paradigms.

Reviewing the history of readings of Bourdieu's studies is a productive employment of Bourdieusian work to position a project in literacies studies and education. This project enjoys the distinctive sociological understanding of the position it adopts in our field, a normative project that proposes a critical Realpolitik for research and practice. Employing and making a case for Pierre Bourdieu's reflexive sociology is strategic within the field of literacy studies and education. Bourdieu's reception in the field of education, and specifically literacy education, mirrors to a degree how he has been read in the American academy in general. With this history in mind, in the following chapters, literacy education scholars from around the world productively and generatively engage with Bourdieu's intellectual legacy.

References

Albright, J. (2006) Literacy education after Bourdieu. *American Journal of Semiotics*, 22(1–4), 107–28.

Anyon, J. (1980) Social class and the hidden curriculum. *Journal of Education*, 162, 67–92.

Arnot, M. (2002) *Reproducing Gender? Essays on Educational Theory and Feminist Politics*. London: RoutledgeFalmer.

Aronowitz, S. and Giroux, H. A. (1993) Reproduction and resistance in radical theories of schooling. In *Education Still Under Siege* (2nd edn). Westport, CT: Bergin and Garvey, 65–110.

Bourdieu, P. (1967) Systems of education and systems of thought. *Social Science Information*, 14, 338–58.

Bourdieu, P. (1973) Cultural reproduction and social reproduction. In R. Brown (ed.), *Knowledge, Education and Cultural Change*. London: Tavistock, 71–112.

Bourdieu, P. (1974) The school as a conservative force: scholastic and cultural inequalities. In J. Eggleston (ed.), *Contemporary Research in the Sociology of Education*. London: Methuen, 32–46.

Bourdieu, P. (1977) *Outline of a Theory of Practice*. Cambridge, UK: Cambridge University Press.

Bourdieu, P. (1979) Symbolic power. *Critique of Anthropology*, 13(14), 77–85.

Bourdieu, P. (1983) *Field of Cultural Production: Essays on Art and Literature*. New York: Columbia University Press.

Bourdieu, P. (1984) *Distinction: A Social Critique of the Judgment of Taste*. Cambridge, MA: Harvard University Press.

Bourdieu, P. (1988) *Homo Academicus*. Cambridge, UK: Polity Press.

Bourdieu, P. (1989) Social space and symbolic power. *Sociological Theory*, 7, 14–25.

Bourdieu, P. (1990a) La domination masculine. *Acts de la Recherche en Sciences Sociales*, 84, 2–31.

Bourdieu, P. (1990b) *The Logic of Practice*. Standford, CA: Stanford University Press.

Bourdieu, P. (1993) Concluding remarks: for a sociogenetic understanding of intellectual works. In C. Calhoun, E. LiPuma, and M. Postone (eds), *Bourdieu: Critical Perspectives*. Chicago: University of Chicago Press, 263–75.

Bourdieu, P. (1998) *Practical Reason: On the Theory of Action*. Stanford, CA: Stanford University Press.

Bourdieu, P. (1999) The social conditions of the international circulation of ideas. In R. Shusterman (ed.), *Bourdieu: A Critical Reader*. London: Blackwell, 220–8.

Bourdieu, P. (2001) *Masculine Domination*. Stanford, CA: Stanford University Press.

Bourdieu, P. and de Saint Martin, M. (1974) Scholastic excellence and the values of the educational system. In J. Eggleston (ed.), *Contemporary Research in the Sociology of Education*. London: Methuen, 338–71.

Bourdieu, P. and Haacke, H. (1995) *Free Exchange*. Stanford, CA: Stanford University Press.

Bourdieu, P. and Passeron, J. (1979) *The Inheritors: French Students and their Relation to Culture*. Chicago: University of Chicago Press.

Bourdieu, P. and Wacquant, L. (1989) Towards a reflexive sociology: a workshop with Pierre Bourdieu. *Sociological Theory*, 7(1), 26–63.

Bowles, S. and Gintis, H. (1977) *Schooling in Capitalist AMERICA*. New York: Basic Books.

Brown, N. and Szeman, I. (eds) (2000) *Pierre Bourdieu: Fieldwork in Culture*. Lanham, MD: Rowman and Littlefield.

Brubaker, R. (1993) Social theory as habitus. In C. Calhoun, E. LiPuma, and M. Postone (eds), *Bourdieu: Critical Perspectives* (pp. 212–34) Chicago: University of Chicago Press.

Calhoun, C. (1993) Habitus, field, and capital: the question of historical specificity. In C. Calhoun, E. LiPuma and M. Postone (eds), *Bourdieu: Critical Perspectives*. Chicago: University of Chicago Press, 61–88.

Calhoun, C., LiPuma, E., and Postone, M. (eds) (1993) *Bourdieu: Critical Perspectives*. Chicago: University of Chicago Press.

Caro, J.-Y. (1980) La sociologie de Pierre Bourdieu: Elements pour une theorie du champ politique. *Revue Francaise de Science Politique*, 30(6), 1171–97.

Carrington, V. and Luke, A. (1997) Literacy and Bourdieu's sociological theory: a reframing. *Language and Education*, 11, 96–112.

Chouliaraki, L. and Fairclough, N. (2000) Language and power in Bourdieu: on Hasan's "The disempowerment game." *Linguistics and Education*, 10, 399–409.

Circourel, A. (1993) Structural and processual epistemologies. In C. Calhoun, E. LiPuma and M. Postone (eds), *Bourdieu: Critical Perspectives*. Chicago: University of Chicago Press, 89–105.

Collins, J. (1993) Determination and contradiction: an appreciation and critique of the work of Pierre Bourdieu on language and education. In C. Calhoun, E. LiPuma and M. Postone (eds), *Bourdieu: Critical Perspectives*. Chicago: University of Chicago Press, 116–38.

Collins, J. (2000a) Comments on R. Hasan's "The disempowerment game: Bourdieu and language in literacy". *Linguistics and Education*, 10, 391–98.

Collins, J. (2000b) Bernstein, Bourdieu and the new literacies studies. *Linguistics and Education*, 11, 65–78.

Corson, D. (2000) Freeing literacy education from linguistic orthodoxies: A response to R. Hasan's "The disempowerment game: Bourdieu and language in literacy." *Linguistics and Education*, 10, 411–23.

Dreyfus, H. and Rabinow, P. (1993) Can there be a science of existential structure and social meaning. In C. Calhoun, E. LiPuma and M. Postone (eds), *Bourdieu: Critical Perspectives*. Chicago: University of Chicago Press, 35–44.

Dumais, S. (2002) Cultural capital, gender, and school success: the role of habitus. *Sociology of Education*, 75, 44–68.

Fowler, B. (1997) *Pierre Bourdieu and Cultural Theory: Critical Investigations*. London: Sage.

Giroux, H. A. (1997) *Pedagogy and the Politics of Hope: Theory, Culture, and Schooling*. Boulder, CO: Westview Press.

Giroux, H. A. (2001) Pedagogy of the depressed: beyond the new politics of cynicism. *College Literature*, 28(3), 1–32.

Goldstien, T. (2003) Contemporary bilingual life at a Canadian high school: choices, risks, tensions, and dilemmas. *Sociology of Education*, 76, 247–64.

Gorely, T., Holroyd, R. and Kirk, D. (2002) Muscularity, the habitus and the social construction of gender: towards a gender-relevant physical education. *British Journal of Sociology of Education*, 24, 429–48.

Grenfell, M. and James, D. (1998) *Acts of Practical Theory: Bourdieu and Education*. London: Falmer Press.

Grenfell, M., and Kelly, M. (eds) (1999) *Pierre Bourdieu: Language, Culture and Education. Theory into Practice*. Bern, Switzerland: Peter Lang.

Harker, R., Mahar, C. and Wilkes, C. (1990) *An Introduction to the Work of Pierre Bourdieu*. London: Macmillan.

Hasan, R. (1999) The disempowerment game: Bourdieu and language in literacy. *Linguistics and Education*, 10, 25–87.

Hasan, R. (2000) Bourdieu on linguistics and language: a response to my commentators. *Linguistics and Education*, 10, 441–58.

Horvat, E. (2003) The interactive effects of race and class in educational research: theoretical insights from the work of Pierre Bourdieu. *Penn GSE Perspectives on Urban Education*, 2(1), 1–45.

Johannesson, I. A. (1993) Principles of legitimation in educational discourses in Iceland and the production of progress. *Journal of Education Policy*, 8, 339–51.

Kelly, U. A. (1997) *Schooling Desire: Literacy, Cultural Politics and Pedagogy*. New York: Routledge.

Krais, B. (1993) Gender and symbolic violence: female oppression in the light of Pierre Bourdieu's theory of social practice. In C. Calhoun, E. LiPuma and M. Postone (eds), *Bourdieu: Critical Perspectives*. Chicago: University of Chicago Press, 156–77.

Lane, J. F. (2000) *Pierre Bourdieu: A Critical Introduction*. London: Pluto Press.

Lareau, A. and Weininger, E. (2003) Cultural capital in educational research: a critical assessment. *Theory and Society*, 32, 567–606.

Lash, S. (1993) Cultural economy and social change. In C. Calhoun, E. LiPuma and M. Postone (eds), *Bourdieu: Critical Perspectives*. Chicago: University of Chicago Press, 132–212.

LiPuma, E. (1993) Culture and the concept of culture in a theory of practice. In C. Calhoun, E. LiPuma, and M. Postone (eds), *Bourdieu: Critical Perspectives*. Chicago: University of Chicago Press, 116–38.

Luke, A. and Freebody, P. (1997) Critical literacy and the question of normativity: an introduction. In S. Musprat, A. Luke, and P. Freebody (eds), *Constructing Critical Literacies: Teaching and Learning Textual Practice*. Cresshill, NJ: Hampton Press, 1–18.

Miller, D. and Branson, J. (1987) Pierre Bourdieu: culture and praxis. In D. J. Austin-Broos (ed.), *Creating Culture: Profiles into the Study of Culture*. Winchester, MA: Allen and Unwin, 210–25.

Min, E. (1996) *Can Political Economy of Communication be Incorporated with Cultural Studies in the Postmodern Era?* (ERIC Document Reproduction Service No. ED351735).

Nahrwold, C. (1996) *Shifting Capital: Electronic Publishing on Bourdieu's Linguistic Market*. Paper presented at the Annual Meeting of the Conference on College Composition and Communication, Milwaukee, WI.

Nash, R. (2002a) The educated habitus, progress at school, and real knowledge. *Interchange*, 33, 27–48.

Nash, R. (2000b) Inequality/difference in New Zealand education: social reproduction and the cognitive habitus. *International Studies in Sociology of Education*, 13, 171–91.

Nash, R. (2003a) Progress at school: pedagogy and the care for knowledge. *Teaching and Teacher Education*, 19, 755–67.

Nash, R. (2003b) Social explanation and socialization: on Bourdieu and the structure, disposition, practice scheme. *Sociological Review*, 51, 43–62.

Olson, K. (1985) Habitus and body language: toward a critical theory of symbolic power. *Philosophy and Social Criticism*, 21(38), 23–49.

Postone, M., LiPuma, E. and Calhoun, C. (1993) Introduction: Bourdieu and social theory. In C. Calhoun, E. LiPuma and M. Postone (eds), *Bourdieu: Critical Perspectives*. Chicago: University of Chicago Press, 1–13.

Prosise, T. O., Miller, G. R. and Mills, J. P. (1996) Argument fields as arenas of discursive struggle. *Argumentation and Advocacy*, 32, Winter, 111–28.

Reay, D. (1997) Feminist theory, habitus and social class: disrupting notions of classlessness. *Women's Studies International Forum*, 20, 225–33.

Reay, D. (2000) A useful extension of Bourdieu's framework? Emotional capital as a way of understanding mothers' involvement in their children's education? *Sociological Review*, 48, 568–85.

Reay, D. (2004) Cultural capitalists and academic habitus: classed and gendered labour in UK higher education. *Women's Studies International Forum*, 27, 31–9.

Rex, L. (2002) Exploring orientation in remaking high school readers' literacies and identities. *Linguistics and Education*, 13, 271–302.

Robbins, D. (2000) Bourdieu on language and linguistics: a response to R. Hasan's "The disempowerment game: Bourdieu and language in literacy." *Linguistics and Education*, 10, 425–40.

Shusterman, R. (1999) *Bourdieu: A Critical Reader*. London: Blackwell.

Simeoni, D. (2000) Anglicizing Bourdieu. In N. Brown and I. Szeman (eds), *Pierre Bourdieu: Fieldwork in Culture*. Lanham, MD: Rowman and Littlefield, 65–86.

Stabile, C. A. (1995) Resistance, recuperation and reflexivity: the limits of a paradigm. *Critical Studies in Mass Media*, 12, 403–22.

Swartz, D. (1997) *Culture and Power: The Sociology of Pierre Bourdieu*. Chicago: University of Chicago Press.

Taylor, C. (1993) To follow a rule . . . In C. Calhoun, E. LiPuma and M. Postone (eds), *Bourdieu: Critical Perspectives*. Chicago: University of Chicago Press, 45–60.

Thompson, P. (2000) The sorcery of apprenticeships and new/old brooms: thinking about theory, practice, "the practicum" and change. *Teaching Education*, 11, 67–74.

Wacquant, L. J. D. (1987) Symbolic violence and the making of the French agriculturalist: an inquiry into Pierre Bourdieu's sociology. *Australian and New Zealand Journal of Sociology*, 23, 65–88.

Wacquant, L. J. D. (1989) Toward a reflexive sociology: a workshop with Pierre Bourdieu. *Sociological Theory*, 7, 26–63.

Wacquant, L. J. D. (1990) Sociology as social-analysis: tales of *Homo Academicus*. *Sociological Forum*, 5, 677–89.

Wacquant, L. J. D. (1992) Towards a social praxeology: the structure and logic of Bourdieu's sociology. In P. Bourdieu and L. J. D. Wacquant (eds), *An Invitation to Reflexive Sociology*. Chicago: University of Chicago Press, 2–59.

Wacquant, L. J. D. (1993a) Bourdieu in America: notes on the transatlantic importation of social theory. In C. Calhoun, E. LiPuma and M. Postone (eds), *Bourdieu: Critical Perspectives*. Chicago: University of Chicago Press, 235–62.

Wacquant, L. J. D. (1993b) From ruling class to field of power: an interview with Pierre Bourdieu on *La Noblesse d'Etat*. *Theory, Culture, and Society*, 10(3), 19–44.

Wacquant, L. J. D. (1993c) Solidarity, morality and sociology: Durkheim and the crisis of European society. *Journal of the Society for Social Research*, 1, 1–7.

Wacquant, L. (ed.) (2005) *Pierre Bourdieu and Democratic Politics*. Cambridge, UK: Polity Press.

Webb, J., Schirato, T. and Danaher, G. (2002) *Understanding Bourdieu*. London: Sage.

Willis, P. (1977) *Learning to Labour*. Lexington, MA: DC Heath.

Chapter 3

Pierre Bourdieu

A biographical memoir

Claire Kramsch

Bourdieu's biographical trajectory and the position he occupied in the French intellectual landscape are important to understanding the social and moral aspects of his work. As he himself acknowledged in his last writing, *Esquisse pour une auto-analyse* (2004), published posthumously, his biography gives a clue to the passion and commitment he invested in educational issues. In a somewhat heteroglossic style, inspired by the reading of "Bourdieu in America" (Wacquant, 1993), this chapter reflects on Pierre Bourdieu, the French intellectual, in the light of my own biographical trajectory—from my French educational training to my American teaching practice. It explains the enormous value given to literate language in French educational practice, the disciplinary and social class discrimination Bourdieu had to fight against, and the decisive impact the war in Algeria had on his intellectual development. Bourdieu's five major concepts—*habitus, field, capital, distinction, symbolic violence*—are discussed in light of his personal experience with farmers in Kabylia and in his own community in the Béarn, and that experience is juxtaposed with my experience reading Bourdieu while teaching in America. Such an interweaving of biographical trajectories allows for an empathetic reading of Bourdieu, thus revealing a deeply humanistic aspect of his work that is often overlooked on both sides of the Atlantic. After reflecting on some of the reasons why Bourdieu has been misunderstood (or only too well understood) both in France and in the United States, the chapter ends on a discussion of what a Bourdieusian stance in literacy education might look like.

Biographical trajectories

I first encountered the writings of Pierre Bourdieu in the early 1980s, as I was teaching French and German at the Massachusetts Institute of Technology (MIT). With a degree in German language and literature from the Sorbonne, I had been in the United States for 15 years and was growing increasingly frustrated with the way my teaching kept missing the mark. My students, who were mostly from very modest social backgrounds, did not seem to have the general education—Bourdieu would say the *cultural capital*—that went with studying at a prestigious institution such as MIT, even though they were very bright. I, in turn, did not know how to tap into their strengths. In 1982, a French exchange student from the *Ecole Normale* brought into my office Bourdieu's *Ce que parler veut dire* (1982), which was making a splash in intellectual circles in Paris. The book took my breath away. Bourdieu dared put a name to the shortcomings of the French education I had received—an education that was in part first-rate and the source of my academic success in the United States, in part the reason for my failure to reach my American students.

Coming as he did from a modest, rural family in one of the poorest regions in southern France, the Béarn, Bourdieu had gone through the same elite education in the Paris of the 1950s as I had—*baccalauréat, hypokhâgne, khâgne, Ecole Normale, agrégation.*[1] He studied philosophy, which was then the prestige discipline. After completing his military service in Algeria, however, he started doing ethnography among the peasants of Kabylia, a mountainous region in Algeria, and switched over to sociology, a field that allowed him to combine both theory and practice. Upon his return to France, radicalized by the war in Algeria, he started studying the tragic plight of peasants in his own community in the Béarn (Bourdieu, 1962), then turned his sociological analysis to the French system of higher education that had brought him to the top of the academic hierarchy (Bourdieu, 1984/1988; Lane, 2000).

I empathized with Bourdieu's biography. I, too, had been seduced by philosophy, even though in 1959 I ended up getting a degree in German, which was then the language of academic power and was more likely to get me a job. By expatriating myself and emigrating first to Germany, then to the United States, I, too, opened myself up to doubts about the universal validity of my French education. I, too, recycled myself later into another field—applied linguistics—that was considered, in some quarters of the American academy, less "noble" than my original one. Reading "Bourdieu in America," I recognized both the thrill of the rigorous intellectual training I had received in my home country, and its inexplicable failures abroad.

Bourdieu's ambivalence helped me to understand mine. For example, I was reminded how, in the French *lycée*, the most brilliant students came to class bragging about how they had not studied for the examination, yet they passed with flaming colors while others, who had worked all night, did not. Why was it so desirable to look disinterested in hard work and its rewards? Bourdieu would explain this disdain for labor or "interest in disinterestedness" as a mark of *symbolic distinction*. The French educational system not only seemed to reward innate talent rather than hard work, it also seemed to put a premium on rhetorical skills at the expense of any personal conviction. For instance, teachers would repeatedly reject any personal opinion on the part of the students ("Miss X, your opinion is of no interest to us") in the name of factual objectivity ("Just tell me what the text says"). Bourdieu again would explain that the field of cultural production is all the more prestigious as it is distanced from such subjective reactions as personal emotion, passion or enthusiasm.

The overemphasis on language and style in the French educational system has deep roots in the belief, which goes back to the court in Versailles and the French Revolution, that the French language is a cultural treasure, that its elegant mastery is a sign of superior thought and a clear mark of class distinction. Such a belief can sometimes lead to an overemphasis on rhetorical skills. Vacuous eloquence and self-promotion in the media, especially on the part of philosophers and literary critics, were the targets of Bourdieu's particular ire. In school, I remember the endless compositions we had to write where style counted more than content. My style was invariably criticized as "pedantic," "heavy," "unclear"—adjectives that, as Bourdieu observed, subtly passed judgment not only on how we wrote but on who we were. Genre separation was strictly enforced, the objective and subjective treatment of topics being clearly separated in the French intellectual tradition. In a literary essay one was supposed to write with elegance, wit, and panache; a philosophy paper demanded depth and complexity (teachers would scribble in the margin: "This is supposed to be a literary essay, not a philosophical treatise!"). The educational system seemed to expect on the examination evidence of skills we had never been taught, thus, as Bourdieu would say, sanctioning an "inherited" knowledge that many of us did not have. Teacher remarks such as, "I am disappointed in you. You can do better than that," exercised a subtle form of what Bourdieu would call *symbolic violence*.

No doubt we were expected to get from home many of the skills necessary to be successful in school. But my mother was a foreigner who knew little French and did not understand the French educational system; my French father was an engineer who was better at math than at the mysteries of literary style. In the absence of the right home environment, I made out of necessity a virtue. I became known for my unconventional ideas—a risky position to take in a system that rewarded not originality but conformity to academic norms of distinction. Thus I naturally gravitated toward thinkers who put institutional conventions and rationalities into question: Pascal, Ricoeur, Bachelard, Merleau-Ponty, the existentialists Sartre, Camus, and Gabriel Marcel, the German philosophers Nietzsche, Heidegger, and Jaspers. Now in Bourdieu, I found echoes of all these writers but also a key to understanding their value in the French intellectual world that had been mine. I realized that by virtue of my higher education I was expected to use my knowledge of these writers, not to put the educational institution into question, but to reproduce the dominance of the class I had been trained to belong to. I had not been aware of belonging to any class, race, or ethnicity. I was French, and that was enough for me. My failures, I thought, were due to my own personal deficiencies. Bourdieu proposed a social explanation for the feelings of personal guilt so many students experienced when they failed to meet the school's expectations. It is in the interest of institutions, he said, to conceal the symbolic power they wield to reproduce the social hierarchy. In France, personal guilt for school failure was all the more pervasive as the French public school and university system took great pride in being democratically open to each and every one, irrespective of gender, race, ethnicity, or social class, so that the individual had only him/herself to blame. But in fact, said Bourdieu, the system was so designed as to reproduce the ways of speaking and writing of a bourgeois elite, who often prized elegance of style over originality of content.

Now, in the United States, my situation was different. My French education had helped me secure an academic position at a prestigious university, but it did not help me understand the needs of my American students. Moving to America, I discovered that race and ethnicity took precedence over class, which my students insisted did not exist in America. But I soon realized that, even though the game was played differently, it was still the same old competition for distinction, except that talk about class had, in the United States, seemingly become taboo. I learned to see myself privileged not by my class but by my race. I also became aware that racial inequalities are, in the United States, fundamentally different from class inequalities, and that they permeate the whole educational system in ways that are different from those described by Bourdieu for social class in France (see, e.g., Prendergast, 2003). But the contemptuous silences and condescending smiles, the compensatory effusions and forced invisibility, are all familiar to those on the receiving end of discrimination, whether it be race- or class-related.

In American academia, I found myself at the bottom of the disciplinary totem pole because I was a language teacher, not a philosopher or a literary scholar. Bourdieu refers to the way French philosophers viewed certain disciplines as "the inferior caste of linguists, ethnologists and even, especially after 1968, sociologists" (Bourdieu, 2004: 26, my translation). In America, I had become associated with a field that belonged to an inferior caste. My colleagues in philosophy ridiculed the claims that teaching language was more than teaching the mechanics of grammar and vocabulary: "You say you teach culture? Are you an anthropologist?" Those in literary studies made fun of my efforts to teach text comprehension: "Because you still believe that texts have meaning, do you?" The French philosophers I had loved and admired were read and discussed in the United States by scholars in the prestige disciplines (e.g., literary and cultural studies, rhetoric, philosophy), not by my fellow language teachers and the researchers in foreign language education. In the 1980s, none of my American colleagues had heard of Pierre Bourdieu. Of course, the social power structure that Bourdieu talks about was there all right, but it was distributed differently. So I started reading Bourdieu from my new perspective as an American academic and an applied linguist.

Bourdieu talked and wrote very little about his life, but it is not difficult to imagine what it meant for a first-generation academic from "the provinces" to make it into the top circles of the Parisian intelligentsia. As I said, he had studied philosophy, like many of his contemporaries before him—Sartre, de Beauvoir, Merleau-Ponty, Levi-Strauss, Foucault.[2] After passing the *agrégation* in 1954, he taught philosophy for a short while at various *lycées* in France and

Algeria. Planning to obtain a doctoral degree, he proposed to his adviser, George Canguilhem, a dissertation topic drawing on the work of Merleau-Ponty—"The temporal structures of affective experience"—already then showing an interest in dealing academically with social and emotional issues he had encountered in his own life. After his military service, he remained in Algeria to do ethnographic work and thought of using his study of Kabyle peasants to write a dissertation in sociology with Jules Vuillemin. But he finally abandoned the idea of a PhD altogether and published his study directly as *Outline of a Theory of Practice* (1972/1977; see Lane, 2000). After 1982, Bourdieu applied the major concepts he had developed in *Outline* and his *Logic of Practice* (1980/1990)—habitus, field, capital, distinction, symbolic violence, which I discuss in the next section—to concrete, empirical studies of the French educational system (*Homo Academicus*, 1984/1988; *State Nobility*, 1989/1996b), that he had focused on earlier with Jean-Claude Passeron. He studied class-based tastes and values (*Distinction*, 1979/1984), the world of art and literary criticism (*Rules of Art*, 1992/1996a), and the world of the immigrants and the disenfranchised (*Weight of the World*, 1993/2000b). His reference to Blaise Pascal in his last important monograph, *Pascalian Meditations* (1997/2000a), reminded me of the central place that the two seventeenth-century philosophers, Pascal and Descartes, still play in French intellectual life. Unlike René Descartes, whose famous *Metaphysical Meditations* (1641/1999) demonstrated the power of scholastic reasoning ("*cogito ergo sum*") to prove the existence of God and solve human problems, Pascal spent his life warning against an exclusive reliance on Cartesian rationality. Man is a complex being, he argued, both powerful and powerless, full of paradoxes and contradictions that cannot be resolved by cold reason alone (see Pascal's famous statement: "The heart has its reasons that reason knows not of"). By placing his ultimate reflections on his work under the aegis of Pascal, Bourdieu resignified Descartes' *Meditations* into a meditation on the power of society—which, he said, was the modern incarnation of God—to shape and be shaped by human action. Bourdieu thus ended up integrating two major strands of French philosophy into his new reflexive sociology, thereby endowing his own discipline with new titles of nobility.

Bourdieu's major concepts

Bourdieu developed his major concepts early on, based on his extensive ethnographic work in Algeria. Trained as he was in a highly theoretical discipline, he was suddenly confronted with the concrete reality of life in rural communities, where peasants had quite a different logic from the logic of academia. Indeed, their *sens pratique* or logic of the practice was both more subjective than the structuralist explanations given by anthropologists such as Levi-Strauss, and more objective than existentialist philosophers such as Sartre would have you believe. Their rituals and matrimonial practices seemed perfectly matched to the demands of their environment even though they were not able to account for them in so many words. Unlike many ethnographers, Bourdieu had one advantage: he understood this logic because it was the logic of his very own family and the surrounding peasant community in the Béarn. In particular, the extensive practice of gift-giving and the attendant expectations of a countergift that should be not too big and not too small, not too expensive and not too cheap, offered not too early and not too late, created bonds of mutual obligation that were both economic and symbolic. These obligations regulated much of the power relations within and among Kabyle and Béarn peasant families, especially regarding who was allowed to marry whom.

Bourdieu saw that the exchange of symbolic goods (family or class honor, debts and obligations) was reproduced on a larger scale by the French educational system, which gave students symbolic recognition in the form of grades and diplomas, but only for achievements that reinforced the social hierarchy. It expected all students to acquire urban, middle-class tastes, thoughts and behaviors, and then enact these in the rest of their lives, thus reproducing the inequitable distribution of knowledge and cultural capital that they had benefited from. After studying peasant communities, Bourdieu decided to subject to a rigorous sociological analysis the very structures of power that had shaped his biographical trajectory. For that, he developed conceptual tools. I discuss below the five major concepts for which he has become well-known: habitus, field, capital, distinction, symbolic violence. I use as examples my own biographical trajectory as described in the previous section.

Habitus

The notion of *habitus*, which is central to Bourdieu's theory of practice, puts a name on the way I was socialized in the French educational system. I developed, like others, an individual habitus, that is, a set of durable dispositions or tendencies to think and act in certain ways, that is inculcated and structured by my family and the school, and enabled me to become integrated into French society—to become "French." For example, I had internalized the values attached to language, the premium placed on textual exegeses, and the disdain for affective engagement in intellectual matters. Unlike students from more modest backgrounds, I learned how to downplay the work I put into my studies, disparage outward signs of success, and disdain any monetary gain. This habitus was quite unconscious. As Bourdieu described it:

> The habitus entertains with the social world which has produced it a real ontological complicity, the source of cognition without consciousness, of an intentionality without intention, and a practical mastery of the world's regularities which allows one to anticipate the future without even needing to posit it as such.

(1987: 12)

My habitus was, as I saw it, my "natural" self. As my parents, teachers and neighbors all confirmed that I was acting in conformity with their expected norms, I took my habitus to be the natural, universal way of being. It was a perception scheme that I would transpose to all other contexts. My individual habitus coincided with that of others around me, who belonged to the same class of people in tastes, behaviors, and way of life. It was thus both subjective and objective. I did not have to think, rationally, of how to behave or what to say. My body knew. My habitus was in my body, and my body was part of the objective world. It was embodied history.

In turn, my habitus structured and reproduced the very social structure I lived in through the words I uttered and the actions I performed. For example, by learning to disparage hard work (all the while that I did what was necessary to succeed), I was perpetuating the existing division and social hierarchy between intellectual and manual labor in French society. Such a perception scheme of society was typical of a certain bourgeois middle class. This habitus was neither imposed on me, nor did I choose it freely: I chose to be that which I was socially destined to be. We spent days in philosophy classes discussing free will and determinism, individual and society, and not once did I ever entertain the thought that my ability to discuss these topics might have less to do with my intrinsic talents than with my position in the social hierarchy.

Field

It was only when I failed to meet my teacher's expectations that I started to become aware of a discrepancy between who I was and who the school wanted me to be. According to Bourdieu's theory, my habitus was in a dialectical relationship with the *field* of educational practice as I encountered it in school. The educational field, like the medical, scientific, literary, or philosophical fields, is a relational, multidimensional space of activity where agents—that is, students, teachers and administrators—take up and occupy positions according to how much capital they have (see discussion below). It is immersed in the larger field of power held by institutions that reproduce the values of those individuals who hold the most economic, cultural, and symbolic capital in a given society.

I came to the realization that the field of my family relations did not quite match the field of schooling. My family encouraged fantasy and outlandish ideas; the school insisted on form, precision, and conventional thinking. But I realized that the picture was more complex than that. Fields were not fully autonomous. For example, through my own participation in them, several fields of experience came into contact that had not totally overlapping values—travels to England and Germany, sports, Girl Scouts, literature—each field itself was not as monolithic as it seemed. In my own family, my French father, who came from the Parisian bourgeoisie, upheld the mainstream values of the school, while my English mother, who was from Jewish/Hungarian/Polish background, prided herself on being a foreigner, thus not bound by any French social or cultural conventions. Even the field of schooling was not totally homogeneous: some teachers, such as my German teachers, prized ideas above all, while others, such as my French teachers, penalized me for my awkward style. Thus each field was a site of struggle among conflicting forces. Each field constituted different forms of capital. Growing up consisted in finding out how to convert these forms of capital into symbolic power in various fields of activity. Unable to change the system, I developed strategies to maneuver myself into a position of strength within the field of education. If I did not have the elegant style, then at least I could have interesting ideas. I chose to capitalize on being out of the ordinary. In Bourdieu's words, my habitus made out of necessity a virtue.

It should be said that the narrative I have just given makes my habitus look much more rational and voluntaristic than it really was. I did not calculate my chances, devise strategies, and decide how to beat the system. My logic of practice, as Bourdieu would say, was neither the result of setting goals for myself nor of executing goals set by others. My embodied habitus was merely adjusting to the objective conditions of action (producing elegant style) and transforming these conditions by producing action of a different sort (producing interesting content), hoping that I would get away with it. Sometimes I did, sometimes I did not. What pushed me in the direction I took was not financial need (although I was happy to get a scholarship), but the need to maximize my chances of symbolic survival (saving face vis-à-vis myself and the teacher, and gaining the respect of my family and friends). Bourdieu called this maximizing one's "profit of distinction" in the struggle for symbolic power, that is, enhancing one's symbolic capital.

Capital

It was clear that I had to enhance my symbolic value as I was aware that my family was not like the other, more traditional French families that lived in my hometown, Versailles, and that I had much more of a French habitus than my family had. Bourdieu's notion of *capital* helps me now understand how I positioned myself within the French educational field. Even though the term echoes Marxian economic theories of wealth, capital in Bourdieu's terminology denotes a more general "capacity to exercise control over one's own future and that of others" (Postone et al., 1993: 4) through economic or symbolic (i.e., social or cultural) means. It is true that, economically speaking, my parents with their seven children and no inherited wealth had less capital than others. In my family, we could only afford one pair of shoes and had to save on heating, but our family background ensured us a particular kind of symbolic capital that would enable us to look to the future with confidence and to take a certain amount of risk. It was a capital inherited from my bourgeois family on my father's side, but it was, on my mother's side, the capital that immigrants and outsiders bring with them, that is, a knowledge of other languages, other cultures, and a capacity to imagine other worlds.

As I said, I was not aware that I belonged to any bourgeois middle class. I discovered that only when I came to the United States. There, my individual and class habitus clashed with those of many of my American students at MIT, where there was a much greater variety of habitus and capital among the students than at *Ecole Normale* and the Sorbonne. The symbolic capital that I had brought with me across the Atlantic legitimized my pedagogy as a teacher of French and German. I had not only naturalized my habitus but essential-ized it as that of a French national. I thought the reason why I could not understand my students was because I was French and they were American. It was only when I had to explain to them terms we encountered in the readings, such as French *petit bourgeois* and *vulgaire*, or German *kitsch*, that I realized many of my American students did not share my tastes, values, and class criteria that Bourdieu found to be characteristic of the French bourgeois class. Their dis-may at my negative judgments on what were, in fact, their own family tastes and values made me realize how bourgeois I, in fact, was.

Distinction

In the United States, I found that the pursuit of happiness was often a pursuit of distinction. Bourdieu calls *distinction* any enhancement of one's symbolic position within a field. A *profit of distinction* is the result of a struggle to be noticed, validated, respected, admired. In French society, it can be gained by adopting ways of speaking that associate you with the educated segments of society, that is, that display your membership in the bourgeois class, or, if you are already in a position of power, by allowing yourself to speak like the little guy as a display of solidarity with the working class—what Bourdieu calls a *strategy of condescension*—that may earn you additional distinction. In the United States, I found there were many more ways to acquire distinction than in the French society I had left. You could enhance your symbolic value in the fields of business, computer industry, entertainment, and not only in the academic field. Educated language seemed to play less of a role in this pursuit of distinc-tion and, in some cases, even be a handicap. However, in the educational field, distinction was definitely linked to speaking the legitimate language and possessing the right academic knowledge required by the institution.

For distinction, like habitus, is not merely a subjective feeling of superiority or of being someone special. It is socially legitimized and consecrated by institutions. It is through institutions such as the family, church, government, academia, that distinction is conferred upon individuals, literally making them into "boys" or "girls," "Christians" or "Muslims," "citizens" or "immigrants," "students" or "dropouts." Schools in particular confer, through an act of social magic, distinction upon some and shame upon others, by the mere administer-ing of tests and examinations. As Bourdieu writes, "between the last person to pass and the first person to fail, the competitive examination creates differences of all or nothing that can last a lifetime" (1982: 120). Institutions can give or refuse individuals the very social reality they need to survive in society.

Symbolic violence

Bourdieu uses the word *violence* to designate the symbolic power exercised by those who possess symbolic resources over those who do not: elders over younger family members, men over women, schools over students, scholars in prestigious fields over those in less prestigious fields, and so forth. Those who are subjected to symbolic violence are not passive recipients; on the contrary, by taking their subjection as the natural and necessary order of things, they are actively complicit in their own subjection. The term "violence" might seem too strong a word for an effect that is not primarily physical but social psychological. Yet Bourdieu felt it captured the deep personal distress he had observed again and again in those individuals who, forced into positions they had not chosen, collaborate in their own submission because "that's how life is." For example, in his last autobiographical essay, *Esquisse pour une auto-analyse* (2004), he referred to the initial study he had done 40 years before, which had been the impetus for his whole life's work—the tragic fate of the eldest son in Béarn peasant families and the symbolic violence done to him (Bourdieu, 1962). In this male-dominated community, the son who had been designated by the elders as the inheritor was, says Bourdieu, "condemned" to celibacy by the unwritten rule that the patrimony should be passed on, intact, from one generation to the next. The obligation to remain on the farm (and not, like the girls or the younger sons, leave for the city or seek a fortune in America) coupled with the increasing difficulty of finding a wife who would be ready to share the hard life of a farmer, virtually ensured that the eldest son would not have a family of his own. Ultimately, however, individual destinies get engulfed in larger geopolitical forces beyond their control. A rule that had ensured the economic survival of the family in a rural economy led to its demise in an increasingly urban, industrial economy because the family thus deprived itself of progeny that could take over the farm and the land, and ended up having to sell its patrimony. However tragic and harsh the inheritance rule was for the eldest son, it was not, however, imposed upon him against his will. Typical of a domination that is symbolic rather than physical, it could be successfully exercised precisely because the inheritor was complicitous in upholding the symbolic values of his family. These symbolic values and the strategies put in place to maintain them were, in turn, related to the economic capital with which the family's physical survival was bound up. Bourdieu's moving description of the village ball in his home community—*le bal des célibataires*—where the "unmarriageable" men, proudly resigned to their fate, stood watching the couples dance, formed the affective impetus for his whole theory of habitus and symbolic violence.

Who's afraid of Pierre Bourdieu?

Pierre Bourdieu has been both understood and misunderstood, admired and criticized, on both sides of the Atlantic. He told uncomfortable truths and debunked the very educational system that gave him the symbolic power to be heard and listened to. Even though he applied his concepts to his own work (hence his term "reflexive" sociology) and thus acknowledged its limitations, he always upheld an ontological claim for his kind of sociology and insisted on its universal validity to explain human affairs. There are thus many reasons why some people have been afraid of Bourdieu or have rejected his work.[3]

In France, the French general public has found his style difficult to read (even in French). The academic establishment criticized his explicit and personalized attacks on its existing hierarchical structures of power, for example, in *Homo Academicus*. Philosophers, in particular, resented his claim to replace philosophy with sociology as the ultimate explanatory framework in the human sciences (e.g., Monod, 1999). They rejected his efforts to blur the distinction between those disciplines, such as sociology, that are supposed to study objective facts of social life, and those such as philosophy or literary criticism that study human subjectivity (Mounier, 2003: 53). His colleagues and students in sociology praised again and again his personal generosity and his modesty, but some complained about his intellectual intransigence and his lack of dialogue with his fellow scholars (p. 15). The notions elaborated for Kabylia with great complexity and differentiation in *Outline* and *Logic*, when applied to French society in *State Nobility*, *Distinction*, and *Rules of Art*, seem to have become more deterministic, possibly because of Bourdieu's personal rage against the "system." The accusation of determinism has been made even by former students of Bourdieu. Some of them, while acknowledging their enormous debt to their mentor, have proposed ways of applying his theory to the more differentiated and multicultural society that France has become (Corcuff, 1999; Lahire, 1998). They offer fruitful avenues of research that continue to expand the work of Pierre Bourdieu in the field of education. I return to those in the conclusion.

Anglo-American readers, too, have perceived his work as too "deterministic," even though he insisted again and again that it was not (Guillory, 2000). But their reasons have to do with the different resonances that the translation of his work has in English as compared to the original French. The American reproach of determinism stems from an American tradition of voluntarism and the widespread belief in the possibility of social change brought about by individual free will. Bourdieu's notion of habitus seems antithetical to the notion of free will, of equal opportunity coupled with the freedom and willingness to struggle for success. After a lecture on Bourdieu, my American undergraduates invariably ask, "But where is individual agency?" If, as Bourdieu asserts, habitus does adapt to and is changed by various fields, American readers want to know how quick one's habitus is likely to change, for example, through schooling; and how many habitus an individual has, since his/her life is likely to have intersected with many different fields in many different countries. Bourdieu does not deny individual agency and the possibility of change, but he never separates the individual from his/her social make-up and from his/her personal and collective history.

The second difficulty raised by Bourdieu's work has to do with his economic metaphors. American readers tend to understand terms such as *capital* and *strategies* within a discourse of economic maximization and strategic rationalism, which Bourdieu rejects as being economically liberal and politically conservative (Boudon, 2004). Furthermore, while he uses economic, utilitarian calculation metaphors (capital, strategies, profit, exchange) to explain human behavior, he rejects economic/material interest as the exclusive motive of human action (Guillory, 2000). For Bourdieu, the power that is being transacted is not only material but for the most part symbolic, even among the working class and rural poor. In the United States, where success is measured in terms of material wealth and social class is reduced to level of income, his economic metaphors have led readers to believe he was describing a *homo economicus* intent on maximizing his economic profit. But, in fact, Bourdieu was a forceful advocate of more state regulation against globalization, and has always fought for the symbolic dignity of the working poor.

The third obstacle to the application of Bourdieu's ideas in the United States is linked to the different societal structures in the two countries. American society seems to be more loosely structured than the French social hierarchy described by Bourdieu. The notion of field, applied to such areas of expertise or activity as religion, higher education, sports, medicine, literature, philosophy, and so forth, lacks clear and empirically founded boundaries (Lahire, 1999c). The notion of social class and the rigid class system Bourdieu describes for France seem inapplicable in a multiple differentiated society such as the United States. Because field is so vague, and social class (by contrast with socioeconomic status) so difficult to define, American educators have generally focused on habitus, which seems easier to grasp, especially if understood as the result of early socialization. But in so doing, they tend to ignore the fact that habitus does not exist independently of its dialectic relation with a field within a theory of action.

Finally, and most importantly, the affective component of Bourdieu's work seems to have been lost in the translation to English. While in the French original his rather abstract style was meant precisely to preclude any suspicion of subjective bias, yet retain subtle markers of affect and political stance, the English translation hardly bears any trace of his human compassion and his personal commitment to social and political change (Simeoni, 2000). Thus American educators have not been sufficiently aware of his deep conviction that it is only by "help[ing] agents to grasp the meaning of their actions" that social change can come about (Postone et al., 1993: 6).

For all these reasons, Bourdieu has not been as popular on American campuses as, say, Foucault or Bakhtin, who address the relation of individual and society, language and power on a more abstract, general level (Wacquant, 1993: 242). However, in the past three years, Bourdieu has gained in resonance among undergraduate and graduate students. They are increasingly aware of the invisible ceilings placed on their upward mobility: the symbolic prestige associated with the names of certain universities, fields, and professors; the symbolic value given to certain listings on their curriculum vitae; the symbolic power that comes with certain accents, behaviors and activities. In particular, they are more conscious than they used to be of the symbolic dimensions of the language they see used in academe and in the media, and they are more receptive to Bourdieu's ideas. His concern for the little guy, his very ambivalence over his own brilliant career, resonate with many students who come from modest backgrounds and with first-generation academics who try to make it into a society in which "nobility of birth," money, and connections seem to weigh ever more than school credentials for access to real power and success.

For a Bourdieusian stance in literacy education

Bourdieu has left us with a treasure trove of theoretical concepts that are broad enough to be applicable to a variety of social contexts where language is used and taught. But as important as the concepts themselves is the stance of inquiry that led him to tie them together into a theory of the practice. Like many French thinkers, Bourdieu was an educator at heart, with an acute sense of social and moral justice. It is therefore particularly appropriate to reflect on what a Bourdieusian stance can contribute to research and practice in literacy education

Bourdieu's main contribution to education is a deep appreciation of the fundamental paradox of literacy as being both liberatory and conservative, an instrument of both social change and social reproduction. The ability to live with this ambivalence and the humility to accept its sobering entailments are not easily achieved in a profession that believes in the power of literacy to automatically increase the chances of upward mobility. It is also politically risky because it makes visible the invisible institutionalized obstacles and ideological barriers that serve to prevent upward mobility for all. However, even though it does not resolve this paradox, a Bourdieusian stance enables educators to better understand their own and their students' successes and failures, and thus turns the paradox into a creative experience.

This experience is not the result of an ever more effective education but of a more *reflexive* one. A Bourdieusian research stance is an eminently reflexive stance. Researchers make explicit whom or what they are directing their research against, what social and personal factors have triggered their research interests, what institutional and political conditions of possibility have made their object of study into what it is. They are aware of how their research will be used by powers beyond their control, and how they themselves are complicit in the economy of knowledge and the academic game of distinction. Bourdieu has shown the way for a kind of research that manages to combine both a rigorous quantitative and qualitative ethnographic methodology and a subject- ive empathy for one's object of inquiry, and an awareness of one's own socio- historical subject position as a researcher. His is an ethically responsible research.

For the educator in the classroom, a Bourdieusian stance combines the awareness of the theory and the empathy of the practice. For example, literacy teachers have to teach the genres of power but, at the same time, they have to help their students demystify the power of the dominant genres. Students learn to distinguish between what they owe to the school in order to succeed and what they owe to themselves in order to maintain their self-respect; they learn to recognize that their personal value is not limited to the grades they receive. In a similar manner, teachers become reflexive of their own practice. Like Bourdieu, they acquire the ability to play the game required by the institution but, at the same time, they are in a position to critically reflect upon the game and to play an active role in bringing about the social and political conditions necessary to change its rules.

Finally, a Bourdieusian stance in literacy education encourages teachers to research their own practice on the micro level of classroom and institutional interactions. This is not something that Bourdieu himself engaged in, since he conducted mostly large-scale ethnographic and sociological investigations on whole segments of the population. But some of his associates have started to apply his stance of inquiry to illuminate how individual and collective habitus get formed, shaped, and transformed, and how symbolic violence gets exer- cised in interaction with different fields. Two of them, in particular, are work- ing to adapt Bourdieu's thinking to our more decentered times. Lahire (1998, 1999b), who has researched elementary school literacy and has worked with discourse analysts such as Aaron Cicourel, proposes a psychological sociology that focuses on the ways in which the social order is constructed and subverted on the grid of turns-at-talk in individual utterances and dialogic exchanges. He suggests applying a Bourdieusian stance to empirical work done in social inter- actionism, conversation analysis, and language socialization studies. Corcuff (1999) attempts to revise Bourdieu's theory of the singular individual in order to account for today's hybrid, heteroglossic subject engaged in various forms of action. He acknowledges that even "such post-Bourdieusian efforts are necessarily a homage to the work of Pierre Bourdieu" (1999: 118, my translation).

In the end, Bourdieu's legacy for literacy scholars lies not only in his theory but also in his biographical example. Like many educators/researchers, he suffered from the confrontation of academic knowledge and the practical real- ities on the ground. With unique empathy and compassion, he applied his immense intellectual capital to exploring both the transmission of practical knowledge in everyday life and the production of academic knowledge at educational institutions. He discovered that both were various forms of struggle for symbolic power. At the end of the autobiographical essay he wrote a few months before his death, Bourdieu summarized best what we may gain from learning about his life.

> [I hope that my readers will be able to] appropriate my work actively, [with] sympraxy rather than sympathy, oriented toward creation and action. Indeed, it turns out that, paradoxically, historicizing an author . . . gives readers a means to come closer to him and to transform this author, embalmed and imprisoned as he is in the bandages of academic commentary, into a real alter ego, or better, a fellow traveler, someone who has also both trivial and serious problems, like everyone else. . . . Nothing would make me happier than to know that I have managed to help some of my readers recognize their experiences, their difficulties, their questions, their sufferings, etc. in mine, and that they draw from this realistic identification (that is quite the opposite of an idealistic projection) the means to do and live a tiny bit better what they have been living and doing.
>
> (Bourdieu, 2004: 142, my translation)

Acknowledgments

I wish to thank Jim Albright and Allan Luke for inviting me to write this chapter and to write it in this unusual biographical genre. It has allowed me to put into words the great intellectual debt I personally owe Pierre Bourdieu.

Notes

1   The *baccalauréat* is both a high-school graduation and a university entrance exam. The *Ecole Normale Supérieure* is a separate higher education track for the recruitment of elite civil servants teaching in the national education system. Admission is highly competitive and can be sought only after two years of intensive preparation in *classes préparatoires* (*hypokhâgne* and *khâgne*) and the passing of a national *concours*. Those who have been admitted pursue graduate studies both at the *Ecole Normale* and at the University (e.g., Sorbonne). They ultimately take the written and oral *agrégation*, the highest discipline-specific diploma that allows one to teach at both the secondary and the post-secondary levels. The *agrégation* is distinct from the *doctorat* or PhD in that it is not a research degree.

2   In her memoirs, especially *La force des choses* [Force of circumstances] published in 1963, Simone de Beauvoir gives a good testimony of the prestige accorded to philosophical studies at the time and the intellectual consecration that an *agrégation de philosophie* represented.

3   Bourdieu's work has been the object of a large number of critical studies both in Europe and in the United States, before and after his death in February 2002. Since my perspective here is more biographical than strictly scholastic, I refer the reader to: Bonnewitz (2002); Calhoun et al. (1993); Swartz (1997); Brown and Szeman (2000); Harker et al. (1990); Lahire (1999a, 1999b); Lane (2000); Mounier (2001); and Robbins (2000) for excellent critical introductions to his work.

References

Bonnewitz, P. (2002) *Pierre Bourdieu: Vie, œuvres, concepts*. Paris: Ellipses.

Boudon, R. (2004) *Pourquoi les intellectuels n'aiment pas le libéralisme*. Paris: Odile Jacob.

Bourdieu, P. (1962) Célibat et condition paysanne. *Etudes Rurales*, 5–6, 32–135. (Reprinted in *Le bal des célibataires: Crise de la société paysanne en Béarn*, 2002, Paris: Seuil)

Bourdieu, P. (1977) *Outline of a Theory of Practice* (R. Nice, trans.) Cambridge, UK: Cambridge University Press. (Original work published 1972)

Bourdieu, P. (1982) *Ce que parler veut dire: L'économie des échanges linguistiques*. Paris: Fayard. (Modified translation published as *Language and Symbolic Power*, by J. Thompson, ed., G. Raymond and M. Adamson, trans., 1991, Cambridge, UK: Polity Press)

Bourdieu, P. (1984) *Distinction: A Social Critique of the Judgment of Taste* (R. Nice, trans.) London: Routledge and Kegan Paul. (Original work published 1979)

Bourdieu, P. (1988) *Homo academicus* (P. Collier, trans.) Cambridge, UK: Polity Press. (Original work published 1984)

Bourdieu, P. (1987) *In Other Words: Essays Towards a Reflexive Sociology*. Stanford, CA: Stanford University Press.

Bourdieu, P. (1990) *The Logic of Practice* (R. Nice, trans.) Cambridge, UK: Polity Press. (Original work published 1980)

Bourdieu, P. (1996a) *The Rules of Art: The Genesis and Structure of the Literary Field* (S. Emanuel, trans.) Cambridge, UK: Polity Press. (Original work published 1992)

Bourdieu, P. (1996b) *The State Nobility* (L. C. Clough, trans.) Cambridge, UK: Polity Press. (Original work published 1989)

Bourdieu, P. (2000a) *Pascalian Meditations* (R. Nice, trans.) Stanford, CA: Stanford University Press. (Original work published 1997)

Bourdieu, P. (2000b) *The Weight of the World: Social Suffering in Contemporary Society* (P. P. Ferguson, trans.) Cambridge, UK: Polity Press. (Original work published 1993)

Bourdieu, P. (2004) *Esquisse pour une auto-analyse*. Paris: Editions Raisons d'Agir.

Brown, N. and Szeman, I. (eds) (2000) *Pierre Bourdieu: Fieldwork in Culture*. Lanham, MD: Rowman and Littlefield.

Calhoun, C., LiPuma, E., and Postone, M. (eds) (1993) *Bourdieu: Critical Perspectives*. Chicago: University of Chicago Press.

Corcuff, P. (1999) Le collectif au défi du singulier: en partant de l'habitus. In B. Lahire (ed.), *Le travail sociologique de Pierre Bourdieu: Dettes et critiques*. Paris: Editions la Découverte, 95–120.

Descartes, R. (1999) *Meditations and Other Metaphysical Writings* (D. M. Clarke, trans.) London: Penguin Books. (Original work published 1641)

Guillory, J. (2000) Bourdieu's refusal. In N. Brown and I. Szeman (eds), *Pierre Bourdieu: Fieldwork in Culture*. Lanham, MD: Rowman and Littlefield, 19–43.

Harker, R., Mahar, C. and Wilkes, C. (eds) (1990) *An Introduction to the Work of Pierre Bourdieu: The Practice of Theory*. London: Macmillan.

Lahire, B. (1998) *L'homme pluriel, les ressorts de l'action*. Paris: Nathan.

Lahire, B. (1999a) Champ, hors-champ, contrechamp. In B. Lahire (ed.), *Le travail sociologique de Pierre Bourdieu: Dettes et critiques*. Paris: Editions la Découverte, 23–57.

Lahire, B. (1999b) De la théorie de l'habitus à une sociologie psychologique. In B. Lahire (ed.), *Le travail sociologique de Pierre Bourdieu: Dettes et critiques*. Paris: Editions la Découverte, 121–50.

Lahire, B. (ed.) (1999c) *Le travail sociologique de Pierre Bourdieu: Dettes et critiques*. Paris: Editions la Découverte.

Lane, J. F. (2000) *Pierre Bourdieu: A Critical Introduction*. London: Pluto Press.

Monod, J. C. (1999) Une politique du symbolique? In B. Lahire (ed.), *Le travail sociologique de Pierre Bourdieu: Dettes et critiques*. Paris: Editions la Découverte, 231–54.

Mounier, P. (2001) *Pierre Bourdieu, une introduction*. Paris: Pocket/La Découverte.

Postone, M., LiPuma, E. and Calhoun, C. (1993) Introduction: Bourdieu and social theory. In C. Calhoun, E. LiPuma, and M. Postone (eds), *Bourdieu: Critical Perspectives*. Chicago: University of Chicago Press, 1–13.

Prendergast, C. (2003) *Literacy and Racial Justice*. Carbondale: Southern Illinois University Press.

Robbins, D. (ed.) (2000) *Pierre Bourdieu* (vols 1–4) London: Sage.

Simeoni, D. (2000) Anglicizing Bourdieu. In N. Brown and I. Szeman (eds), *Pierre Bourdieu: Fieldwork in Culture*. Lanham, MD: Rowman and Littlefield, 65–86.

Swartz, D. (1997) *Culture and Power: The Sociology of Pierre Bourdieu*. Chicago: University of Chicago Press.

Wacquant, L. J. D. (1993) Bourdieu in America: notes on the transatlantic importation of social theory. In C. Calhoun, E. LiPuma, and M. Postone (eds), *Bourdieu: Critical Perspectives*. Chicago: University of Chicago Press, 235–62.

Chapter 4

Bourdieu and "literacy education"

Monica Heller

The title of this book, *Bourdieu and Literacy Education*, invites reflection on the ways some of Bourdieu's key concepts might help us understand particular activities of what we understand to be literacy education. My purpose here is to take one step further back, and use some of Bourdieu's ideas to ask what "literacy education" means.

"Literacy education" as field and discourse

My argument is simply that we can understand it in Bourdieu's sense as a field or market (Bourdieu, 1982), that is, as a discursive space in which certain resources are produced, attributed value, and circulated in a regulated way, which allows for competition over access and, typically, unequal distribution.

By referring to "discursive" space, I mean to emphasize that the processes of regulation and attribution of value to resources—indeed, their very constitution as resources—are embedded in processes of signification. They make sense within conceptual spaces shot through with power, within ways of understanding the world that are deeply interested, and that can be understood as regimes of truth in the Foucauldian sense: shared frames of reference and practices of signification that construct, legitimate, and mask relations of power (Foucault, 1970). The term "resources" in this sense comprises interchangeable material and symbolic practices or things, whose sense is part of the knowledge–power nexus to which both Foucault and Bourdieu attached so much importance. (Indeed, Bourdieu insists frequently on the role of the exchangeability of material and symbolic forms of capital in processes of social reproduction; see, for example, his discussion of matrimonial practices in Bourdieu, 1972.) Discursive spaces are therefore sites of struggle. It is an empirical question as to how closed they may be, that is, how reproductive of current arrangements of difference and inequality; or, conversely, how open they may be to forms of social action aimed at, and perhaps achieving, social change.

To understand literacy education as such a discursive space, then, is to understand it as a space where symbolic and material resources are constituted as valued resources, whose regulation serves as a site of production and reproduction of relations of power which, while they might well involve acts of coercion, are more likely to take the form of practices of symbolic domination (that is, of consensus through misrecognition, or the convincing of all participants in a discursive space that current arrangements of power are legitimate; Bourdieu, 1977; Bourdieu and Passeron, 1977). Finally, to see literacy education this way invites a more fundamental question: Why does it operate as such a discursive space?

My goal here is less to provide anything like a definitive answer to this question, and more to raise questions—questions about the historical constitution of literacy education as a discursive space, about the nature of the resources regulated there, about the interests and social positionings of the actors and relations of power involved. Critiques inspired by the New Literacy Studies (Street, 1984) opened the concept of literacy to analysis as an ideologically defined construct within historically and socially situated discursive spaces. My goal is to take off from that insight and examine how those spaces shape stakes, and hence meanings, for social actors with different positions and therefore different interests, with respect to the resources circulating in those spaces and connected to the concept of literacy. This will mean seeing literacy not simply as practice, but as practice embedded in the interested construction and legitimation of social difference and social inequality, and literacy education as a particular site for the regulation of access to resources ideologically constructed as connected to the concept of literacy. It means locating literacy, and literacy education, within the framework of concerns about access to symbolic and material resources, which informs much of Bourdieu's work on education and its role in the production and reproduction of social difference and social inequality (Bourdieu and Passeron, 1977). It also means exploiting Bourdieu's understanding of how social actors get positioned differentially in a system of unequal distribution of resources, developing different orientations to and understandings of that system (Bourdieu, 1982) as a way of capturing who has what interest in constructing literacy education in certain ways.

In what follows, I will first examine some of the ways in which the New Literacy Studies help to deconstruct the idea of literacy itself, re-embedding it as a form of communicative practice within complex sets of relations of power, institutions, and technologies. I will then return to the notion of literacy education as a discursive space to rethink it within the idea of symbolic domination and to raise questions about how literacy is understood, by whom, and why, in a kind of genealogical account situating literacy within ideologies of language and communicative practice emerging in the context of the rise of capitalism and the shifting role of the state in the last two centuries—a genealogy in which academic studies of language and literacy, of course, have their own place.

I will then turn to some specific questions about literacy and literacy education which emerge in the context of the globalized new economy, a space in which communicative practice itself is more and more directly tied to economic activities. In particular, I will consider some of the ways in which the current political economic context favors the understanding of communicative practice as a measurable skill, thereby favoring the reproduction of a certain discourse of literacy education as a neutral field of transmission of techniques necessary for economic integration—the kind of discourse Bourdieu would likely have considered central to the operation of the field of literacy education in social reproduction, that is, to the masking of the mechanisms of symbolic domination actually operating within or across it. If we think of literacy as communicative practice within a specific discursive space that is traversed by practices of symbolic domination, we are forced to ask in whose interests it lies to understand literacy that way. Finally, we must ask what the basis of legitimacy and authority might be, of those who get to define what counts as literacy, and of the practices constituted as literate themselves (Bourdieu, 1977). This necessarily includes us, as producers and circulators of discourse, as well as any other stakeholders or affected parties.

"New Literacy Studies" and the deconstruction of literacy

Most readers of this volume will be familiar with Street's (1984) by now well-known distinction between so-called "autonomous" and "ideological" concepts of literacy. For my purposes, I will only recall here the ways in which this distinction captures different ontological positions about literacy.

The so-called "autonomous" model, consistent with prevailing views in linguistics about the autonomy of the linguistic system, sees literacy as an objectively existing set of technologically mediated tools for the advancement of cognition. The so-called "ideological" model recasts literacy as a set of historically contingent social practices, necessarily embedded in the ideological frameworks which allow for the reproduction of regimes of truth. The strand of work, known as the New Literacy Studies (NLS), which emerged from the ideological perspective, largely takes the position that to understand literacy as related to cognitive and also social development runs the risk of falling into social Darwinism or, at best, the kind of linear models of progress that characterize the ontology of Western modernity since the nineteenth century. Such models are universalizing and hierarchizing and, viewed from more current postcolonial perspectives, serve largely to justify European and North American claims to superiority and the right to undertake the civilizing missions which underlie Western hegemony. They can be seen as part of the construction of Western symbolic domination, part of the discourse which legitimizes Western colonialism and neo-colonialism. And they can be seen to play a central role not in the processes of coercion, which certainly characterize those relations of power, but in those of symbolic domination carried out through a variety of institutional means, not the least of which, as Bourdieu and Passeron argued, is education.

Related arguments can be made about the ways in which autonomous models of literacy can be seen to be bound up in the production of relations of power within states, to the extent that "literacy" is understood to be a requirement for full citizenship, that is, for adequate access to and participation in the politically defined public sphere (Bauman and Briggs, 2003). "Literacy" can then be understood, from an NLS perspective, as an ideologically loaded term, with roots in the specific conditions of the emergence of the bourgeois, expansionist nation-state, and therefore tied to the interests of the architects of that state and to the reasons why the state took the shape it did. It becomes a technology of mass communication permitting the "imagination of communities" in the hands of print capitalists (Anderson, 1983).

But literacy is more than that since, in an NLS view, what counts substantively as literacy is culturally defined. Indeed, many NLS studies are devoted to the documentation of communicative practices that can be argued to be literate but which escape the notice of mainstream institutions, especially educational ones, who are quick to categorize as illiterate people whose literacy practices merely differ from those understood as such by the institution in question (e.g., Martin-Jones and Jones, 2000, assemble a large number of case studies of multilingual literacy practices usually completely invisible in a world where only majority language monolingualism tends to count). If that is the case, then the question arises of who gets to decide what counts as literacy, and who gets to decide who gets access to it. In other words, literacy is also available as a terrain for assertion of control over the definition of the legitimate language—in Bourdieu's (1977) terms, of the language that is authorized, that must be heard—and, hence, over processes of selection of legitimate speakers, that is, of those who can require others to hear them. In Bourdieu's terms, literacy becomes available as a site for social selection.

But if NLS has shown that literacy is not an autonomous system or foundation of modes of thought, that it must be understood as historically located and socially embedded in relations of power, it has failed thus far to address the question of how we should understand it analytically. We can show, every day if need be—the data are that evident—that literacy is a working element of the discourse of public space in the developed world. There are plenty of programs funded by governments, supranational organizations and non-government organizations for the promotion of literacy and literacy education; literacy figures prominently in school curricula, in programs for immigrants, in programs preparing people for the new labor market. It is understood as an issue not just in monolingual spaces but in multilingual ones as well (Luke, 2003; Martin-Jones and Jones, 2000). While NLS insists that literacy be understood as a practice, not a system or a technology, it still allows for a certain degree of autonomy, granting that there is something about literacy that is analytically different from other communicative practices. Hence, perhaps also NLS's greater orientation to Vygotskian social constructivism, in a paradoxical continuity with literacy studies' tendency to focus on the cognitive, than to theories of social structuration which are the other side of what counts as "culture" (Luke, 2004).

I propose here that we take the NLS position to its logical conclusion, that we see literacy as an ideological construct, relating to a variety of forms of communicative practice that are, for reasons we can empirically discover, understood to be somehow different from other forms of communicative practice. If NLS shows us anything, it is that it is the very concept of "literacy" that requires problematization. It is with this notion of literacy as an ideological construct that I wish to begin, in order to see how taking it as such allows us to ask a series of questions about how it operates in the construction of symbolic domination.

Literacy, the nation, and citizenship

Bauman and Briggs (2003) point to the ways in which language standardization in the nineteenth century was bound up in processes of constructing the notion of the modern nation-state. They focus in particular on some legitimacy dilemmas of the new political formation, related to bourgeois and masculine interests in retaining control over capital and property, while being seen to champion democracy and equality. These are, of course, the very dilemmas which dog us to this day. They note (see, in particular, pp. 59–69) that a central way of solving this dilemma was to set up language as a pure, neutral terrain on which to construct the kinds of ways of thinking that are best suited to the production of social order and social progress; that is, to oppose modernity, rationality, social order, and clear thinking to primitiveness, emotionality, chaos, and cognitive muddle. This is the kind of legitimizing ideology central to Bourdieu's ideas about mystification and misrecognition; it is an example of how participants get convinced of the naturalness and rightness of prevailing patterns of unequal distribution of resources. The next step was to get to work on defining the forms and practices of "civilized" language, through the production of grammars, dictionaries, and other tools of authorization, and to organize their distribution through education. However, as Bourdieu pointed out, one of the points of education as we know it is to mask the operation of social selection by imposing discourses of meritocracy in a system in which one cannot succeed without already mastering the tools of the system (Bourdieu and Passeron, 1977).

Grillo (1989) and Anderson (1983) also argue that the concept of literacy as a set of distinct practices becomes particularly important as emerging nation-states try to establish modes of organization—and, Foucault (1975) would add, of social control—across stretches of time and space, greater than other political formations had yet encountered. Viewed like this, the notion of literacy looks like part of a set of privileged and authoritative modes of gathering and distributing the information required for the functioning of the state, for its ability to muster coercive and persuasive forms of authority and legitimacy, and for its ability to protect and foster the interests of bourgeois capitalism which underlie its existence.

The link between literacy and education thus begins with an ideology of language that serves the interests of bourgeois, nationalist capitalism; it serves to legitimate the dominant discourse of the public sphere, and the political apparatus that controls it, by defining what counts as legitimate language in a very particular way; namely, as a language of reason, disconnected from the mess of everyday life, and therefore seemingly "disinterested." The successful linking of specific linguistic forms and practices, and the construction of a "purified" (Bauman and Briggs, 2003), specialized sphere of language with reason, progress, and authority, allows for the construction of legitimate and illegitimate subjects (Bourdieu, 1977). It becomes possible, indeed necessary, to distinguish between those who may act as full citizens by virtue of their mastery of the "purified," standardized language forms and associated practices, and those who require either protection or elimination by virtue of their inability to communicate and therefore to think "clearly" for reasons that can be constructed as having to do with their personal failure to profit from access to the legitimate language or with their membership to particular gender, race or class social categories understood to be constitutionally unable to master it. The very idea of literacy is linked to this legitimizing ideology, as a form of linguistic practice which requires active learning, and which can be constructed as distinct from the natural and socially embedded practices of talk by virtue of its ability to transcend the immediate and of its location in technologically mediated interaction.

In this way, we can understand literacy as a discursive field set up in a particular socio-historical context in ways which correspond organically to the exercise of symbolic domination. In particular, its institutionalization, through the production of specialized materials, the development of dedicated technologies, the identification of particular practices, and the regulation of the distribution of all of the above in specific sites, involving selected actors, allows for literacy to function simultaneously as a regime of social control, of social selection, and of symbolic domination. This institutionalization renders the concept of literacy available for the production of legitimate citizens, and for the definition of acceptable and authoritative discourse, both in the active sense of providing for the deep socialization of those who will belong to the definers and selectors, and in the negative sense of providing means for identifying those people and practices which require policing, and techniques of marginalization and control.

We can see clearly how this constitution of literacy and standard language is connected to class interest, insofar as we are convinced by theories of the nation-state which attribute its rise to the ability of the emerging capitalist bourgeoisie, to harness the apparatus of political power and control to advance its interest in constructing conditions for the expansion of their activities and for control over materials and markets (see Grillo, 1989; Higonnet, 1980;

Hobsbawm, 1990; Ives, 2003; Wolf, 1982). Bauman and Briggs take pains to point out that this discourse is also traversed by ideologies and inequalities of gender and race, in ways that have been explored in the literature in a variety of ways. And, of course, the state as an institution never acted alone; religious institutions, notably, have been bound up in these processes in important ways (see, e.g., Fabian, 1986; Kapitzke, 1993; or Meeuwis, 1999).

Outram (1987), for example, demonstrates the ways in which the discourse of the French Revolution created oppositions between the vigorous and new versus the old and decadent, which not only depended heavily for effect on prevailing gender ideologies (the *ancien régime* characterized as frivolously, corruptly female, and, indeed, overly influenced by actual women) but also in the practice of discursive production, necessarily marginalized Revolutionary women who, in Bourdieu's terms, could not possibly ever be legitimate producers of Revolutionary discourse. To the extent that this connection carried over into the construction of democratic nation-states in the nineteenth century—and, as Higonnet (1980) points out, the Revolution in the final analysis was carried out by an emerging bourgeoisie for itself—with the same interests on the part of bourgeois men for control over the labor of women and for minimization of their access to power, we can see how the linkages between reason, clarity, and the social order are tied not just to the bourgeoisie but also to masculinity.

Cameron (1995) explored the ways in which this linkage has consistently operated on the terrain of language since the nineteenth century to tie femininity both to incompetence and to danger, two sides of the coin of the process of exercise of symbolic domination; what does not fit must be contained either through coercion or persuasion. Her work also illustrates the profound ways in which the social order, which reproduces difference in the service of reproducing inequality, is strongly tied to a sense of the moral order; and how panic over threats to the social order can be read in moral panics over grammar, linguistic style, and other domains of linguistic form and linguistic practice. Once again, we encounter "purified" language as a terrain of social control and symbolic domination.

Finally, race was of course the central trope of legitimacy of the construction of the nation-state. Since it was crucial to mask the specific class interests behind the idea of the democratic state, what emerged as a legitimating ideology was the concept of a nation based on shared values and shared practices, whether on the French Revolutionary model or the German Romantic one. Indeed, Higonnet (1980) argues that the privileging of French monolingualism in Revolutionary discourse was a direct result of bourgeois reaction to peasant and worker claims on both aristocratic and bourgeois property. In his view, the legitimacy of the Revolution was precisely its pretence at universality, but its claims, taken to their logical conclusion, proved too threatening to the property interests of the Revolutionary bourgeoisie. To skirt around this, Higonnet claims, the leaders of the Revolution began to focus instead on other forms of sharedness—sharedness of a more symbolic kind, in linguistic and cultural practices that would come to define French citizenship in ways that could be made to appear democratic and neutral—while deflecting any critical gaze from the class-based forms of inequality that emerged from the Revolution and that can be argued to have been at its core (a classic Bourdieusian mystifying move).

Certainly once the concept of nationality became available, it could be and was used as a means to legitimate the construction of nation-states through means less violent than the Revolution. Hobsbawm (1990) argues that this move had the consequence of opening up as a terrain of struggle the definition of what would constitute a nation, of the important kind that gets legitimately to claim a state. Many groups laid claim to such a status, and still do today, as we see in the continuing politics of ethnolinguistic minority movements in places such as Catalonia, Brittany, Wales, Corsica, or Quebec. Hobsbawm traces nineteenth-century discussions which, he says, can be seen in the end to focus on criteria that are fundamentally economic: underneath discussions of authenticity there lay discussions of economic viability. The putative nation-state had to represent a market of production and consumption adequate to bourgeois capitalist interests. At the same time, it had to present the conditions of legitimacy and authority of control of such a political and economic space, hence the attention paid notably to the standardization of language. The question was simply whether or not the "nation" in question could lay claim to shared linguistic forms and practices which, on the one hand, could be demonstrated to have historical depth (and, hence, act as marks of authenticity, a key legitimating function) but which also, on the other hand, could be demonstrated to correspond to the modernist, rational ideal of the purified, technical language (a key authorizing function). Groups that meet those conditions get access to the status of nation, understood in an organic and fundamentally racial sense, and these conditions help us understand the emergence of subfields of linguistics, such as language planning.

What this requires, then, is a set of criteria for determining who counts and who does not, and invites the elaboration of legitimating theories which authorize selection and therefore exclusion. On this basis, we can understand the enthusiasm for means of objectively ranking nations, on a developmental or absolute scale, especially considering that the results of such rankings serve to legitimate expansion at the expense of others; that is, various forms of internal and external colonialism, or more recently, in the postcolonial or neo-colonial discourses of "development" (Luke, 2004). Particularly interesting, for our purposes, is the role that language, and linguistics as a discipline, plays in the identification of criteria and scales of evaluation (somewhat in the spirit of Bourdieu's furious 1977 attack on a linguistics that insists on understanding language as a reified system, rather than as social practice embedded in the construction of relations of power).

Understood in historical and political economic terms, the concept of literacy is tied to the concept of the kind of decontextualized, institutionalized, and "technicized" language that served as a central discursive space for the development of ideologies and practices of the bourgeois, capitalist, homogenizing nation-state in ways that not only helped legitimize class, race, and gender inequality but also in many ways served to actively construct them. These ideas are still current and can be seen in active circulation in the form of policy debates regarding literacy and immigration, as well as literacy and citizenship education in schooling more generally. One dimension of these debates concerns the aptitude of immigrants as putative citizens to engage in the public sphere of the state, based on their mastery of literacy skills, defined more or less automatically as skills in the majority language of the state in question. While there are concerns about whether these are skills that should be evaluated as a criterion for granting immigrant status, or whether they are teachable once immigration is completed and whether they are transferable across languages or not, in all cases there is an assumption that the concept itself is relevant to our understanding of citizenship.

While NLS showed us that the naturalization (among other things, through academic work) of this concept of literacy served these particular interests and helped marginalize other practices which could quite well, looked at through different lenses, equally aspire to the status of literacy practices, it has been less successful in addressing the historical and political economic bases of the very concept of literacy. Without such an analysis it is difficult to grasp the reasons why literacy is effectively constructed as a discursive space, and how it operates to reproduce particular relations of difference and inequality; and it is here, of course, that Bourdieu invites us to begin.

I will return to this problem later. First, however, I want to examine some of the ways in which the concept of literacy is taken up in contemporary conditions related to the globalized new economy; ways, I will argue, which are consistent with the notion of literacy as a privileged, or at least specialized, set of communicative practices, but which set literacy more squarely in the realm of the economic. The issue here is less one of literacy as a key to individual participation in public space as a full citizen or to collective participation in the community of nation-states, and more one of individual and collective economic integration into the capitalist activities of high modernity. This can be seen as an extension of Bourdieu's interest in the modern state and state agencies to the private sector, which is so closely tied to it.

Literacy, "skills," and the globalized new economy

While one of the premises of modernity has been political equality (as discussed in the preceding section), the other has been not economic equality but rather equal access to competition for economic resources and to participation in economic progress. One of the hallmarks of high modernity (Giddens, 1990) has been realignment of the relationship between states and the private sector in the regulation of the economy (Castells, 2000), whose globalized characteristics are arguably not so much radically new as somewhat reshaped. Perhaps, more importantly, high modernity is characterized by a shift in economic activity, with the greatest expansion coming from the tertiary sector (Castells, 2000), connected to a crisis in the modes of industrial production underlying the emergence of the bourgeois nation-state. This has consequences for the role that modern ideas about language play in legitimizing relations of difference and inequality related to new(ish) modes of production.

Gee and colleagues (1996) have shown how the crisis of industrial capitalism has resulted not only in production of new commodities (more service and information, fewer manufactured objects) but also in the reorganization of modes of production, whatever the product. This reorganization requires new forms of legitimization, new modes of social control, and the ones that emerge are closely connected to the role of language—or to use the terms of the discourse itself, of literacy—in the social organization of work in the new economy. They show that work is more and more mediated by a variety of forms of technologized communication, with the result that various kinds of linguistic practices, including the technologically mediated ones that we think of as literacy, come to the forefront as the means through which work-related competence is judged.

This shift, they go on to argue, is the result of greater competition within the context of increased possibilities for profiting from global inequalities; it is easier than it used to be to produce the kinds of things the new economy produces using cheap labor and cheap infrastructure, once too far away or too difficult to access. The result in the developed world is the flattening out of workplace hierarchies and a focus on flexibility. The first is presented as democratization; Gee and colleagues (1996) argue that it is instead a means of increasing competitiveness by eliminating expensive managers. The second is presented as providing greater freedom and autonomy to workers, and a greater chance for them to invest in (literally and ideologically) and profit from their labor; Gee and colleagues argue that it is instead a means to eliminate union-won benefits and security packages. Most importantly for my purposes, however, this shift requires the active involvement of workers in the discursive dimensions of both production and social control.

French sociolinguists following the transformation of the workplace in the 1990s (Boutet, 2001; Kergoat et al., 1999), as well as other authors (see Cameron, 2001; Heller, 2003), make similar arguments about how this shift involves more persuasion and less coercion in the construction of workplace authority. In Bourdieu's terms, the high modern workplace places a greater emphasis on modes of symbolic domination than did the modern industrial one. These authors also point out how the combination of language-centered products, language-centered modes of production, and language-centered modes of social control converge to produce a concept of communicative competence and, in particular, of literacy as a measurable and commodifiable skill (which thus entails an even greater interest in rejecting Bourdieu's ideas about language as social practice, although his notion of capital could easily get appropriated and reinterpreted). Boutet asserts:

> In taylorism, talking and working are considered antagonistic. Talking makes you lose time, distracts you, prevents you from concentrating on the (physical) action you need to perform. . . . The introduction of new modes of production, and in particular of automation, robotization and computerization of activities, along with the introduction of the management of workers (participative management, responsibilization, semi-autonomous teams, self-direction . . .) end up having two major consequences for the place of language at work. The first is the general spread of engagement with the written word (reading, writing) in all activities and trades, including unskilled ones. . . . The second is the emergence of a work-related communicative competence.[1]
>
> (2001: 56, my translation)

To provide one example, in call centers where we have recently been conducting research (see Boudreau, 2003; Roy, 2003),[2] the workforce consists mainly of representatives who do the actual (communicative) work of customer service. Some are selected as "peer coaches," who have the responsibility of inspecting the work of subsets of other representatives, by listening in on calls online or reviewing taped calls. They do this with the representative in question, and time is allocated to regular meetings between representative and coach, in forms of discipline that have more to do with self-criticism than authoritarian sanctioning. There is co-production of the discourse of social control between actors constructed as "peers" (and, in fact, the coaches get little in the way of compensation for the role they play; perhaps privileged access to choice of shifts, more control over their allocation of time, occasionally a little more money). At the same time the product, the quality of which is being inspected, is a linguistic one—partly oral (the exchange between representative and client), partly written on-screen (the actual trace of the product in the shape of computerized forms which representatives fill out, and occasionally in the shape of email)—although the product is also achieved with the use of reading on-screen or paper texts and the support of handwritten notes kept frequently on a pad beside the computer. The work is thus multimodal (see the New London Group's 1996 appeal to a concept of "multiliteracies"). It nonetheless requires transparent criteria of evaluation in order for the new forms of management to retain legitimacy and authority. Communication becomes a skill, to be treated in the same way as other skills.

This view of literacy is also present in a great deal of current policy concern (Street, 2000). Alongside the problem of literacy and political citizenship discussed above, the current conditions permit the explicit emergence of a commodified notion of literacy, or "communicative competence" as Boutet (2001) more broadly refers to it, linked to integration in the job market. The policy concern for literacy now revolves as much, if not more, around the acquisition of literacy skills for the job market as it does around literacy skills for participation in public debate (see Budach, 2003; Lamoureux et al., 2003). Indeed, the two can be seen as linked; that is, it is now through demonstration of integration into the job market that one shows oneself to be a full citizen. "Communicative competence" is displaced toward the first step, but remains essential to legitimacy in a discursive space understood as much as a market as a nation-state, if not more so.

However, the mechanisms of definition of communicative competence for the nation-state—the grammars, dictionaries, and standardizing language classes in school—turn out to be not so easily transferable to the new conditions. Our research is showing how hard this seems to be, in fact, to achieve. Managers and peer coaches in call centers can be very precise about what they look for in the way of content, and certainly in the way of output (Is a sale made? Are the requisite numbers of calls made in a given amount of time? Are forms filled out correctly?) but find themselves floundering when it comes to what to look for in the way of "quality service." The same is true in other new economy workplaces we have been investigating. Peer coaches use their old-school knowledge of grammar and vocabulary to evaluate representatives' language without knowing whether or not, and certainly not how, such features are indeed connected to customer satisfaction.

One way in which they address this problem is to impose standard practices, fixed interactional routines the content of which is meant to convey management values. This has the advantage of having a history and some tools that can be mobilized for the new purpose. This strategy, however, is from the start doomed by its conflict with one central standard of quality service, namely authenticity and personalization (Cameron, 2001; Roy, 2003). It also makes workers feel like robots, and thus undermines management attempts to have them invest ideologically in the concept of teamwork. There are gaps in the construction of mystification.

Another way is to outsource language work. In Canada at least, there are important numbers of self-employed consultants, sometimes working alone and sometimes in small firms, who produce language products, usually in the form of texts, from scratch or in the form of translation. Occasionally, someone in-house who has the training to do this kind of work is called upon to do so, although such tasks may not in fact formally figure in his or her job description. These kinds of "literacy workers" use the tools of the standardized nation-state type of literacy, which seems to work because the product is precisely one which is decontextualizable.

Two other interrelated strategies work in precisely the opposite direction: they minimize the specialized nature of these skills, treating them as innate and natural, or, on the other hand, not in fact very important. They institutionalize variability and redefine quality as whatever works. They emerge mainly in less routinized, more deeply socially embedded forms of linguistic performance or production. The first is evident where multilingual skills are involved; rather than use standardized tests or fixed lists of criteria, managers will call on any employee who claims to speak the language required to carry out the work, whether it is interpreting an email or evaluating a job candidate, and fail to scrutinize the results (they all say it seems to work). The second is simply to ignore the issue unless an actual problem arises, in which case management is hard pressed to find solutions using anything other than intuitive criteria.

We can see similar signs of destabilization at the institutional level. Recent studies of francophone literacy centres in Ontario (Budach, 2003; Lamoureux et al., 2003) have shown how these sites are traversed by the overlapping and sometimes contradictory discourses of nation and skill. Francophone nationalist mobilization in Canada over the last 40 years or so has more or less successfully established the principle that francophones need to be treated as a homogeneous nation with political rights to the modernist institutions of the state, or at least to homogeneous institutions distributing state resources (such as schools; see Heller, 2002a). The original legitimacy of this argument was strengthened by the demonstrable marginalization of francophones from sources of wealth and power in Canada, leading to specific efforts to set up schooling, early childhood and adult education programs to facilitate access to mainstream measures of success. In Ontario, by standard measures in the 1970s, the francophone adult population was shown to have a disproportionately high rate of illiteracy; the state response was to set up a network of francophone literacy centers parallel to, but separate from, the mainstream adult literacy programs.

By the late 1990s, the state was making institutionalized distinctions between programs for anglophones, francophones, and members of the Deaf and Aboriginal communities—each one conceptualized as distinct and internally homogeneous, but all subject to the same planning which tended to be developed first for the majority and then adapted, or simply applied, to the minority. The state's discourse on adult literacy also shifted away from literacy as empowerment, and literacy and identity, towards literacy as preparation for the job market with, of course, new sets of evaluative criteria for the distribution of resources.

In the meantime, the putative population base of the francophone literacy centers seemed to have shifted. Set up to provide basic literacy skills to an undereducated monolingual population, the centers seemed to receive students who corresponded less and less to that profile. Most of the (at least putative) clientele were job seekers educated and literate in English, seeking literacy skills in French for the new job market. Some of them could be classified by almost any criteria as second-language learners of French. Others were francophone refugees and immigrants, often educated in French but possessing no English, seeking means to gain skills that would help them gain entry to the bilingual job market. This gap between the legitimizing ideology of the centers (as sites of ethnonational empowerment), the institutional structures regulated by the state (based on a reductionist but easily administered notion of distinct communities), and what diverse members of the population were seeking was difficult to manage for literacy workers who depended on performance evaluation measures defined by the state for access to resources and maintenance of existing structures. It was also difficult to manage at the program level, given the diverse kinds of linguistic resources brought to the centers by the clientele, the lack of clarity around what kinds of resources people like that would actually need to have to fulfill their goals of bilingual employment, and the constraints imposed by the state on what resources such centers could legitimately provide.

The new conditions clearly challenge (although they do not seem to have entirely replaced) established criteria for defining and regulating what is to count as legitimate language and who counts as legitimate speakers. They multiply its forms and make it relevant to an increasing number of people within an ideology that insists more and more on democracy and autonomy in the service of reproducing discrepancies of wealth. They do nothing, however, to destablize the prevailing notion that there is such a thing, and that mastery of it is a sign of full competence as a member of society and perhaps, more importantly, as a credible job candidate.

The notion of literacy, if anything, has spread and become more diffuse. In academia, as we have seen, the concept of multiliteracies has been introduced to capture the kinds of complex, variously mediated practices that characterize the experience of more and more people. Street (2000: 19, 20) has voiced concerns that such an approach runs the risk of simply multiplying reified and internally coherent objects, that is, of reproducing an ideology of literacy as monolithic and autonomous. In public debate, it seems clear that the idea of literacy has also slid into a more general idea of specialized, mediated knowledge; for example, my local newspaper recently ran a small piece in which "health literacy" was glossed as an ability not only to read instructions on packets of medicine, or things such as nutritional guidelines published by public health authorities, but also to understand what the doctor tells you when you are in his or her office (Kesterton, 2004).

This is, I think, not an accident, nor even necessarily a bad thing. It is instead a sign that the social, political and economic conditions in which we live are still saturated with modernist notions of expertise, and of specialized forms of linguistic practice whose authority derives from the fact that their technological mediation allows for exercise of control over access to those practices, to the ability to imbue them with meaning, and to use them to develop discourses of legitimation of modernist, capitalist forms of power. Those forms of power have certainly changed in the past two or three decades, but in ways which are more consistent than not with modernity (which is indeed the reason Giddens, 1990, refers to "high modernity" rather than "post modernity"). They may very well, however, be coming unstuck; an example from a slightly different realm concerns the perplexity of many multinationals faced with having to invent ways of evaluating the multilingual "skills" of their language workers, especially in customer service domains (Heller, 2002b).

The contradictions between democracy, diversity and inequality, and the ways that the relative success of bourgeois capitalism has brought about ever more obvious manifestations of these contradictions, destabilize the dominant discourses in which the autonomous model of literacy played such an important role. But they only destabilize; they do not displace entirely. The notion of literacy remains a powerful one in this context, although we can see in academic discourse various ways in which we have tried to confront the contradictions, by appealing to multiple literacies, multimodality, and literacy practices understood as cultural and social processes and forms of social action (Ahearn, 2001; Street, 2000). It has not been possible under high modern conditions to completely sustain the autonomous model, but neither has it seemed possible to deconstruct the notion of literacy entirely.

In the final section of this chapter, I will discuss how Bourdieu's notions invite us not to deconstruct it entirely, but rather to take it as an object of discursive analysis instead of an objectively existing phenomenon. Bourdieu invites the analysis initiated by NLS to complete its path, problematizing literacy as an element of processes of symbolic domination, rather than as a specialized form of communication or social interaction.

The dilemma of "literacy"

This rather oversimplified and somewhat breathless account has tried to situate literacy, and by extension literacy education, in the context of a historically situated discourse giving rise to naturalized ideas about technicized, standardized and specialized language in the service of political economic ideologies, specifically, ideologies linking the political structures of the nation-state to the economic structures of capitalism. My argument is simply that this is the context in which the notion of literacy has emerged and makes sense. Taken in this way, we can see some of the ways in which it has been constituted as a Bourdieusian field, supported by institutionalized practices, especially educational ones.

In this way, I am arguing that contemporary prevailing discourses of literacy, subsumed generally under the heading of "New Literacy Studies," fail to actually engage with the political economic bases of the concept itself. Bourdieu, I want to argue, pushes us to envisage any discourse as constituted within very particular, historically situated systems of distribution of resources. Until we can provide analyses of why we even bother with the concept of literacy, and why certain kinds of socially situated actors take the positions regarding literacy they do, we cannot fulfill the NLS agenda of understanding how literacy is bound up in the construction of relations of power.

Concerns over what is to count as literacy clearly identify it as a terrain of struggle over the resources that underlie contemporary relations of power. The problem is whether to accept the rules of the game as they are set, at least insofar as acquiescing to the relevance of a notion of "literacy" as a specialized field; or to contest them, opening up the concept to the broader idea of communicative practice, which some (such as Boutet) suggest may be more relevant to the current recognition of the multiplicity of the practices involved, and retaining a critical analysis of the stakes involved in the discourse of literacy as it stands now.

My own view is that we are best served by asking such questions as: Who has an interest in maintaining a distinct set of concepts and the institutions that go with it? What are the resources produced and distributed via literacy education, by whom and to whom? What kinds of practices are defined as "legitimately literate," by whom and why? What processes of symbolic domination traverse the field of literacy? In this view, literacy education becomes a discursive space in which resources are produced and distributed—although its role as a space in which value is attributed to resources is perhaps less clear; Bourdieu and Passeron showed clearly how education is about legitimizing regimes, not constituting them—and in which actors are legitimized or marginalized, consecrated or stigmatized, in complex processes of social selection involving exchanges among a wide variety of forms of material and symbolic capital.

As analysts, we cannot assume we know in advance who gains and loses what from current or imagined literacy education arrangements. I want to argue that Bourdieu precisely invites us to first ask what such arrangements actually produce and for whom—and, I would add, why—before taking a stand. For while Bourdieu has often been criticized for ignoring agency, his concepts, I believe, actually help us locate it. Within the kind of political economic analysis I have suggested here, his framework suggests we look closely at how linguistic practices are bound up in active struggles on specific terrains. We, too, are players in those spaces, with interests in understanding literacy and education in certain ways, and abilities to use our tools of analysis to understand why literacy education makes sense, how and to whom, in specific historical and social formations. Probably most importantly, Bourdieu invites us to look for the political economic underpinnings of specific arrangements of discursive spaces, as well as for their consequences for the exercise of control over the production, distribution and attribution of value to symbolic and material resources as a first step toward deciding how we feel about that, and what, if anything, we want to do about it.

Notes

1   Boutet, 2001: 56:
     Dans le taylorisme, parler et travailler sont considérés comme des activités antagonistes. Parler fait perdre du temps, distrait, empêche de se concentrer sur les gestes à accomplir. . . . La mise en place de

nouveaux modes de production et en particulier l'automation, la robotisation et l'informatisation des activités, comme la mise en place de nouveaux modes de gestion des salariés (management participatif, responsabilisation, équipes semi-autonomes, auto-contrôle . . .) auront deux conséquences majeures en ce qui concerne le statut du langage au travail. L'une c'est la généralisation du recours à l'écrit (lecture et écriture) dans tous les métiers et activités y compris déqualifiées. . . . L'autre c'est l'émergence d'une compétence de communication.

2   This research was funded by the Social Sciences and Humanities Research Council of Canada (1997–2000 and 2001–04). It has involved at various times team members from the University of Toronto, the Université de Moncton, the Université de Montréal, the University of Calgary, the Université d'Avignon, and the J. W. Goethe-Universität, Frankfurt/Main.

References

Ahearn, L. (2001) Language and agency. *Annual Review of Anthropology*, 30, 109–37.

Anderson, B. (1983) *Imagined Communities*. London: Verso.

Bauman, R. and Briggs, C. (2003) *Voices of Modernity: Language Ideologies and the Politics of Inequality*. Cambridge, UK: Cambridge University Press.

Boudreau, A. (2003) *Le vernaculaire comme phénomène de résistance. L'exemple d'un centre d'appel*. Paper presented at the *Contacts de langue et minorisation* conference, Sion, Switzerland.

Bourdieu, P. (1972) *Esquisse d'une théorie de la pratique*. Geneva, Switzerland: Droz.

Bourdieu, P. (1977) The economics of linguistic exchanges. *Social Science Information*, 16, 645–68.

Bourdieu, P. (1982) *Ce que parler veut dire*. Paris: Fayard.

Bourdieu, P. and Passeron, J. (1977) *Reproduction in Education, Society and Culture*. London: Sage.

Boutet, J. (2001) Le travail devient-il intellectuel? *Travailler. Revue Internationale de Psychopathologie et de Psychodynamique du Travail*, 6, 55–70.

Budach, G. (2003) *Diskurs und praxis der alphabetisierung von erwachsenen im frankophonen Kanada*. New York: Peter Lang.

Cameron, D. (1995) *Verbal Hygiene*. London: Routledge.

Cameron, D. (2001) *Good to Talk?* London: Sage.

Castells, M. (2000) *The Information Age: Economy, Society and Culture* (vols 1–3). Oxford, UK: Blackwell.

Fabian, J. (1986) *Language and Colonial Power*. Cambridge, UK: Cambridge University Press.

Foucault, M. (1970) *L'ordre du discours*. Paris: Gallimard.

Foucault, M. (1975) *Surveiller et punir*. Paris: Gallimard.

Gee, J., Hull, G. and Lankshear, C. (1996) *The New Work Order: Behind the Language of the New Capitalism*. Boulder, CO: Westview Press.

Giddens, A. (1990) *The Consequences of Modernity*. Berkeley, CA: University of California Press.

Grillo, R. (1989) *Dominant Languages*. Cambridge, UK: Cambridge University Press.

Heller, M. (2002a) *Éléments d'une sociolinguistique critique*. Paris: Didier.

Heller, M. (2002b) Globalization and the commodification of bilingualism in Canada. In D. Block and D. Cameron (eds), *Globalization and Language Teaching*. London: Routledge, 47–64.

Heller, M. (2003) Globalization, the new economy and the commodification of language and identity. *Journal of Sociolinguistics*, 7, 473–92.

Higonnet, P. (1980) The politics of linguistic terrorism and grammatical hegemony during the French Revolution. *Social Theory*, 5, 41–69.

Hobsbawm, E. (1990) *Nations and Nationalism Since 1760*. Cambridge, UK: Cambridge University Press.

Ives, P. (2003) *Gramsci's Politics of Language: Engaging the Bakhtin Circle and the Frankfurt School*. Canada: University of Toronto Press.

Kapitzke, C. (1993) *Literacy and Religion*. Amsterdam: John Benjamins.

Kergoat, J., Boutet, J. and Linhart, D. (eds) (1999) *Le monde du travail*. Paris: La Découverte.

Kesterton, M. (2004) Social studies: a daily miscellany of information. *The Globe and Mail*, April 14, A16.

Lamoureux, S., Lozon, R. and Roy, S. (2003) Bilinguisme et accès des jeunes au marché du travail. In N. Labrie and S. Lamoureux (eds), *L'éducation de langue française en Ontario: enjeux et processus sociaux*. Sudbury, Canada: Prise de Parole, 187–202.

Luke, A. (2003) Literacy and the other: a sociological approach to literacy research and policy in multilingual societies. *Reading Research Quarterly*, 38, 132–41.

Luke, A. (2004) On the material consequences of literacy. *Language and Education*, 18, 331–6.

Martin-Jones, M. and Jones, K. (eds) (2000) *Multilingual Literacies*. Amsterdam: John Benjamins.

Meeuwis, M. (1999) Flemish nationalism in the Belgian Congo versus Zairean anti-imperialism: continuity and discontinuity in language ideological debates. In J. Blommaert (ed.), *Language Ideological Debates*. Berlin, Germany: Mouton de Gruyter, 381–424.

New London Group. (1996) A pedagogy of multiliteracies: designing social futures. *Harvard Educational Review*, 66, 60–92.

Outram, D. (1987) Le langage mâle de la vertu: women and the discourse of the French Revolution. In P. Burke and R. Porter (eds), *The Social History of Language*. Cambridge, UK: Cambridge University Press, 120–35.

Roy, S. (2003) Bilingualism and standardization in a Canadian call center: challenges for a linguistic minority community. In R. Bayley and S. Schecter (eds), *Language Socialization in Multilingual Societies*. Clevedon, UK: Multilingual Matters, 269–87.

Street, B. (1984) *Literacy in Theory and Practice*. Cambridge, UK: Cambridge University Press.

Street, B. (2000) Literacy events and literacy practices: theory and practice in the New Literacy Studies. In M. Martin-Jones and K. Jones (eds), *Multilingual Literacies*. Amsterdam: John Benjamins, 17–29.

Wolf, E. (1982) *Europe and the People without History*. Cambridge, UK: Cambridge University Press.

Chapter 5

Pedagogy as gift

Allan Luke

There is another metaphor for explaining the teaching and learning of reading and writing in Bourdieu's (1990) early explorations of traditional systems of exchange. I want to reconsider *reading and writing as gifts*, and begin discussing the possibilities this might hold for explaining the education of those students who currently do not do well within state education systems. My argument is that many students who fail in early literacy are refusing a form of cultural exchange that is increasingly marked out as commodity exchange—an institutional exchange with costs and benefits from ostensive "buy in," and rewards that often are inaccessible and invisible. This institutional exchange increasingly is dominated by corporate texts and legislated pedagogical scripts.

I model a pedagogical economy where literacy education is taken as cultural gift, with reciprocal entitlements and responsibilities. There are elements of this notion of reciprocity in dialogical approaches to radical and democratic pedagogies, process, and rhetorical approaches to the teaching of writing, and, interestingly, in attempts to teach reading comprehension using reciprocal teaching and intercultural models. All have demonstrated some success at the re-engagement of students alienated from mainstream pedagogy. These models typically are located on the "student-centered" or progressive end of comparative pedagogical continua, set in opposition to teacher-centered, direct instruction and traditional didactic authority relations. One possible cultural historical approach is to see whether elements of a pre-capitalist exchange can be reappropriated in literacy pedagogical exchanges, in the institution that is both designed to service the historical nexus of print and capitalist exchange, and, increasingly, has come under the ambit of corporate commodified textual knowledge.

There are two lines of argument here. First, that teacher-centered, highly "ritualized" elements of pedagogy need not be part of a commodification process, but can be reframed as moments of pedagogic gifting. We find this both in pre-capitalist exchange and in the current digital and online exchanges that begin to model post-commodified social relations—where participants are motivated by ritual, reputation, altruism, and curiosity. I want to explore whether such a construct of literacy can offer a means to bridge the binary divide that has characterized the great debates over literacy. Typically these have been characterized as debates between traditionalism and progressivism, direct and indirect instruction, foci on code and on meaning, literary and functional, "high" and "low" classification and framing, print and digital, and, indeed, between autocratic and democratic education (Alexander, 2000). My aim is to reinstate elements of "overt instruction" (New London Group, 1996) within a critical, dialogic model of literacy. I propose that traditional customary and ritual elements of exchange have a potential value in altering the persistent patterns of failure that curricular policy mandates of direct, scripted pedagogy purport to address. One way to do so is to remake ritual responsibilities of gifting and riposte between elders and youths, teachers and students. This will require a theoretical and practical uncoupling and reappropriating of overt instruction from its commodity form.

This is meant as an alternative to attempts by governments and schools to discipline pedagogy, students and literacy into accountable, countable and quantifiable entities. These current conditions might, indeed, benefit from an attempt to reframe literacy instruction as a traditional cultural exchange entailing reciprocal gifts of culturally significant texts and textual practice, with reflexive responsibilities for readers and writers as members of a cultural community. This would involve a historical re-culturing of literacy instruction, with directions already well-established in the literature on the education of cultural and linguistic minorities in New Zealand, Australia, the US and Canada.

Writing as gift

This text is a "gift" that was given and received in an economy of exchange from my parents and sisters, from my teachers and the other writers and critics who speak through this text. This text is, in many ways, an intergenerational taking of turns across space and time, a mediated "riposte" (Bourdieu, 1990: 100) to their pedagogic practices and assumptions, their insistent statements, and didactic presence that remains in this text, in this work, and in its surrounding pedagogic fields. My experience of learning to read and write was very different from that described by Claire Kramsch in this volume (see Chapter 3). I grew up in the 1950s among the Chinese-American community in Los Angeles. I was the object and product of post-war American meritocratic and progressive schooling—IQ-tested, streamed, enriched, and remediated: neither model student nor model minority. This text is the product of that field of textual and linguistic exchange, and all of its reciprocal moments and responsibilities, of artifacts produced and exchanged, of writing done at home with siblings and at school under the watchful eye of teachers, in church, at Chinese school, and in community groups. There are also traces of my teachers' work of reading H. G. Wells' *History of the World* aloud at the end of each school day, of our daily 45 minutes with *Dick and Jane*, my father's second-hand set of *Harvard Classics*. My learning was not solely and simply an economic or ideological determination, either in retrospect or in structure. Nor was it simply fixed in the "C" mark I received in my fourth year of schooling for English, reading and language arts, and whatever the fallout at home that might have been.

Becoming a writer and reader is, inter alia, a set of reciprocal obligations and exchanges between mentors and prospective literates, between elders and children, between virtual or distant author and new reader/writer, and, yes, between the pedagogic institution of the school and the individual. Likewise, the refusal of these exchanges can become a de facto marker of community membership, of solidarity against a particular form of symbolic violence. The hidden curriculum of literacy constituted an unwritten and often unspoken social and cultural contract—but one that was potentially as binding, as inviolable and as powerful as any mortgage, catechism or writ. In the migrant Chinese-American views of my father and mother, aunties and uncles, economic trajectory and vocation played a part. But this was later on, after the contract was enacted and sealed. And it is within and in relation to that contract—an originary field of cultural exchange—that my habitus as writer, reader, and thinker exists.

Writing is in part a pedagogic gifting—however pretentious and self-important this may sound, however willing and unwilling, receptive and resistant you may be. It is an act of self-objectification—itself tied up in authority and responsibility, authority of speakers/writers and readers, responsibility of scholarship, and the other felicitous conditions that are presupposed when one writes or reads a chapter such as this. While far from an ideal speech situation, it is a pedagogic act—however successful or unsuccessful, playing into the fields of reputation built by prior exchanges we might have had—and it is a production and voicing of the pedagogic act of having learned to write. Describing the relationship between gifting and intergenerational and interfamilial learning, Bourdieu puts it this way:

> the whole dialectic of challenge and riposte, gift and counter-gift, is not an abstract axiomatics but the sense of honour, a disposition inculcated by all early education and constantly demanded and reinforced by the group, and inscribed in the postures and gestures of the body (in a way of using the body or the gaze, a way of talking, eating or walking) as in the automatisms of language and thought.
>
> (1990: 103)

Entry into community and one's domestic space requires gifting. Gifting, and its forms of affiliation, entails reciprocity of exchange. The basis for pre-capitalist exchange was gifting, a "total social phenomenon" (Mauss, 1990: 3) beginning from kinship relations and encompassing all orders of social and cultural life. This evolved, with substantive moral and political economic consequences and contradictions, into barter systems and marketized commodity exchange. Gregory (1997) describes this as a shift from qualitative relations between human subjects to a focus on quantitative relations between objects.

Writing, whether here or on a blog, is a reputational act, signaling entry into and status within an interpretive community. As a pedagogic exchange, it has implied reciprocal conditions and obligations. However altruistic and counterfactual this might sound, writing is an act of gifting. Despite the now ubiquitous ethic that all literacy is functional literacy, there might be no necessary capital benefit or debt incurred in the reading. But you take with it a particular cultural and social, scholarly and academic responsibility, of having to respond in some specific way. There are cognitive and symbolic uses entailed in writing and reading that do not involve or imply the exchange of economic capital. This might involve transportation to other possible worlds, whether parochial or cosmopolitan, global or local—literacy can provide a ticket more or less for free, with degrees and kinds of responsibility for riposte.

Contrast this with the model of literacy in schools. Writing and reading have become commodity exchanges between corporation and consumer, between facilitator and client. With national literacy programs in the US and UK, the pedagogic exchange between literate and aspiring literate, between teacher and student, between school and individual, is mediated and shaped by the corporate commodity of the instructional package, with all of its affiliated patterns, rules and systems of reward, performance and institutional accountability. In spite of, or perhaps as a result of, the publishers, governments and systems of accountability are pushing to fix and contain the inevitable idiosyncrasy of local classroom discourse, the idiosyncrasy of the local curriculum-in-use.

Teaching and learning as commodity exchange

Three decades of research document the interactional, conversational, and linguistic features of early literacy teaching. Interactional structures have distinctive cognitive, social, and developmental investments and consequences for learners. The political economy of literacy pivots around commodification: the increased use of standardized pedagogical scripts and highly ideologically regulated and structured texts, whether prescribed in textbook series, the official syllabus guidelines of curriculum documents, or simply internalized as the instructional norm by teachers and schools (e.g., Larson, 2005). These are language-in-education policy bids to fix early literacy as a social and educational problem, particularly for the lower quartile of children from linguistic minority, indigenous, and lower socioeconomic communities. Beginning from Bourdieu and Passeron (1990), it would appear that the matter can be defined in terms of the social reproduction of differential cultural capital, forms of symbolic imposition, and the complicity of schooling in the selection and production of class and distinction, taste and habitus.

Although the argument here is principally historical and philosophical, I want to illustrate it by reference to some of the features of classroom exchange. This is a Singapore Year 3 primary classroom literacy lesson described by Ruth Wong in her study of literacy teaching in three primary schools.

T:	1.	OK, today we are going to be doing a topic on oceans. OK? Yes, sorry? Did you all say yes? Adam?
Muhd A:	2.	I like the ocean.
T:	3.	You love the ocean?
P:	4.	Yes.
T:	5.	But Jerome, there are so many stuff still on your table. I said to put everything away. . . .
:	6.	Why do you like the oceans? Anybody been in the ocean?
P:	7.	Ya, I've been.
T:	8.	So many of you have been IN the ocean?
Ps:	9.	Yes. (laughter)
T:	10.	You have?
P:	11.	Sometimes.
T:	12.	Sometimes? When?
P:	13.	// Maybe one time only.
P:	14.	// I gone to Canada Ocean. I gone to Canada Ocean.
T:	15.	Yes?
		(A pupil from another class enters the room and approaches the teacher)
P:	16.	I want to see Audrey.
T:	17.	Audrey? Audrey. In 3C? Please go to 3C, please.
:	18.	OK. Anyway, OK, we are going to read a passage about the ocean and hopefully we will learn a little bit more about the ocean. Some of you know quite a bit, some of you have read on your own OK, about the ocean. I see quite a few of you borrowing books on the oceans and creatures of the oceans from the library, from the school library. Yap, there, Cheryl has got a book on whales. The other time you had a book on?
Cheryl:	19.	Fish.
T:	20.	The different fishes that you can find in the oceans. Is that right? Fadli had that? Anyone else?
:	21.	Ya, so, some of you have read some books on your own, some not. So, for the benefit of those who have not and who have no idea what goes on in the ocean itself or what it is all about, OK? We are going to learn a little bit more about it.

The lesson queues and frames the social relations of teaching and learning. From our quantitative studies we can conclude that it is a generalizable pattern of interaction in Singapore primary schools. As conventional instructional strategies, a number of key moves are identifiable: the pre-reading discussion introduces a topic (1), and then solicits interest, background knowledge and prior experience (1, 3, 6, 10, 12). With some regulative, behavioral asides (5, 15, 17), the initiate–response–evaluate pattern consists of a set of symmetrical solicit moves on the part of the teacher, whose responses to content claims are open-ended and encouraging. Moves 18–21 mark out and frame a shift in phase, toward a more formalized invitation to the class.

Shortly thereafter, as the children begin reading a passage assigned by the teachers, the rules of the pedagogic exchange are made more explicit:

T: 1. OK. We're going to learn a little more about the ocean. So- and I need you to pay attention, because at the end of everything, you have a worksheet to complete for me based on what we are going to read now. OK?

 : 2. So pay attention.

P: 3. Can we don't write dolphin, can we write stingray?

T: 4. Is it in the passage? Is it in the paragraph? Can you see here? What does it say, paragraph 2? Is stingray in the paragraph 2?

    5. . . .

    6. You're making up your own stories now. I said whatever you can find IN the passage. What does the passage tell you about Midnight Zone? Anthony?

    7. . . .

    8. Wrong! There is nothing in the passage that tells you that shark and seahorses- Seahorses have big mouths, big stomachs, is it? . . .

This transition marks out a shift in phase and oscillation of activity structure from what nominally appears as a pre-reading introduction into a more for-malized activity, with the teacher (1) restating a content cue ("we're going to learn a little more about the ocean") initiated in line 18 above. But what kind of symbolic and economic exchange are the students being invited into? The teacher is quite explicit: "I need you to pay attention, because at the end of everything, you have a worksheet to complete for me based on what we are going to read now" (1). From this point on in the lesson, subsequent student responses are corraled toward that task. In this way, the interactional exchange is mediated by and focused upon the cultural production of the instructional commodity of the "worksheet." The worksheet is a principal token of exchange in Singapore primary school pedagogy.

This exchange is accepted by some and, inevitably, rejected by others who find themselves differentially positioned in the social field of the school. In the case of Singapore, they are children from lower socioeconomic backgrounds, with a disproportionate number of Malay and Chinese dialect speakers form-ing up the lower quartile of literacy achievers in the early years. In other states, children of linguistic minorities, indigenous communities and the urban poor would be similarly positioned in early literacy education (Organisation for Economic Co-operation and Development (OECD), 2005). Here I want to re-theorize the problem of persistent literacy failure as a refusal of a particular form of commodity exchange.

Reproduction and ritual in pedagogy

Literacy is defined in curriculum as a quantifiable psychological or cognitive process or skill. This is but one possible characterization of the social practices of reading and writing. In romantic literary and psychoanalytic traditions, writing is invented as a solipsistic creative act, as a moment of aesthetic or intellectual commission, or as a moment in the realization of self, of ego/identity equilibrium. In this volume, we conceptualize writing variously as craft, as labor, as semiotic production and cultural practice, with specific ideological and material consequences. Each definition is historical, enacted and realized in a social field of text production and exchange. Each official policy or syllabus definition stands in its own context as a legitimated objectification of self, of the other (the "un"- or "non"-literate), and a particular set of institutional conditions for its production and reproduction.

Our debates over the "right" ways of describing, studying, and teaching literacy are less matters of scientific truth and more disputes over how the practice will be normatively shaped toward the production of varied forms of bodily habitus and capital. The economic and historical base of social and economic relations establishes the enabling conditions of mode of information, textual production, and representation, reception, and use. These conditions, in turn, reflexively fix and mediate their own cultural relations of representation: how they are presented and spoken about by parents and public, students and teachers, bureaucrats, media, and politicians. A selective tradition of literacy creates narrative folklores and sciences around itself, establishing the necessity of its own self-objectification and logics of practice. Teachers and parents, policymakers and the media offer competing folkloric explanations of the optimal signs of the power of literacy, its developmental narratives, consequences, and uses. In Singapore, teacher accounts of their practice often focus upon a "worksheet culture," where the production of and completion of worksheets, many from commercial packages and programs, constitute markers of curricular and instructional progress, signs of the successful achievement of school literacy. Many parents, in turn, gauge successful pedagogy in terms of the production of finished worksheets in homework and classroom settings.

As economic bases, as modes of cultural production and information shift, as globalized flows of production cross boundaries and borders, so does the nature and structure of literate relations and relations within its allied symbolic economies. Media convergence enables new inscription practices online and in multimodal environments (Sefton-Green, 2006). It also has generative local impacts on both digital and print practices—altering relations of authorship, ownership, production, and accessibility of traditional print texts, their linguistic forms and their uses (Kapitzke and Bruce, 2006). In such a context, print literacy becomes a base ground for debates over the normative cultural uses of the "old" technology of print, themselves destabilized by new relations and emergent rules of exchange. This is most visible where old criteria for writing and reading sit against new. Consider, for example, the Australian media critique that the OECD's Program for International Student Assessment (PISA) writing assessments did not include formal assessment of grammatical and spelling error. The place of handwriting, whether students should or must produce correct spelling, the developmental hierarchicization of genre, all constitute nodal points in the teaching of literacy open to destabilization and contestation.

Paradigm wars thus have at their base different foundational assumptions about the "nature" of literacy—different objectifications of this particular technology of objectification, different parceling up and prioritizing, foregrounding and backgrounding of its possible scientific and cultural, empirical and aesthetic, reproductive and critical practices. The initial critical move is to objectify these objectifications. That is, to make transparent the ideological and epistemic constructions competing to fix what counts as literacy in schooling, in state systems, and in dominant modes of information. This has entailed descriptive and analytic demystification; that is, a making transparent of the rules of exchange and networks of discourse within which writing sits—taking apart its folklore and its habituation, its embodiment and sublimation in everyday use. But this isn't to say in any absolute sense that each or any such objectification is, in and of itself, right or wrong, true or false, effective or ineffective. Different objectifications of literacy education constitute and contribute to different economies of symbolic exchange, hierarchical relations of power, identity and capital, both local and more generalizable. Hence, the question of efficacy pivots around what kinds of exchanges are being culturally formalized in classrooms and schools, churches and mosques, work places and play spaces—and how these have the potential to produce, regulate, and habituate adjacent fields that the literate may engage with.

There is now a relentless empirical demonstration and critique of how education systems consistently and systematically fail to engage students from lower socioeconomic classes, linguistic minorities, and culturally subordinated groups. Whatever its intents, literacy education comes to mark out a dividing rod of class and cultural disparity, where unequal access and deployment of economic capital, available discourses and practices tends to be reaffirmed and reified in the fields of the school. International comparative data show telling differences in the effects of social class between national systems, with indications that some national systems appear to produce and reproduce literate practices defined by conventional assessment measures in more strongly socially stratified patterns than others (OECD, 2005). That is, some systems, notably Finland, Canada, and Ireland, rate high on equity and quality, while others demonstrate a higher correlation between socioeconomic backgrounds of students and literacy achievement (McGaw, 2006). Yet the overall results are consistent: the bottom end of normal and abnormal curves of achievement are disproportionately populated by the children of socioeconomically and culturally marginalized groups. School systems, and the networks of available social, economic, and symbolic capital that they sit within, contribute to this stratification of educationally acquired capital.

Our efforts to offer plausible, powerful positive theses and pedagogical reforms seem frustratingly blunt in policy, action, scale, and generalizability. The reform of literacy education often feels like small-scale groundwork in the face of tectonic forces of class, capital, and state. So in the context of the policy "fixes" and critical debates over phonics, scripted pedagogies, notional targets and outcomes, and the ostensive "evidence" of the efficacy of legislative and practical efforts, we should and must ask again: is the everyday classroom work of literacy education indeed locked into the reproductive "iron cage" that is attributed, however accurately, to Bourdieu and Passeron's (1990) analysis of the post-war French education and social class system? Might there be an alternative normative "objectification" of literacy that is not about the inequitable reproduction of habitus, capital, and class? Part of the answer lies in coming up with public policy alternatives that define the social fields and possibilities of literacy education differently, actual acts of resistance to and re-appropriations of neo-liberal policy. Other work can be done in the remaking of the systems of exchange in classrooms. But these require normative cultural models.

Despite the anthropological turn in "new literacy studies" (e.g., Street, 1984), ritual has not been a focal point of research on school literacy. The originary power of writing is a theme in analyses of the history of literacy, from Jack Goody's anthropological work, cited in Bourdieu's (1990) preface to *The Logic of Practice*, and marking a departure point for Scribner and Cole's (1989) socio-cultural study of the Vai. Goody (1977, 1987) describes writing as a key onto/phylogenetic moment in the development of spoken cultures—a thesis developed *contra* Levi-Strauss. Like Luria (1976), he views literacy as an architectonic force, reshaping cognition and culture, social and economic relations. I describe the sociological qualification of such claims in Chapter 17 of this volume.

Goody (1987) explains the shift from religion of the word to religions of the book. Writing began to supplant the spoken and embodied word as the domain of the sacred. This marked a reorganization in authority relations and political economies, with power moving from shaman and patriarch to those who held control of sacred texts, inscriptions, archives, codes, and interpretations. This theme is taken up in the Canadian communications tradition by Innis (1951) and McLuhan (1962), who argue that fundamental economic and cultural reformation is "biased" by communications technologies such as literacy. It is restated by Benedict Anderson (1992), who identifies the tie between nation, nationalism, and "print capitalism" both in the formation of the European nation-state and in the emergent forms of modernity in postcolonial states. The historical link between the current logics and practices of literacy teaching, national ideology, identity, and economic production is well established.

Goody described oral language and earlier historic forms of writing as ritu-alized, intergenerational cultural exchanges, in some contexts ridden through-out with residual forms of responsibility and reciprocity, patriarchy, and paternalism. Bourdieu's (1977, 1990) work on gifting and time amongst the Kabyle offers some keys. In some of his earliest formulations of the model of habitus, field, and capital, Bourdieu makes the connection between education, pedagogy, and the gift.

Gifting is a central component of pre-capitalist cultural exchange, system-atically marking out community and familial membership, initiation into cul-tural patterns of patriarchy, the spatial boundaries of territory and home, and punctuating seasonal and generational time. In anthropology, it is exemplified in studies by Levi-Strauss (1969) and continues to be a focus of current field-work. Hardly benign, in traditional societies gifting was central to the constitu-tion of a patriarchal moral order that centered on the giving of women as gifts, establishing systems of exchange for patriarchy, hierarchy, and exclusion (Irigaray, 1997). As Bourdieu (1990) points out, amongst the Kabyle the obliga-tion of reciprocity in fact can constitute both hierarchical relations and a prototype of symbolic violence, where the recipient's obligation to reciprocate is not negotiable.

Since Mauss's (1990) description of the logic and systematicity of gifting, a key theme in anthropological and economic research has been the differences between gift, barter, and market economies. Gifting was a type of economic behavior where kinship relations and their attendant taboos were established on principles of reciprocity and symmetry of social relations (Levi-Strauss, 1969). Polanyi (1944) contrasted this with the marketized redistribution of goods, which was premised on centrist relations regulated by the state and market. The shift from gift to market exchange, according to Gregory (1997), marks out a change in focus from cardinal to ordinal distinctions, from quality to quantity, from communicative and social relations to those of relations between objects. The model of gifting has been used as a means of critique and reappropriation of alienated labor and capitalist commodity exchange (Mauss, 1990; see also Schrift, 1997).

Gifting entails, Bourdieu argues, unspoken rules around obligation and res-ponsibility. Above all, like pedagogy, it requires acknowledgment and "riposte." Gifting thus is not simply ritual and customary exchange, but a central form of traditional social relations and economy. As Gregory (1997) acknowledges, any simple binary attributing "positive exchange" to gifting and "negative exchange" to market relations is reductionist. The question, he reminds us, is how the exchange structures in any specific cultural or institutional setting are established and negotiated. Gifting then constitutes a different cultural and economic approach to exchange and a different marking out of relationships of power and capital. Bearing these cautionary comments in mind, I use gifting as a metaphor which can be turned on and against current debates over the marketization and corporatization of schooling, and the commodification and standardization of literacy teaching and learning.

Joining critical and traditional pedagogies

Bourdieu provides a sociological vocabulary for explaining the bodily, linguistic, and institutional machinery of educational failure, marginalization, and disenfranchisement. We can explain the social construction of habitus (Luke, 1992; Collins, 1993; see also Pahl, Chapter 10 of this volume)—we can trace cultural and linguistic, economic and social constructions into and across the formal institutions of schooling, where we watch various forms of pedagogic action grind away at the symbolic violence of schools, colleges, and universities. We can empirically observe and interpret the various kinds of sociological uptake, internalization and agency in response to the social fields of the school. And finally, we can longitudinally track and follow the complex bundles of capital that the "educated" take out into the systems of exchange of work, further education, civic life, and face-to-face and virtual relations of power, hierarchy, and structure. The analyses of the market relationships of teaching and learning constitute a powerful sociological agenda for literacy research.

Yet the model of reproduction has been subject to critique; for example, that it is a species of structuralist determinism, that while it can explain relations of exchange, it can do little to remediate them, and that the Bourdieusian system does not enable a normative model of equitable pedagogical change. Is there a pedagogical positive thesis in Bourdieu? Is there a model of education and pedagogy, however explicit, that speaks of the capacity of pedagogic action to construct productive, transformative and agentive literate subjects?

Relatedly, is there a mode of classroom exchange that is not always already shaped as a fixed capitalist commodity transaction, where existing cultural capital is differentially and unequally converted into certified textual skill and power with subsequent market value in a process structurally determined by the prior class, taste, and distinction of teachers and students?

There are at least three possibilities for a positive pedagogic model. First, there are attempts to build critical, self-reflexive pedagogy, akin to Bourdieu's reflexive sociology. In this model, student-inquirers are taught not only to interrogate the grounds for pedagogy, but also to explore, analyze, weigh and critique the social fields where educational acquired capital is deployed. This—nothing new—features prominently in the extension of critical pedagogy to discourse analysis proposed by Fairclough (1992). The analysis of possible textual positionings and effects can entail an expansion of the instructional focus on audience in rhetorical and reader–response approaches to literacy to engage in a social and cultural analysis of the social fields of exchange and power where texts and discourses are deployed; that is, classroom analysis of what Fairclough calls the "conditions of reception" where dynamics of class, gender, race, and power come into play. This can include an analysis of the parameters of the classroom as field of exchange.

Second, an affiliated approach sets out to create a normative habitus that is disruptive—that is, forms of social identity, practice and embodiment that are potential free radicals in the social fields of exchange that they are set into. We find this modeled in the critical pedagogy and multiculturalist work that focuses strongly on engaging student "voice" as an alternative to dominant discourses and ideologies (e.g., Comber and Simpson, 2001). Though perhaps appearing to be a more radical proposal, this is another normative agenda that is linked, broadly, to a reconceptualist model of curriculum: asking what kind of social subject can and should be shaped, and encouraging the development of an agentive literate habitus that can "position take" within and around the various "positioning" devices in any given social field (Luke and Carrington, 2002).

Both of these models highlight a central problem of critical pedagogy. The practice of dialogic exchange has proven itself able to the task of critical social analysis and creating a space for "voice." This is ably documented in the numerous case-based and documentary descriptions of critical pedagogy in action in schools and informal sites. There are, further, conditions in state schools and curricula that can handle a bit of interactional trouble, and where pedagogies can foster bids at the dialogic analytic and material transformation of social fields. The implementation of critical literacy as a component in mainstream state literacy education in the Australian states, New Zealand, Ontario and some areas of New York are cases in point.

Yet the anomaly of the historical durability of elements of explicit, didactic and teacher-centered pedagogy remains. In the pedagogy of multiliteracies work, we called this "overt instruction" (New London Group, 1996): instances where characteristics of the textual design required direct, expert transmission. Many kernel elements of print literacy pedagogy are remarkably resilient, sustained across colonial, postcolonial, and industrial curriculum settlements with very different ideological orientations. The teaching and learning of literacy across cultures and historical periods has entailed some element of direct instruction in elements of the code, memorization, rote reproduction of the symbol system, enforced bodily discipline, and training. These elements of training entail heightened classification and framing of knowledge (Bernstein, 1990). I refer to those didactic pedagogies that are centered on prior knowledge, expertise, and experience with the technology that are held by elders, masters, and mentors. They are about reshaping the disposition of the literate in particular normative forms. These include passage study and memorization of culturally significant texts, oral recitation, call and response reading, manual training in orthography, poetic and musical rhyme and meter, and a formal semantic or syntactic parsing of text. Much of this is training in what Bourdieu refers to as "mnenotechnic devices," with "poetry, the conservation device *par excellence* in non-literate societies" (p. 125).

Unfortunately, many of these practices typically are represented in ideological forms, driving fundamentalist debates around "the basics" and defined in opposition to dialogics, critical analysis and local "voice." They have become the central focus of attempts to regulate and script both the instructional interactions and the developmental sequences of early literacy pedagogy through the use of standardized, corporate textbook packages. But separating them from their reification and commodification by neoconservative and neoliberal educational projects, and from their commodity and accountability functions—they might very well fall under a different light.

Overt instruction in cultural codes of text, as McNaughton's (2002) current work on the reading comprehension of lower socioeconomic class Maori and Pacifika students shows, is crucial to mastery of the technology particularly amongst those who are not "schooled before schooling." For McNaughton (2006), the problem is not whether we use direct instruction but the degree to which students have the expertise to engage in a shunting from direct instruction into contextual application. He points out that direct instructional models in both code and meaning can generate gain scores by conventional indicators. In Singapore research, we called this "weaving" (Luke et al., 2004)—teachers' and students' capacity to move from text to context, from known to new, from direct and teacher-centered work to more hands-on, student-centered research.

The question—sitting underneath the whole language/phonics wars in the US—is not whether they are done, but how, when, and as part of what kinds of systems of exchange. At the heart of sociocultural explanations of literacy is a focus on how apprentice literates can engage with the advanced tool making and use knowledge and expertise that sits beneath teachers' epistemic authority. And it is this epistemic authority that often appears to be given away in the dialectics of critical and progressive pedagogies. The policy response noted above effectively fetishizes the "basics," and turns them into a fundamental code that can only be acquired through heavily scripted, automated, and "quality assured" industrial pedagogy. Part of the challenge, then, is how these didactic, traditional elements of literacy instruction can play a role in a critical education, where and when. The matter is one of pedagogic movement and weave between distinctive pedagogical phases with different rules of exchange, rather than the assumption of the isomorphism between singular method of literacy education, pre-specified exchange relations, and the acquisition of rudiments of practice.

How might we account for traditional didactic modes and reappropriate them as part of a critical, redressive agenda? If we can theoretically reframe them, we can come some way in addressing the concerns about the necessity and sufficiency for non-dialogic knowledge and skill instruction to alter the relativities of literacy as class reproduction (Bernstein, 1990; Delpit, 1996). One approach has been to incorporate them into pluralistic models of practice, such as the Four Resources Model (Freebody and Luke, 1990). This describes coding as "necessary but not sufficient" for practice and then working to avoid hierarchical models of skill development. Another model has been to argue that literacy pedagogies consist of systematic "weaves" or shunts between kinds and levels of instruction orchestrated by highly skilled teachers. This defines classroom interaction as a kind of alternating and shifting zone, where relationships around the technology take different interactional shapes. The affiliated view is of a dynamic social field of pedagogy where the rules of exchange and value vary from phase to phase in the interests of building particular kinds of literate practices and habituses.

Yet the pluralistic models lack theoretical specificity. They might describe programs that yield better "outcomes" on a number of scales of value. They provide a vocabulary for the parsing of literacy education at the curriculum and lesson, classroom and work program planning level. They may also yield better measurable results and less residualization and threshold effects. But they do not offer a normative analysis of current practice, its reproductive effects, or how they might be reformed. While they might create a space for a non-commodified literacy, they stop short of theoretical description of what that space might be, other than "balanced" or "better achieving" or "empowered" learners or more flexibly expert teachers. How, then, might we free these traditional elements of overt literacy teaching from the commodity form that is currently enforced upon systems at the expense of the kinds of critical engagement advocated in the first two models noted above?

One way is to change the philosophic warrant of direct instruction from that of claims about psychological efficacy to the imperative for the intergenerational transfer of wisdom and technological expertise. That is, rather than take a modernist scientific explanation of the efficacy of direct instruction, we can shift to a traditional, customary explanation—one that argues that overt instruction gains its salience, its power, and its efficacy because of its warrant as a mentor-apprentice, elder–youth relationship; as a form of cultural gifting, rather than as marketized exchange.

On pedagogy and gifting

The third model is the model of pedagogy as gift, as pre-capitalist exchange. It is based upon a pedagogic ideal, however counterfactual: the notion of reading and writing as a practice normatively expected and reflexively constructed in reciprocal acts and exchanges with elders. I speak not of an ideal literacy event—but rather of a literacy that is insured and assured by contract between elders and youths, families and schools, cultures and civic societies, by a moment of "positive reciprocity" (Polanyi, 1944) in the dialectics of cultural gifting. This amounts to a different form of life of literacy education, where teachers and students stand in reciprocal obligation—an obligation of riposte, of uptake, of exchange. It is already a feature of culturally substantive literacy learning environments, whether they are Freirian or didactic, whole language or process. It is in part contingent upon student recognition of the teachers' authority and expertise as cultural elder, the teachers' demonstrative mastery of and epistemic authority over culturally significant texts and affiliated practices, and the teachers' capacity to translate that authority into a structured, reflexive set of ritual exchanges built around positive reciprocity. This recognition of the significance of the pedagogue remains central to many cultural systems of education, specifically those of some East Asian and European systems that retain didactic traditions (Alexander, 2000; see also McHoul, 2006).

Bourdieu's discussion of the Kabyle describes gifting as systems of customary exchange. Systems of customary exchange depend upon moral obligation and the honor of the participants. In that nomadic culture, these may involve coercive forms of inculcation into cultural norms, interfamilial exchange and rivalry, and gendered kinship relations. Bourdieu notes:

> Accepting the gift requires forms of formal ritualization. This may seem spurious in the face of conditions that suggest that the habitus that children bring to schools is increasingly complex. What characterizes ritual exchange is a tacit understanding of the rules of exchange, the responsibility of riposte and the costs/benefits of acceptance of the exchange.
>
> (1990: 125)

Where literacy education is based upon customary exchange—for instance, in non-secular education, in some forms of informal education, in community language and culture schools—it is interesting to note that "failure" and "deficit" are backgrounded. This is in part because it is based on the broad assumption that all children can and will learn, that there is a familial, community or transcendental imperative to respond. In this way, expected patterns of volition and participation in the exchange go without saying. Similar cultural principles were central in Au's (1993) work with indigenous Hawaiian children, and Malcolm and colleagues' (1999) pedagogy for Aboriginal education. Both designed a match between the dynamics of face-to-face exchange, and their attendant authority structures in community and in early reading instruction. In the case of Au's (1980) work in the Kamehameha Early Education Program (KEEP), the interactional patterns of reading comprehension instruction were remodeled to fit children's prior habitus, semiotic cues, and verbal markers. In such contexts, the exchange gains value in and of itself as a qualitative marker of ritual membership, rather than as a means for the quantitatively marked, psychometric evaluation of skill. As in traditional gifting, such institutions tend to be based upon principles of enfranchisement, inclusion, and membership—rather than individuation and stratification. The focus, further, is on the quality of the relationship between subjects, rather than its individuated objectification.

In various cultures, customary literacy teaching historically has involved oral recitation of sacred passages, reciprocal choral exchanges (e.g., between priest and lay, teacher and student), poetry, song, and narrative (e.g., Kapitzke, 1995; Scribner and Cole, 1989). This serves purposes of the scripted reproduction of historical and cultural memory, the disciplining of the body, the demonstration of alacrity and automaticity with linguistic code. Practice is galvanized and habituated around customary exchange, which in turn marks out membership in an interpretive community.

The problem arises, as Bourdieu and Passeron (1990) later recognize, when the institution engages in formalized impositions that entail misrecognition of cultural resources and gifts, and recast these as "official" institutional exchanges, hence symbolic violence. The problem is a complicated and potentially contradictory one—particularly if literacy itself has been objectified as part of the move toward the modernist rationalization of knowledge, self and, indeed, industrial and corporate exchange. Bourdieu adds:

> By detaching cultural resources from persons, literacy enables a society to move beyond anthropological limits—particularly those of individual memory—and liberates it from the constraints implied by mnemotechnic devices such as poetry . . . it makes it possible to accumulate the culture previously conserved in the incorporated state . . . and to perform the primitive accumulation of cultural capital, the total or partial monopolizing of the society's symbolic resources in religion, philosophy, art and science, through the monopolization of the instruments for appropriation of these resources (writing, reading and other decoding techniques).
>
> (1990: 125)

The link between literacy and the reorganization, accumulation, and control of society's "symbolic resources" is drawn directly from Goody. Bourdieu goes on to recognize that: "capital is given the conditions of its own full realization only with the appearance of an educational system" (p. 125). That is, the formalization of access to symbolic resources through the school in effect sets the very conditions for marketized exchange in adjacent social fields. By this definition, the school is the institution for codifying and stratifying capitalist exchange of societal symbolic resources.

> [T]he whole process of rationalization that is made possible by . . . objectification in writing, are accompanied by a far-reaching transformation of the whole relationship to the body, or more precisely of the use made of the body in the production and reproduction of cultural artifacts.
>
> (p. 73)

The reframing of initial and early literacy pedagogy within a ritualized gifting process would be based upon high permeability between community and school, and a systematic weaving between systems of classification and framing. This would involve a shunting between word and world, text and context, new and known, everyday and scientific, and, indeed, overt and indirect pedagogies. As such, it could also set the grounds for a critical education, a bid to reappropriate the remaking of the body from systems of marketized exchange. It can be structured to set out moral/normative and ethical conditions of reciprocity for early literacy, other than those of commodity exchanges of worksheets, leveled readers, and test results. This would not nor could it dislodge schooling from a preparation for a marketized political economy of "hypercapitalism" (Graham, 2005). But it could provide foundational grounds for literacy teaching around a moral responsibility for cultural memory, discourse inquiry, and, potentially, critique.

I began this chapter by describing literacy failure as a refusal of this institutional exchange among at least a decile of students in postindustrial educational systems—whether conceived of as symbolic violence or pedagogic action—consistently by those segments of the school-aged population most marginal from mainstream systems of economic exchange. The position I have put here is that this constitutes a refusal of the gift, perhaps a lack of tacit understanding about its consequences and value, and a turning away from the pedagogical responsibility of riposte. Further, we could argue that the school has misrecognized students' capital, and introduced them into a series of pedagogic exchanges that are not immediately recognizable as customary or valuable, based as they are on a curricular symbolic violence. Regardless of where we choose to emphasize the agency or good faith of student, teacher and/or institution here—suffice to say that the exchange has broken down.

Yet the response of systems has been to further tighten the enforcement, codification, and standardization of that exchange. This response is based on two interlocking assumptions. First, the fundamentalist assumption is that all children, regardless of habitus, are lacking and require a uniform version of the basics sourced in the institutional package and not in community or even common, secular culture. Second, current policy assumes that the local variables and idiosyncrasies of the exchange are the problem, whether generated by context, teacher or student habitus. The result is a policy bid to centrally control and quality assure the exchange by steering via grids of performativity. In this regard, the current policy is an attempt to industrially manage and define literacy education, its shapes and forms. This entails a mis-culturalization of literacy education, a further distancing it from community life forms and practices, textual traditions residual and emergent. The potential of gifting has been replaced with commodity forms, regardless of variable student and teacher habitus and their variable customary sense of exchange.

It is a categorical mistake to confuse the significance of overt pedagogy, of teacher pedagogic and epistemic authority, and of the need for technical mastery of the code with its commodity form. In his comparative studies of primary schooling, Alexander (2000) maps a binary continuum from democratic to autocratic pedagogic form. This work is accurate in the degree to which structure/agency dialectics are built into particular models of pedagogy. Yet, intentions aside, it remakes the student/teacher, didactic/progressive binaries that have been a key feature of pedagogical and curricular debate since Dewey (1991). The assumption that democratic, agentive pedagogy will necessarily disrupt the patterns of social reproduction has common-sense appeal: that the school should not be a site for the symbolic violence of imposition of life-world and practice. Further, the progressive critique has argued against scripted pedagogy on democratic and egalitarian principles: that direct instruction shapes a habitus, which is a kind of domestication and stratification of working classes, and a reproduction of "unprincipled" (Edwards and Mercer, 1987) and, indeed, undemocratic imposition.

Yet while these claims stand against commodified and official forms of direct instruction, they may neglect elements of the customary pedagogy. My point is that didactic pedagogy and overt instruction has its place in a critical educational agenda, that many traditions of literate practice and their durability in traditional instruction may serve a central educational function: of defining literacy as an intergenerational gift, as a ritual demand for membership in a community that necessitates riposte, response, and engagement with a sociocultural contract. This is compatible with Freire (2005) and others' versions of literacy education as membership of a cultural circle, or even early whole language models of learning as initiation into a club, and the current "community of practice" literature. Membership of a cultural circle requires learning the responsibilities of riposte.

A ritual exchange mode would redefine literacy education as community and cultural action, warranted by elders and with reciprocal elements of ritual, honor, and obligation. I am aware of the historical irony and contradiction here. The proposal presupposes that literacy—a technology that is historically and ontogenetically linked to the production of modernity and capital exchange—could be reappropriated in a mock pre-commodified exchange that is less about individuation and more about membership in community. There is a possibility that literacy teaching can be ritually insulated in ways that defer its formal economic rationalization.

What might such an approach look like? Part of the task would be to enlist approaches that have previously been undertaken in the fields of cross-cultural and indigenous education internationally:

- *The participation of community/family elders*—whose demonstration of expertise would constitute and would set out reciprocal responsibilities of riposte. This would involve the engagement of elders and experts of all ages, with mastery of both (oral and print) residual cultures and emergent (digital) cultures. The responsibility of these elders would be to model literacy practices, old and new, and to formally establish an intergenerational contract between students and teachers of reciprocal rights and responsibilities, functions and purposes around reading and writing practices. We find elements of this model of the teacher both in European traditions of teachers as "pedagogues" and in Confucian traditions, as well as approaches to indigenous education (e.g., Malcolm et al., 1999; Shields et al., 2005).

- *A focus on culturally significant texts*—not trivialized and purpose-built texts, but rather those forms of cultural memory and narrative that have visible significance in explaining the "dreaming" of how things came to be and how things could be. These would include texts of historical, literary and cultural belief, value and significance, and emergent digital texts which are making and constituting the cultural present and future.
- *An alteration of the exchange structures to approximate those of gifting*—that involve reciprocal responsibilities to speak, read and write from immediate point of entry into schooling. This involves a setting of an environment where writing and reading count—not just institutionally—but culturally, as a ubiquitous cultural practice that comes with customary routines. It would reappropriate everyday, community and familial exchange patterns into pedagogic practice, such as modeled by Au (1980), Malcolm and colleagues (1999), McNaughton (2002) and others with indigenous learners.
- *A formal ritualization of more traditional aspects of pedagogy*—including choral and oral reading, singing around culturally significant texts, and memorization and induction into the physical craft of inscription and its cultural mnemonics.
- *A routinized weaving of those elements of rote pedagogy into more dialogic, critical education*—this would involve a systematic and predictable weaving between foci on word and world, text and context, code and meaning, overt instruction with critical analysis, and open discussions of a repertoire of reciprocal obligations and responsibilities.
- *An engagement with both residual and emergent traditions and modes of representation*—encouraging the weaving between digital, print, and oral traditions wherever possible, with transliteration between spoken, written and digitally represented texts.

Centrally, such an approach would involve a reframing of the role and preparation of the teacher to afford a traditional position of cultural elder and technological craftsperson: the position of master multiliterate with an obligation to perform and profess a range of significant cultural practices and texts. The deskilling of teachers through scripted instruction and testing would deter such a move.

But to speak of a re-culturing of literacy education would require an expansive, contemporary understanding of the dynamics of cultures in societies already caught in the cultural contestation and blending of globalization and transnational capital exchange. The necessity to avoid cultural essentialism is a practical one, given the cultural heterogeneity of experiences brought to classrooms and the diversity of student populations. We would therefore have to consider several critical caveats. First, that any "tradition of the new" based upon gifting would build and reinforce a determinate cultural economy. Traditional exchange can entail "negative reciprocity" (Gregory, 1997), with high cultural and practical consequences for refusal. Cushla Kapitzke (1995) offers the case of religious gifting, which entails a hierarchical assertion of intergenerational, patriarchal power with doxic structures of guilt and retribution for non-compliance. The formation of the modern secular school built around a common curriculum was in part a move to free children from the symbolic violence of some community cultures. This is still an imperative.

But by "going back" we would return to the foundational questions about the teleology of state schooling, rather than a return to a pre-modern. I propose here a "traditionalism of the new," rather than a return to the pre-modern, a bringing together of residual and emergent, community and secular, print and digital traditions, rather than a romantic revisiting of the license of patriarchy and intergenerational control prior to the industrial school.

Such a ritualization of early literacy education thus would have to be based upon a modern version of literate culture in the community—with elders and masters of the craft. This would involve print and digital literacy forms, as well as a refocus on oral practice. This would involve chants, songs, and the lodging of literacy education in culturally significant texts on a daily, routinized basis. The purpose of this would not be to better skill students, though this would be of value. It would be to re-instill the community responsibility to read and write, to engage with and learn the code, and to use these for culturally significant purposes and practices.

From commodity to custom

In a recent analysis of the new economic structures of the internet—the new mnemotechnic device—economist John Quiggin (2006) argues that the social fields of the new technologies break and elude many traditional expectations about how markets work. He argues that the dot.com crash was not simply the product of investment speculation, but the result of a misestimation of the regularities and norms of behavior by users and participants in online communities. He goes on to make the case that behavior is driven, in part, by motivations and patterns that are uncharacteristic of late capitalist markets, including: reputation and status, anti-authoritarian behavior, and, notably, altruism and gifting. Bergquist and Ljungberg (2001) further argue that the "power of gifts" is a principal focus of the organization of social relationships in open source communities. They argue that the gift giving creates "openness" but also is a way of "guaranteeing the quality of the code." While the conflict between "pay-per" markets and "creative commons" continues (Kapitzke and Bruce, 2006), these analyses partly account for the difficulty of mainstream economic models for accounting for the patterns of exchange, economic and discursive/communicative, on the new media.

There is evidence that other, hybrid models of communication and exchange are possible in the conditions of "hypercapitalism" (Graham, 2005)—that some emergent institutions and media can be shaped differently, or in ways that are on the edges or outside fully commodified and marketized capitalist exchange. The emergent capacities and structures of the new media, still visibly in formation and with shifting centers of power and innovation, are seedbeds for both residual and emergent traditions of human agency. And they are sites where the shape and contexts of the archive are being expanded and altered by different human agents, institutions and agencies (Lam, 2006). What is notable in descriptions of information and attentional economies is deliberately counter-capitalist and anti-market behavior, belief, and motivation. In the virtual worlds of hypercapitalism, some youths and adults are reinventing and reappropriating residual cultural traditions: via gifting, altruism as high modernist ideal, and resistance as a means of political statement and corporate subversion.

Shifting the patterns and motivations of exchange in the "modern" school is a more difficult challenge, for all of the aforementioned political and economic reasons. But it should not go wanting of alternative theoretical and historical models. My aim here has been to argue that we can address the issues of stratified achievement amongst economically and culturally marginalized students, and we can redefine the binary debates over pedagogy by re-envisioning literacy education as a counterfactual ideal, one that brings together old worlds with new, the oldest media with the newest, traditional with digital cultures. That the structures constructed by young and old in digital communities can reflect those values that are defined in contra-distinction to the market and to traditional commodity exchange, marks new possibilities of community, identity, and persistent resistance to structures of capital.

Conflict around the "uptake" of reading and writing instruction in part entails a clash of residual and emergent traditions, a clash between literacy pedagogy as "gift" and literacy pedagogy as commoditized, capitalist economic exchange, epitomized in the hundred-year campaign of Western educational systems to convert literacy education into a secular, industrial training. In search of a positive thesis for literacy education that supplants the reproductive effects of this economic reductionism, I have explored whether notions of gift and reciprocal exchange offer us cultural grounds for remaking, rebuilding, and reworking the everyday classroom exchanges that plague the system now—where socioeconomically marginalized students refuse the commodity exchange that have been legislated in schools for the "taking" and "uptake" of literacy.

Would such a model simply prime the pump for a willing consent into a hegemonic literate culture that is built in and through the new corporatist curriculum settlement? On this, Bourdieu is suitably ambiguous, leading us back to the dialectical dilemmas noted by Dewey and Freire. We might use Bourdieu's comments on the role of social science to frame up the possibilities and problems with literacy education:

> The object of social science is a reality that encompasses all the individual and collective struggles aimed at conserving and transforming reality, in particular those that seek to impose the legitimate definition of reality, whose specifically symbolic efficacy can help to conserve or subvert the established order, that is to say, reality.
>
> (1990: 141)

Whether and how literacy education can expand to encompass "all the individual and collective struggles aimed at conserving and transforming reality, in particular those that seek to impose the legitimate definition of reality" and whether and how "it can help conserve and subvert the established order" is, ultimately, in the hands of teachers and students. They have as available resources blends of traditional and radical, didactic and dialogic, rote and constructivist pedagogies.

This has been but one proposal of how we might shift early literacy education from its commodity form. The symbolic violence of the commodity form is refused by many students. This codifies literacy as prerequisite for entry and defined through systems of marketized, individuated exchanges. The refusal of that codification acts to confirm the very class structures that it is based on. Yet we should not confuse the commodification of literacy with its ostensive pedagogical focus on overt instruction. The current context requires radical alternatives and new historical syntheses. I have suggested here bringing together traditional teaching based on teacher technological and epistemological expertise, canonical and critical cultural knowledge—with pre- and post-capitalist notions of gifting, altruism, and reciprocity. Through a critical ethics of literacy that originates as an obligation and responsibility to and marker of community, students might be in a position where they can conserve and subvert the gift of writing—rather than reject it and in so doing reproduce the market.

Acknowledgments

My thanks to Ruth Wong for use of the transcripts from her study of Year 3 Singapore reading classrooms; to colleagues for critique, advice and correction: Carmen Luke, Don Sanderson, Cushla Kapitzke, Phil Graham, Jim Ladwig, Linda Graham, Jim Albright, Dennis Kwek, Masturah Ismail and Barbara Comber.

References

Alexander, R. (2000) *Culture and Pedagogy*. Oxford, UK: Blackwell.

Anderson, B. (1992) *Imagined Communities*. London: Verso.

Au, K. H. (1993) *Literacy Instruction in Multicultural Settings*. Belmont, CA: Wadsworth.

Au, K. H. (1980) Participation structures in a reading lesson with Hawaiian children: analysis of a culturally appropriate instructional event. *Anthropology and Education Quarterly*, 11, 91–115.

Au, K. H. and Mason, J. M. (1983) Cultural congruence in classroom participation structures: achieving a balance of rights. *Discourse Processes*, 6, 145–67.

Bernstein, B. (1990) *Class, Codes and Control: Vol. 4. The Structuring of Pedagogic Discourse*. London: Routledge.

Bergquist, M. and Ljungberg, M. (2001) The power of gifts: organising social relationships in open source communities. *Information Systems Journal*, 11, 305–20.

Bourdieu, P. (1977) *Outline of a Theory of Practice* (R. Nice, trans.). Cambridge, UK: Cambridge University Press. (Original work published 1972)

Bourdieu, P. (1990) *The Logic of Practice* (R. Nice, trans.). Cambridge, UK: Polity Press. (Original work published 1980)

Bourdieu, P. and Passeron, J. C. (1990) *Reproduction in Education, Society and Culture* (2nd edn). Beverley Hills, CA: Sage.

Collins, J. (1993) Determination and contradiction: an appreciation and critique of the work of Pierre Bourdieu on language and education. In C. Calhoun, E. LiPuma, and M. Postone (eds), *Bourdieu: Critical Perspectives*. Chicago: University of Chicago Press, 116–38.

Comber, B. and Simpson, A. (eds) (2001) *Negotiating Critical Literacies in Classrooms*. Mahwah, NJ: Lawrence Erlbaum Associates.

Delpit, L. (1996) *Other People's Children: Cultural Conflict in the Classroom*. New York: New Press.

Dewey, J. (1991) *The School in Society and the Child in the Curriculum*. Chicago: University of Chicago Press.

Edwards, D. and Mercer, N. (1987) *Common Knowledge*. London: Routledge.

Fairclough, N. (ed.) (1992) *Critical Language Awareness*. London: Longman.

Freebody, P. and Luke, A. (1990) Literacies' programs: debates and demands in cultural context. *Prospect: Australian Journal of TESOL*, 5(3), 7–16.

Freire, P. (2005) *Education for Critical Consciousness*. London: Continuum.

Goody, J. (1977) *Domestication of the Savage Mind*. Cambridge, UK: Cambridge University Press.

Goody, J. (1987) *The Logic of Writing and the Organisation of Society*. Cambridge, UK: Cambridge University Press.

Graham, P. (2005) *Hypercapitalism*. New York: Peter Lang.

Gregory, C. A. (1994) Exchange and reciprocity. In T. Ingold (ed.), *Companion Encyclopedia of Anthropology*. London: Routledge, 911–39.

Innis, H. A. (1951) *The Bias of Communication*. Toronto: University of Toronto Press.

Irigaray, L. (1997) Women on the market. In A. D. Schrift (ed.), *The Logic of the Gift*. London: Routledge, 174–89.

Kapitzke, C. (1995) *Literacy and Religion*. Amsterdam: John Benjamins.

Kapitzke, C. and Bruce, B. C. (eds) (2006) *Cybraries*. Mahwah, NJ: Lawrence Erlbaum Associates.

Larson, J. (ed.) (2005) *Literacy Teaching as Snake Oil*. New York: Peter Lang.

Lam, W. S. E. (2006) Culture and learning in the context of globalisation: research directions. *Review of Research in Education*, 30(1), 213–37.

Levi-Strauss, C. (1969) *Elementary Structures of Kinship*. London: Routledge.

Luke, A. (1992) The body literate: discourse and inscription in early literacy instruction. *Linguistics and Education*, 4, 107–29.

Luke, A. and Carrington, V. (2002) Globalisation, literacy, curriculum practice. In R. Fisher, M. Lewis, and G. Brooks (eds), *Language and Literacy in Action*. London: Routledge/Falmer, 231–50.

Luke, A., Cazden, C. B., Lin, A. and Freebody, P. (2004) *A Coding Scheme for the Analysis of Singapore Classroom Practice*. Singapore: National Institute of Education, Centre for Research in Pedagogy and Practice.

Luria, A. (1976) *The Nature of Human Conflicts*. New York: Norton.

Malcolm, I., Haig, Y., Konigsberg, P., Rochecouste, J., Collard, G., Hill, A., et al. (1999) *Towards More User-friendly Education for Speakers of Aboriginal English*. Perth: Education Department of Western Australia.

Mauss, M. (1990) *The Gift* (W. D. Halls, trans.) London: Routledge.

McGaw, B. (2006) *Education and Social Cohesion* (Dean's Lecture Series). Melbourne: University of Melbourne.

McHoul, A. (2006) The twisted handiwork of Egypt. Unpublished manuscript, Murdoch University, Perth, Western Australia.

McLuhan, M. (1962) *The Gutenberg Galaxy*. Toronto: University of Toronto Press.

McNaughton, S. (2002) *Meeting of Minds*. Auckland, New Zealand: Learning Media.

McNaughton, S. (2006) Effective literacy instruction and culturally and linguistically diverse students. Paper presented at the Future Directions in Literacy Conference, Sydney, Australia.

New London Group. (1996) A pedagogy of multiliteracies: designing social futures. *Harvard Educational Review*, 66, 60–92.

Organisation for Economic Co-operation and Development. (2005) *School Factors Related to Quality and Equity*. Paris: Author.

Polanyi, K. (1944) *The Great Transformation*. New York: Rinehart.

Quiggin, J. (2006) Non-economics of information. Paper presented at the Centre for Creative Industries Researcher Symposium, Queensland University of Technology, Brisbane, Australia.

Scribner, S. and Cole, M. (1989) *The Psychology of Literacy*. Cambridge, MA: Harvard University Press.

Schrift, A. D. (ed.) (1997) *The Logic of the Gift*. London: Routledge.

Sefton-Green, J. (2006) Youth, technology and media cultures. *Review of Research in Education*, 30(1), 279–306.

Shields, C. M., Bishop, R. and Mazawi, A. E. (2005) *Pathologizing Practices*. New York: Peter Lang.

Street, B. (1984) *Literacy in Theory and Practice*. Cambridge, UK: Cambridge University Press.

Part II

Producing the field

Chapter 6

The field of Arabic instruction in the Zionist state

Allon J. Uhlmann

Arabic in the Arabic schools is a living language that is spoken, and written, and heard. In Hebrew schools the Arabic language is taught as if it were a dead language that is not spoken and written, like Latin is taught, for instance.

> (A senior Arab academic at an Israeli university, department of Arabic language and literature, personal communication[1])

Teaching a language is never merely a technical, pedagogical issue, and the teaching of Arabic in the state of Israel is particularly charged. Zionism's continuing ambivalence toward Arab existence in historic Palestine has shaped Arabic instruction in various, often contradictory, ways.

It is, indeed, Israel's peculiar polity—or field of power—that emerges as critical in shaping its unique dynamics of Arabic instruction. Israel's polity is marked by Zionism, the nationalist-sectarian project that constitutes Jews as a distinct nation, and seeks to mobilize them as a group to assert Jewish collective supremacy in Palestine. By analyzing the field of Arabic instruction in Israel, this chapter aims to develop an analytical approach that draws on Bourdieu's sociology of practice, and to adapt it to societies whose polity is marked by a collective project of sectarian domination.

Before continuing, some elementary contours of the education system in Israel need to be clarified. The Israeli public school system is divided into various streams. The most elementary division is between the Hebrew-language stream which caters predominantly to Israel's dominant Jewish population, and the Arabic-language stream which caters to Israel's Palestinian citizens and residents. Israel's tertiary education system is tiered, with universities forming the top tier, and colleges—mostly teacher colleges—forming the second tier. All universities and most colleges teach in Hebrew (Amara and Mari, 2002).

This chapter focuses on the teaching of Arabic in the Hebrew school stream, and on the instruction at university departments of Arabic language and literature. The teaching of English is used as a comparative backdrop to help tease out the dynamics of Arabic instruction. After identifying some differences between the way English and Arabic are taught, I use Bourdieu's notion of cultural capital to outline the systemic significance of these differences. I then rely on Bourdieu's notion of field to explain the systemic logic of Arabic instruction in Israel. At the end of the chapter I draw some implications for the deployment of Bourdieu's heuristic apparatus in societies such as Israel's, which are dominated by a sectarian project.

Language instruction in Israel— English versus Arabic

While English is taught as a living second language, Arabic is Latinized: it is generally taught in the Hebrew sector as if it were a textually based, dead language, to be decoded and interpreted but not creatively used for communicative purposes. Thus, Arabic is taught in the Jewish school sector and at universities in Hebrew. In fact, most of the Jewish schoolteachers of Arabic, and a substantial number of university lecturers in Arabic, are unable to speak fluently, write or teach in Arabic. This is aggravated by the paucity of Arabs teaching either at Jewish schools or at universities. By contrast, schoolteachers and university lecturers of English are predominantly native speakers of English, and teaching is conducted in English. In fact, English teachers in many schools have a policy of speaking only English with students, even outside of class.

At Hebrew schools, English is taught as a compulsory subject from primary school, normally Year 3. It is usually only at Year 7 that pupils have to choose between Arabic or French as a second foreign language. English is a compulsory subject for matriculations and is taught at a level equivalent to a major or near major in academic high schools. By contrast, the second foreign language (Arabic or French) is typically taught up till Year 10, and is not a required matriculation subject. (Arabic is nonetheless available for matriculation both as a major and as an elective.) Furthermore, schools invest considerably in maintaining and supporting immigrant English-speaking students' native knowledge. Many schools run special classes for English speakers or, at the very least, support English speakers with special assignments. By contrast, knowledge of Arabic from home meets with no support from within the school system.

In English classes there is a great deal of effort put into developing and enhancing the capacity of pupils to express themselves by emphasizing creative usage through such assignments as compositions and conversational exercises. By contrast, both instruction and matriculation examinations of students of Arabic overvalue grammatical skills such as the conjugation of verbs and desinential inflection (إعراب) and emphasize passive understanding, while undervaluing the capacity to construct meaningful sentences and express ideas.

These differences are accentuated at the tertiary level. Advanced English instruction at university assumes a much higher level of proficiency among students compared with advanced Arabic. Thus the amount of Arabic reading required is substantially less than the amount of English reading at equivalent departments of English, and students are expected to write and present in English very much more than in Arabic.

On the face of it, all this is a rather strange state of affairs. Given that more Israelis speak Arabic than English—mostly Palestinian Arabs, but also Arab Jews (Amara and Mar'i, 2002)—one might expect there to be a large enough pool of teachers who are proficient in Arabic, and for Arabic to be taught as a living language. Moreover, university standards for Arabic proficiency need not be less than for English.

Language and literacy are elements of what Bourdieu has dubbed *cultural capital*, that is, knowledge, skills, and dispositions that are acquired through social interactions (Bourdieu, 1986). These are conceptualized as capital because they carry with them value, which is ultimately interchangeable with other forms of capital. This value is not fixed. It depends on the way social agents evaluate it, and this evaluation is a product of ongoing social and political processes.

Pedagogical policy and practice carry profound implications for the differential valuations of literacy and fluency. In the case of Arabic, educational practice devalues native knowledge of the language while, by contrast, native fluency in English is greatly valued. Moreover, the fact that university departments of Arabic language and literature carry out instruction in Hebrew creates a strong overvaluation of Hebrew literacy as compared to Arabic literacy. In fact, the capacity to speak Hebrew and write English is necessary for appointments and promotion within university departments of Arabic. Arabic proficiency is of secondary importance. In other words, the value of the cultural capital of Jews is inflated, even in this area, at the expense of the cultural capital of Arabs.

In this way the diasporic knowledge of Arab Jews is also greatly devalued, in sharp contrast with the equivalent diasporic knowledge of European Jews. This devaluation can be situated within the broader Zionist project of de-Arabizing Arab Jews—a project which is a necessary component of the ideological constitution of a distinct Jewish nation in the Middle East (see Brosh and Ben-Rafael, 1994).

The revaluation of cultural capital reproduces in the realm of literacy the social structure and the prevalent self-image—or as Bourdieu would have it, the dominant vision of social division—of Israeli society. Here we see, in other words, how the valuation of cultural capital mirrors and reproduces social structure at large, with Jews dominant over Palestinian Arabs, and Europeans dominant over Arab Jews.

The field of Arabic educational policy and practice

The prevailing social order greatly conditions the place of Arabic and the patterns of its instruction, but it does not determine these patterns. To understand the systemic nature of the continuously evolving practice of Arabic instruction we must incorporate Bourdieu's notion of *field*, a heuristic device aimed at identifying the historical dynamics that shape reality (Bourdieu, 1985; Bourdieu and Wacquant, 1992).

In order to interpret the logic and dynamics of a particular area of social practice, a social analyst must bracket off a relatively autonomous area of practice as a field. For the purposes of the current discussion, the relevant field can be designated as the field of Arabic educational policy and practice.

Fields do not exist independently of the consciousness of the agents who operate within them. Rather, fields are produced and reproduced by the agents who operate within them, and it is the consciousness of these agents that motivates their practice within the field. By the very same token, the consciousness of social agents—their very agency—is shaped by their experiences within the fields in which they operate. In other words, agents' consciousness and the field are mutually constitutive, and it is in this relationship of mutual constitution that we must search for important dynamics of historical reproduction and change (Bourdieu, 1981).

Bourdieu uses the term *habitus* to capture this process whereby agency, itself a product of the field, produces and reproduces the field. In what follows, the discussion of the field of Arabic instruction will integrate an analysis of the consciousness of social agents—their dispositions. This consciousness will at the same time be interpreted as a product of the field and the agents' place within it—their positions.

A comprehensive analysis of the field of Arabic instruction is well beyond the scope of this chapter. Here I will offer a preliminary analysis that will seek to derive some of the dynamics that shape the field. The main practices of Arabic instruction—such as the separation between a Hebrew stream and Arabic stream, the exclusion of Arabs from the Arabic teaching staff in Hebrew schools, the status of Arabic as an elective second foreign language—crystallized in the 1930s and 1940s, in the days of the British Mandate over Palestine. At the same time, the main struggles in the field took shape, such as over the language of instruction of Arabic and the status of Arabic as non-compulsory.

The politics of schooling

One originary trait of the field is the subversion of official policy at the local level of practice. For instance, there seems to have always been a general consensus among policymakers that Arabic should be made compulsory for Hebrew-speaking students, and that Arabic is best taught at school in Arabic (see the collection of policy documents and pedagogical debates in Yonai, 1992, and Landau, 1961). But no less remarkable than such ongoing consensus is the failure of such policies to materialize in practice. They are repeatedly subverted at the local level of schools and school districts, and the policymakers have so far been unable to force the issue.

Currently, official ministerial policy requires that Arabic should be made compulsory at Hebrew schools from Year 7 until Year 10, and then should be included at the matriculation at the minimal level of one unit. These policies have been decided at the education ministerial level but are progressively watered down as one goes down the rungs of the bureaucratic ladder all the way to the classroom. In most schools it continues to be offered as an optional second foreign language. There is a general enforcement of the availability of Arabic in Hebrew schools between Years 7 and 9, although this, too, is by no means comprehensive. There is no enforcement of the compulsory inclusion of Arabic in the matriculation examinations.

This state of affairs is remarkable, given the impressive weight of the forces that push for the expansion of Arabic instruction. These include academics, the professionals involved in teaching Arabic such as supervisors at the Ministry of Education and Arabic teachers, and sympathetic Ministers of Education. In this they are allied with the very powerful security apparatus—most importantly, the Military Intelligence—with its insatiable need for Arabic speakers.

Military Intelligence is probably the most powerful driving force in the promotion of Arabic instruction in Israel. Military representatives have participated in virtually all commissions of inquiry into Arabic. The military is also represented on the Arabic Language Subject Committee, which steers Arabic instruction within the Ministry of Education (see Military Intelligence, 2004).

Military Intelligence is involved not only at the level of policymaking and implementation but also with the actual teaching of Arabic. This involvement takes various forms, including special educational camps and intelligence paramilitary training to young cadets, the creation of links between suitable candidates and intelligence units before the military service, and the provision of a whole array of speakers, teaching aids and other material to support teachers. Military Intelligence has also funded educational development and has endorsed instruction material used at schools. Furthermore, the military provides some schools, usually junior high schools in peripheral towns, with conscripts who are trained to teach Arabic (Military Intelligence, 2004).

The rationale provided by Military Intelligence for the promotion of Arabic is straightforward: Israel needs people who understand Arabic to help protect the Jewish state from the Arab threat, and also to facilitate contact with the peoples of the region. This need is particularly acute now that the generation of Jews who had immigrated from Arabic-speaking countries is retiring or dying out and is not being replenished.

The open involvement of Military Intelligence in supporting Arabic instruction at Jewish schools is important. Much of the informal curriculum, and a substantial part of the formal curriculum, revolves around preparing students for their compulsory military service. Building up the significance of Arabic for the security needs of the Zionist state is thus a critical aspect of creating a positive attitude among students toward the subject, lifting the prestige of learning Arabic, and attracting the "good" students to the subject. Teachers, for their part, actively seek military involvement in their classes as an effective means to raise the motivation of Arabic students.

Ironically, the Zionist establishment is not alone in calling for deepening of the instruction of Arabic. It is the autonomous nature of the field that allows for contradictory social forces to come together and, in this case, it is also Israeli Arabs who are greatly concerned to lift the status of Arabic in the country and in the educational system. Thus, in the report of the Knesset (parliament) Education Committee investigation into the teaching of Arabic, it was Arab Communist Member of Knesset Tawfiq Tubi who outdid his colleagues by issuing a minority recommendation to the effect that the Knesset should legislate to make the teaching of Arabic compulsory throughout the education system (Knesset, 1986). No doubt, Military Intelligence would have happily seconded this proposal.

More remarkable than the constellation of forces that militates in favor of deepening the instruction of Arabic at schools is the fact that it has so far been singularly unsuccessful. These initiatives from above are thwarted from below, as it were, by pupils, parents and principals.

The critical areas where decisions are subverted are the prioritization of resource allocation to schools and, more significantly, the local action of teaching staff and students, especially principals. For their part, principals direct resources (teaching time and budgets) to subjects that are tested at the matriculation level, and away from non-examined subjects. This is sometimes achieved by highly irregular means. Some principals go as far as handing out bogus term grades to students after completely canceling the compulsory Arabic instruction in their school. The supervisory staff at the Ministry of Education generally turn a pragmatic blind eye to such practices.

Such pragmatism is a mixture of recognition of two main facts. One is that a full implementation of all official curricular policy is unrealistic given the resources available. Rather, official policy is seen as, at best, a wish list or, at worst, as a cynical political statement for public consumption with no practical significance. The other fact is the limit of the supervisory powers to confront a coalition of principals and parents. There is a diffuse concern that in such situations being too dogmatic may end up in a political blowout. Moreover, there is a split within the Ministry between those functionaries who are in charge of ensuring the smooth operation of schools—by making realistic compromises—and the subject supervisors who act as advocates for their own particular subjects. It is, in fact, the negotiations between these two sets of mid-level functionaries that shape such pragmatic compromises.

Parents and pupils support the principals' concentration of resources on "important" subjects. In fact, many pupils resort to additional means to avoid wasting energy on subjects that are not examined at the matriculation level. In the last two decades, many students have been taking advantage of a mushrooming private market in educational psychology to "buy" exemptions from the study of a second foreign language so that they can focus on the subjects that matter (such as English and mathematics).

To further understand the motivations of parents and pupils, we must consider the political economy of foreign language literacy. Even though Arabic is nominally an official language, Hebrew is the language of business, the administration, the law, and so forth. In fact, English has a greater currency than Arabic does. The segregation of Israeli society is such that very few Jews have the opportunity to interact with Arabic speakers beyond some superficial, laconic exchanges. The moment they operate outside the narrow confines of Arab society, Arabs, too, operate in Hebrew. There is not even a single recognized Arabic university in the Israeli system. Moreover, in calculating university entrance scores, universities add bonus points for preferred subjects such as English, Arabic attracts no bonus (Amara and Mar'i, 2002). The nominal status of Arabic as an official language is an anachronistic relic of different times and carries negligible practical significance, other than providing a false liberal gloss to Zionist linguistic sectarianism. This means that Arabic is of greatly reduced value as cultural capital even beyond the narrow confines of language instruction—a vicarious measure of the power relations between Jews and Arabs.

Consequently, the most profound ideological difference between the instruction of Arabic and English in the Hebrew stream is the way the two are articulated to the personal and national interest. Learning English is motivated by personal interest, that is, by the benefits such knowledge bestows upon its bearer as an individual. It is taught so as to help pupils in their later years. A good mastery of English is a prerequisite for entry into university and is a highly valued skill in the labor market. It is deemed essential for professional, financial, and personal success.

Learning Arabic is not of personal value as such, but rather of national significance. Its benefits lie not in immediate palpable personal gain, but rather within the national interest, that is, the Zionist project. Maintaining a reservoir of Jews who can understand Arabic is deemed to serve this interest. While majoring in Arabic may lead one to an interesting career with the public service, it makes little utilitarian sense to study Arabic for any other reason.

This explains how social agents whose habitus incorporates Zionist ideological dispositions may come to adopt contradictory positions in the field. Zionist policymakers, as guardians of the national interest, are motivated by their sectarian concerns to strengthen Arabic instruction. The very same Zionist aesthetics produce in parents, children and principals contradictory strategies and practices. This clearly exemplifies that habitus and field cannot be fully understood in isolation. That the two must be approached together is further reinforced by the ironic coalition between opposed dispositions that are embodied on the one hand in the Zionist pedagogical and security establishments and, on the other hand, in an Arab Communist Member of Knesset.

To the differences between the interests of bureaucrats on the one hand, and parents and pupils on the other, must be added a general hostility among many Jews toward Arabic, which stands as a practical metaphor for Arabs (see Brosh and Ben-Rafael, 1994: 341–4). One Jewish Arabic teacher recounted how after one suicide attack in the centre of Israel, she came into her Year 10 classroom to find "Death to Arabs" written across the blackboard. This was not unusual. Several teachers and supervisors observed that the continuing conflict creates a mental block in some students toward Arabic in particular, and Middle Eastern studies more generally.

The role of universities

The urgency, or rather, the lack thereof, of Arabic instruction at Hebrew schools is one of the interesting contours of the field of Arabic instruction. Another is the methodology and quality of Arabic instruction, that is, how Arabic is conceptualized as subject matter and what methodology is adopted for its instruction. Here, too, the field serves to depress the value of Arab cultural capital compared with Jewish/Hebrew cultural capital.

The role of universities in this respect is critical. Israeli departments of Arabic language and literature are heirs to a long tradition of European Orientalist scholarship. They conceive of the study of Arabic as the study of alien textual codes, and accordingly conduct the bulk of their instruction in Hebrew.

Actual teaching policies do vary. Departments that have Arabs on their staff, such as Haifa and Tel Aviv, tend to incorporate a greater amount of Arabic instruction. Thus at Tel Aviv University, a few lecturers have taken to lecturing very slowly in rather simple Arabic, providing Hebrew summaries during or at the end of the lesson. Still, many of the tenured Jewish lecturers in Arabic are, in fact, unable to teach in Arabic. One head of department confessed that this made it practically impossible to implement a policy of teaching in Arabic. Another insisted that in any event, his department does not aim to be a place to teach language skills. This is done mostly by the military as well as by private bodies such as Berlitz. Rather, his department focuses on the teaching of culture through texts.

But Israeli academia goes much further than that in tipping the balance away from Arab knowledge of Arabic. In teaching Arabic grammar and syntax, Arabic schools, in line with the education system in the Arab world, organize their grammar and syntax along traditional Arab approaches; Israeli universities and Hebrew schools follow the European Orientalist method.[2] (The only partial exception here is Haifa University, whose first-year curriculum offers separate Arabic grammar and syntax classes to graduates of Arabic and Hebrew schools.) This methodological discrepancy between Israeli Arab schools and universities serves to alienate Arab students. It comes in addition to the fact that Arab students are taught Arabic grammar and syntax at school in Arabic, and are thus doubly alienated in the university classroom where they are taught in Hebrew. The consequence of all this is that Jews outperform Arabs at grammar and syntax.[3]

The domination of the European Orientalist approach in academic pedagogy is intertwined with the ethnic composition of the academic staff. Israeli university departments of Arabic are overwhelmingly dominated by Israeli Jews, many of whom do not speak Arabic as a mother tongue. Thus the Department of Arabic at the Hebrew University—Israel's oldest—has only ever had one permanent academic staff member who was Arab. This is in stark contrast with equivalent departments of English, for example, which are overwhelmingly dominated by native English speakers, or speakers with native proficiency, who have studied English as a living language at anglophone universities.

Israeli academia thus reflects the dispositions of those who dominate it. Conceptualizing language proficiency as cultural capital makes it possible to see an important aspect of social dynamics in action. Specifically, we see how Jews, mostly Western, through exercising their superior political and economic power end up increasing the value of their own cultural capital while debasing that of Arabs.

Orientalist sensibilities, then, and the domination of non-native-speaking Jews are mutually constitutive. The devaluation of Arabic proficiency in teaching and appointments—a by-product of the European Orientalist approach—neutralizes one of the major advantages of Arab scholars. This, however, is only a partial explanation for the paucity of Arab academics in Arabic.

There is also a strong element of self-elimination out of teaching Arabic, something that readers of Bourdieu and Passeron (1990) might expect. But the dynamics are different here. Bourdieu and Passeron were grappling with the realization that social agents from subaltern social spaces seem to voluntarily exclude themselves from educational opportunities and upward mobility. They argued that because such social agents are faced with exceedingly low chances of success, expressed in the paucity of previously successful agents from disadvantaged backgrounds, they opt out of the race from the start, thereby actively ensuring their failure.

By contrast, self-elimination of Arabs in Arabic is motivated by somewhat different dynamics. Relatively few Arabs major in Arabic at school. It is of little use-value, as it were, in Hebrew-dominated Israel. Moreover, it is of depressed value in the calculation of university entry scores (Amara and Mar'i, 2002).

At the undergraduate level, Arabs have a reduced incentive to major in Arabic. Career options for Arabs in Arabic are rather restricted compared with those for Jews. Most Jewish graduates of Arabic can expect to join the state apparatus, especially the security and diplomatic services from which Arabs are excluded. Therefore, there is comparatively little to be gained by Arabs from studying Arabic. This explains why, as one Jewish head of the Arabic department complained, the good Arab students seem to gravitate away from Arabic.

Indeed, they do, but the mechanisms of their self-elimination are different from those that Bourdieu and Passeron have described for France. The difference in mechanisms also carries implications for the political significance of self-elimination, a point I will take up below.

Those Arabs who do claw their way through the system to the doctorate level tend to take much longer than Jews, mostly because they have to combine their academic pursuits with a heavier involvement in the labor market. This is probably a reflection of the fact that Arab students have less of an economic basis for surviving without fixed incomes, and are more likely to develop pressing family commitments before completing their doctoral degrees. At the Hebrew University and others, this brings potential Arab candidates up against the university's preference not to appoint older candidates for beginning positions. This academic preference, which forms another barrier, is itself an expression of the profound extent to which Israeli universities are organized around typical Jewish career paths.

Maintenance of the pedagogic status quo

Institutionally, universities set the tone throughout the field of Arabic instruction in many ways. They are the main producers of Arabic teachers. Academia is also critical in directing the educational policies of schools; for instance, through its dominant role in the Ministry of Education's Subject Committee which directs the teaching of Arabic at school, and in the many commissions of inquiry that have investigated the teaching of Arabic. Academia is thereby greatly responsible for the fact that Arabic in Jewish schools is taught in Hebrew. A senior official of the Ministry of Education lamented that most Jewish university graduates of Arabic who become teachers could not communicate in Arabic (except for those who had been trained to do so during their military service and deployed accordingly). This is one of the major stumbling blocks for numerous reform initiatives that have sought to have teachers teach Arabic in Arabic.

We thus see how the poverty of Arabic proficiency among teachers—both at university and at school—reproduces itself down the generations in the system. Departments that lack Arabic proficiency produce graduates who lack proficiency. This is one example of the conservatism, or historical inertia, born of the autonomy of the field. The field follows its own internal logic. Furthermore, this inertia may be getting more entrenched, and its effects more widely felt.

Many veteran schoolteachers and university lecturers of Arabic report a palpable decline in the Arabic language skills of Hebrew high school graduates who major in Arabic. This might be part of a general, pervasive drop in the standards of Israeli schooling. But a probable additional cause is the changing demographic nature of the Arabic teaching workforce in the Jewish sector. In earlier decades the workforce was dominated by Arab Jews, especially Iraqis.

But with the waning of immigration from the Arab world, and the ageing of the last generation of immigrants, the ratio of Israeli-trained teachers has increased, and with it a palpable drop in the Arabic communication skills and literacy among teachers.

There is, of course, a seemingly straightforward way to overcome the paucity of teachers who can communicate in Arabic, namely, the integration of Arab teachers of Arabic. But the persistent segregation of the teaching force even in such conditions is a reflection of the fact that the autonomy of the field of Arabic instruction does not amount to independence. The segregation of Israeli society in general—an integral part of the field of power—is thrown here into sharp relief.

Currently, Arabs are estimated to account for a meagre portion—fewer than 5 percent of Arabic teachers in the Hebrew stream (about 50 of 1,200 teachers). This state of affairs is rarely publicly challenged. Officially, there is no policy of segregating the teaching force. When questioned, ministerial administrators normally offer two kinds of explanations for this paucity of Arab teachers. One kind doubts the compatibility of Arab teachers to teach in the Jewish sector; such explanations highlight, for instance, difficulties that face native speakers who teach their own mother tongue as a second language.[4] These causes, while they may apply to individual instances, are unlikely to account for much of the lack of integration of Arabs into the Jewish system. English is taught predominantly by native speakers of English, French is taught predominantly by French teachers, and there is no inherent reason why the same should not apply to Arabic.[5]

Another set of explanations, though, seems to account more directly for the lack of integration, and that is the resistance of Jewish principals, parents, and teachers to integrating Arab teachers. This takes essentially two forms: one is the refusal on the part of principals to deploy Arab teachers; the other is the continued harassment by students, parents, and other staff, of Arab teachers who have already been employed.

An experimental program to train Arab teachers of Arabic to teach Arabic at Hebrew schools was abandoned in the 1980s when it became clear that virtually all of its graduates dropped out of the system very quickly. A senior supervisor who is closely familiar with this aborted initiative went so far as to suggest that Arabic is the toughest subject for an Arab teacher to teach in a Jewish school. The topic itself is emotionally charged, and confounds attitudes toward Arabs with attitudes toward Arabic, profoundly straining the classroom interaction for Arab teachers of Arabic to Jews.

Furthermore, the resistance can be further aggravated by some vested interests. When I raised with one Jewish teacher the question of integrating Arab teachers into the Jewish sector, her first response was to protest that this would deprive the Jewish teachers of Arabic from work. She then proceeded to add that this may not be a good idea also "for security considerations." She could not expand on what kind of security breach such a scenario would entail, other than the general sense that it would be simpler, safer, and less worrisome if Arab teachers were kept away from Jewish children.

While this resistance from below, as it were, to the integration of Arab teachers is real, its acceptance by the policymakers at the highest ranks of the ministry is remarkable. Needless to say, no principal would be able to refuse to accept Jewish teachers of Russian or Moroccan origin, or justify the exclusion of any Jewish minority members. Those ministerial professionals who had run the aborted teaching program for Arab teachers came crashing against the limits to the autonomy of their field. Subsequently, the same professional staff have come to redirect their efforts toward focusing on increasing Arabic literacy among the Jewish teachers already in the system. They and others are currently trialing various programs to help improve Jewish Arabic teachers' Arabic, and hopefully have them teach in Arabic. This sub-optimal option seems more realistic. Such pragmatic compromises inevitably reinforce the segregation. They also demonstrate one of the ways by which agents come to discover the limits of what is realistically possible.

The analysis so far has relied on Bourdieu's heuristic apparatus, especially his notion of field, to develop a systemic understanding of the historical evolution of Arabic instruction in Israel. The critical significance of other areas of practice to the field is obvious, exemplified among others in the influence of the labor market on pupils' strategies, in the needs of Military Intelligence, and in popular Jewish attitudes toward Arabs. But no less significant is the autonomy of the field, exemplified among others by the unique coalitions among agents within the field, and the ongoing struggle between different agents within the field. Moreover, the inertia within the field, exemplified in the difficulty of shifting to Arabic instruction in Arabic, is a major product of the field's autonomy.

But the analysis has also raised some interesting departures from the findings of Bourdieu and his collaborators in their numerous equivalent analyses in Europe. These departures stem from the difference between the overarching field of power in bourgeois liberal democracies on the one hand, and sectarian regimes such as Israel on the other. In the remainder of this chapter I will draw out some of the implications of this difference to the way Bourdieu's approach can be applied to societies such as Israel's, which are marked by a project of sectarian domination.

Applying Bourdieu to sectarian polities

The official pretence of no segregation, and the contradictory reality that belies it, is typical of much of the Zionist establishment's policy and practice toward Arabs. This strategy dates back to the lead-up to the United Nations' partition resolution of 1947, when the Zionist establishment-cum-state of Israel sought to present a liberal inclusive façade to the international community, while in practice forcing through its sectarian agenda. The public secret surrounding the status of Arabs derives from the contradiction at the very ideological core of the Zionist state, the one between the ideal of a liberal democratic state and a Jewish state. A great deal of ideological and material effort is put into maintaining the fiction of a democratic state as a cover for sectarian Zionist practices.

This duality spawns many other public secrets that pertain to Arabic and its instruction. For instance, in theory, Arabic is an official language alongside Hebrew; in practice, Hebrew is the single official language. Officially, there is no policy of segregation of the teaching force, too. Practice, though, is radically different. Officially, Arabic is taught as a compulsory subject; the reality is different. Of course, few are fooled by the public secret. Yet the collective pretence that covers it up is a common collective Zionist strategy. The investigation of such strategies is important for the analysis of fields.

The concept of the public secret has proven useful especially for situations in which an oppressive regime intimidates the public from freely acknowledging the reality of political oppression (e.g., Taussig, 1999). This, however, is not the case among the Jews in Israel, who enjoy relative freedom of expression. The maintenance of the public secret among the Jews in Israel is not achieved through coercion and intimidation, but rather largely through the active participation of willing agents. Therefore, Zionist public secrets among Jews in Israel are better approached as a collective group project.

Bourdieu's concept of *officializing strategies* (Bourdieu, 1977) could lend itself to further theorizing the public secret within the field, where this depends on the willing participation of social agents rather than coercion. Bourdieu used the concept of officializing strategies to describe the terms in which people represent acts and relationships in order to maximize their prestige and apparent propriety—that is, their symbolic capital. As such, officializing strategies serve as legitimizing strategies.

Bourdieu illustrates his point by reference to matrimonial negotiations among the Kabyle. In practice, the negotiations may be conducted by women along networks that are maintained by women. However, the matrimonial deal is formally sealed and handled as if conducted between men, along culturally privileged networks of patrilineal relationships (Bourdieu, 1977). By analogy, it is the bureaucrats and security personnel who, like women, operate in the concealed realm of realpolitik, and who conduct the effective business of Zionist domination. Thus, a deputy commissioner in the Ministry of Education would vet Arab candidates for teaching positions on behalf of the Shabak, Israel's secret service (Dayan, 2004). It is up to the politicians and other spokespersons to put the legitimizing gloss over the practices of the bureaucracy.

Bourdieu himself did not elaborate on officializing strategies in his subsequent analyses of fields. Rather, in his analysis of situated agency within the field he generally conceived of agents in the field as taken by the game—genuinely taken by the prevailing mystification.

In a polity such as Israel's, where part of the collective project of the dominant group is to deny much of the nature of its very project of domination, the deception is often a conscious collective act, or perhaps willful ignorance, rather than a matter of doxa. The creation and promulgation of the secret is an orchestrated effort and a well-differentiated project. Some people or agencies generate the official ideology, the ideological apparatus distributes it, and at the broadest level it is consumed and echoed by the ordinary folk. This differentiation reflects the successful mobilization of the social category of Jews around the formal and semi-formal Zionist national establishment. Much of the imperative to sustain and maintain the secret is motivated by a pervasive sense that the ongoing realization of the Zionist project requires the "bending" of reality in the greater interest of collective well being.

For the majority of Jews in Israel, the veracity of public pretence is simply a low priority. Of course, the subjugated groups are not easily taken by any of this mystification. Indeed, while Zionism seeks to establish hegemonic control over Jews, its domination of Arabs is mostly non-hegemonic. The public secret is part of the broader phenomenon of mobilization of social agents into a collective project of domination. This project itself requires theorization. As part of its radical sectarianism, the Zionist state constitutes Jews as a discrete nation, which it seeks to organize and on whose behalf it acts. Accordingly, the state structure and a myriad of semi-official Jewish bodies seek to mobilize and organize Jews, thereby turning them from a social category into a group.

The failure of the experimental program to train Arab teachers to teach Arabic at Hebrew schools is an example of the negotiation of the collective project in practice. The program was championed and run by professionals in the Ministry of Education, whose motivation was not to subvert the Zionist agenda but to optimize the teaching of Arabic. The resistance to their action came from below: teachers, pupils, parents, and principals. The program failed. The resistance attests to the great extent to which the Zionist project is internalized by Israeli Jews, and not merely directed from above. The segregation of Arab from Jew remains an inherent aspect of Zionist practice, even if at times it is taken so far as to subvert the aims of the sectarian élite. By contrast, instances of segregation at the local level among Jews have usually been defined as a problem and attracted corrective government policies.

Such collective projects pose a challenge to Bourdieu's analysis of fields. Bourdieu developed his notion of fields in relation to class society. He therefore tended to highlight how agents who pursue their own interests within the field end up, inadvertently perhaps, reproducing the social order. Bourdieu conceived of classes as fractured entities riddled with often antagonistic factions. He did not systematically theorize collective sectarian mobilization, and the effect of such a mobilization on the dynamics and evolution of the field of power.

The organization of the field of power around the production and promotion of sectarian domination is all-pervasive. It inflects and modifies dynamics which at first might seem quite similar to those that prevail in liberal democracies. The process of self-elimination is a case in point. Earlier I argued that the lack of suitable Arab candidates for appointment at the Hebrew University is, in part, the result of self-elimination. But the dynamics involved in this self-elimination are fundamentally different from those that Bourdieu had in mind when discussing the French education system.

Bourdieu's notion of self-elimination is circular. The subalterns have a lesser chance of succeeding. Consequently, they are more likely to drop out of the race and select themselves out of the competition, thereby spontaneously, as it were, achieving their pre-destiny. This, in turn, legitimizes pre-destiny by making it appear as individual achievement. In other words, this is an instance of a self-fulfilling prophecy, whose ideological power stems from the fact that it remains implicit, and the fiction of equal opportunity is maintained.

But in Israel the fiction of equal opportunity is only partially maintained. The mechanisms that exclude Arabs from profitable careers in Arabic are not implicit. The security and diplomatic apparatuses, the main employers of university graduates of Arabic, are directed against Arabs. Arabs are excluded from those sensitive and responsible tasks, whose main aim is precisely to control and contain them. This is a great disincentive to invest in tertiary studies of Arabic. The lack of success among Arabs in such conditions lacks the hegemonising effect of reconstituting social pre-destiny as individual achievement. Exclusion is not experienced as resulting from individual failure, but rather as the product of an external force. Significantly, then, both the nature of this self-elimination and its ideological consequences are quite different in a sectarian state from that in a liberal democracy. Of course, when it comes to differences among Jews, self-elimination is more similar in its structure and effect to that which prevails in class-divided liberal democracies such as France.

It is this sectarianism that ultimately also fixes the relative value of capital within the field. Arabs are often limited in various fields from using their capital in a similar way to Jews. The value of Arabic proficiency for a Jew and an Arab is completely different in the field of Arabic instruction and in general. Jews can accrue material and symbolic capital from proficiency in Arabic in ways that Arabs cannot, for instance, through a well-paying prestigious career in the security apparatus, from which Arabs are excluded. The situation here is radically different from the inequality Bourdieu and his followers have variously described in liberal democracies. In the latter, members of the dominated class have restricted access to capital, and the inequality takes the form of inequality in the distribution of capital. What we are facing here, however, is an additional and essentially different dynamic whereby even in instances where they possess a similar, or greater, value of capital, the Arab possessor's opportunities to use this capital are restricted compared with a Jew.

This means that in such contexts, the dominant species of capital is that kind of capital whose variants include Jewishness and Arabness. This kind of capital is not social capital in Bourdieu's sense. Social capital—the value of one's concrete social networks—is extremely important, and in the Jewish-dominated state Jews are more likely to have valuable contacts than Arabs. But the distinction between Jewish and Arab is significant, independent of the social networks of particular Jews or Arab. Rather, in such instances, Jewishness and Arabness should be seen as physical capital—essentially inherited traits with profound implications for social trajectories. This transformation of hereditary social traits—being either a Jew or a non-Jewish indigene—into physical capital is what makes the overarching field of power in sectarian states such as Israel radically different from liberal democracies such as France. This kind of physical capital is not generally a quantitative trait but rather a qualitative trait, and forms the basis for the valuation of all other forms of capital.[6]

In sum, the peculiarities of Arabic instruction that were described at the beginning of the chapter—Arabic's Latinization and marginalization—largely arise from the sectarian project which dominates the field of power in Israel. The aspects that are particularly important seem to be the significance of physical capital (Jewishness versus Arabness), and the collective mobilization (of Jews) in favor of the sectarian (Zionist) project. These, in fact, make the whole field of literacy education in Israel substantially different in its systemic logic from similar fields in bourgeois liberal democracies.

To understand the logic of practice in this field we must therefore reformulate some of Bourdieu's heuristic apparatus, most notably by reconceptualizing physical capital and its significance. This makes it possible to rely on the powerful conceptual apparatus of field, capital, and habitus to account for the emerging practices of Arabic instruction, including such technical issues as the language of instruction. Approaching practice as the expression of the habitus of social agents within social fields allows us to link the broad macro level (e.g., sectarian political structure) to local micro situations (e.g., the relationship between pupils and teachers) without reducing the latter to a mere enactment, or epiphenomenon, of the former. The formation of different species of capital, their revaluation, and the all-pervasive domination of physical capital in Israel's polity are the historical product of the unfolding of the dynamics in the different fields of practice that make up Israeli society.

Notes

1   The research that informs this chapter includes participant observation, observations and interviews. Given the sensitivity of some matters that are raised in this chapter, I have taken care not to identify my interviewees in order to protect them.

2   European grammarians of Arabic (e.g., W. Wright's classic *Grammar of the Arabic Language*) emphasize function, while Arab grammarians (e.g., Al-Sakkākī's centuries' old *Miftāḥ al-ʿulūm*) emphasize form.

3   The consensus among lecturers and students I spoke with is that Jews are better at grammar and syntax, and at textual analysis. The latter is commonly ascribed to a greater emphasis in Jewish schools on creative critical thinking, as opposed to a greater emphasis in Arab school on rote learning. By contrast, Arab students are

better at Arabic comprehension and communication, both written and verbal. It is also commonly held that Arab students are generally much less assertive in the classroom than Jewish students. Such seeming systematic differences in learning style are often interpreted in the Jewish sector as the problem of poor teaching in Arab schools. Remarkably, none of the educators I spoke with seemed to conceive of differences in learning style as such, or translate such differences into pedagogical policy consideration.

4   Such rationalizations are by no means new. For an early version see the 1946 background briefing by the supervisor of Arabic in the Education Department of the Jewish Assembly in Palestine (Ben Zeev, 1946).

5   It is quite possible that what is misdiagnosed as the difficulty Arab teachers have in teaching their mother tongue as a second language may, in fact, be a problem of differences in cognitive styles and educational culture between the Arab and Jewish education systems.

6   This formulation of physical capital is obviously much broader than earlier similar conceptualizations (physical, embodied or bodily capital) that were limited to the physical body (e.g., Shilling, 1991; Wacquant, 1995). This broadening of scope is a necessary analytic response to the sectarian organization of Israeli society.

References

Amara, M. H. and Mari, A. (2002) *Language Education Policy: The Arab Minority in Israel*. Dordrecht, Netherlands: Kluwer.

Ben Zeev, I. (1946) The instruction of Arabic in the year of 1946 [in Hebrew]. *Yonai*, 2002, 36–8.

Bourdieu, P. (1977) *Outline of a Theory of Practice* (R. Nice, trans.). Cambridge, UK: Cambridge University Press.

Bourdieu, P. (1981) Men and machines. In K. Knorr-Cetina and A. V. Cicourel (eds), *Advances in Social Theory and Methodology: Toward an Integration of Micro- and Macro-sociologies*. London: Routledge and Kegan Paul, 304–17.

Bourdieu, P. (1985) The genesis of the concept of habitus and field. *Sociocriticism*, 2, 11–24.

Bourdieu, P. (1986) The forms of capital. In J. G. Richardson (ed.), *Handbook of Theory and Research for the Sociology of Education*. New York: Greenwood Press.

Bourdieu, P. and Passeron, J. (1990) *Reproduction in Education Society and Culture* (2nd edn). London: Sage.

Bourdieu, P. and Wacquant, L. J. D. (1992) *An Invitation to Reflexive Sociology*. Chicago: University of Chicago Press.

Brosh, H. and Ben-Rafael, E. (1994) Language policy versus social reality: Arabic in the Hebrew school [in Hebrew]. *Iyyunim Behinukh*, 59–60, 333–51.

Dayan, A. (2004) Teachers' pests [electronic version]. *Haaretz*. Retrieved September 30, 2004 from www.haaretzdaily.com/hasen/pages/ShArt.jhtml?itemNo=483006

Knesset (1986) Report of the Knesset Education Committee. *Yonai*, 1992, 174–80.

Landau, J. M. (ed.) (1961) *The Teaching of Arabic as a Foreign Language: Selected Articles* [in Hebrew]. Jerusalem, Israel: School of Education of the Hebrew University and the Ministry of Education and Culture.

Military Intelligence. (2004) טל"מ (section on development of the study of Orientalism). Retrieved February 5, 2004, from www1.idf.il/aman/Site/EnterTelem/EnterTelem.asp

Shilling, C. (1991) Educating the body: physical capital and the production of social inequalities. *Sociology*, 25, 653–73.

Taussig, M. (1999) *Defacement: Public Secrecy and the Labour of the Negative.* Stanford, CA: Stanford University Press.

Wacquant, L. J. D. (1995) Pugs at work: bodily capital and bodily labour among professional boxers. *Body and Society*, 1, 65–93.

Yonai, Y. (ed.) (1992) *Arabic at Hebrew Schools* [in Hebrew]. Jerusalem, Israel: Ministry of Education and Culture, Branch of History of Education and Culture.

Chapter 7

Wireless technology and the prospect of alternative education reform

Mark Dressman and Phillip Wilder

In this chapter we examine the data from a two-year study of the impact of wireless technology on the students, teachers, and school curriculum of an alternative middle school in a Midwestern, mid-sized city in the United States. The middle school students (Grades 6–8) enrolled at Prairie Academy, as we will call it here, all shared a common history of struggle in school and yet, as we noted in a previous study (Dressman et al., 2005), the etiology of their struggles and the ways in which those struggles manifested themselves in their learning and social behavior varied quite widely and significantly.

Introduction

In 2001, the school, in partnership with a local university, received a grant of 30 wireless laptops from a major corporation that also included a mobile cart and transmission station, printer, digital camera, two web-based instructional programs, and several thousand dollars to support curriculum development at the school and a mentor program that brought together the students and staff at Prairie with pre-service teachers and their instructors at the university. A second expansion grant a year later bought nine more laptops and more funds for faculty development.

While the staff at Prairie was renowned for its expertise in dealing with the social and behavioral "baggage" that students brought with them, expectations for student achievement and expertise in how to engage students in sustained academic activity were sometimes lacking. The belief of the university personnel and staff at Prairie who were involved in the writing of the grant—a belief that was articulated in the grant proposal, reports to the funding corporation, and in many informal conversations about why and how the technology would be used—was that the laptops and supporting materials would support a significant shift in students' attitudes toward school and their own capacities as students; a shift in the ways that teachers and pre-service teachers organized instruction and taught; and a dramatic shift in the ways that teachers, pre-service teachers, and the educational community within Prairie City as a whole perceived the students and the program at Prairie.

We also projected significant shifts in the ways teaching and learning would take shape at Prairie. Beyond increases in efficiency, we assumed that the use of word-processing programs would dramatically increase the quantity and quality of students' writing and revision activities, as well as provide new avenues for publication via desktop publishing. We imagined new possibilities for self-expression as students learned to compose web pages that incorporated hypertext, sound, and graphics, and joined the worldwide community of the internet. We spoke of the simulations in science and math that would dramatically demonstrate complex concepts to students and of the ways that chatroom-like programs could revolutionize patterns of classroom discourse, and assumed that in time teachers would begin to collaborate across disciplinary boundaries. Our strong hope was that all of these innovations would ultimately result in a shift in the position of the students at Prairie from culturally and symbolically undercapitalized to advanced, skilled players within the educational community of the school district and beyond.

A year after the close of the program, however, we could point to little curricular change at Prairie, and to even less of a shift in the attitudes of the pre-service teachers who worked as mentors, the staff at Prairie, or the community as a whole toward the struggles of students there. In part this has been because of a shift in district administration toward more "accountability" in terms of test scores (with concurrent pressures to "teach for the test") as well as significant budget cuts. But this shift came at the end of the two-year project and did not directly impact the program there until the year after the project ended. Rather, we would argue, as does Cuban (2003), that longstanding structural conditions were largely responsible for the failure of technology to produce the sort of significant curricular and instructional changes that we wanted—and, we would argue, many educational technologists today continue to want—so desperately to believe in.

In his analysis of the introduction of advanced computer technologies into multiple schools in the San Francisco Bay Area, Cuban detailed the astonishing amounts of money, effort, and speed with which the schools he studied became fully equipped with computers, software, and full internet access. Yet he concluded that despite the extraordinary success of the logistical project of equipping schools with technological hardware and software, few gains in efficiency, productivity, curricular reform, or vocational preparation were achieved, nor were likely to be achieved in the future. Instead, Cuban documented the extent to which technological resources were either not used at all or used in ways that automated traditional teaching and assessment practices, rather than revolutionized them. A few students might take to technology and become very savvy, but this learning usually occurred outside of classroom instruction and often at home rather than at school.

To account for this lack of change in the face of real opportunity and encouragement, Cuban located his study of technology-as-reform within the history of reform movements within the United States, from the introduction of kindergarten in the early 1900s to the desegregation of US schools in the 1960s and 1970s, to calls in the 1980s and 1990s for accountability; and showed how seldom, if ever, any of these reforms had achieved their goals. He argued that because of a fundamental lack of change in the organizational structure of schooling, the ways teachers are prepared to teach, and views of what constitute knowledge, learning, and educational achievement, all attempts to reform such practices are predicated on inverted notions of cause and effect and will inevitably fail.

Cuban's analysis could lead to the conclusion that the implementation of computers into schools is a waste of time and energy. Yet, as Cynthia Ching (2005) argues, to ignore the extraordinary possibilities for instructional reform that the ubiquitous use of computer technology—and in particular, we would argue, wireless laptop technology—offers is likely to prove as grave a mistake as assuming that merely because resources are provided they will be used in optimal ways. We would agree with Ching's argument and suggest that the obvious potential of technology warrants not abandonment of the promises of reform through technology, but rather a more fine-grained analysis of how and why technology sometimes succeeds and often fails to produce change.

Moreover, although Cuban's findings parallel our own in some significant ways, we find little in his historical analysis that suggests a practical direction in which to turn. The lesson that Cuban drew from his study was that without some sort of radical epistemological shift on the part of educators and the public in the United States toward schooling, all efforts at systemic reform, be they technological or otherwise, would be doomed to be absorbed into and essentially neutralized by the existing school culture and its practices. That lesson—or, rather, the conversion experience it calls for on the part of much of the population in order for it not to apply—seems rather disingenuous to us, since Cuban offers little in the way of a scenario for how it might either happen spontaneously or be encouraged to happen.

For these reasons, in accounting for how wireless technology came to Prairie Academy, what was done with it, and how it both succeeded and failed in its mission, we have turned not to the largely empirical analysis of Cuban but to a more interpretive analysis of the project's outcomes—the theoretical work of Pierre Bourdieu (1989, 1990, 1993)—a turn that we believe provides a more hopeful, if also more complex, account of the implications for meaningful, sustained change in education via technological applications.

We became interested in framing our analysis in Bourdieusian terms after we noticed some ironic parallels between tensions in Bourdieu's account of relations between conditions of social reproduction and cultural production—that is, between characterizations of his theory of social order as relentlessly deterministic and his own characterization of his theory as providing possibilities for agency and social change—and our own experience at Prairie Academy of educational intransigence in the face of what we perceived to be the revolutionizing possibilities of wireless technology.

Bourdieu himself addressed this tension between "structuralist" readings of his work and his own more "constructivist" intentions in a lecture, "Social space and symbolic power" (1989). For Bourdieu, the confusion between his own intentions and the interpretations of his Anglo-American readers stemmed from a misunderstanding over the use of the term *structuralism*, which, he argued, he used not in the same sense as Saussure or Levi-Strauss—that is, to claim that he was describing the "essential nature" of social phenomena in genetic or deterministic terms—but rather to describe ingrained patterns of social perception and behavior that are materially conditioned over time within a relatively stable social group, and that are, therefore, malleable.

Misunderstandings of his work are exacerbated further, Bourdieu has argued, by prevailing distinctions made in the social sciences between "objective" or "physical," and "subjective" or "psychological" approaches to understanding social phenomena, and the perceived "dialectic" or irresolvable polarity of these two approaches (pp. 14, 15). Bourdieu rejected the assumed polarity of these approaches, noting that objective claims of social science are always constructed from subjective positions within a field of activity, whereas subjective claims are always necessarily made from some objectively situated position within social space that is seldom acknowledged or understood by the subjectivist social scientist who makes them. As a result of this widely held distinction, according to Bourdieu, his critics have routinely misunderstood his work as being thoroughly, *structurally* "objective"—that is, as positing a view of social reality that is mechanically or physically as deterministic as the reality described by any "hard" (physical or biological) science. But this is not the case, Bourdieu has responded. It is his critics, and not he, who have confused the social maps or diagrams of fields in works such as *Distinction* (1984) with the actual dynamics of lived social reality; the constructs of his work have never been meant to be read as anything more than tentative representations, or abstractions, of particular social fields.

The tentativeness of the "objectivity" he claims for his theory has allowed Bourdieu to argue for a *reflexive sociological* approach to the construction of social theory, one in which the "constructed" condition of the "structures" one identifies remains radically apparent. In such a paradigm, the "semantic elasticity" (1989: 20) of the signs—for example, the commodities, preferences, gestures— by which individuals and social groups differentiate and so identify themselves is acknowledged, so that the meaning of any text, or web of signs, remains contingent not on the reading that the social scientist would give to it but on the ways that social groups and individuals within particular contexts make use of it. Thus, the possibility of a shift in meanings, and so a shift in the social positions of individuals and groups who make use of those meanings, remains an imminent possibility within social space.

Moreover, Bourdieu has argued, while people's perceptions are guided by the "structuring structure" of the habitus, they (like he, the social scientist) remain capable of some limited understanding of that habitus and its effects on their own and others' behavior, and so are also capable of acting in ways that effect some modification or challenge to what prevails as "common-sense" expectations for social behavior. Through these two conditions—and, we would also note, through a third, the possibility of a radical change in the material conditions of the social space itself, which would call for an "improvisation" on the habitus that cannot be predicted in advance—changes in people's social positions can and sometimes do occur.

But, does Bourdieu protest too much? In our reading of studies such as *Distinction* (1984) or "The Kabyle House" in *The Logic of Practice* (1990), or *Reproduction in Education, Society, and Culture* (Bourdieu and Passeron, 1977), we have found much to suggest a rendering of the social order as highly repro-ductive and static, and little to suggest ways in which individuals or social groups might act to produce significant change in their own social position or in the structure of their own societies. The enduring paradox of Bourdieu's work for us remains that, while in theory the social order remains pregnant with possibilities for change, the "objective" empirical evidence and analysis presented in his own work seems to suggest that just the opposite is the usual outcome.

Our own analysis of the effects of wireless technology on educational reform in Prairie brings us to a very similar paradox. At the risk of revealing too much too soon in this chapter, we will report here that despite the best intentions, the highest hopes, and an overflow of material and professional support, we found little evidence of any significant shift in the ways that teachers taught or stu-dents learned during the two years of the grant project. Yet against this portrait of failed reform, like Bourdieu, we must protest that *the possibilities for change are still there*—in the proven technical capacities of computer technology, wireless or otherwise; in the brief or partial responses of one teacher and several marginalized students whom we observed; in changing material conditions that require a shift in practices; or, perhaps, in the course of time itself. The search for these possible avenues of change, via a reading of our data and framed by our reading of Bourdieu, is the subject of our concluding analysis. But first, we have a story to share.

Context of the study

Prairie Academy is an alternative middle and high school program funded and administered by the school district of a mid-sized city. The program is housed in a refurbished elementary school in an ageing residential neighborhood north of downtown. Prairie's program was developed in 1995 in response to "safe schools" legislation in the state, and was originally housed in a storefront in the downtown area. Its original intent was largely "vocational" in its emphasis, that is, to serve as an interface through which students who were perceived as having little prospect of graduating from high school, either because of aca-demic failure or their school behavior, would pass on their way into the workforce. Shortly after its establishment, however, local citizens groups such as the National Association for the Advancement of Colored People and the Urban League protested that the program at Prairie was racially discriminatory, since the overwhelming majority of the students sent there were African-American and male. Under threat from a federal lawsuit, the school was moved to a remodeled elementary school and its curriculum redesigned so that the school operated as an academic unit whose curriculum largely mirrored that of students' "home" schools. In addition, Prairie was designated a "school of choice" within the district and began to market itself as a place with low teacher–student ratios (approximately one to seven), a caring staff, and the promise of a "project-based" curriculum.

Despite these changes, the stigma of enrollment at Prairie Academy remains to this day. Although the elementary school into which the program moved was spacious and thoroughly renovated, community members could also note that it was located in a predominantly African-American area of the city (suggesting that it was a school for "Black kids who misbehaved") and that at 100-plus years, the building was the oldest facility in operation in the district. School board members noted the expense of operating a school that served less than 125 students but that required a staff of 15 or more teachers, two administrators, and a social worker. Disapproval from the media was also evident. For example, in the first year of the grant, Mark arranged for local television and newspaper coverage of Prairie Academy students' visits with their pre-service teacher–mentors to the University of Illinois at Urbana-Champaign (UIUC) campus—coverage that praised the program and the corporation for its generosity but that disparaged the student population of Prairie on air and in print as disinterested in college and "below average" in school achievement.

During the period of our involvement, from fall 2000 to spring 2003, the staff at Prairie worked to educate approximately 50 high school and 50–60 middle school students with a history of chronic struggle, sometimes academic and sometimes social, in school. In 2001–02, slightly less than 80 percent of the student body was African-American, 6 percent was bi-racial, approximately 15 percent was White, and 1 percent each was Asian-American and Latina/o. Seventy-eight percent of the students participated in the free/reduced lunch program, but in fact virtually every student was working class or working poor. The circumstances under which the overwhelming majority of students came to Prairie Academy—through referrals from their home schools following disruptive behavior and/or academic failure—had a profound impact on student and teacher morale at Prairie. Although teachers and administrators demonstrated a constant concern for the academic, social, and emotional well-being of the students in their interactions with them, it was difficult to engage students in sustained academic work and so to make demonstrative progress in subject areas such as math, science and literacy.

It might seem from this description of Prairie's history, location, building characteristics, and the general discourses that circulated about the program within the school district and local media, that, from a Bourdieusian structural analysis, Prairie's institutional role within the school district was so over-determined that no amount of intervention of any variety or volume would be likely to interrupt its socially and culturally reproductive practices. But, at the beginning of the 2001–02 school year, we could also point, in Bourdieusian terms, to the "semantic elasticity" of Prairie's redesignation as a "school of choice" and an "alternative program" in the district, and to the positive publicity that would come from inviting local newspaper and television coverage, as one harbinger of a change in public opinion about Prairie, and so about students' attitudes about being at Prairie. Moreover, we noted the raised awareness of Prairie's faculty and director that "something had to be done" about the curriculum and the public image of the school, and that this grant was their "big chance" to make that change. In addition, we believed that the material change brought about by the presence of the wireless laptops would exert a gradual effect on the practices of students as learners and teachers as curriculum developers and instructors.

Taken together, these shifts in the language by which Prairie was characterized, in the awareness of Prairie's staff, and in the material conditions of education in the program also offered some hope, from a Bourdieusian analysis, that the introduction of wireless technology to its middle-school program would produce some structural change—change that could lead to a "new start" for Prairie as an institution.

Data collection

During the school year prior to the grant project, Mark, Phil, and a second research assistant, Julia Conner, conducted ethnographic life and literacy case histories of eight middle-school students at Prairie Academy. Data collection from that research project, which extended over one-and-a-half school years, included a range of ethnographic data sources, such as field notes, interviews, and artifacts; a range of cognitive measurements, including an informal reading inventory and assessment for orthographic proficiency; and a review of stories about Prairie, lawsuits filed against the school district for discriminatory practices, and state legislation for alternative education. As a result, the grant project and its data collection activities were informed by extensive knowledge of the political and curricular history of the school, deep personal knowledge of many of the students in the middle school program, and strong personal relationships with the principal staff members involved in the project.

Data collection for the grant project focused mainly on providing ongoing information about the implementation and progression of use of the 30 laptops in the school curriculum, for the purposes of making bimonthly and yearly reports to the granting corporation. Data collection practices included interviews with Prairie students and staff and with university students/pre-service teachers, field notes, the collection of email exchanges between the university and Prairie students, and standardized test scores. In addition, Mark met with Prairie's director each week, and more informally with science teacher Sam and math teacher Jane to discuss progress in the implementation of the laptops and accompanying materials. Mark also sat in on several training sessions for the web-based curriculum program (which we will call *Coordinator*) and instructional software (which we will refer to as *Participation*) that were included in the grant.

From September to December 2001, our main goal in data collection was to record and collect as much data as possible from as many sources as possible, in order to make a general survey of the initial period of introduction. Once the students began to use the laptops regularly, however, we were overwhelmed by the amount of observation that was required and began to search for ways that we might observe what was going on in more limited, but systematic, contexts. In January 2002, Phil narrowed the focus of his observations to a few students who might serve as case studies. Yet the problem of observing and recording precisely where students "went" when they used the internet and linking that activity to classroom assignments and other less official activities remained difficult, as were the pace and circumstances in which students gained proficiency in the multiple tasks of proficient laptop use—for example, keyboarding, emailing, sending attachments, using Microsoft Word and Excel, and cutting and pasting pictures into reports. In the second year of the program (2002–03), data collection efforts were focused mainly on the collection of field notes and artifacts from the revised pre-service teacher–student project, and on the collection of "hard data"—that is, test scores—that would provide "hard evidence" of the project's impact on student achievement.

Narrative of events

Year One (2001–02)

As Mark wrote the grant during the spring of 2001, he spent several afternoons brainstorming projects with Prairie's director and with Sam and Jane. Prairie's director was excited about the impact the computers would have on the program's profile within the community and was very agreeable to a plan to have eight to ten pre-service teachers at the school for their fall field placement, to obtain email addresses for all the students so that they could share with their university pre-service mentors, and to have students from Prairie visit the university campus for a "day at college." With little or no hesitation, Sam and Jane described multiple innovative uses for the laptops, including online research and data recording, the use of simulations, and an overnight camping trip to a local state park where students would use the laptops to collect data and record field notes about the history and geology of natural landmarks. Mark included all these ideas in the timeline and list of possible activities in the grant proposal.

The laptops and accompanying hardware arrived in early October 2001. Initial access to the computers on the part of the students was slow, largely because of concerns for security and that the students might treat the equipment roughly. By mid-November, only one eighth-grade class was using the computers regularly. But these concerns quickly evaporated after specific students were assigned to work with the same computer every day and as it became apparent that the students treated the computers with great respect. They were, in fact, very careful about how they carried and cared for what they described as *their* computers. By the beginning of January 2002, all seventh and eighth graders were using the computers on a regular basis in science, and on an increasing basis in math. By the end of the month, the sixth graders, who had caused the most concern, were also using the computers regularly.

As we waited in August and September 2001 for the laptops to arrive, faculty and research/teaching assistants at the university began to plan the field trip that Prairie students would take to the UIUC campus in October to meet their pre-service teacher–mentors. Our original plan was to pair individual students with individual mentors and allow them the morning to tour the campus, visiting museums, the student union, and even going to classes if that was possible, before returning to the education building for a boxed lunch. But when the students arrived, it became apparent that both the pre-service teachers and the Prairie students would be more comfortable working in small groups. For the most part, this visit was a very stimulating one, particularly for the university students, who were eager to follow up with email messages to the students at Prairie. However, a lag in the start-up of services by Coordinator, the web-based service provided through the grant, prevented students at Prairie from receiving email addresses until after the Christmas break. In early February 2002, we tried to rekindle the relationships that had begun in October with field trips by the university pre-service teachers to visit the students at Prairie Academy. Again, the pre-service teachers reported their eagerness to exchange email with the students at Prairie, but a range of problems, from students returning to their home schools at the end of the semester in February to a lack of significant contexts for interaction, prevented many serious bonds from being formed.

By January also, both Sam and Jane had begun to experiment with the use of the instructional software program in their classes, and to use the computers in an increasing number of instructional formats. Prairie's director became intrigued by the potential of the Coordinator program to bring the school's curriculum and instructional planning into alignment with state and district standards, and he began to work with Sam and Jane as lead teachers on this project. By February, use of the computers had expanded into the hallways and other teachers' classrooms. Mark had already met with the director several times to discuss possibilities for a project that might integrate the use of technology across the middle school curriculum.

After several meetings with the faculty, a decision was made to take a problem-based approach to remodeling the school's attic. The eighth graders were divided into four working teams, the last (elective) period of the day was devoted specifically to the project, and each subject area teacher brainstormed ways to involve their students in studying the attic and constructing a proposal for remodeling it. Sam involved students in his science classes in the use of architectural software and discussions of the physical science of building. Jane worked with her students in math to draw up blueprints and used Microsoft Excel to produce a budget for the project. The art teacher began to work with the students on art projects that involved net searches for information about artists and art movements. The social studies teacher planned to involve the students in archaeological work (Prairie's main building is over 100 years old). And the reading/language arts teacher and Mark sponsored a reading program and a writing contest among the seventh and eighth graders for stories, poems, and essays related to the theme of "attics."

Work on this project began in March and continued through the end of the school year, with mixed results. Blueprints were drawn and budgets were constructed, and 17 entries to the writing contest were submitted. But for health-related reasons—the attic had become a loft for wild pigeons—students were not allowed into the attic, and this put a serious obstacle in the way of the hands-on projects that were planned by the science and social studies teachers.

Assessing outcomes of Year One

Thus, the first year of the project might accurately be characterized as a flurry of activities designed to overcome technical issues and to get students and teachers at Prairie and pre-service teachers at the university using the resources provided by the grant. Prior to the introduction of this wireless classroom, students at Prairie Academy had limited exposure to the use of computer technology. There were a few iMacs in each classroom that students used for occasionally surfing the internet, writing short reports, and a remedial reading program called Read 180™. Access to and interest in computer technology, from our observations, seemed to be limited to only a few students, most of whom were male. Both the staff at Prairie and researchers from the university were concerned that students might be frustrated at first by the complexity of the computers' operation and the multiple functions that we expected them to use the computers for.

But for the most part these concerns were unfounded, partly, we suspect, because several students already had had some experience with personal computers at home, but also because of a phenomenon that we had rarely observed prior to the introduction of the computers: students teaching each other. Through an elective that Sam taught during the last period of the day, a handful of the most avid students had the chance to "play around with" and so "pick up" a number of "tricks," such as Google searches, cutting and pasting images, importing and creating short animations, and converting images into customized wallpaper. The informal, spontaneous sharing of this information spread rapidly, first through the eighth grade, then the seventh, and finally the sixth grade. By February, when the pre-service teachers visited, every computer was customized and nearly every student could demonstrate proficiency in accessing and sending email, surfing the web, bookmarking favorite pages, opening and closing files and Word documents, basic word processing, and participating in sessions with Participation. The only serious stumbling block to full proficiency with the computers as a tool was the lack of keyboarding skills. The addition of a basic keyboarding program to each computer (downloaded free from the web) helped somewhat, and many students became very skilled at "hunting and pecking," as indicated by several lengthy stories that were produced during the Attic Writing Contest. But from our observations, at the end of the school year, many students still struggled to type in URLs accurately and to type extended passages, both formally as in written assignments and informally as in the sending of email messages.

Beginning in November, Sam began to integrate the use of the internet as a research tool into his teaching with seventh and eighth graders. Jane followed, but partly, she argued, because her math curriculum was more prescribed by the district and partly because a lack of relevant programs for teaching the math content, integration of the technology into the math curriculum was limited. Both teachers embraced Participation as a mechanism for testing and informal assessment, but its use as a tool for actual discourse was limited, in part because of the students' lack of keyboarding proficiency, in part because of the short battery life of the teacher's computer (this was a chronic problem; in the middle of a session the computer would suddenly "die" and the teacher would have to quickly switch batteries, boot up, and start all over again), and in part because the program itself did not promote discourse or direct exchanges among students without teacher mediation.

However, the most surprising and perhaps the strongest indication that wireless technology was becoming fully integrated into the academic life of the school came from the students' spontaneous integration of the computers into classes and assignments outside math and science. In January, we noted that students from other classes began coming into Sam's classroom to borrow their computers for class-related work. In some cases, the use of the computers in reading/language arts, art, and social studies was initiated by teachers, but in many cases it was initiated by students who were realizing that the computer might be used as a research tool for a class project or to more easily write a report. By the time we began to plan the Attic Project in February, all the teachers involved had either formally or informally become enthusiastic participants in the use of the wireless laptops.

Perhaps the best way to illustrate the power of this technology to engage students with highly individual needs is to present an event in Sam's classroom in which Phil worked with David (pseudonym), a hyperactive but very bright seventh grader with a long history of school failure, due largely to his inability to complete any assignment. One day, Sam brought the class together to work on a project in which they were to select a moon or planet in our solar system, research its characteristics, and come up with a plan for colonizing it. The following excerpt is taken from Phil's field notes and a later account of the incident in a paper written for a doctoral course at the university:

Sam uses repeated pauses to try to gain the attention of distracted students. Students get up to go get their computers, but are told to sit back down because Sam hasn't told them to get them yet. Most students sit back down and listen to the final instructions, but David stands by the computers, calls me (Phil) by a playful nickname, "Billy-Bob," and appears to ignore his teacher's off-handed request to sit back down. Before they are allowed to assemble in their "planet group," Sam instructs students that they should "use Yahoo! to search for basic facts on your selected planet— temperature, how much water is on the planet, size of the planet, etc.— because you're going to try and colonize the planet with about 100 people. Write down these facts in your planet book or type them into a Microsoft Word document." Even before his last words are spoken, students have converged on the computer station, grabbed their laptops and convened with their group. Randy and David are a group. Nathan works alone since his partner is absent, and the four girls work together just like they have for the entire year and a half of my involvement in their classes.

I pull up a chair next to David and Randy immediately includes me in the group by peppering me with questions about the planets. "Which planet is farthest away?" "How big is Triton?" Meanwhile, David has taken the reigns of the computer, found Yahoo!, and typed in "pictures of planets" as an opening search. He takes little time to scan the results but clicks on the first result. He's obviously done this before. Before I can articulate my suggestion that we should take more time looking at a web page, he has hit the back button, returned to the results page and clicked on a second result. Both boys continue to search for information on all of the planets and avoid selecting one planet until they know more about all of them. Using the computer, he shows us a Hubble photograph of an icy area of Triton and suggests that we should include it in the PowerPoint if they decide to colonize Triton. Randy begins searching for photos on his own laptop.

David and I spend the next several minutes trying to find a photo of an oxygen tank for his planet PowerPoint and trying to find "space music" to use in his PowerPoint. I suggest something from *2001: A Space Odyssey*, and David agrees to look for the music. With quick clicks of the mouse, he peruses various web pages, using the "back" button to re-access the search results from Ask Jeeves. He navigates back and forth between RealPlayer, Internet Explorer and PowerPoint with ease and knows how and where to save his documents. He finds a few bits of information on the size of the planet and he immediately highlights the text, right-clicks on it, selects "copy" and then pastes the text into a PowerPoint slide. When I try to show him how to set up the custom animation of his slides, he quickly cuts me off and proceeds to set up the custom animation on his own without my assistance. Images are inserted in the slides, re-sized and ordered to enter from the bottom of the screen with a few speedy clicks of David's mouse. Whenever he and I are waiting for a page to load or when he gets bored with searching Ask Jeeves for photos of oxygen tanks, he quickly opens up RealPlayer and plays a rap video. Then he lets it play in the background while we continue the search for more information.

Admittedly, the PowerPoint presentation remains partially finished. One slide exhibits only bits of seemingly fragmented text while other slides show only an image. The presentation even contains one blank slide. To some degree, this is not surprising considering David's history of not finishing assignments. However, it is also apparent that David has constructed some knowledge of Triton, even if it appears incomplete by our standards. Images represent conceptual understanding of the planet and the oxygen tanks illustrate his recognition that we could not breathe on the planet without them. One image and David's accompanying written text, "This is how we'd melt the ice on Triton," signifies not only his knowledge of the temperature and climatic conditions on the planet, but that he, like one of our most skilled scientists, is not sure how we could melt the ice and survive on Triton. Finally, another purloined image illustrates his recognition that food would need to be grown on Triton using hydroponics. The laptop, internet, and PowerPoint presentation engaged him in a process of constructing his knowledge by using a project-based learning unit that aligns more accurately with the literacy activities experienced in his home.

Assessing curricular and instructional change

In his analysis of the event just described, Phil concluded:

> Only through transactions with multiple texts and the social construction and transformation of traditional and electronic texts can David achieve meaningful, engaged learning. Colonizing Triton was a start. Creating a slide presentation on the types of clouds was another effective learning experience for David. But, if David is to succeed in school, all of his teachers need to take a participatory approach to text and learning that builds off of his multiple literacies and gives David the opportunity to generate his own knowledge and to make his own interpretation of the varied texts he encounters.

Despite successes with students such as David, our findings suggest a note of caution, for two reasons. First, it seems almost certain to us that there is a direct correspondence between proficiencies that individual students possess prior to the introduction of the wireless laptops and their capacity to make full use of it as a tool for learning. While it was very encouraging, indeed, to enter a classroom and see all the students eagerly engaged in a Yahoo! search, closer observation and interaction with many of these students indicated wide variation in their ability to distinguish between sites that might be useful for their purposes and sites that were not. Even when many students did access a site that was a potentially useful source of information about, for example, a moon of Jupiter, they often seemed confused about how to take notes and how to synthesize information into a report. Students might become adept at cutting and pasting images, but the text that accompanied them was often very limited. Similarly, while we were surprised and pleased that 17, or approximately one-third, of the seventh and eighth graders produced entries for the Attic Writing Contest (and that those entries ranged from one-page poems to "novellas" with multiple chapters), it should be noted that two-thirds of the students did not, largely, it seemed, because of poor writing—not keyboarding—skills. During their free time (or when supervision was loose), when students were allowed to surf the net, it was not unusual to see students who read and wrote at grade level or above visit sites such as "Who Wants to be a Millionaire?" while other students who did not read or write as well visited their favorite music site to watch a music video. In other words, the basic literacy of the students tended to be the determining variable in their productivity as users of the internet.

In retrospect, we should not have been surprised by this. But, in fact, we were surprised and somewhat disappointed, largely because we had hoped that the use of technology in the classroom would be the "magic bullet" that provided the engagement to bring everyone's level of proficiency up to par. We can point to individual cases in which it did seem that a magical transformation was in progress—cases in which students who had shown little interest in their studies became intrigued by a topic whose presentation was technologically mediated, and cases in which students such as David who were highly literate but unmotivated became motivated—but we can point to few cases of students whose basic skill levels were demonstrably raised after approximately six months of use, merely by the introduction of wireless technology into the academic program. Although in the long run it may come to pass that levels of proficiency will be increased for all students, at the present time our observations suggest that those students with better basic skills benefited from the use of wireless technology far more than did those who struggled to read and write—that is, computer technology helped the already successful to become even more successful at a greater rate than it helped those students who were chronically less successful in school.

The second reason that we suggest a note of caution regarding the potential long-term impact of the wireless laptops on students' learning at Prairie Academy is that, with the exception of Sam, none of the other teachers at Prairie showed much interest in considering how the use of wireless technology might "build off," as Phil put it in his field notes, students' multiliteracies in ways that would "[give them] the opportunity to generate [their] own knowledge and to make [their] own interpretation of the varied texts [they encountered]." Jane, who was described as a lead teacher and who supported the grant proposal enthusiastically, actually made minimal use of the laptops in her teaching. She actively resisted participation in the Attic Project and only agreed to collaborate to the extent that the drawing of blueprints for renovation of the attic could be justified by the district curriculum. Other teachers were equally resistant to the idea of "surrendering" time from their content areas or rescheduling classes to facilitate the project's time frame. They might tolerate the use of the laptops in their classrooms to do word processing or when students had "completed their assignments," but in staff meetings they made it clear to Prairie's director that they were not "turning over" their classrooms or their curriculum to "someone from the university." And even though funds were allocated in the grant budget for substitute teachers and summer in-service projects, none of that money was spent, save for the financing of one trip by Jane to a statewide math conference.

Wireless technology and teacher education

Although the extended contact and mentoring that we hoped the project would promote between the pre-service teachers and Prairie's students did not occur as planned, there were many indirect benefits from the arrangement. The visits by the students at Prairie to the university campus and by the pre-service teachers to Prairie stimulated much discussion during Mark's class sessions and on the web-based course discussion board. By virtue of the criteria whereby students are accepted for admission to the university, all of the pre-service teachers in the program were highly successful in their own middle and high school careers. These pre-service teachers are placed in field experiences in local schools throughout the teacher education program, but their personal contact with students who struggle remains limited. Having the chance to interact with the students at Prairie, away from the supervision of teachers and the confines of classroom walls, was very challenging for many of the pre-service teachers and made the content of Mark's courses, which focused on teaching in diverse settings, real to them in ways that it otherwise would not have been.

Yet while the pre-service teachers were impressed by the resources and students' ability to use the laptops after only a few weeks of practice with them, they also offered a critical perspective that we lacked. One pre-service teacher, for example, noted on the course discussion board that perhaps the portability of the laptops could be a liability as well as an asset:

> It mustn't be very efficient to have to drag out those laptops, boot them up, and log on the students every class period, not to mention trying to keep the students on task in the face of the internet's myriad distractions. At the

same time, the laptops seem to be a resource that has the potential to make the classroom more exciting and enthusiastic [sic]. I guess these things will be ironed out over time.

This student's comment and others like it led to increased interest and discussion in Mark's class about how the integration of technology into the curriculum might require teachers to rethink the organization of their classrooms and their instruction in radical ways, rather than see the computer as something "added on" to existing resources and practices. Yet even after Mark began to use wireless laptops routinely in his own teaching with these pre-service teachers at the university, and even as the pre-service teachers used laptops to complete group work, do research, compose PowerPoint presentations, and send and receive documents with a facility and in ways that would not otherwise have been possible, use of wireless (or any computer) technology in their lesson plans and curriculum projects remained largely perfunctory.

Year Two (2002–03)

An extension grant in the second year of the program, which increased the capability for wireless access throughout all middle school classrooms and brought additional funds for staff development as well as auxiliary battery packs that extended the use of each laptop, led to some modifications in the focus of the project, particularly in its teacher education component. In the second year, the focus of efforts became more multidisciplinary, if not interdisciplinary.

Much of the activity of Year Two was mitigated by pressure at the district level for changes in Prairie's program and mission. A new superintendent had been hired to "do something" about the ongoing lawsuit, charging the district with discriminatory policies and a gap in achievement between minority (largely African-American) and White students in the district. The new superintendent was highly critical of the "caring" philosophy that brought students who struggled actively and passively in school to Prairie, and of the expense of a program that demonstrated so few "hard results" in terms of achievement, that is, increased test scores. A new plan for the school called for students who did not have "behavioral problems"—that is, those who were not "disruptive" in class—to be returned to their home schools, and for the institution of a program in which students who were under threat of suspension or expulsion were sent to Prairie for short terms, where they would be taught by a skeletal staff, largely through online, programmed curricular packages. Prairie's director and teachers, with some support from the community, resisted full implementation of this plan with some success, but support staff were eliminated and orders were given to pay more attention to student achievement as measured by the state's year-end achievement test.

These threats to Prairie's continued existence provoked several frank meetings between Mark and Prairie's director about how the school's curriculum might be restructured and how the technology from the grant project might be most advantageously used. Because of changes in district enrollment policies, fewer than 30 students were enrolled in Prairie's middle school program. The five main academic classrooms in the middle school—math, science, social studies, language arts, and reading—all opened onto the same short hallway. Moreover, "airports" acquired through the expansion grant had made wireless access throughout all five classrooms practical and dependable. Mark argued that because of these factors, students should be allowed to have their own individual laptops and be allowed to carry them from class to class; and the extremely small size of some classes—there were only four sixth graders enrolled, for example—should encourage collaboration across grade levels and content areas.

But while Prairie's director showed some interest in these possibilities, the teachers themselves resisted any changes in scheduling or the sort of extensive use of laptops that Mark was suggesting. Rather, they began to look for ways that the available technology might raise test scores. Participation, the software program enabling teachers to monitor the responses of students on laptops to assessment items electronically and individually, was used more frequently in both the math and the science classrooms. For example, Jane designed a "controlled experiment" in which she used Participation regularly to assess math skills with one eighth grade class, while she used paper-and-pencil assessments with another eighth grade class as well as pre- and post-test measures of the state achievement test. In addition, she became intrigued by a program she had seen demonstrated at a workshop for teaching geometry and began to introduce it into her teaching of the district's geometry curriculum on a regular basis. Other teachers also made increasing use of the laptops to do web-based research and word processing, but always within the confines of their content area and predetermined curriculum topics.

Because of uncertainty about the direction that the school program at Prairie might take, participation of pre-service teachers enrolled in Mark's university class was suspended during the fall semester. When Prairie's situation stabilized later in the semester, Mark obtained a small grant through the university's technology and teacher education program, which provided the impetus for a much-revised project that would provide a more meaningful and sustained context for interaction between Prairie's students and pre-service teachers enrolled in Mark's middle school literacy methods class in the spring. After extensive negotiations with the teachers and director at Prairie, Mark rearranged his teaching schedule and course syllabus to allow 15 of the 25 preservice teachers enrolled in his class to spend a minimum of 25 hours in field experience at Prairie, working in groups of two to three with small groups of students on projects that extended a Prairie teacher's math, science, language arts, or social studies curriculum. Modeling the use of wireless laptop technology extensively in classes at the university, Mark worked with the 15 pre-service teachers to design projects that extended the curriculum in the classrooms in which they were placed and that involved extensive use of the wireless laptops.

Finally, in an attempt to measure some gain in student achievement before and after the introduction of the wireless laptops, Mark hired a research assistant to conduct a statistical analysis of student test scores from 2000–01 (the year before the grant) and from the 2001–02 and 2002–03 school years.

Assessing outcomes for Year Two

In assessing the effects of the wireless laptops and accompanying materials in Year Two of the grant, we can point to many of the same responses of teachers, pre-service teachers, students, and staff at Prairie and the university as in Year One. Student enthusiasm for the laptops was as high as ever. Incoming students were quickly inducted into the technological culture created by returning students from the first year—logging on as a user, selecting wallpaper, bookmarking favorite sites, and evading whenever and wherever the surveillance of adults in the classroom as well as protocols for using the laptops instructionally. We also continued to note that significant differences in the ways that students were able to use the computers as writing, research, and study tools had much to do with their prior level of literate proficiency.

The director of Prairie Academy also reported that teachers seemed not to grasp the full possibilities of the computers as instructional tools, and complained that when teachers made deliberate use of them, it was largely for writing or word-processing assignments. He wished repeatedly that he could get more teachers interested in using Coordinator, particularly the lesson planning feature, for aligning instructional activities with state standards. He expressed some interest in Mark's suggestion that students each be given a laptop to carry around all day, and at the vision Mark presented—of wireless laptops largely replacing paper and pencils and textbooks, of the use of the internet as a primary resource in social studies and science, and of the simulation and demonstrative potential of the laptops in the teaching of Math—but stopped short of presenting that idea to the teachers.

Ethnographic data revealed little change in the overall culture of the school, particularly in the ways that the teaching staff as a whole characterized the students' abilities as learners, conceived of computers as instructional tools, or thought of themselves as teachers or of their subject matter. The expansion grant that was awarded at the end of Year One provided funds to pay all the teachers at Prairie a week's summer salary to allow them to develop curriculum for the coming school year, but the money was not spent. At the end of the two-year project as before it began, and despite two significant attempts to engage the staff in interdisciplinary, computer-based units of study, students moved from class to class in 42-minute periods and teachers taught individual subjects in their own rooms with little, if any, extended teaming or concern for interdisciplinarity; while the laptops and accompanying software were largely regarded as supplementary, if not exotic, luxuries.

The 15 pre-service teachers in Mark's middle school literacy methods class were very excited about their placement at Prairie and quickly bonded with the teachers and students there. They avidly used wireless laptop technology at the university in designing and preparing a small-group project for the students with whom they had been placed at Prairie, and understood that one of their main goals was to use the wireless technology available at Prairie in writing and research activities. But in the end, of six group projects designed, only two made any use of wireless laptops in their activities. Even though each project had been planned to extend and enhance the curriculum of the classrooms in which these pre-service teachers were placed, and the teachers at Prairie had approved of the project in advance, in the end projects were either abandoned in favor of more general tutoring activities or the pre-service teachers "never got around" to using wireless laptops in their work with the students. While all 15 pre-service teachers reported that their time in the program had been their best (most engaging and most extensive) field placement, and cited the relationships they had developed with individual Prairie students as the reason, none cited or even made mention of the use of technology.

Finally, extensive efforts to measure differences in student achievement, behavior, and attendance between the years before and during the project were hindered by a combination of low student numbers and student transience. The study conducted by Jane in the spring of the second year of the program, in which math scores on the state's achievement test were compared, was similarly thwarted.

Positive effects continued to be demonstrated, however, in the attitudes and activities of individual teachers and students. Sam, for example, was deeply interested and somewhat proficient in the use of computer technology prior to the grant, and made extensive, experimental use of the computers' capacities as tools for web-based research, computer simulations, and graphic design in his teaching. In the second year, Jane and the art teacher also began to experiment tentatively with multiple uses of the computer and available software. While nearly all the students enjoyed using the computers whenever and wherever possible, several of the students in the program used the computers to write more extensively than ever before and to master programs such as PowerPoint as media for projects and reports. Several of the teachers also noted the same change in David, the student whom Phil had documented the year before. Like Phil, they also concluded that the "multitasking" capability provided by the laptops ironically enabled David to remain more focused in his attention to schoolwork, and thus reduced his level of social interaction with peers—a level of interaction that had often been inappropriate and that got him into frequent trouble with teachers.

Conclusion

Turning to a Bourdieusian perspective, particularly his concept of practice, may help to account for the failure of the wireless technology to effect the level of change in educational practice that we expected at Prairie Academy. In Bourdieu's (1990) view, social organizations, cultural practices, and indeed the very beliefs and ideologies that people use to justify those practices, are formed through adaptive responses to the material, structural conditions in which they are embedded. When people are presented with something "new" to their cultural environment, the almost invariable tendency is to make sense of, and practically incorporate, that which is new—be it technology, an idea, or an individual—into pre-existing organizational or cultural structures and beliefs, and so preserve the unity, stability, and productive function of the cultural body as a whole. Thus, it becomes axiomatic that the more things change, the more they remain the same. Yet Bourdieu also recognized that this was clearly not always the case. In some instances, when something "new" is encountered in the face of some shift in the material conditions of the culture, people may take up the new in improvisational and innovative ways. In other instances, when an individual is not "of a piece" with the "cultural body" she or he finds himself or herself a part of, that individual may take up that which is new as a way of improvisationally improving his or her own conditions.

From this point of view, the lack of cultural change in the program at Prairie in the face of overwhelming espousals of enthusiasm for the educational possibilities of computer technology by the school's staff as well as university collaborators and pre-service teachers, is attributable to little or no accompanying change in the material conditions into which the wireless laptops and paraphernalia were introduced. Rather, the tendency throughout the two years of the program was always to try to accommodate the use of the laptops within pre-existing schedules and practices, both at Prairie and at the university. For example, while the Participation software program that came with the laptops provided opportunities for teachers to develop open-ended questions to invite students to explore their own understanding of basic concepts, and for teachers to engage in assessment and dialogue with the students on an individual basis, the software was used only as a means of electronically testing students through "closed" questions to which only one correct short answer was allowed. The overall result was an adaptation to the introduction of computer technology in which as little actual change as possible—in order to avoid the political and cultural catastrophe of upsetting any group's center of power—became the tacit, unconscious, cultural goal of all participants.

Findings from this two-year project in the use of wireless laptop technology as an engine of curricular change and its analysis á la Pierre Bourdieu suggest that providing open, largely no-strings grants of sophisticated computer technology to schools, no matter how apparently interested in innovative practices they may claim to be, may be a generous and well-intentioned but often ineffective action toward the promotion of curricular change. However, a Bourdieusian analysis of outcomes from this project also brings us back to the three possible ways that outcomes from similar future projects might be increased, so that the structural exigencies in which Prairie was caught might be mitigated.

The first of these stems from the "semantic elasticity" that Bourdieu (1989) argued is inherent within even the most reproductive and "set" social fields. Semantic elasticity refers to the multiplicity of meanings that any object or sign may be given within a social field. Perhaps the most dramatic and illustrative examples of this sort of bending or stretching of meanings in the United States come from working class or working poor African-American youth (which in turn derive from long-standing practices in African-American culture), in which something that is "bad" is something good, or in which wearing pants pulled down to reveal baggy boxer shorts or wearing pants with one leg rolled up to the knee—all of which flaunt middle-class White standards of taste and "appropriate" behavior—reverse conventional meanings in ways that raise the status of their innovators within their own communities and, through commercial marketing (and some would say, exploitation), their symbolic and cultural capital within the popular culture at large. In the case of Prairie Academy, we would argue that the very presence of 30 high-tech wireless laptops in a school whose enrollment consisted largely of the district's "fail-ures" effected a dramatic—if, we admit, incomplete—shift in the ways that students at Prairie defined themselves, from students who had "lost" academ-ically to students who were "high tech" and worth the investment of such expensive and glamorous equipment. Several students told us this directly and, through continual references to *their* laptops, the time spent customizing each computer with their favorite websites and wallpaper, and the care with which new students were introduced to the care and use of the laptops, showed us as much as well. That we and the school did not pick up sooner on this shift in pride, and use its symbolic power to more profitable advantage in designing curriculum and sending messages to students about their changed status as students in the school and district, is something we are very sorry for.

Closely related to the positive shift in attitude that we noted was the way that some students and teachers were able to exert some agency within the exercise of the habitus that normally guided their actions. As Bourdieu (1989) again would predict, the individuals who seemed to make the most innovative use of the laptops at Prairie over the two years of the program were almost invariably those students and teachers who seemed the most "at odds" with peers and the general culture of the program itself, and in some need of alternative processes. Sam, for example, had a notably different ethic about teaching, and particularly about being a teacher at Prairie, than did most of the rest of the staff. He and the director had been associated with Prairie from its very earliest days of existence and took stances toward students at Prairie that were markedly different from the other staff, who tended to see the students as down-and-out or to patronize them and ignore or deny that they had any real academic potential. Sam was also the only staff member who was not originally from the area and had not attended a regional state university, and was more liberal politically and in terms of his educational perspective. Thus, he stood on the margins of the professional culture of the district and even the school itself, and seemed to embrace the potential of wireless technology as a part of his identity as a science educator in ways that the other more mainstream teachers in the school did not.

Similarly, David, the "underachieving" student with attention deficit hyperactivity disorder, who was among the most marginalized of an already marginalized student body, along with a handful of other students (including one White student from a poor rural background), embraced the laptops and their potential in ways that enhanced their own identities and, in turn, their performance as students. It was these most marginalized individuals, in the end, who found in the use of technology a way to construct identities and practices that were highly empowering to them; and who, had there been even more time, we believe, would have begun to challenge the status quo of the school's culture. Thus, if we were to repeat this project we might begin by providing key individuals within a cultural body who were themselves "structurally in need" and prepared to use new technology in innovative ways, and then work with those individuals to act as agents of change within the cultural body itself.

Finally, although Bourdieu does not directly suggest a third possible means of structural change, we will point out that the materiality of his structuralist position—which argues that habitus, fields, and practices are all reflexively constructed in response to historical and prevailing physical environmental conditions—implies that a radical shift in those conditions should produce a reflexive shift within practices and in time within people's habitus and the fields in which they are actors. Thus, we wonder in closing whether the need to recognize the full potential of wireless technology might not ultimately be contingent on providing it within contexts where material conditions have shifted in some strategic, if not dramatic, way, on the axiomatic premise repeatedly expressed in Bourdieu's work that cultural production occurs as people struggle to make "a virtue of necessity" (see *Distinction*, 1984); in other words, to live by the maxim that "necessity is the mother of invention." Suppose that wireless technology were introduced to educational circumstances in which no textbooks or other text materials were available, or in which other media of writing and graphic expression, such as paper and pencil, photocopiers, or art supplies were available. Or suppose that the physical circumstances of teaching were changed, in which teachers were no longer able to teach in the isolation of their own classrooms. In such cases, innovation and improvisation would become a necessity, not an add-on or something to be ignored or deprecated. Yet how that necessity would shape the resulting habitus, practices, and fields that would necessarily also be the historical continuation of prior existing structures is not clear, and, in the face of our own lack of perspicacity, is not an outcome we feel confident to predict.

References

Bourdieu, P. (1984) *Distinction: A Social Critique of the Judgment of Taste*. Cambridge, MA: Harvard University Press.

Bourdieu, P. (1989) Social space and symbolic power. *Sociological Theory*, 7, 14–25.

Bourdieu, P. (1990) *The Logic of Practice* (R. Nice, trans.). Stanford, CA: Stanford University Press.

Bourdieu, P. (1993) *The Field of Cultural Production* (R. Johnson, trans.). New York: Columbia University Press.

Bourdieu, P. and Passeron, J. (1977). *Reproduction in Education, Society, and Culture*. London: Sage.

Ching, C. (2005) Book review of *Oversold and Under Used: Computers in the Classroom. Journal of Curriculum Studies*, 37, 235–40.

Cuban, L. (2003). *Oversold and Under Used: Computers in the Classroom*. Cambridge, MA: Harvard University Press.

Dressman, M., Wilder, P. and Conner, J. (2005). Theories of failure and the failure of theories: A cognitive/sociocultural/macrostructural study of eight struggling adolescents. *Research in the Teaching of English*, 40, 8–61.

Chapter 8

Toward a pedagogy of the popular

Bourdieu, hip-hop, and out-of-school literacies

Marc Lamont Hill

In this chapter, I argue for a closer examination of the complex and varied literacy practices that students engage in outside of school. Given hip-hop's popularity among urban youth and its growing influence on American popular culture, I develop a theoretical and practical framework for connecting the literacy practices of the hip-hop community to the classroom. To illustrate the potential of this framework, I use Bourdieu's theory of practice to initiate a new perspective on the use of hip-hop literacies within the classroom. Drawing from ethnographic data taken from "Hip-Hop Lit," a hip-hop-centered high-school English literature course, I demonstrate how the redistribution of capital within the classroom field vis-à-vis popular culture can enrich learning and reconfigure classroom power relations in varied, complicated, and often highly problematic ways. Specifically, I use two ethnographic vignettes to address the following questions: How does the infusion of the popular into the classroom lead to the reconfiguration of classroom knowledge and power? How do teachers and students negotiate these reconfigured notions of knowledge and power?

In *Reproduction*, Bourdieu and Passeron (1977) argue that schools commit acts of symbolic violence and reproduce inequality by imposing and privileging arbitrary cultural forms reflective of dominant class interests. Those who are in possession of particular bodies of knowledge, tastes, resources, academic investments, and so forth, known as *cultural capital* (Bourdieu, 1972/1977), are able to more successfully negotiate the schooling process; while those with little or no formally recognized cultural capital experience great difficulty because of the undesirable exchange rate between home and school capital. Within the traditional classroom *field*, the cultural capital that is recognized and valued comes in the form of "school literacies," which can be defined as:

> The learning of interpretive and communicative processes needed to adapt socially to school and other dominant language contexts, and the use or practice of those processes in order to gain a conceptual understanding of school subjects.

> (Gallego and Holingsworth, 2000: 5)

These literacies are the primary currency with which students gain access to educational success. Further, the hegemonic position of these literacies precludes the possible co-existence of alternate but equally viable forms of literacy (that is, "literacy" instead of "literacies").

There is an important and growing body of literacy scholarship that focuses on alternate, more expansive conceptions of literacy that account for the non-prestigious literacy practices of various communities that do not comfortably fit within the cultural logic of schooling. Some of the most important insights have come from the field of New Literacy Studies (e.g., Gee, 1996, 2000; Street, 1993, 1995), which has demonstrated through ethnographic research that school literacies (also referred to as "academic literacies") compose one of multiple forms of literacy. Through this research we are able to expose and reassess the value of out-of-school literacy practices that are perennially obscured by hegemonic Western notions of decoding text, cultural literacy, and particular communicative practices.

While current research has persuasively demonstrated the importance of developing an expansive notion of literacy and connecting it to classroom practice, there remains a dearth of scholarship that addresses the crucial process of *reconnaissance* (recognition). As Bourdieu argues, the power and privilege that derive from possessing capital and the amount of recognition that the capital receives within a particular field of social relations are directly proportionate (Bourdieu, 1991). It is through this process of recognition within a field that cultural capital becomes symbolic capital. In other words, while it is widely recognized that youth do possess alternative literacies, we know little about how it is that these alternative literacies gain or retain cultural capital within the classroom.

In order to privilege out-of-school literacy practices within the classroom, educators must effectuate a radical redistribution of symbolic capital that results in the decentering of traditional academic literacies. This suggests that the transport of out-of-school literacies into the classroom does not automatically or necessarily countervail reproductive forces. In fact, the inclusion of out-of-school literacies in a limited or superficial way could reinforce the falsely obvious distinctions made between unrecognized and recognized forms of capital, thereby reifying the in-school/out-of-school binary. Equally important, the successful decentering of traditional literacies has the possibility of creating irremediable theoretical and practical tensions within the classroom as a consequence of the syncretism of multiple fields. It is in this regard that the New Literacy Studies focus on expansive notions of literacy, and the critical literacy/pedagogy discourses surrounding democracy, student voice, and emancipation are indispensable but ultimately insufficient for making sense of the practical consequences of using out-of-school literacies in the classroom.

Framing the popular

The use of hip-hop within the classroom creates apprehension among many literacy educators who are concerned about the relationship between students and popular culture. These educators often presume the existence of a unidirectional relationship between reader and text that positions students as passive recipients of latent and problematic textual features, such as racist, sexist, or capitalist messages. Consequently, popular culture is banished from official classroom activity or becomes the object of critical analysis for the sole purpose of exposing its insidious aspects to unwitting students, which has been the primary educative purpose of many critical media literacy projects (e.g., Alverman et al.,1999). This perspective is problematic, as it tacitly reifies elitist Frankfurt School notions (Adorno, 1998; Adorno and Horkheimer, 1944) of high culture as the exclusive transcendent space wherein human agency and counter-hegemonic practices can be asserted. Moreover, it obstructs the entry of many popular literacy practices into the classroom under the well-intentioned but misguided premise of responsible pedagogy.

An alternative to the elitist posture assumed by many literacy educators is the celebratory approach to popular culture. This approach focuses on the use of popular texts for exclusively divergent, resistant, and emancipatory purposes (e.g., Fiske, 1979, 1987, 1989). While this perspective coheres with many progressive educators' attempts to transport the popular into the classroom, it is theoretically inadequate for analyzing the hegemonic aspects of popular culture because of its overestimation of the subject's ability to identify and respond to latent textual messages.

The fundamental problematic with regard to these two perspectives is not their respective dispositions toward the popular per se. Rather, these perspectives index an epistemological and ontological orientation that prefigures the relationship between individuals and the social world. The belief that individuals are unable to resist the influence of the culture industry reflects a structural determinist position that subordinates individuals to the objective structures with which they interact. Conversely, the belief that these structures can be successfully negotiated reflects an expectation of self-determinism and subjectivity when negotiating the popular. In order to move beyond this dichotomy, I look to Bourdieu's (1972/1977) theory of practice, which allows for the theoretical reconciliation of the elitist and celebratory positions through its treatment of subjective and objective structures.

In his attempt to make sense of the relationship between individuals and contexts, objective structures and human practices, Bourdieu examines the ways that observed structures are identifiably structured and structuring. For Bourdieu, the false dilemma between objectivism and subjectivism—or structuralism and phenomenology (Bourdieu and Wacquant, 1992)—can be resolved through a dialectical approach that accounts for the constitutive potential of both objective structures and human subjectivity. To realize this,

Bourdieu provides and develops the terms *field* and *habitus*. Within his theory of practice, a field is an objective set of social relations that determines human activity and facilitates social reproduction. This conception of field is under-girded by the structuralist expectation of a predictable relationship between and among individuals within this system. Habitus is "an acquired system of generative schemes objectively adjusted to the particular conditions in which it is constituted" (Bourdieu, 1972/1977: 95). These schemes, which can also be described as dispositions, attitudes, or habits, allow for subjective responses to the field.

Although Bourdieu's theory of practice is expressly designed to move beyond the structure–agency, objective–subjective dichotomies, it admittedly fails to accomplish this completely. While the concept of habitus allows for human agency, this agency is at all times circumscribed by the objective structures within which it is asserted. Bourdieu argues:

> Because the habitus is an endless capacity to engender products—thought, perceptions, expressions, actions—whose limits are set by the historically and socially situated conditions of its production, the conditioned and conditional freedom it secures is as remote from a creation of unpredict-able novelty as it is from a simple mechanical reproduction of the initial conditionings.
>
> (1972/1977: 95)

Consequently, the agency that subjects use to negotiate a field is itself consti-tuted by that field. This is because of Bourdieu's belief that, while the subjectiv-ist/objectivist binary is problematic, the objectivist position is less problematic (Bohman, 1999; Jenkins, 1992). While this lack of complete reciprocity between habitus and field does not absolve Bourdieu from structural determinism, it provides a useful framework for analyzing popular literacies in a way that accounts for the celebratory and elitist positions while allowing for practical possibilities that extend beyond the binary.

By viewing the popular as a contested terrain, educators are theoretically encouraged to access the out-of-school literacy practices that are most salient to students without losing unnecessary ideological ground to the culture indus-try by failing to attend to ideological critique. Also, by understanding that popular culture provides a site where individuality and creativity (however constrained) exist, educators can make important connections to students' out-of-school lives by exploiting the popular literacy practices that reflect or inform the various subjective and objective structures that students negotiate.

It is important, however, not to conflate this Bourdieusian approach to the popular with the traditional Gramscian or "neo-Gramscian" (Storey, 2003) approaches that have dominated cultural studies and critical pedagogy litera-ture in recent years. While both look at popular culture production as a site of contestation, resistance, and ultimate reproduction through the *doxa* (Bourdieu,

1980/1990) or hegemony (Gramsci, 1971) of particular fields, the latter is inadequate for examining the consequences of engaging in out-of-school literacy practices within the traditional school field. The Bourdieusian project, however, demands close sociological attention to the relationships of power and practice that develop when the in-school and out-of-school fields are brought together. Further, it forces literacy educators to interrogate the veracity of critical claims of emancipation, democracy, and social transformation vis-à-vis the valorization of popular culture.

Hip-hop literacy

Partly because of the relative paucity of hip-hop scholarship, there is a decided ambiguity within the literature with respect to the meaning of the term "hip-hop." Though many recent musicologists, critics, and even artists have employed the term for narrowing purposes, that is, distinguishing between highbrow and lowbrow forms of rap music, I accept Tricia Rose's definition of hip-hop as "an African-American and Afro-Caribbean youth culture composed of graffiti, breakdancing, and rap music" (1994: 2). While Rose's definition fails to include the important fourth component of "turntablism" or "DJing"—the art of playing, mixing, and scratching records—it nonetheless represents a more comprehensive definition of hip-hop than many earlier ones. In assuming a Bourdieusian stance, I am also compelled to problematize and ultimately disregard the "distinction" (Bourdieu, 1984) between high and low culture that accompanies narrowing definitions of hip-hop. As Bourdieu argues, such judgments are not the product of a transcendental aesthetic, but a reflection of particular class interests.

Although Bourdieu's basic thesis regarding the relationship among taste, class position, and reproduction is useful, his analysis is problematic for several reasons. As Hall (1992) argues, Bourdieu's focus on class fails to account for the complexities of status distinctions based on other factors, such as race, gender, and sexual orientation, all of which are critical when analyzing hip-hop culture. Within the US context, race is particularly confounding to the Bourdieusian framework, given its persistent influence on access to economic capital (Conley, 1999; Hacker, 1992; Oliver and Shapiro, 1995), access to basic material resources (Massey and Denton, 1993; Orfield et al., 1997), and academic performance (Steele, 1997), all of which contribute to social mobility and reproduction.

Bourdieu also partially shares the Frankfurt School's obsession with high culture, as evidenced by his generous readings of high artistic productions such as Manet and Flaubert (Reed, 2003; Roberts, 2000; Szeman, 2002) and his pessimistic readings of television (Bourdieu, 1996/1998). Further, Bourdieu's analysis focuses primarily on the processes of distinction that reflect the upper class *weltanschauungen*, thereby ignoring the processes, struggles, and doxas of popular culture production. This is particularly problematic with regard to hip-hop, which is both the product of "common culture" (Willis, 1990) and a form of "race music" (Ramsey, 2003). It is these weaknesses that necessitate a closer examination of some of the literacy practices particular to hip-hop culture.

The term "hip-hop literacy" has been utilized in popular and academic circles to signify the ability to understand or comfortably maneuver through hip-hop culture. Although useful, such a definition reduces hip-hop literacy to a set of observable competencies, such as mastery of hip-hop vernacular and dress, and knowledge of current music trends. Drawing on literature from multiple fields, I provide an alternate, more expansive operational definition of hip-hop literacy as *the ability to read and write in a manner that allows one to decenter dominant (hegemonic) conceptions of reality and relocate the specific experiences, values, and codes of the hip-hop community from the periphery to the center.* It is important to stress, however, the indispensability of the "observable competencies" discussed above. A thorough understanding of hip-hop vernacular, fashion, and other aesthetic features of the culture is an essential component of the hip-hop literacy project. If hip-hop literacy is to be viewed as a viable and valuable end to a pedagogical process, it is important that a person who participates in such a process is capable of functioning within hip-hop-centered contexts.

Critical literacy serves as the theoretical springboard for my conception of hip-hop literacy. Hip-hop literacy shares critical literacy's commitment to "challeng[ing] the status quo in an effort to discover alternative paths for social and self-development" (Shor, 1999: 1). Like critical literacy, hip-hop literacy is concerned with reading "the word and the world" (Freire and Macedo, 1987) in a way that calls dominant ideology into question with the expressed intention of recognizing the pervasiveness and complexity of power relationships and ultimately transforming them.

Hip-hop literacy's preoccupation with examining and undermining asymmetric power relations arises from hip-hop's organic connection to political struggle. Nearly since its inception, hip-hop has been a fecund terrain for cultural critique. Beginning with the message rap of the early 1980s, hip-hop has been instrumental in spotlighting inner-city suffering in full view of the mass public. Since 1982, when Grand Master Flash and the Furious Five released "The Message," a devastating critique of inner-city conditions, explicit critiques of race, class, and gender relations in post-industrial America have been consistently present in the world of rap music. Though usually occupying marginal positions, excluding the commercially successful political rap movement of the late-1980s and early 1990s, political rappers have been an integral part of hip-hop culture (Allen, 1996). Artists such as dead prez, who admittedly use rap music to further their grassroots political organizing by appropriating previously inaccessible sociopolitical theory and moving it into the public sphere, have assumed the role of what Mark Anthony Neal (2003) calls "celebrity Gramscians." Unlike Gramsci's notion of the organic intellectual, who emerges from subaltern groups and serves as an organizing intellectual force

(Gramsci, 1971), the celebrity Gramscian connects her political agenda to her fame in order to mainstream the message. The prominent positioning of the celebrity Gramscian is important, as it causes a relocation of leadership and canons of knowledge from local to public (commercial) spaces (Hill, in press).

Rap music has also provided an otherwise nonexistent space for urban youth to apply and examine cultural critiques vis-à-vis their own lived experience. An excellent example of this is top-selling rapper Jay-Z's song, "A Ballad for the Fallen Soldier," which critiques America's post-9/11 anti-terrorist fervor and simultaneous indifference to ghetto suffering:

> The World is facin' terror
> Bin Laden been happenin' in Manhattan
> Crack was anthrax back then
> Back when
> Police was Al Qaeda to Black men.
> (Jay-Z, 2002, disc 2, track 11)

By placing this frequently posited argument within an urban context—in terms of content and commercial accessibility—Jay-Z facilitates the development of politicized discussion within new spaces.

Despite its strong connection to critical literacy, hip-hop literacy attempts to address the aspects of critical literacy that are insufficient with respect to the particular needs of the hip-hop community. While critical literacy posits that the reader's worldview necessarily mediates his or her reading of a text (Freire, 1970; Hunt, 1991), hip-hop literacy advocates the use of the rhetorical and narrative strategies of the hip-hop community, which are deeply rooted in the African-American oral and literary traditions (Dyson, 2003; Rose, 1994; Smitherman, 1997) in order to foreground the values and perspectives of the hip-hop community. These strategies include *signifyin(g)* and *narrativizing* (Richardson, 2003; Smitherman, 1994, 1997).

Hip-hop literacy decenters Eurocentric communicative practices by privileging alternate modes of speech employed by members of the hip-hop community, namely signifyin(g). Signifyin(g) is a narrative tool connected to the Afro-diasporic oral and literary traditions (Gates, 1988; Mitchell-Kernan, 1972; Smitherman, 1997). The valorization of signifyin(g), which can be described as a tactic used in verbal dueling, a way of encoding messages through indirection, or as an overarching trope of Black experience (Potter, 1995; Richardson, 2003; Smitherman, 1997), is an essential part of the hip-hop literacy project as it contributes to a reappraisal of the previously marginalized cultural values and norms of the hip-hop community.

Narrativizing, which is the primary discursive vehicle for hip-hop expression, is a strategy used by practitioners of hip-hop to decenter both mainstream discursive strategies and master narratives themselves. The production of counter-narratives, or alternate stories, through storytelling connects to critical race theory and its focus on placing marginalized stories at the center of public discourse (Delgado Bernal, 2002; Guinier and Torres, 2002; Ladson-Billings, 1998). As legal scholar Derrick Bell (1995) notes:

> Analysis . . . through fiction, personal experience, and the stories of the people on the bottom illustrates how race and racism continue to dominate our society. The techniques also help in assessing sexism, classism, homophobia, and other forms of oppression.
>
> (p. 144)

Bell's assertion coheres greatly with hip-hop's emphasis on storytelling as a primary form of expression. Even when hip-hop texts are not explicitly or intentionally political, their presentation of alternate possibilities has the potential to disturb mainstream notions of reality.

The importance of hip-hop's counter-narratives as a counter-hegemonic force is further buttressed by hip-hop's focus on what Murray Forman (2002) calls "the extreme local," which alludes to its unprecedented focus on specific cities, neighborhoods, zip codes, area codes, and housing projects within rap texts. By focusing on the extreme local, hip-hop's counter-narratives attach faces and names to otherwise abstract notions of ghetto life. With respect to hip-hop literacy, this suggests that in order to attempt to understand the hip-hop community, one must avoid generic, essentialized notions of its members, focusing instead on the specific experiences of a local body of subjects negotiating specific realities within a particular historical moment.

Hip-hop pedagogy

Perhaps the most important philosophical underpinning of the hip-hop pedagogy approach is, as Bourdieu frequently argues, the inextricability of theory and practice. It is therefore necessary that the theoretical shift that accompanies the hip-hop literacy approach be met with an equally radical shift in pedagogical practice. The most distinctive aspect of this shift in practice is a genuine and ongoing engagement with hip-hop literacy that allows traditionally alienated aspects of students' lives into the classroom. It is worthwhile to stress that hip-hop pedagogy should not be viewed as a set of strategies or activities for reaching ostensibly disaffected youth. In fact, the very notion of hip-hop pedagogy as a "how to" guide for hip-hop literacy is an affront to the intensely intellectual spirit of the project through its tacit offer of flattened, generic procedures, and simple answers to complex issues. Rather, hip-hop pedagogy reflects an alternate vision of pedagogy that reconsiders the relationship between curriculum and instruction, reader and text, and teacher and student.

Curriculum and instruction

One of the most formidable challenges when attempting to infuse hip-hop pedagogy into the curriculum is recognizing and capitalizing upon appropriate curricular spaces and pedagogical moments for its implementation. Despite the nascent body of important research using hip-hop in the classroom, most of the work done has consisted largely of curricular interventions within English classrooms (e.g., Bruce and Davis, 2000; Mahiri, 1998; Morell, 2002; Morell and Duncan-Andrade, 2002; Rice, 2003). While these works have provided extraordinary insight into the concrete ways that hip-hop texts can be brought into the classroom, hip-hop pedagogy reflects an ongoing engagement with the popular that extends beyond the co-optation of student culture for infinitesimally small segments of students' overall schooling experiences. Instead, we must search for ways of weaving students' lived culture into the very fabric of the curriculum. An example of this effort can be found in my own work within an urban high school.

As part of a larger research project that examined the effectiveness of hip-hop texts in teaching literary interpretation, as well as the specific and local interactions between students and hip-hop texts within formal pedagogical spaces, I co-constructed and co-taught a hip-hop-centered high-school English literature course entitled "Hip-Hop Lit," which used hip-hop texts as primary sources for teaching literary interpretation. Based on the principles of hip-hop literacy, I established the following three broad goals for the course: 1) provide students with the analytic tools for interpreting, critiquing, and discussing literature; 2) create a space in which the literacy practices of the hip-hop community are moved from the margins to the center of the curriculum; and 3) create a space for student voices to be heard in a way that validates their particular experiences and interests. The one-year elective course was divided into six thematic units: Love, Roots of Hip-Hop and Literature, Family, Neighborhoods, Politics, and Despair.

Each unit contained eight texts: four that were selected by my co-teacher and I, and four that were selected by individual students, subject to teacher approval. At the beginning of each class meeting, students were asked to answer journal questions that linked the day's topic to their personal experiences. For example, the first text that the class read from the Love unit was Lauryn Hill's "Manifest," a first-person narrative about a romantic relationship gone bad. Prior to reading the text and engaging in more formal analysis, students were asked to journal about their own experiences with love. The students then shared their personal narratives and engaged in a lengthy discussion. Like many of the students in the class, Natasha, a 17-year-old African-American female, cited these types of activities as reasons for the effectiveness of the course:

This was my favorite class ever 'cause we learned a lot and I could relate to it. Like when we read [*Manifest*] . . . We learned about hyperbole and imagery and all that but I liked the fact that we got to talk about real stuff too. Plus we got to tell our own stories too. Why can't it always be like this?

By allowing students' personal narratives to co-exist with and speak to the "official texts," we were able to construct a full-fledged, hip-hop-centered curriculum.

Natasha's question ("Why can't it always be like this?") reflects the sentiment of many critical and otherwise progressive educators, whose work implicitly or explicitly forecasts a neat accommodation of the in-school and out-of-school fields through careful investigation and engaged pedagogy. Within this logic, the decentering of school literacies and the prioritization of student voice and experience are worthwhile processes because of their transformative potential. However, an under-examined question persists: What is at stake when out-of-school literacies are privileged within the traditional classroom?

When designing Hip-Hop Lit, my co-teacher and I made a deliberate decision to discard traditional Western texts and replace them with hip-hop texts in order to attract and engage disaffected students. Despite our success, it is important not to romanticize or fetishize our use of popular texts. By relying on hip-hop texts instead of canonical texts, we deprived students of access to forms of cultural capital that would be valued in larger fields (e.g., college). On its own, this type of practice, which is often the form that classroom engagement with the popular takes, enables social reproduction by preventing students from developing a feel for the game(s) of power. It is in this vein that Delpit (1995) is instructive:

> Students must be taught the codes needed to participate fully in the mainstream of American life, not by being forced to attend to hollow, inane, decontextualized subskills, but rather within the context of meaningful communicative endeavors; that they must be allowed the resource of the teacher's expert knowledge, while being helped to acknowledge their own "expertness" as well; and that even while students are assisted in learning the culture of power, they must also be helped to learn about the arbitrariness of those codes and about the power relationships they represent.
>
> (p. 45)

Clearly, by not using the Western canon, we were valuing local forms of capital in the form of student expertise at the expense of other forms. It would be inaccurate, however, to suggest that in doing so we facilitated social reproduction. Because the class's focus was on the process of literary interpretation, and it was offered as an elective, we felt that we made a worthwhile sacrifice. The students in Hip-Hop Lit developed a formal vocabulary of literary critique that would be of value in a mainstream literature classroom. By acknowledging student "expertness" vis-à-vis the hip-hop texts, and allowing them to engage in formal criticism using the texts, we were also able to create a space where students could question the privileged and highly arbitrary position of the Western canon. Also, from a pragmatic perspective, our use of hip-hop texts provided a suitable "hook" that sustained the students' interest. Without such a hook, the students may not have maintained strong attendance, which was the case with other traditional English courses within the program.

Reader and text

When implementing hip-hop literacy approaches in the classroom, it is important to account for the highly unpredictable links that emerge between readers and texts. Although critical literacy scholars (e.g., Giroux, 1996; Kellner, 1995) create theoretical space for multiple readings of popular culture, their actual readings of popular texts (typically films) allow little room for alternate interpretations (Daspit and Weaver, 1999; Dimitriadis, 2001). By failing to account for alternate readings, and succumbing to the meanings inscribed upon texts by power blocs, educators become unequipped to respond to the unpredictable ways in which students interpret and employ hip-hop texts.

An excellent example of reader/text unpredictability emerged during a Hip-Hop Lit class in which Ricky, a 16-year-old White male student, brought in "If I Had" by Eminem for the class to read and analyze. Partly because of the explicit nature of the text, but more importantly to Eminem's larger corpus of violent, misogynistic, and homophobic songs, I decided that the song was unacceptable for classroom consumption. The following day, instead of responding to the assigned journal question, Ricky wrote the following:

> I don't understand why we can't read "If I Had" in class. I know [Eminem] don't say everything that he is supposed to but who else is representing for me? The same way he came into the game as the only White boy and did his thing like he said in the song, that's how I'm trying to be around here. I don't agree with everything he says but why do we have to agree with everything to read him?

For many, including myself, Eminem's music offers some of the most egregious examples of hate and intolerance within popular music. For Ricky, Eminem's extraordinary success despite his minority status within the hip-hop community mirrored his own position as the only White male (along with three White females) in a class of 20 students. As he would indicate throughout the semester, Ricky felt compelled to prove that he "belonged" in the class. As such, Eminem represented the possibility for a White male to comfortably fit within a predominately African-American context.

This account provides a clear example of the danger of assuming predictability between readers' interpretations and the meanings attributed to texts by dominant voices. The assumption that a text is solely hegemonic, facilitates social reproduction, or is otherwise problematic can inform curriculum and pedagogy in ways that delimit possibilities, thus effecting or fortifying the very structures of domination that the infusion of popular literacies into formal pedagogical spaces attempts to undermine. To remedy this, I echo Daspit and Weaver's (1999) call for the decentering of critical pedagogical approaches to reading the popular. They explain:

> Decentering implies we see the reading of popular culture texts primarily as counter or independent readings that flow within or alongside of our own narratives . . . Creating a decentered critical practice of reading popular culture texts also implies the need to reconfigure the epistemological foundations that undergird our notions of knowledge and method. That is, we need to ask how we, as academics, come to understand the ways in which students, teachers and administrators read popular culture texts and construct multiple readings of these texts, or how do we construct the reader/viewer of popular culture texts?
>
> (p. xxiii)

The practical implication of this reconfiguration of knowledge and method is that much of the power of those sanctioned to interpret the popular *for* students (scholars, cultural critics, teachers, and so on) must be ceded to students. This is not to suggest that student readings and uses of the popular should not be scrutinized, problematized, and challenged. In fact, such activity (as demonstrated in the following section) is central to the hip-hop literacy project's larger mission of creating and expanding democratic spaces. However, this project must begin with a firm understanding of students' relationships with and to the popular that can only come from a "deep listening" (Schultz, 2003) to student voices.

Teacher and student

In order to facilitate a classroom that engages in hip-hop pedagogy, teachers must commit themselves to a sustained dialogue with students regarding their relationship to the popular. This dialogue must be reflective of the transfigured power relations that accompany hip-hop pedagogy because of the radical redistribution of symbolic capital within the classroom. Traditional classrooms, which have tacitly rejected youth culture by excluding it from the curriculum or using it in sporadic, opportunistic ways, must be replaced by spaces in which teachers and students engage in critical dialogue about the meaningful, valuable, and problematic aspects of popular culture.

The reconfigured relationship between teachers and students for which I argue is not unproblematic. Students' reluctance to expose vital and personal aspects of their lived experience in full public view must be carefully considered and addressed when attempting to transport the popular into the classroom. Even under the most optimal conditions, the emergence of hip-hop pedagogy will (and should) be met with tremendous apprehension from students who are fearful of putting their lives on display for academic scrutiny. For this reason, teachers must resist the urge to position themselves as arbiters of youth culture when engaging in critical dialogue about the popular. Again, this is not to suggest that the troubling aspects of student culture should not be called into question. Rather, the critical dialogue that must take place between teachers and students surrounding the popular must not degenerate into an officially sanctioned moral and ethical attack on students' lives and values. In attempting to balance these two concerns, irreconcilable tensions will often emerge. To illustrate, I return to Ricky.

After reading Ricky's journal entry defending his choice of Eminem, I delayed that day's lesson and asked the entire class to share their opinions about the situation. Many of the boys in the class agreed with Ricky's choice and felt that it was unfair not to allow "If I Had" into the curriculum because of my personal disapproval of Eminem's work. Nearly all of the girls in the class, however, were adamant about not reading Eminem's songs in class. Kara, one of the older girls in the class, said the following:

> I know that we can't always read stuff that we agree with . . . but he talks about killing his baby mom and throwing her in the river. I mean he got skills and everything but he always talk about killing gays and doing drugs. I mean, do we got to hear about that stuff in school too?

After nearly an hour of intense debate, it seemed that most of the class agreed with Kara, and Ricky reluctantly decided to choose another song. Although I would not have permitted the song even if the students had deemed it acceptable, the dialogue was nonetheless useful. By creating a space where students could discuss their feelings about the text, both Ricky and I were able to gain insights that would help us to better negotiate the course and understand the diversity and complexity of textual positions that students assume.

It is important, however, not to romanticize the above exchange with Ricky, as it demands a closer examination of the effects of hip-hop pedagogy on the classroom field. As mentioned earlier, the negotiation of the classroom field is mediated by a very specific set of rules, values, capitals, and so forth that are recognized within the space. Despite the expressed curricular goal of allowing student experiences, counter-narratives, and interpretations to play a constitutive role in the daily practices of the course and ultimately lead to the redistribution classroom capital, several contradictions emerged that undermined this goal.

My refusal to allow Ricky's chosen text into the classroom reflects a contradiction between classroom and textual authority that is inevitable when engaging in hip-hop pedagogy. While the acceptance of unpredictability between reader and text allows for a certain amount of interpretive freedom, this freedom failed to translate into legitimate classroom power in the above incident. Despite Ricky's ostensibly redemptive use of the Eminem text, my own politics prompted me to leverage my classroom authority in a way that ultimately trumped the textual authority that Hip-Hop Lit afforded Ricky. As such, Ricky's agenda became subordinate to mine.

When faced with the contradiction between our respective goals, both Ricky and I retreated to the traditional habitus of the classroom field. Despite our expectation of shared expertise and authority, I immediately appealed to my position as teacher to place Ricky in a position in which he had to justify his choice of the text. Although I engaged in an apparently democratic dialogue with him and the other students, my own decisions were never subject to change unless I wanted them to. That no one challenged my approach or ultimate decision speaks of the pervasiveness and permanence of the *doxa* of formal schooling within our classroom. Bourdieu (1980/1990) defines doxa as:

> the coincidence of the objective structure and the internalized structure which provides the illusion of immediate understanding, characteristic of practical experience of the familiar universe, and which at the same time excludes from that experience any inquiry as to its own conditions of possibility.
>
> (p. 26)

To be fair, the students' acquiescence may have been arisen from several reasons: the students may have genuinely decided that the text was inappropriate, the students disagreed with my decision but accepted my authority, or the students were indifferent to the process. Nevertheless, each of these possibilities, as well as many possible others, reflects an uncritical acceptance of certain aspects of the classroom field.

Another important factor when considering the students' acceptance of my decision was my particular position as an expert within the classroom. Unlike my co-teacher, who was conspicuously silent during the two-day period, the students repeatedly deferred to my expertise as a hip-hop journalist and scholar throughout the semester. Also, my own subject position as an African-American male may have provided me with a degree of authenticity with regard to the class and the incident, which made my decision more palatable. Although I did not explicitly interrogate these points during the incident, they are empirically buttressed by the following section, which shows the difficulties that emerge when a teacher is not considered an expert.

Dilemmas in deliberation

To this point, my consideration of hip-hop literacy and pedagogy has examined the ways in which a redistribution of capital within the classroom field can affect students. Often at stake in this redistribution of capital, however, is the teacher's ability to successfully negotiate this reconfigured field. This is particularly problematic with regard to popular literacies, as issues of difference (race, class, generation, and so on) may render many teachers ineffective. In this section, using Bourdieu's theory of practice as a guiding framework, I perform a discourse analysis of the Hip-Hop Lit curriculum deliberations with my co-teacher, Mr Columbo, in order to demonstrate some of the contradictions that emerge when decentering traditional literacies.

Although my experience as a hip-hop journalist and lifelong consumer of hip-hop provided me with great insight into its culture and rap music, I had little knowledge of local and national English education standards and no formal experience teaching English literature. Consequently, I decided to rely on the expertise of an experienced English teacher. I approached Mr Columbo, a friend and former colleague, who enthusiastically agreed to co-construct and co-teach the course with me. Despite his lack of familiarity with hip-hop, he brought an interesting background that contrasted mine: Mr Columbo was a 30-year-old White classroom teacher with four years of English teaching experience and little knowledge of hip-hop; I was a 24-year-old African-American graduate student, former high school Spanish teacher, and active member of the hip-hop community. It was my belief that our respective areas of expertise would contribute equally to the construction and implementation of Hip-Hop Lit. We decided to begin meeting weekly in order to construct the basic framework for the course.

The first task of our curriculum deliberation was to outline and begin collecting a set of central texts that would form the initial curricular framework for the course. Like the other aspects of course design, we expected this process to be smooth, democratic, and constructive. Nevertheless, crucial issues prevented the process from being any of these things. The following two vignettes, both from the first day of curriculum deliberations, provide insight into the problems that quickly emerged with respect to the distribution of symbolic capital. While the first vignette does not directly address the issue of hip-hop literacy, it provides an important contextual backdrop and crucial point of comparison for the second vignette, which occurred moments later.

Academic speak

One of the major problems that emerged as Mr Columbo and I attempted to construct a hip-hop-centered curriculum was our inability to find and employ a rich, mutually intelligible curriculum. Although I was sensitive to the frequently posited arguments from classroom teachers regarding the often inaccessible language of the academy, I was equally concerned with discarding powerful and nuanced academic language in order to accommodate Mr Columbo's potential concerns. The following excerpt from our first deliberation meeting provides a lucid example of the asymmetric power relations that quickly developed as a result of this tension:

1: Me:	We need to find a way to organize the class by beginning with central texts and letting the students . . .
2: Col:	I thought we were using songs
3: Me:	We are but . . .
4: Col:	But we're writing them down
5: Me:	That too but when I talk about text I'm talking about various things like TV, video
6: Col:	So it's NOT text
7: Me:	Well I use a more expansive notion of text . . . [pause] kinda postmodern
8: Col:	What's postmodern?
9: Me:	Well for this it's a way of looking at multiple kinds of text and challenging interpretations.
10: Col:	Whatever. What's next?
11: Me:	Well, I wanted to think of what kinds of texts to use.
12: Col:	Well?
13: Me:	What do you think?
14: Col:	I think whatever you think. This is your kid. I'm just babysittin'.

In this transcription, what began as an ostensibly democratic dialogue quickly degenerated into a conversation that effectively silenced Mr Columbo. What I considered to be a clear and innocuous use of the term "text" (in line 1) triggered an exchange that privileged academic language at the expense of Mr Columbo's comfort.

Bourdieu's notion of social activity as a game (Grenfell and James, 1998) provides a useful construct for analyzing our interaction. Unlike sports, which provides explicit rules of interaction, social activities are largely replete with tacit instructions for success within the particular set of relations of which they are composed. With respect to the above interaction, this was reflected in my employment of a particular "discourse," which Norman Fairclough (2003) defines as "a particular way of representing" which "figures in the representations that are always a part of social practices—representations of the material world, of other social practices, [and] reflexive self-representations of the practice in question" (p. 26). The very use of the term "text" in the postmodern sense, as an all-encompassing signifier of cultural production, assumed a knowledge not only of academic discourse in the generic sense but of a particular academic discourse that accepted (or at the very least discussed) "a more expansive notion of text" (line 7). While one could argue that this allusion to another body of knowledge, or "intertextuality" (Fairclough, 2003), is extremely useful and perhaps necessary as a form of intellectual shorthand, it can prove quite problematic for those outside of the particular discursive community. As such, my apparently ambiguous use of the word "text" and subsequent failure to provide an adequate explanation during this first meeting helped to tacitly establish an important rule for future deliberations: academic discourse would be the language of choice.

It could be argued that Mr Columbo could (and should) have resisted the positioning of academic discourse as the dominant language of our interaction. However, such an argument would ignore both Mr Columbo's efforts to do just that, as well as the extent to which particular discourses have power over others. For example, Mr Columbo attempts (in line 4) to receive clarification for my use of the word "text" by offering that it was the act of writing that made the aforementioned signifiers texts. While his offering did not cohere with my intended meaning, his statement provided me with an opportunity to offer an alternate, more understandable response. At this point I could have provided a clear, non-academic explication of how I was defining and using the word "text." As a former teacher in the school and colleague of Mr Columbo, I had a firm grasp of the standard "teacher talk" that would have appealed to him and made the conversation more comfortable. Instead, I further complicated matters by bringing another academic (and equally ambiguous) term into the conversation: "postmodern" (line 7). It is clear that I had consciously decided to position myself as an academic, as opposed to a fellow or former teacher, within this conversation.

Nevertheless, I am afforded yet another opportunity to employ a different type of discourse when Mr Columbo asks for a definition of "postmodern" (line 8). Although I attempt to offer a quick (and clearly inadequate) definition of postmodernism, I also assert a particular type of intellectual authority by beginning my response with the phrase, "Well, for *this* . . ." By beginning my response with this phrase, I make it clear that any definition that I gave him would not be thorough. Rather, I was providing him with merely enough information to allow him to function in this particular conversation, thereby reiterating his subordinate position within the conversation. In Bourdieusian terms, I was not only establishing the rules of the game, I was positioning myself as the arbiter. Again, this positioning was directly related to my decision to represent myself as an academic and not a teacher.

By reasserting the need to engage in an academic discourse, I constrained Mr Columbo's ability to employ alternate forms of representation or discourses. This is buttressed by the following comment that Mr Columbo made to me as we were ending our meeting:

> Damn. That meeting reminded me of why I hated grad school. Everybody talks this shit that nobody understands and when you try to talk regular, everybody looks at you like you're the [pause], like you don't [pause], you're not as smart because you don't want to talk in riddles. But [pause] that's the way it is over there.

Mr Columbo's comments reflect more than his obvious disaffection with the academy. More importantly, he makes an important connection between our deliberations and what he considers to be pedantic academic discourse. By saying, "that's the way it is over there," he does two things: he distances himself physically and ideologically from the academy, and he concedes to the necessity of academic discourse in particular social spaces. In short, Mr Columbo has submitted to the rules of a game that he feels obligated but unequipped to play. In order to unpack the reasons for Mr Columbo's decision to submit to the rules of the game, it is helpful to return to the concepts of structure, agency, field, and habitus within Bourdieu's theory of practice. These concepts are embodied in the remainder of the conversation between Mr Columbo and me.

At this point (line 10), Mr Columbo expressed his frustration by disregarding my definition of postmodernism ("Whatever") and attempting to move on to another topic ("What's next?") Clearly, Mr Columbo had lost interest in, or at the very least given up on, clearly understanding my usage of "text" and "postmodern." Moreover, he openly assumed a subordinate position in the conversation (in lines 12 and 14), where he expressed his desire to follow my lead. Despite his assertion of agency by dismissing my definition of postmodernism and attempting to change the subject, he had submitted to the immutability of the larger structure (academic discourse), an act that he admitted to in his post-deliberation comment, "that's the way it is over there."

From a Bourdieusian perspective, this conversation structured Mr Columbo by causing him to invoke certain dispositions that he connected to the academic enterprise. His association of our deliberations with being in graduate school would logically cause him to conjure a particular habitus that is mediated by his personal experiences. Nevertheless, Mr Columbo was able to effectively resist the structure of the academic field by exhibiting behaviors typically unassociated with appropriate academic discourse, namely sarcasm and disengagement. It is important to stress that Mr Columbo's resistance to the structure (that is, the deliberation) is realized solely within the larger hegemonic framework of academic discourse. This coheres with the Bourdieusian notion that domination and resistance never occur in a pure form. Mr Columbo was "allowed" to resist the structure provided that he accepted the permanence of the structure.

Hip-hop (il)literacy

Given our expressed concern with renegotiating the relationship between teacher and student, Mr Columbo and I were committed to including student voices in our curriculum deliberations. Although our curriculum allowed for students to include their own texts (both original and selected from popular media) within the Hip-Hop Lit course, we also wanted student input during the design process. We asked Jamal,[1] a student at the school whom we expected to take the class, to join us in our curriculum deliberations as we were discussing the particular types of texts to use in the course. The following exchange occurred moments after the first:

15: Me: What kind of songs do y'all want to use?
16: Jamal: I don't know. Real stuff. Y'ah mean?
17: Col: [laughing] In *English* Jamal.
18: Jamal: I'm *sayin'*, dog. Real stuff.
19: Col: But . . .
20: Me: *I* got you. But what else?

At this point Jamal lifts his chair and turns toward me, moving Mr Columbo from his direct line of view to his periphery.

21: Jamal: Some jiggy shi . . . stuff, [laughs lightly] some underground stuff, and some gully stuff.[2] But nothin' ol' school.
22: Me: Cool. What kind of stuff do ya'll want to talk about?
23: Jamal: Street shit, love, guns, [pause] everything.

Moments later, a teacher calls Jamal out of the room and he does not return. At this point, Mr Columbo appeared noticeably irritated, and I began to worry about the likelihood that we would be able to successfully co-construct and co-teach the course. By the end of the deliberation, I knew that a huge problem was developing but I was uncertain about how to improve the situation. Mr Columbo seemed completely disinterested in participating, and his following statement provided me with great insight into the reason why:

> I'm tired of waitin' for this kid. Besides you two can handle this yourselves. I don't know anything about what he's talking about. [looks at my notes] Jiggy? Gully? Underground? I thought postmodern was bad. At least I'd heard o' that before. [laughing] Maybe you and Jamal can teach the class . . . I'll watch.

Moments later, Mr Columbo suggested that we end our meeting and reconvene on the same day the following week.

My statement (in line 15) signaled an important discursive shift in our deliberation. My use of the word "y'all" in reference to Jamal's classmates signified the acceptability of African-American Vernacular English (AAVE) in the deliberation. Jamal followed my lead by responding in AAVE (line 16), asserting that he wanted the text to be "real" or, in hip-hop vernacular, authentically connected to the experiences of the hip-hop community (Hill, ms in preparation). At this point, Jamal and I had managed to do what Mr Columbo could not: change the discourse of the conversation to suit our particular goals. As the arbiter of the game (as discussed in the previous section), it was reasonable to expect that I had the authority to shift the conversation from academic to colloquial discourse vis-à-vis AAVE. That Jamal had an equally pivotal role in effecting this shift reflects a crucial power dynamic that was becoming more apparent as the deliberations continued. Not only was Mr Columbo subordinate to me, he was quickly assuming a tertiary (and in his mind expendable) position now that Jamal was involved in the conversation.

Despite Mr Columbo's discomfort with academic discourse, he nonetheless attempted to assert authority by alluding to its necessity (in line 17). By demanding that Jamal speak "in English," that is, Standard English, he seemed to be trying to place Jamal in the same uncomfortable position within the conversation that he occupied earlier. Jamal, much like Mr Columbo in the first vignette, resisted this by essentially repeating his previous statement (line 18). Before Mr Columbo could reassert what I anticipated to be a protest (line 19), I quickly interjected and indicated that I understood what Jamal was saying. Although my decision to interject was made to avoid a time-consuming repeat of the previous vignette, as well as to prevent Mr Columbo from subjecting Jamal to what I expected to be culturally insensitive verbal harassment for his use of AAVE, it did far more than that.

The stress that I placed on the personal pronoun "I" (in line 20) suggested that my understanding of Jamal's statements superseded that of Mr Columbo's in terms of its importance. Instead of asking Jamal to restate his comments in Standard English or "translating" them to Mr Columbo, I allowed Jamal's comments to stand as they were, further distancing Mr Columbo from the deliberation. The discursive and ideological distance that was being established became reified through Jamal's decision to reposition his chair. Although it is unclear whether or not his move was deliberate or unconscious, it nonetheless marked a significant moment in the interaction. Mr Columbo was now officially removed from the conversation.

Bourdieu's theory of symbolic activity and capital provides a useful tool to analyze the second vignette. Returning to the notion of social activity as a game, Bourdieu (1972/1977) states that success depends not only on knowledge of explicit rules, but also a *sens practique*, or a feel for the game. As Grenfell and James (1998) suggest, effective strategies for success are "the result of combining practical good sense and commonly accepted practices, often in an implicit, semi-automatic manner" (p. 19). In the first vignette, Mr Columbo develops, though begrudgingly, a feel for the game. He has full knowledge of what he needs to possess (familiarity with academic discourse) and how he needs to behave (willingness to engage in academic discourse) in order to be successful; he simply chooses to resist these requisites for success because of lack of interest and/or ability.

Jamal's presence in the second vignette, however, represents the commencement of a different game. Although Mr Columbo may not recognize it, he is entering into a new set of social relations with its own set of values. Mr Columbo's disorientation with the new field is evident as he unsuccessfully attempts to chide Jamal for his use of AAVE (line 17). It was only after Jamal's successful resistance, partly because of my support, that it became obvious to Mr Columbo that he was engaged in yet another game for which he was unsuited. Bourdieu argues that the rules and principles of the social game are played out in terms of the products of a particular field, or symbolic capital (Bourdieu, 1973; Grenfell and James 1998). This is evidenced in the radical redistribution of cultural capital that occurred when Jamal enters the deliberation. My position as arbiter, as established in the first vignette, allowed me to change the game and restructure what was valued.

Although my decision to change discourses was done to accommodate Jamal, this further marginalized Mr Columbo. Although academic discourse was no longer privileged in the conversation, it was replaced by African-American and hip-hop vernaculars that were equally alien to him. The intertextual references to postmodern theory were merely replaced by intertextual references to the hip-hop lexicon ("gully," "underground," "jiggy"). Jamal's and my cultural capital, in the form of our speech, knowledge of hip-hop terminology, and familiarity with hip-hop texts, was suddenly foregrounded. As such, the traditional teacher–student power relation between Jamal and Mr Columbo was momentarily inverted because of my presence. Also, I made a conscious decision to privilege my teacher–student relationship with Jamal over my teacher–teacher relationship with Mr Columbo in a way that enabled me to control the situation and marginalize him.

Bourdieu's notion of *illusio* is helpful for understanding Mr Columbo's involvement in these two vignettes. Even in his resistance to the first conversation, there remained for Mr Columbo an illusio, or sense of importance, of the game itself. Bourdieu (1996/1998) states:

> *Illusio* is in the fact of being interested in the game, of taking the game seriously. *Illusio* is the fact of being caught up in and by the game, of believing the game is "worth the candle," or, more simply, that playing is worth the effort. In fact, the word interest initially meant very precisely what I include under the notion of *illusio*, that is, the fact of attributing importance to a social game, the fact that what happens matters to those who are engaged in it, who are in the game.

(p. 76)

In the second vignette, when Mr Columbo expressed his dislike of the conversation, he seemed far more willing to withdraw from the conversation. Given that he did not particularly enjoy either situation, this suggests that he did not attach the same level of importance to the second game as he did to the first. Although he saw Hip-Hop Lit as an acceptable class for students such as Jamal, his actions suggested that he did not view it as a completely legitimate and worthwhile project. For Mr Columbo, the "real" literacy education was taking place somewhere outside of our classroom.

The implications of Mr Columbo's position are enormous within the context of hip-hop pedagogy or any other pedagogical intervention that focuses on a body of students whose cultural experiences are largely different from those of the majority teaching force. By refusing to participate (or, in Mr Columbo's case, half-heartedly participating) in such interventions, teachers tacitly reiterate dominant narratives about the inherent superiority of traditional literacies and the consequent inferiority of all other literacies.

Although the reconfiguration of classroom power was one of our expressed goals, Mr Columbo and I naively focused solely on how it would affect the students. At no point in our discussion of course goals did we attempt to account for how this redistribution of power could alienate a teacher. Although one of the primary reasons for my decision to co-construct and co-teach the course with Mr Columbo was his knowledge of both content and pedagogical content (Shulman, 1987), his expertise was quickly marginalized. Although this was only the first day of deliberation, at no point did we appeal to Mr Columbo's expertise or position him as a valued member of the deliberation. By disempowering him early in the deliberations, we may have undermined his effectiveness for future deliberations as well as in teaching the course.

New directions for Bourdieu, hip-hop, and out-of-school literacies

As I have demonstrated in this chapter, Bourdieusian theory yields enormous insights for understanding the practical limitations of traditional Gramscian and neo-Gramscian approaches to popular culture and critical pedagogy. Through Bourdieu's theory of practice, we are better equipped to understand the inexorability of asymmetric power relations within the classroom and the need for constructing a pedagogy that attends to the inevitable redistribution of symbolic capital that accompanies the transport of hip-hop and other out-of-school literacies into the classroom. From a Bourdieusian stance we can also begin to examine the contradictions of a classroom field with redistributed capital that exists within a larger context that does not recognize capital similarly.

In addition to exposing the shortcomings of current critical educational discourses, these insights also invite greater reflexivity and further exploration of emancipatory possibilities within Bourdieusian theory. As such, the various tensions between structure and agency that pervade this chapter must be reconsidered outside of not only the guarded optimism of neo-Gramscian theory, but also the deterministic constraints of traditional Bourdieusian approaches. This type of post-critical posture has important implications for workers within the fields of hip-hop studies and out-of-school literacies, for whom an examination of the potential and impotence of various habiti is essential for effecting transformative praxis within the classroom vis-à-vis the exploitation of hip-hop literacies.

This chapter also raises important questions about hip-hop and other out-of-school literacies that can only be addressed through further investigations and field analyses: What effect does bridging the in-school and out-of-school within the classroom have on other, larger social fields? How does the redistribution of cultural capital enable or constrain teaching and learning? Such considerations are critical as we attempt to locate new methods for constructing a sturdy bridge between students' in-school and out-of-school lives.

Acknowledgments

I would like to thank James Albright, Allan Luke, and Kara Jackson for their generous and insightful critiques of this chapter.

Notes

1   Jamal is a pseudonym used to protect the identity of the student.
2   In hip-hop vernacular, *gully* means "reflective of . . . urban life" (Hill, ms in preparation: 62); *underground* refers to "non-commercial hip-hop culture" (p. 115); and *jiggy* means "commercial hip-hop culture" (p. 71).

References

Adorno, T. (1998) On popular music. In J. Storey (ed.), *Cultural Theory and Popular Culture: A Reader*. Athens: University of Georgia, 197–209.

Adorno, T. and Horkeheimer, M. (1944) *Dialectic of Enlightenment*. New York: Continuum.

Allen, E. (1996) Contours and contradictions of message rap. In W. E. Perkins (ed.), *Droppin' Science: Critical Essays on Rap Music and Hip-hop Culture*. Philadelphia: Temple University Press, 158–91.

Alvermann, D., Moon, J. and Hagood, M. (1999) *Popular Culture in the Classroom: Teaching and Researching Critical Media Literacy*. Newark, DE: International Reading Association.

Bell, D. (1995) *Faces at the Bottom of the Well*. New York: Basic Books.

Bohman, J. (1999) Practical reason and cultural constraint: agency in Bourdieu's theory of practice. In R. Shusterman (ed.), *Bourdieu: A Critical Reader*. Malden, MA: Blackwood, 129–52.

Bourdieu, P. (1973) Cultural reproduction and social reproduction. In R. Brown (ed.), *Knowledge, Education, and Cultural Change*. London: Tavistock, 71–112.

Bourdieu, P. (1977) *Outline of a Theory of Practice* (R. Nice, trans.). Cambridge, UK: Cambridge University Press. (Original work published 1972)

Bourdieu, P. (1984) *Distinction: A Social Critique of the Judgement of Taste* (R. Nice, trans.). Cambridge, MA: Harvard University Press. (Original work published 1979)

Bourdieu, P. (1990) *The Logic of Practice* (R. Nice, trans.). Cambridge, UK: Polity Press. (Original work published 1980)

Bourdieu, P. (1991) *Language and Symbolic Power*. Cambridge, UK: Polity Press.

Bourdieu, P. (1998) *On Television* (P. P. Ferguson, trans.). New York: New Press. (Original work published 1996)

Bourdieu, P. (1998) *Practical Reason: On the Theory of Action*. Cambridge, UK: Polity Press. (Original work published 1994)

Bourdieu, P. and Passeron, J. (1977) *Reproduction in Education, Society, and Culture*. London: Sage.

Bourdieu, P. and Wacquant, L. J. D. (1992) *An Invitation to Reflexive Sociology*. Chicago: University of Chicago Press.

Bruce, H. and Davis, B. (2000) Slam: hip-hop meets poetry. A strategy for violence intervention. *English Journal*, 89, 119–27.

Conley, D. (1999) *Being Black, Living in the Red: Race, Wealth, and Social Policy in America*. Berkeley, CA: University of California Press.

Daspit, T. and Weaver, J. (eds) (1999) *Popular Culture and Critical Pedagogy: Reading, Constructing, Connecting*. New York: Garland.

Delpit, L. (1995) *Other People's Children: Cultural Conflict in the Classroom*. New York: New Press.

Delgado Bernal, D. (2002) Critical race theory, Latino critical theory, and critical raced-gendered epistemologies: recognizing students of color as holders and creators of knowledge. *Qualitative Inquiry*, 8, 105–26.

Dimitriadis, G. (2001) *Performing Identity/Performing Culture: Hip-hop as Pedagogy, Text, and Lived Practice*. New York: Peter Lang.

Dyson, M. (2003) *Open Mike: Reflections on Philosophy, Race, Sex, Culture, and Religion*. New York: Basic Civitas.

Fairclough, N. (2003) *Analyzing Discourse*. London: Routledge.

Fiske, J. (1979) *Reading Television*. London: Routledge.

Fiske, J. (1987) *Television Culture*. London: Methuen.

Fiske, J. (1989) *Understanding Popular Culture*. London: Routledge.

Forman, M. (2002) *The 'Hood Comes First: Race, Space, and Place in Rap and Hip-hop*. Hanover, NH: Wesleyan University Press.

Freire, P. (1970) *Pedagogy of the Oppressed*. New York: Herder and Herder.

Freire, P. and Macedo, D. (1987) *Literacy: Reading the Word and the World*. South Hadley, MA: Bergin and Garvey.

Gallego, M. A. and Hollingsworth, S. (2000) *What Counts as Literacy: Challenging the School Standard*. New York: Teachers College Press.

Gates, H. (1988) *The Signifying Monkey: A Theory of African American Literary Criticism*. New York: Oxford University Press.

Gee, J. P. (1996) *Social Linguistics and Literacies: Ideology in Discourses* (2nd edn). London: Falmer.

Gee, J. P. (2000) New people in new worlds: networks, the new capitalism and schools. In B. Cope and M. Kalantzis (eds), *Multiliteracies: Literacy Learning and the Design of Social Futures*. London: Routledge, 43–68.

Giroux, H. (1996) *Fugitive Cultures: Race, Violence and Youth*. New York: Routledge.

Gramsci, A. (1971) *Selections from Prison Notebooks*. New York: International Press.

Grenfell, M. and James, D. (1998) *Bourdieu and Education: Acts of Practical Theory*. London: Falmer Press.

Guinier, L. and Torres, G. (2002) *Miner's Canary: Enlisting Race, Resisting Power, Transforming Democracy*. Cambridge, MA: Harvard University Press.

Hacker, A. H. (1992) *Two Nations: Black and White, Separate, Hostile, Unequal*. New York: Scribners.

Hall, J. R. (1992) The capital(s) of cultures; a nonholistic approach to status situations, class, gender and ethnicity. In M. Lamont and M. Fournier (eds), *Cultivating Differences; Symbolic Boundaries and the Making of Inequality*. Chicago: University of Chicago Press.

Hull, G. (1993) Critical literacy and beyond: lessons learned from students and workers in a vocational program and on the job. *Anthropology and Education Quarterly*, 24, 308–17.

Hunt, R. (1991) Foreword. In J. M. Newman, *Interwoven Conversations: Learning and Teaching Through Critical Reflection*. Toronto: OISE Press; Portsmouth, New Hampshire: Heinemann, pp. vii–xii.

Hill, M. L. (Manuscript in preparation) Vocab: a dictionary of hip-hop slang.

Hill, M. L. (in press) Critical pedagogy comes at halftime: Nas as Black public intellectual. In M. E. Dyson and S. Daulatzai (eds), *Nas: Illmatic 10th Anniversary*. New York: Basic Civitas.

Jay-Z. (2002) A ballad for the fallen soldier. On *The Blueprint 2: The Gift and the Curse* [CD]. New York: Roc-A-Fella/Def Jam.

Jenkins, R. (1992) *Pierre Bourdieu*. New York: Routledge.

Kellner, D. (1995) *Media Culture: Cultural Studies, Identity and Politics Between the Modern and the Postmodern*. New York: Routledge.

Ladson-Billings, G. (1998) Just what is critical race theory and what's it doing in a nice field like education? *Qualitative Studies in Education*, 11, 7–24.

Mahiri, J. (1998) *Shooting for Excellence: African American Youth Culture in New Century Schools*. New York: Teachers College Press.

Massey, D. S. and Denton, N. A. (1993) *American Apartheid: Segregation and the Making of the Underclass*. Cambridge, MA: Harvard University Press.

Mitchell-Kernan, C. (1972) Signifying and marking: two Afro-American speech acts. In J. Gumperz and D. Hymes (eds), *Directions in Sociolinguistics*. New York: Blackwell, 161–79.

Morell, E. (2002) Toward a critical pedagogy of popular culture: literacy development among urban youth. *Journal of Adolescent and Adult Literacy*, 46, 72–7.

Morell, E. and Duncan-Andrade, J. M. R. (2002) Promoting academic literacy with urban youth through hip-hop culture. *English Journal*, 91(6), 88–92.

Neal, M. A. (2003) Still a riot goin' on: Fela Kuti, celebrity Gramscians, and the AIDS crisis. Retrieved January 1, 2004, from www.popmatters.com/columns/critical-noire/030226.shtml

Oliver, M. L. and Shapiro, T. (1995) *Black Wealth/White Wealth: A New Perspective on Racial Inequality*. New York: Routledge.

Orfield, G., Eaton, S. E. and Jones, E. R. (1997) *Dismantling Desegregation: The Quiet Reversal of Brown v. Board of Education*. New York: New Press.

Potter, R. (1995) *Spectacular Vernaculars: Hip-hop and the Politics of Postmodernism*. Albany: State University of New York Press.

Ramsay, R. F. (2003) Transforming the working definition of social work into the 21st century. *Research on Social Work Practice*, 13, 324–38.

Reed-Danahay, D. (2004) Tristes Paysans: Bourdieu's early ethnography in Bearn and Kabylia. *Anthropological Quarterly*, 77, (1): 87–100.

Rice, J. (2003) The 1963 hip-hop machine: hip-hop pedagogy as composition. *College Composition and Communication*, 54, 453–71.

Richardson, E. (2003) *African American Literacies*. New York: Routledge.

Roberts, H. (2000) Classification of intellectual capital. In J. E. Gröjer and H. Stolowy (eds), *Classification of Intangibles*. Jouy-En Josas, France: Groupe Hec, pp. 197–205.

Rose, T. (1994) *Black Noise: Rap Music and Black Culture in Contemporary America*. Hanover, NH: Wesleyan University Press.

Shulman, L. S. (1987) Knowledge and teaching: foundations of the new reform. *Harvard Educational Review*, 57, 1–22.

Schultz, K. (2003) *Listening: A Framework for Teaching Across Difference*. New York: Teachers College Press.

Shor, I. (1999) What is critical literacy? In I. Shore and C. Pari (eds), *Critical Literacy in Action: Writing Words, Changing Worlds*. Portsmouth, NH: Heinemann, 1–30.

Smitherman, G. (1994) *Black Talk: Words and Phrases from the Hood to the Amen Corner*. Boston: Houghton Mifflin.

Smitherman, G. (1997) The chain remain the same: communicative practices in the hip-hop nation. *Journal of Black Studies*, 28, 3–25.

Steele, C. (1997) A threat in the air: how stereotypes shape intellectual identity and performance. *American Psychologist*, 52, 613–29.

Storey, J. (2003) *Inventing Popular Culture*. Oxford, UK: Blackwell.

Street, B. (1995) *Social Literacies: Critical Approaches to Literacy in Development, Ethnography and Education*. London: Longman.

Street, B. (1993) *Cross-Cultural Approaches to Literacy*. New York: Cambridge University Press.

Szeman, I. (2002) The limits of culture: the Frankfurt School and/for cultural studies. In C. Irr and J. Nealon (ed.), *Rethinking the Frankfurt School: Alternative Legacies of Cultural Critique*. Albany: State University of New York Press, pp. 59–80.

Willis, P. (1990) *Common Culture: Symbolic Work at Play in the Everyday Cultures of the Young*. Milton Keynes: Open University Press.

Chapter 9

Critical race perspectives, Bourdieu, and language education

Rachel A. Grant and Shelley D. Wong

This chapter discusses the significance of Bourdieu's work in the teaching of English as a second language (ESL), and more generally its implications for bilingualism and literacy education. It is our view that the contributions and implications of Bourdieu's work in the teaching of ESL, World Englishes, and African-American Vernacular English (AAVE) are largely unexplored territory. Bourdieu's *stance* in posing the question, "Who has the right to speak?" enables us to understand the discursive workings of class, race, culture, and power in these fields; it enables us in the Teaching of English as a Second or Other Language/Bilingual Education (TESOL/BE) and literacy education to take a stand with students who have been systematically underrepresented in higher education. Bourdieu's *viewpoint* on the workings of the production and reproduction of legitimate language and symbolic capital is a valuable theoretical resource in the education of "other people's children" (Delpit, 1988). Bourdieu's *method* in asking the question, "Who goes to the university?" (Bourdieu and Passeron, 1977) gives us valuable tools for talking about the ways in which different groups develop the capital resources to achieve and succeed in educational systems. Our purpose here is to openly use and appropriate Bourdieu to stand with those who are the descendents of slaves, colonized and indigenous people, and the sons and daughters of workers, the working poor, and those from rural areas.

Bourdieu and Passeron's analysis of who went to the university in France has a parallel in the analysis of university students in the United States in the late 1960s who asked, "Who rules the university?" and identified themselves as "Third World students in the belly of the beast." On campuses such as the University of California, Berkeley and San Francisco State College, students went on strike for minority admissions, ethnic studies, and to demand the decolonialization of social and educational research, making the case that research should work in the interests and from the standpoints of minority communities. For those of us in language and literacy education who continue to pursue these demands, Bourdieu's stance, viewpoint and method of a sociology of education offer a grounded link to understanding political economy and history.

Womanist and feminist critiques of structural perspectives of reproduction have stressed the need to look at race, consciousness, agency, and subjectivities (Collins, 2000; Luke and Gore, 1992; Pavlenko, 2001). W. E. B. Du Bois (2003) pioneered this work in addressing the relationship between structural inequalities and consciousness by reflecting on the conditions of African-Americans 40 years after the end of slavery. In his extraordinary collection of 14 essays, *The Souls of Black Folk* (2003), his concept of *double consciousness* is an important forerunner to Bourdieu's symbolic domination and production and reproduction of legitimate language.[1] Taking up James Baldwin's question from his 1985 essay "If Black English isn't a language, then tell me, what is?" our aim here is to discuss the pedagogical implications of bilingualism and language diversity for critical multiculturalism in TESOL, bilingual, and literacy education. We want to show that critical race theories (Crenshaw et al., 1995; Tate, 1997) and the linguistic anthropological tradition of Zora Neale Hurston (Boyd, 2003), Luis Moll (Moll and Greenberg, 1990) and others complement and contribute to understanding Bourdieu's sociological method as they are grounded in historical, social, and cultural understandings of language and power, particularly in the intersections of race, class, and gender.

Bourdieu on language: against structuralism and formalism

Whose language is legitimate? Bourdieu is critical of formal approaches to language, specifically those of Comte, Saussure, and Chomsky that do not look at the resource of language in relation to capital and power. Bourdieu quotes Auguste Comte as an example of an apolitical view of language:

> Language forms a kind of wealth, which all can make use of at once without causing any diminution of the store, and which thus admits a complete community of enjoyment; for all, freely participate in the general treasure, unconsciously aid in its preservation. In describing symbolic appropriation as a sort of mystical participation, universally and uniformly accessible and therefore excluding any form of dispossession, Auguste Comte offers an exemplary expression of the illusions of linguistic communism which haunts all linguistic theory.
>
> (Bourdieu, 1994: 43)

Saussure draws on the same metaphor of linguistic treasure, in which the individual has an "inner treasure"—deposited by the practice of speech in subjects belonging to the same speech community—that is the sum of individual treasures of languages or imprints deposited in each brain (Bourdieu, 1994). According to Bourdieu, such approaches vest language either in linguistic structure and system or the psychological capacities and prepossessions of individuals. This ignores "the question of the economic and social conditions of the acquisition of the legitimate competence and of the constitution of the market in which this definition of the legitimate and the illegitimate is established and imposed" (p. 44).

Yet when we shift the study of language to the question of whose language is "official" or "legitimate" or "standard," as Bourdieu and Passeron (1977) do, issues about the hierarchical ownership and control of languages such as English are brought into play, with the hierarchical labeling and controlling of some varieties as "bad" and the speakers "lazy" or "ignorant." Turning to Chomsky, Bourdieu comments, "Chomsky has the merit of explicitly crediting the speaking subject in his universality with the perfect competence which the Saussurian tradition granted him tacitly. . . . In short, from this standpoint, Chomskyian *competence* is simply another name for Saussure's *langue*" (1994: 44).

Both Chomsky and Saussure based their linguistics on an idealized speaker/hearer. Rather than language learning as mimicry and parroting, Chomsky saw cognition as having a "distinctively rationalist flavor" (Chomsky, 1972: 171). To Chomsky a native speaker would make errors in performance because of fatigue, memory limitation, shifts of attention or interest, or other factors that are not a reflection of that person's actual competence or knowledge of what is grammatical. While Chomsky's generative critique of behaviorism showed the ambiguity and cognitive complexity involved in knowing what was "grammatical," something which could not be accounted for through mimicry and repeating, he ignored the issue of power in determining what was grammatical (Wong, 2005).

The ideal speaker–listener

Bourdieu's critique of Chomsky's competence and Saussure's *langue* is doubly significant for TESOL and bilingual education because the "ideal speaker–listener" has historically been defined as White, European, or North American, even as these linguistic communities themselves became more overtly multilingual and culturally diverse. Within the field of educational research, the educational terminology utilized continues to carry assumptions about what is "normal," excluding racial minorities and relegating them to the margins. Banks and Banks (1995) point out that educational terminology reflecting overt perspectives of deficit (terms such as "culturally deprived" and "culturally disadvantaged") have been replaced with terminology (e.g., "inner city," "urban," and "at-risk") that still reflect attitudes and assumptions that place groups in hegemonic opposition to the White standard. "At-risk," "urban," and "inner city" are racially marked terms evoking images of Black children, although in reality most children living in poverty are racially classified as White (Lee, 2003).

The racial or class composition of the ideal speaker–listener in the field of TESOL and Second Language Acquisition has historically been ignored, particularly within the United States where in the area of foreign and second language education, Chomskyian linguistics held particular dominance not only in linguistics departments but also in psychology departments and colleges of education. Indeed in TESOL, because of the behaviorism of audiolingualism that dominated foreign and second language teaching in the United States in the 1950s and 1960s, Chomsky's revolution provided the cognitive psychological foundation and dominant linguistic paradigm for communicative approaches of the 1970s to 1990s. To this day, within the United States, to base TESOL or even mainstream language and literacy preparation courses on, for instance, Hallidayan functional or critical discourse analytic models would be considered unusual or aberrant, although the landscape is changing to reflect Australian, Canadian, and UK influences.

Legitimate language

What Chomsky's rationalism ignored was that the ideal speaker–listener was a speaker of what Bourdieu called *legitimate* language. The limitation of Chomsky's formal approach to grammar, as Bourdieu pointed out, is that it ignores the question of "Whose language is legitimate?" A formal approach hides or obfuscates racial, ethnic, and class divisions, and inequalities in society that determine what is grammatical. As Bourdieu put it:

> Chomsky . . . sidesteps the question of the economic and social conditions of the acquisition of the legitimate competence and of the constitution of the market in which this definition of the legitimate and the illegitimate is established and imposed.
>
> (1991, p. 44)

From our perspective, the strength of Bourdieu in critiquing Chomsky and Comte is in piercing the metaphor of a "common" treasure and show that we (people of all classes, all regions, all ethnic groups) do not share in the same "common" treasure with respect to legitimate language. Instead we have different accents (Lippi-Greene, 1997; Matsuda, 1991), and they bear different values with respect to what is viewed as "legitimate" language (Perry and Delpit, 1998; Rickford and Rickford 2000; Wolfram et al., 1998). By making an ideal abstraction of language, Chomsky made his own competence (educated and standard) grammatical. If, instead, he had used *performance* or actual language to determine what was grammatical, then regional, class, and other variations of concern to linguists such as Gumperz (1986), Scollon and Scollon (1995), and other anthropological linguists could potentially take center stage. Of course, if we use performance instead of an idealized competence, whether linguistic variation is ignored or becomes subterfuge once again depends on *whose* language is the subject of research (Baugh, 1983; Rickford, 1999). We saw with a great deal of mainstream psycholinguistic baby-talk studies that "Motherese" was characterized by research with White, middle-class North

American mothers and babies—this contrasted sharply with Elinor Ochs' (1988) work on language acquisition in Samoan children.

A parallel to the ideal speaker–listener is the "ideal reader" in the field of literacy education, with a narrow monolingual, monocultural model of what it means to "be literate." To make this point clear, we turn to recent work by Meacham (2000). To the question, "What does it mean to be literate?" he used historical frames to detail the workings of dominant political interests in the United States and the manipulation of definitions of literacy, literacy practice and assessment, and literacy policy. Meacham contends, and we would agree, that these dominant political interests affirm and reaffirm prevailing relations of power in a desire to preserve conceptual coherence. "Cultural [and we would add linguistic] diversity is seen as marginal, and even detrimental, to effective literacy, conception and practice" (p. 181).

Throughout the history of schooling in the United States, efforts to incorporate linguistic and cultural diversity into conceptions of literacy have been viewed as chaotic and a threat to the social order (West, 1993). Indeed past and recent debates about the use of Ebonics (that is, the discussion about the implications for educating speakers of AAVE) clearly point to how perceptions of languages and cultures different from the majority can be categorized, manipulated, and even demonized. As a result, barriers to literacy have been maintained for many people of color, the poor, and females as they have been denied access to ownership of literacy. This is reflected in current policy:

> Policymakers believed that it was necessary to promote literacy practices in keeping with a *single* [italics added] cultural and linguistic identity at the expense of cultural and linguistic diversity. . . . In other words, structural *singularity* [italics added] has been the structural hallmark of dominant social visions and literacy practices.
>
> (Meacham, 2000: 182)

In order to maintain this structural singularity, literacy is conceptualized, defined, taught, and assessed through the dominant White monolingual lenses (Willis and Harris, 2000). To ensure the legality of this view, institutions within education (e.g., the National Academy of Sciences) and the literacy profession (e.g., the National Reading Panel) have narrowed definitions of literacy research so that many studies that have examined literacy within the contexts of linguistic and cultural diversity do not meet standards of the carefully crafted definitions of "scientific rigor." This has effectively excluded insightful work on literacy and diversity (Gebhard et al., 2002; Kubota, 2004).

This narrow view of the ideal learner or ideal reader reflects conventional thinking within the field of literacy education and has had differential effects on the educational experiences of language learners (Grant and Wong, 2004). Willis and Harris noted that "the current disregard for the cultural politics of literacy research, which is being used to maintain an illusion of an equal educational system, has failed to suggest the importance of creating more culturally responsive, inclusive, and transformative literacy learning and teaching spaces" (2001: 80). As a result, curriculum reform policy is shaped, teaching practices are advanced, and high-stakes testing measures are employed to sustain singular and English-only conceptions of literacy (Shohamy, 2001; Valdez-Pierce, 2003).

Who owns English?

Indeed the unquestioned universalism or "normative" perspective of Chomsky's competence and Saussure's *langue* blocks out the discussion of questions such as "Who owns English?" (or other languages of colonial expansion such as French or Spanish). Traditionally within the field of TESOL, English was "owned" by native English speakers (Braine, 1999). It was assumed that native speakers were the best language teachers and the best models. Only recently has this assumption been challenged by non-native English-speaking professionals.

Within the field of TESOL the question of who owns English, or the supremacy of British and North American varieties, has been challenged by linguist Braj Kachru and others who have questioned why the English spoken in former colonies of Britain that were populated by White settlers (e.g., the United States and Canada) are considered legitimate standard varieties, but that spoken in former British colonies that are populated by the descendents of Africans who were brought to the colonies as slaves and the indigenous people who were colonized (e.g., India, Singapore, Jamaica, Kenya, and other World English speakers) are viewed as non-standard.

Expanding circles of English

Kachru (1986) developed a model of three concentric circles to represent the varieties of English. The *Inner Circle* includes the United States, Canada, United Kingdom, Ireland, Australia, and New Zealand. The *Outer* or *Extended Circle* includes their former colonies: India, Pakistan, Singapore, Nigeria, Ghana, and so on. The *Expanding Circle* includes areas in which English is studied as a foreign language, such as China, Japan, Russia, Kuwait, Mexico, Brazil, and so on. Because of the spread of English as an international language, there are actually more English speakers in the Outer Circle and Expanding Circle than in the Inner Circle:

- Inner Circle: 400 million speakers
- Outer or Extended Circle: 500 million speakers
- Expanding Circle: 800 million speakers.

The demographic shifts above call for an expansion of the traditional canon and the development of African, African-American, World Englishes, and English curricula in the context of internationalization (Pakir, 1999).

If English is owned by the Inner Circle but spoken by the Outer or Expanding Circles, whose model should be viewed as the "standard" educational model? This debate was taken up in the 1960s as many former colonies in Africa and around the world became independent.

Appropriate models of English

Writing from the standpoint of teaching English in newly independent countries, Halliday and colleagues (1964) had come to question British Received Pronunciation as the only appropriate model for education. They argued for the use of local educated varieties as the standard. Clifford Prator vehemently disagreed with the British linguists. In "The British heresy in TESL" (1968), Prator argued against using local varieties of English, such as Indian or West African English, and that only "mother-tongue" English (British or American) should be used as a model. His stance was based on the French model of foreign language teaching in which Parisian French was unquestioned as the standard. The French government defined and set the standards for the national language, and any suggestion to allow "deviant" pronunciation would be dismissed as absurd.

Prator warned that using diverse models would lower instructional standards:

> The doctrine of establishing local models for TESL [Teaching English as a Second Language] seems to lead inevitably in practice to a deliberate lowering of instructional standards. In the minds of many students it becomes a convenient, officially sanctioned justification for avoiding the strenuous effort entailed in upgrading their own pronunciation. It weakens any sense of obligation a teacher may feel to improve his own speech and makes it impossible for him to put any real conviction into his attempts to encourage or impel his students in the same direction.
>
> (p. 474)

He has been criticized by Kachru (1978), Sandra McKay (1991), Arjama Parakrama (1995) and others for his position on limiting acceptable models for the classroom to North American and British English. Who owns English? Why is it that American English, which also is derived from the descendents of a British colony, is considered "native English" but the language of the "natives" is not?[2] Why is it that the descendants of the White settlers' variety of English is standard, and the varieties of English of the descendants of slaves, indigenous people, and plantation workers are not standard? Is there any reason to assume that a Third World learner of English is less of a person, or from a lesser culture, than a First World learner of another language?

James Baldwin, an African-American intellectual and expatriate, who for many years lived in France, so clearly grasped the implications of colonialism and the discursive workings of culture, race, and power in determining legitimate language for colonized peoples:

> People evolve a language in order to describe and thus control their circumstances, or in order not to be submerged by reality that they cannot articulate. (And if they cannot articulate it, they *are* submerged.) A Frenchman living in Paris speaks a subtly and crucially different language from that of the man living in Marseilles; neither sounds very much like a man living in Quebec; and they would all have great difficulty in apprehending what the man from Guadeloupe, Martinique, is saying, to say nothing of the man from Senegal—although the "common" language of all these areas is French. But each has paid, and is paying a different price for this "common" language, in which, as it turns out, they are not saying, and cannot be saying, the same things: They each have very different realities to articulate, or control.
>
> (Baldwin, 1985: 649–50)

Baldwin's critique of the concept of "common" language is similar to the point Bourdieu made in critiquing Comte and Chomsky. Whereas Baldwin's sympathy was with the conquered, those who had paid the price for the common language, Prator had no sympathy for the colonized who spoke an imperfect version of the colonizer's language. Prator was particularly critical of Indian English:

> After 20 years of testing the English of hundreds of incoming foreign students semester after semester at the University of California, I am firmly convinced that for the rest of the English-speaking world the most unintelligible educated variety is Indian English. The national group that profits least from the University's efforts to improve their intelligibility by classroom instruction also seems to be the Indians; *they can almost never be brought to believe that there is any reason for trying to change their pronunciation* [italics added].
>
> (1968: 473)

Prator's comments reflect limitations in his own ability to understand the implications of colonialism for English language teaching. Prator acknowledged that proposals for the acceptance of local varieties inevitably occurred in former colonies:

> In fact, such proposals seem to arise spontaneously and inevitably in every formerly colonial area where English has been the principal medium of instruction long enough for the people to begin to feel somewhat possessive about the language.
>
> (p. 460)

Prator's comment on "possessiveness" shows that he was not able to understand the implications of colonialism from the standpoint of the colonized. Why is it that White New Zealanders or Canadians or South Africans, whose accents evolved from British English, are considered "native speakers" and Blacks from the former colonies of Rhodesia (now Zimbabwe) or Trinidad are not? Why are Indian and Singapore English varieties or Native Hawaiian pidgin seen as being "incomprehensible"? TESOL scholarship on World Englishes, Black English (or AAVE), and by non-native English language professionals raises the need to address racism in language teaching. Does "native speaker" mean "White"?

Decolonializing research: views from the natives

It was not until the "natives" themselves began to write from their own perspectives that the legitimacy of varieties of English such as Black English, AAVE, or Ebonics became an issue in the public discourse (Smitherman-Donaldson and Van Dijk, 1988). While linguists such as Kachru began conceptualizing a theoretical framework for Indian English as early as 1965, organized efforts to discuss the concept of World Englishes did not occur until the convening of conferences at the East–West Culture Learning Institute in Honolulu, Hawaii and the University of Illinois at Urbana-Champaign in 1978. The study of World Englishes is still a source of struggle and contention (Kachru, 1995). With the growth of English as an international language, professionals are arguing for inclusion of diverse voices as the educated standard and critique of the native speaker as the norm (Brutt-Griffler and Samimy, 1999). Advocates for World Englishes point out that there should be many varieties of English (or French) as the educated standard.

Textbooks that employ English as an International Language (EIL) should have examples from diverse speakers. World Englishes must be incorporated into the textbooks for EIL. An English language learner from Japan should be prepared to speak to others who come from various countries within the region, rather than think of themselves as using English with only North Americans. "The assumption of native speaker authority that underlies teaching inner-circle varieties of English puts the other circles in an inferior position to the native speakers and threatens to undermine Japanese learners' agency as EIL users" (Matsuda, 2003: 722).

As Pennycook (1998) points out, "there are deep and indissoluble links between the practices, theories and contexts of ELT [English Language Teaching] and the history of colonialism" (p. 19). The struggle to decolonialize the teaching of English and the ownership of English is closely related to another dimension of power ignored by formal approaches to language, and that is Bourdieu's concept of the right to speak and to be heard.

The right to speak

Not all speaking subjects will be listened to. Associated forms of power and authority are implicit in recognizing the right to speak. However, dominant psycholinguistic models treat these communicative acts as mere intellectual operations involving, as Thompson (1991) notes, the "encoding and decoding of grammatically well-formed messages" (p. 8).

Like Habermas (1970), Bourdieu identified the problem of the right to speak through an analysis of Oxford philosopher J. L. Austin's speech acts. Austin classified speech acts, analyzing the utterances of everyday language into a very small set of functions (Hatch, 1992). Among Austin's speech acts are *performatives*, in which there is a legal change of state through the speech act; examples of this are marriage ceremonies or christenings. Austin points out, for example, that for the words "I name this ship the Queen Elizabeth" to be "felicitous," they must be spoken by an appropriate person in accordance with conventional procedures.

> The myriad of symbolic devices: the robes, the wigs, the ritual expressions and respectful references that accompany such occasions are not irrelevant distractions. They are the very mechanisms through which those who speak attest to the authority of the institution which endows them with the power to speak, an institution which is sustained in part by the reverence and solemnity which are *de rigueur* on such occasions.
>
> (Thompson, 1991: 9)

Bourdieu emphasizes that conventional procedures are "in accordance with institutional authority," in which the institution defines the conditions (that is, time, place, agent). He points out that analysis of performative utterances must be understood from the standpoint of institutions, rather than a purely "linguistic sphere":

> Austin's account of performative utterances cannot be restricted to the sphere of linguistics. The magical efficacy of these acts of institution is inseparable from the existence of an institution defining the conditions (regarding the agent, the time or place, etc.) which have to be fulfilled for the magic of words to operate. As is indicated in the examples analyzed by Austin, these "conditions of felicity" are social conditions, and the person who wishes to proceed felicitously with the christening of a ship or of a person must be entitled to do so, in the same way that to be able to give an order, one must have a recognized authority over the recipient of that order.
>
> (Bourdieu, 1994: 73)

Controversies regarding the ordination of women or gay and lesbian clergy are an example of a struggle over institutional authority over who is deemed an appropriate agent, that is, who is "authorized" to speak and be recognized as such by others.

One of the studies in TESOL that has utilized Bourdieu's "right to speak" is Bonny Norton's (1998, 2000) study of immigrant women in Canada. Norton contrasted the experiences of two immigrant women: Mai, a Vietnamese-Chinese, and Katrina, who was Polish. Racism was an issue that separated the experiences of White and non-White immigrants. Norton's study challenged the "acculturation" model (Schumann, 1986) that is prominent in second language acquisition literature (SLA) (see Brown, 1987; Ellis, 1994; Larsen-Freeman and Long, 1991; McGroarty, 1998; Spolsky, 1989). Too often in English-speaking host countries such as Canada or the United States, there is hostility toward immigrants for not speaking English and not speaking an "accent-less" English:

> Theories of acculturation in SLA do not pay sufficient attention to the inequitable relations of power that exist between second language learners and target language speakers. Despite their investment in the target language, second language learners may have little opportunity to interact with target language speakers and improve their language learning. It would be both inaccurate and irresponsible to assume, as some people do, that immigrants who have limited proficiency in the target language are necessarily "unmotivated" or "indifferent".
>
> (Norton, 1998: 17)

Norton's work is also significant because she was one of the first to name the issue of race and racism in TESOL. The SLA model which was developed in the United States was a computer sender–receiver model of communication that had no exploration of power issues between interlocutors. Psycholinguistic models of SLA likewise do not address the inequality of speakers with respect to race, ethnicity, class, and gender. That is why Bourdieu's right to speak and right to be heard is so important to us in TESOL/BE and literacy education. By saying that ESL students need the right to speak and the right to reception (to be paid attention to or listened to), Norton was broaching an entirely new issue of power. Her research, comparing different immigrant women, showed differential treatment according to whether they were White ("good" immigrants, assimilable, and like "us") or non-White ("foreigners" and unassimilable).

Norton's questioning of the right to speak also included the right to retain one's own mother tongue (1998, 2000). Again the issue of bilingualism is a question of power (Skutnabb-Kangas, 2000). Historically the indigenous people and African slaves were forbidden to speak their native languages. Patricia Hill Collins (2000) asserts in *Black Feminist Thought* that it is only when oppressed groups can frame their ideas in the language that is familiar to and comfortable for a dominant group that they will be listened to. The issue of bilingualism and language loss for those of "lesser cultures" and less powerful people is an issue of linguistic genocide when it comes to indigenous people, who have no other homeland to go to in order to find speakers of their language (Wong-Fillmore, 2000). If you do not look at the power dimensions and assume a benign equality of speakers, you will wind up blaming the victim for being "unassimilable"; it is the victim's fault for being clannish, "hanging out among themselves."

Language educators cannot take for granted that those who speak regard those who listen as worthy to be listened to, and conversely, that those who listen regard those who speak as worthy to speak (Norton, 2000). In TESOL methodology, classes typically discuss communicative competence as a goal. Norton (1998) suggests that language educators must extend the definition of "competence" to include "the right to speech" or the "power to impose reception." If we ignore the problems of racism, we will blame our students for lacking motivation for speaking their home language instead of learning English to better themselves. The hidden assumptions of English-language dominance must be challenged.

> It is crucial that we acknowledge the inequitable relations of power between target language speakers and second language learners so that we can support learners as they claim the right to speak. Right to speak refers not only to the target language but the mother tongue.
>
> (p. 16)

Validation of an immigrant's language, culture, and history not only serves to maintain the mother tongue among children but can also promote their learning of the target language, particularly with reference to the development of academic literacy (Ball and Farr, 2003).

Symbolic dominance and symbolic power

Bourdieu's notion of symbolic power is essential to the interpretation of social life. Symbolic power is best presented as the power of legitimate authority and order and is critical to Bourdieu's framework, revealing the systemic mechanisms that mask *misrecognitions* of power that sustain the current hierarchy within the social order. The focus is no longer on how individuals navigate the current social systems; instead, attention is shifted to the social world and its important hidden and intrinsic rules. This shift of attention reveals the sources of power that perpetuate systems of domination and subordination (Horvat, 2003).

Bourdieu contends that within the social order dominant groups exercise control in such a way that power and position within the order are unconsciously and uncritically accepted by subordinate groups. Through class, culture, race, and in other ways, individuals establish their membership within a group in particular ways. These *distinctions* or differences that can enhance their cultural or social enterprise allow members to align with a particular group. Bourdieu writes that "the dominant culture . . . contributes to the legitimation of the established order by establishing distinctions (hierarchies) and legitimating these distinctions" (1994: 167). All other groups or subcultures define their positions within the social order by their distal or proximal positioning to the dominant group. These arbitrary distinctions are "defined through a given relation between those who exercise power and those who submit to it" (p. 170). For Bourdieu, unconscious and uncritical acceptance by subordinate groups is the result of misrecognitions because "symbolic violence accomplishes itself through an act of cognition and of misrecognition that lies beyond—or beneath—the controls of consciousness and will" (Bourdieu and Wacquant, 1992: 171, 172).

Bourdieu points out that symbolic dominance occurs through the *habitus*, which enables us to uncover what critical race scholars are concerned about—unequal relations among classes and racial/ethnic groups, and discourse through everyday language practices at home, in the community, and at school. Recognition of the legitimacy of the official language, in Bourdieu's words, is "inscribed . . . through a long and slow process of acquisition":

> All symbolic dominance presupposes on the part of those who submit to it, a form of complicity which is neither passive submission to external constraint nor a free adherence to values. The recognition of the legitimacy of the official language has nothing in common with an explicitly professed, deliberate and revocable belief, or with an intentional act of accepting a "norm". It is inscribed, in a practical state, in dispositions which are impalpably inculcated, through a long and slow process of acquisition, by the sanctions of the linguistic market, and which are therefore adjusted, without any cynical calculation or consciously experienced constraint, to the chances of material and symbolic profit which the laws of price formation characteristic of a given market objectively offer to the holders of a given linguistic capital.
>
> (Bourdieu, 1994: 50, 51)

Critical race perspectives in educational research suggest that we be more inclusive rather than automatically adopt Eurocentric, upper-middle-class or male-as-norm answers to the "nature of the learner" (Lin et al., 2002). Yet what occurs in the production and reproduction of legitimate language is that the dominance of one group's language over others (or what is "regular," "normal," or "standard," and what is "not up to standard") occurs imperceptibly through symbolic violence.

Within the fields of second and foreign language and literacy education, distinctions of language, accent, and dialect work in complex and layered ways, creating distinctions for students who are the descendents of slaves, colonized and indigenous people, the sons and daughters of workers, the working poor, and those from rural areas, and influencing their educational experiences and their positioning within society (Kubota et al., 2003; Smitherman and Villanueva, 2003). An important tenet of symbolic power is the concept of *symbolic violence* as it relates to the dominant social force and all other subordinate or subcultures within the social order. The dominant group defines and controls the social hierarchy through social enterprise that is generated by *distinctions*. With respect to social order, individuals become members of a group by distinguishing themselves in particular ways that make apparent their membership within the group. The resulting actions generate capital or power for the group in society (Zentella, 1997).

Subordinate groups vie for positions within the social order relative to their proximity to the dominant group. One example serves to clarity this point: the inhumane and racialized system of slavery established by Europeans in America and elsewhere ensured Whites a position of power and dominance. "Racial aspects of social systems are viewed as fundamentally related to hierarchical relations among races in those systems" (Bonilla-Silva, 2001: 46). To hold their position within the social order, Whites utilized murder, beatings, mutilations, rape, and legal systems as weapons of mass violence and terror, attempting to strip Africans of humanity to ensure their co-operation and acceptance of the social order. To begin, Whites implemented a system of linguistic terrorism for newly arrived slaves by separating those Africans who shared languages or other means to communicate. Africans were forbidden the use of their cultures, their languages, and even their own names (Baugh, 1999). Often upon threat of death or beating, they could not honor or practice their religion, could not celebrate traditions and customs, and could not use their own music or dance to comfort themselves in an alien and brutal land. One can easily see that for Africans the system of slavery was intended to create unimaginable terror, a sense of displacement and subordination as the means of establishing and controlling the social order.

Over time, slave owners constructed sophisticated social hierarchies within slave communities based on, among others, skin complexion and work tasks to preserve the social order. For example, slaves who possessed a fairer complexion or those fathered by White slave owners were placed higher in the social order. Sadly, a shared bloodline with the dominant group, even one resulting from rape and brutality, could earn one a higher ranking in the social order. Using task assignment and complexion bias, the dominant group generated for slaves the distinctions that established the social enterprise of the various subgroups within the social order. Viewed within Bourdieu's framework, one can easily see how even within a system as perverse and morally bankrupt as slavery, dominant groups establish mechanisms for power and domination within social orders; indeed, systems established centuries ago that have remained firmly in place well into twenty-first century America (DeCuir and Dixson, 2004).

Cultural capital

Bourdieu's contribution to TESOL/BE and literacy education is that his framework enables us not only to have an analysis of inequality in education, but also to utilize that analysis to transform education. Through the concept of *cultural capital*, Bourdieu enables us not only to identify cultural deficit models but also to design literacy instruction that will work to address those structural inequalities that engender the symbolic domination (Collins, 1993). Bourdieu sees power as the way people have access to, use, and produce different kinds of capital within various fields. Crucially, such capital is not simply something one has, but something that has different value in different contexts, mediated by the relations of power and knowledge in different social fields.

Using examples from TESOL, Pennycook (2001) provides a helpful framework within which to view Bourdieu's three forms of capital—economic, social, and cultural. Symbolic capital, in this case knowledge of or access to English, is recognized as having value. Therefore, one with the monetary resources to pay for English classes possesses *economic capital*. Having personal access or the "right" group connections supplies the *social capital* that positions individuals closer to English or those with knowledge of English. Finally, possessing the "trinkets" or proper documents (e.g., required TOEFL scores, teaching certificates, or college degree) affirming one's knowledge of English, supplies the *cultural* or *linguistic capital* that embodies power in the world of TESOL.

Cultural capital, or ways of speaking and literacy practices that are valued in schools as discussed above, involves the habitus. The dispositions that constitute the habitus are inculcated, structured, durable, generative, and transposable. Given that cultural capital values upper-class dispositions, is it possible for education to *transform* those relations of domination?

Implications for TESOL/BE and literacy education

As I understood it, one of the many horrendous violations that slavery wrought was robbing black people of their natural language—their toolbox—and replacing it with that of the slave master. That meant those of African descent who grew up speaking English were being forced to use somebody else's toolbox. A person's natural language, I concluded, is the electricity of his or her soul, and to disconnect it is to shut them down. The more I delved into the complexities and quirks of language, the more I appreciated the power and magic of words.

(Fisher, 2001: 200)

The sociological questions of who is hired, seen as qualified to be a scholar, and admitted to the university and graduate degree programs must be accompanied by a critique of cultural and linguistic deficit models of education. Who conducts educational research? What are the power relationships? Is it research that serves working-class and minority communities? Ethnic and women's studies expand the canon. Funds of knowledge also enable us to link the various forms of capital for democratic participation and economic and community development (Wong, 2000). One implication of Bourdieu's analysis is to look at education from the standpoint of whether it provides working class and racial minority students with alternative pathways as well as academic curricula that will support their full engagement in education and society.

As educators, we can easily fall into what Luke (1995) calls the "hypodermic" trap, that is, reifying a particular methodology (e.g., genre-based approaches or even critical pedagogy such as Freirian pedagogy) and thinking that a particular approach—give them a shot of this or that—will "empower" students to succeed academically. A sociological approach such as Bourdieu's enables us to understand the profundity of Marx's Theses on Feuerbach that "the ruling ideas are the ideas of the ruling classes" in a very complex, not a mechanistic, sense. Bourdieu's approach eschews economic determinism, and yet gives primacy to economic, social, and cultural capital as material forces in the world. Bourdieu, Volosinov (1973) and critical discourse theorists such as Luke (1995), Hodge and Kress (1988), Fairclough (1989) and others enable us to see the workings of capital, power, and ideology, and to have a materialist basis to understand how to transform language, power and education. Luke calls for a:

> broadly based political project for remaking the institutional distribution of literacy and its affiliated forms of capital. . . . Criticism, contestation and difference is not a genre, not a skill, not a later developmental moment, not a reading position, it is, according to Volosinov, a constitutive and available element of every sign, utterance and text. It can be, following Bourdieu, a principal strategy in realizing, converting and contesting economic, cultural and social capital. That is, unless dominant cultures and pedagogical practices, however intentionally or unintentionally, silence it.
>
> (1996: 334)

We agree that for those who have been excluded from education historically, Bourdieu offers not only a framework to analyze the reproduction of social inequality in education but also a framework for transformation. For us in education, transformation entails continuing the struggle of the Third World Strikes of the late 1960s for a political program of ethnic studies, minority recruitment, and research that serves minority communities. As we have discussed above, applying Bourdieu's concept of legitimate language in TESOL/ BE and literacy education requires that we contest English-only standard models of monocultural, monolingual language education (Auerbach, 1995), and critique the traditional canons that exclude women and people of color. We must work as language teachers to educate the public on the myths of the superiority of one language over another (Cummins, 1986). We must dispel linguistic stereotypes (Luke, 1986). This includes making sure that the voices of language-minority speakers are included in the curriculum. It is also critical that language minorities be hired at all levels of the educational system, from elementary schools to the university; and in all capacities from teachers, counselors, and social workers to administrators, professors, educational researchers, and technical and educational support staff (Grant and Wong, 2004). Recognition of multiple languages is a struggle over language policy (Tollefson, 1995). We seek to teach English as an *additional* language, not to replace the home language or dialect with Standard English. To produce curriculum in the home languages of all the students is a struggle for linguistic equality.

The linguistic anthropological traditions of Zora Neale Hurston and Luis Moll complement and contribute to understanding Bourdieu's sociological method as a force for transformation of TESOL/BE and literacy education as they are grounded in historical, social, and cultural understandings of language and power, particularly in the intersections of race, class, and gender. The work of Moll and colleagues in the area of *funds of knowledge* is one of the most significant and promising areas for educational praxis. Moll and Greenberg (1990) and others worked with teachers in after-school programs with working-class Mexican-American children and families in Tuscan, Arizona. They conducted an anthropological investigation of the networks of knowledge that enabled Mexican-American families to support each other (including child care, fixing cars, plumbing, and carpentry). They then incorporated funds of knowledge from the families and communities into the school curriculum.

Hurston and Moll are examples, in our view, of scholarship that attempts to work within this broad political project as we see it. Why are they exemplary? Because they infuse into the academy those working class, descendents of slaves, colonized and oppressed peoples' voices, languages, ways of knowing, doing and speaking that have traditionally not been seen as legitimate or "high culture"; because they challenge, extend or transform traditional aesthetics. Hurston, a pioneer of African-American ethnography, devoted her career to preserving these voices within the Black folk heritage (1984, 1995). In her significant analytical work, *Characteristics of Negro Expression*, Hurston asserts that:

> While he lives and moves in the midst of White civilisation, everything that he touches is reinterpreted for his own use. He has modified the language, mode of food preparation, practice of medicine, and most certainly the religion of his new country.
>
> (cited in Boyd, 2003: 254)

Bourdieu's cultural capital enables us to see how the powerful structures of social inequality, mediated through the habitus, are inculcated. Incorporating funds of knowledge into the curriculum takes an additive rather than subtractive approach to the home language and culture (Osterling, 2001).

We showed that Bourdieu critiqued Comte, Saussure, and Chomsky for sidestepping the issue of whose language was legitimate. Sociolinguists and linguistic anthropologists provide a corrective to this idealized, apolitical view of language by insisting on examining actual spoken language and utterances, and by attending to dialect difference with respect to class, region, ethnicity, and various social groups. But they do not necessarily delve fully into power in that in the ethnography of speaking (Hymes, 1964), the attention to the micro-analysis of speech acts tends to cut off history and ignore the ideological component of all texts. Volosinov's (1973) contribution is that all texts are ideological; not in the sense that ideology is only a negative force of false consciousness and chains of the past, but instead his (and the Bakhtin Circle's) view of ideology is contested, a struggle of various points of view, and heteroglossic (Bakhtin, 1981).

Working for the inclusion of heteroglossic speakers of all English accents into the academy—AAVE, World English speakers from India, Singapore, Jamaica, Kenya, non-native English speakers from the outer and expanding circles, and speakers of other languages—is needed now more than ever in these times of US aggression, military domination, racism ,and chauvinism.

Disregarding international opinion, including its European allies France and Germany, the United States chose to unilaterally invade Iraq. As English language teachers we cannot ignore the fact that English is the language of the occupying armies, the "imperial troopers" (Edge, 2003). It is English that is spoken by the invading forces, it is English that is spoken by the torturers, and it is English that is spoken by those Iraqis who comprise the leadership of the "puppet" interim government. As English language teachers we must speak out. In the words of Randall Robinson (2004):

> It is memory, this unremarked deep core of *knowing* [emphasis in the original] of pain, that joins all of the subjugated, all of the long-suffering browns of the world in a society of empathy for Iraq's pain, not Saddam Hussein's, but Iraq of the greater whole, the ageless Iraq of biblical Baby-lon ... the Iraq of mundane bustling routine, the Iraq of families and hope and love and pride, and the Iraq of small everyday everywhere life, and now, because of America, the Iraq of brutal sudden death, the Iraq of a child's open, lifeless, gray, dust-laden eyes, bombed-down hospitals, markets, and schools.
>
> (p. 108)

Within the United States we face growing anti-Arab and anti-Muslim senti-ments, deepening racial polarization, dismantling of civil liberties under the guise of national security, and a growing division between the rich and the poor. To impose its will the United States has created distinctions, to use Bourdieu's term, to set in place mechanisms that concentrate wealth and power in the hands of the elite and corporate interests. We in TESOL/BE and literacy education must support and build political movements for greater equality. The job at hand requires bold steps and a process of popular mobilization and activism. What is *essential* in our view—and if we are labeled "essentialist," so be it—is the inclusion of the multiple accented voices of racial minorities, descendents of slaves, colonized and indigenous peoples. Oppressed communities must themselves participate in their own liberation, and in the process of a social and political struggle. Participation of their voices infuses life into any political program, without which there is no chance of advancing the struggle.

Notes

1   See W. E. B. Du Bois's allegorical fable of a young man from the Jim Crow South who is educated in the North and returns to the South to teach, only to find that his Northern-educated way of speaking and behaving has "ruined him" (according to the White authorities) and estranged him from the African-American community.
2   Prator acknowledged that the area where second language varieties of English would be needed would be at the lexical rather than the phonological level: "New words are certainly needed to identity things and processes for which there is no name in British or American society."

References

Auerbach, E. (1995) The politics of the ESL classroom: issues of power in pedagogical choices. In J. W. Tollefson (ed.), *Power and Inequality in Language Education*. Cambridge, UK: Cambridge University Press, 9–33.
Bakhtin, M. M. (1981) *The Dialogic Imagination*. Austin, TX: University of Texas Press.
Baldwin, J. (1985) If Black English isn't a language, then tell me, what is? In *The Price of the Ticket: Collected Nonfiction 1948–1985*. New York: St Martin's Press, 649–52. (Reprinted from *The New York Times*, 1979, July 29)
Ball, A. and Farr, M. (2003) Language varieties, culture, and teaching the English language arts. In J. Flood, D. Lapp, J. R. Squire and J. M. Jensen (eds), *Handbook of Research of Teaching English Language Arts*. Mahwah, NJ: Lawrence Erlbaum Associates, 435–45.
Banks, J. and Banks, C. (eds) (1995) *Handbook of Research on Multicultural Education*. New York: Macmillan.
Baugh, J. (1983) *Black Street Speech: Its History, Structure, and Survival*. Austin, TX: University of Texas Press.
Baugh, J. (1999) *Out of the Mouths of Slaves: African-American Language and Educational Malpractice*. Austin, TX: University of Texas Press.
Bonilla-Silva, E. (2001) *White Supremacy and Racism*. London: Lynne Rienner.
Bourdieu P. (1991) *Language and Symbolic Power*. Trans. G. Raymond and M. Adamson. Cambridge MA: Harvard University Press.
Bourdieu, P. (1994) *Language and Symbolic Power*. Cambridge, MA: Harvard University Press.
Bourdieu, P. and Passeron, J. (1977) *Reproduction in Education, Society and Culture*. London: Sage.
Bourdieu, P. and Wacquant, L. J. D. (1992) *An Invitation to Reflexive Sociology*. Chicago: University of Chicago Press.

Boyd, V. (2003) *Wrapped in Rainbows: The Life of Zora Neale Hurston*. New York: Scribner.

Braine, G. (ed.) (1999) *Non-Native Educators in English Language Teaching*. Mahwah, NJ: Lawrence Erlbaum Associates.

Brown, H. D. (1987) *Principles of Language Learning and Teaching*. Englewood Cliffs, NJ: Prentice Hall.

Brutt-Griffler, J. and Samimy, K. (1999) Revisiting the colonial in the postcolonial: critical praxis for nonnative English-speaking teachers in a TESOL program. *TESOL Quarterly*, 33, 13–32.

Chomsky, N. (1972) *Language and Mind*. New York: Harcourt Brace Jovanovich.

Collins, J. (1993) Determination and contradiction: an appreciation and critique of the work of Pierre Bourdieu on language and education. In C. Calhoun, E. LiPuma, and M. Postone (eds), *Bourdieu: Critical Perspectives*. Chicago: University of Chicago Press, 116–38.

Collins, P. H. (2000) *Black Feminist Thought: Knowledge, Consciousness, and the Politics of Empowerment* (2nd edn). New York: Routledge.

Crenshaw, K. W., Gotanda, N., Peller, G. and Thomas, K. (1995) *Critical Race Theory: Key Writings that Form the Movement*. New York: New Press.

Cummins, J. (1986) Empowering minority students: a framework for intervention. *Harvard Educational Review*, 56, 13–36.

DeCuir, J. T. and Dixson, A. D. (2004) So when it comes out, they aren't that surprised that it is there: using critical race theory as a tool of analysis of race and racism in education. *Educational Researcher*, 33, 26–31.

Delpit, L. (1988) The silenced dialogue: power and pedagogy in educating other people's children. *Harvard Educational Review*, 58, 280–98.

Du Bois, W. E. B. (2003) *The Souls of Black Folk*. New York: Modern Library.

Edge, J. (2003) Imperial troopers and servants of the Lord: a vision of TESOL for the twenty-first century. *TESOL Quarterly*, 37, 701–9.

Ellis, R. (1994) *The Study of Second Language Acquisition*. Oxford, UK: Oxford University Press.

Fairclough, N. (1989) *Language and Power*. London: Longman.

Fisher, A. Q. (2001) *Finding Fish: A Memoir*. New York: Harper Collins.

Gebhard, M., Austin, T., Nieto, S. and Willett, J. (2002) "You can't step on someone else's words": preparing all teachers to teach language minority students. In Z. Beykont (ed.), *The Power of Culture: Teaching Across Language Difference*. Cambridge, MA: Harvard Education, 219–44.

Grant, R. A. and Wong, S. D. (2004) Forging multilingual communities: school-based strategies. *Multicultural Perspectives*, 6, 17–23.

Gumperz, J. J. (1986) Interactional social linguistics in the study of schooling. In J. Cook-Gumperz (ed.), *The Social Construction of Literacy*. Cambridge, UK: Cambridge University Press, 45–68.

Habermas, J. (1970) Toward a theory of communicative competence. *Inquiry*, 13, 360–75.

Halliday, M. A. K, McIntosh, A. and Strevens, P. (1964) *The Linguistic Sciences and Language, Class and Power in Language Teaching*. London: Longman.

Hatch, E. M. (1992) *Discourse and Language Education*. Cambridge, UK: Cambridge University Press.

Hodge, R. and Kress, G. (1988) *Social Semiotics*. Ithaca, NY: Cornell University Press.

Horvat, E. M. (2003) The interactive effects of race and class in educational research:

theoretical insights from the work of Pierre Bourdieu. *Urban Education Journal*, *2*(1), 1–25. Retrieved October 8, 2005 from www.urbanedjournal.org/articles/article0009

Hurston, Z. N. (1995) *Hurston: Folklore, Memoirs, and Other Writings*. Washington, DC: Library of America.

Hurston, Z. N. (1984) *Dust Tracks on a Road* (2nd edn). Urbana: University of Illinois Press.

Hymes, D. (ed.) (1964) *Language in Culture and Society*. New York: Harper and Row.

Kachru, B. B. (1978) Models of English for the third world: white man's linguistic burden or language pragmatics? *TESOL Quarterly*, 10, 221–39.

Kachru, B. B. (1986) The power and politics of English. *World Englishes*, 5(1–3), 124–40.

Kachru, B. B. (1995) World Englishes approaches, issues, and resources. In H. D. Brown (ed.), *Reading on Second Language Acquisitions*. Upper Saddle River, NJ: Prentice Hall, 229–61.

Kubota, R. (2004) The politics of cultural difference in second language education. *Critical Inquiry in Language Studies*, 1, 21–39.

Kubota, R., Austin, T. and Saito-Abbott, Y. (2003) Diversity and inclusion of socio-political issues in foreign language classrooms: an exploratory survey. *Foreign Language Annals*, 36(1), 12–24.

Larsen-Freeman, D. and Long, M. (1991) *An Introduction to Second Language Acquisitions Research*. New York: Longman.

Lee, C. (2003) Why we need to re-think race and ethnicity in educational research. *Educational Researcher*, 32, 3–5.

Lin, A. M. Y., Wang, W., Akamatsu, A. and Riazi, M. (2002) Appropriating English, expanding identities, and re-visioning the field: from TESOL to teaching English for globalized communication (TEGCOM). *Journal of Language, Identity and Education*, 1, 295–316.

Lippi-Greene, R. (1997) *English with an Accent: Language, Ideology, and Discrimination in the United States*. London: Routledge.

Luke, A. (1986) Linguistic stereotypes, the divergent speaker and the teaching of literacy. *Journal of Curriculum Studies*, 18, 397–409.

Luke, A. (1995) Text and discourse in education: an introduction to critical discourse analysis. *Review of Research in Education*, 21, 3–48.

Luke, A. (1996) Genres of power? Literacy education and the production of capital. In R. Hasan and G. Williams (eds), *Literacy in Society*. London: Longman, 308–38.

Luke, C. and Gore, J. (1992) *Feminisms and Critical Pedagogy*. New York: Routledge.

Matsuda, A. (2003) Incorporating World Englishes into teaching as international language. *TESOL Quarterly*, 37, 719–29.

Matsuda, M. (1991) Voices of America: accent, antidiscrimination law, and a jurisprudence for the last reconstruction. *Yale Law Journal*, 100, 1329–407.

McGroarty, M. (1998) Second language acquisition theory relevant to language minorities: Cummins, Krashen, and Schumann. In S. McKay and S.-L. Wong (eds), *Language Diversity: Problem or Resource*. Cambridge, MA: Newbury House, 295–337.

McKay, S. L. (1991) Variation in English: what role for education? In M. L. Tickoo (ed.), *Languages and Standards: Issues, Attitudes, Case Studies*. Singapore: SEAMEO Regional Language Centre, 42–50.

Meacham, S. (2000) Literacy at the crossroads: movement, connection, and communication within the research literature on literacy and cultural diversity. In W. G.

Secada (ed.), *Review of Research in Education*. Washington, DC: American Education Research Association, vol. 25, 181–208.

Moll, L. and Greenberg, J. (1990) Creating zones of possibilities: combining social contexts for instruction. In L. Moll (ed.), *Vygotsky and Education: Instructional Implications and Applications of Sociohistorical Psychology*. Cambridge, UK: Cambridge University Press, 319–48.

Norton, B. (1998) Rethinking acculturation in second language acquisition. *Prospect: An Australian Journal of TESOL*, 13(2), 4–19.

Norton, B. (2000) *Identity and Language Learning: Gender, Ethnicity, and Educational Change*. Harlow, UK: Pearson Education.

Ochs, E. (1988) *Culture and Language Development: Language Acquisition and Language Socialization in a Samoan Village*. Cambridge, UK: Cambridge University Press.

Osterling, J. P. (2001) Making the sleeping giant: engaging and capitalizing on the sociocultural strengths the Latino community. *The Bilingual Research Journal*, 25(1–2), 59–89.

Pakir, A. (1999) Connecting with English in the context of internationalization, *TESOL Quarterly*, 33, 103–13.

Parakrama, A. (1995) *De-hegemonizing Language Standards: Learning from "Post" Colonial Englishes about "English"*. New York: St Martin's Press.

Pavlenko, A. (2001) *Multilingualism, Second Language Learning, and Gender*. Berlin, Germany: Mouton de Gruyter.

Pennycook, A. (1998) *English and the Discourses of Colonialism*. London: Routledge.

Pennycook, A. (2001) *Critical Applied Linguistics: A Critical Introduction*. Mahwah, NJ: Lawrence Erlbaum Associates.

Perry T. and Delpit, L. (eds) (1998) *The Real Ebonics Debate: Power, Language, and the Education of African-American Children*. Boston: Beacon Press.

Prator, C. (1968) The British heresy in TESL. In J. Fishman, C. Ferguson, and J. Das Gupta (eds), *Language Problems in Developing Nations*. New York: John Wiley, 459–76.

Rickford, J. R. (1999) *African-American Vernacular English*. Oxford, UK: Blackwell.

Rickford, J. R. and Rickford, R. J. (2000) *Spoken Soul: The Story of Black English*. New York: John Wiley.

Robeson, P. (1971) *Here I Stand: 1898–1976*. Boston: Beacon Press.

Robinson, R. (2004) *Quitting America: The Departure of a Black Man from his Native Land*. New York: Dutton.

Schumann, J. (1986) Research on the acculturation model for second language acquisition. *Journal of Multilingual and Multicultural Development*, 7, 379–92.

Scollon, R. and Scollon, S. W. (1995) *Intercultural Communication*. Oxford, UK: Blackwell.

Shohamy, E. (2001) *The Power of Tests: A Critical Perspective on the Uses of Language Tests*. Harlow, UK: Longman.

Smitherman-Donaldson, G. and Van Dijk, T. A. (1988) *Discourse and Discrimination*. Detroit, MI: Wayne State University Press.

Smitherman, G. and Villanueva, V. (eds) (2003) *Language Diversity in the Classroom: From Intention to Practice*. Carbondale: Southern Illinois University Press.

Spolsky, B. (1989) *Conditions for Second Language Learning*. Oxford, UK: Oxford University Press.

Skutnabb-Kangas, T. (2000) *Linguistic Genocide in Education or Worldwide Diversity and Human Rights?* Mahwah, NJ: Lawrence Erlbaum Associates.

Tate, W. F. (1997) Critical race theory: history, theory, and implications. In M. W. Apple (ed.), *Review of Research in Education*. Washington, DC: American Education Research Association, vol. 22, 191–243.

Thompson, J. (1991) Editor's introduction. In J. B. Thompson (ed.), *Language and Symbolic Power Pierre Bourdieu*. Cambridge, MA: Harvard University Press, 1–32.

Tillman, L. C. (2002) Culturally sensitive approaches: an African-American perspective. *Educational Researcher*, 31, 3–12.

Tollefson, J. W. (ed.) (1995) *Power and Inequality in Language Education*. Cambridge, UK: Cambridge University Press.

Valdez-Pierce, L. (2003) *Assessing English Language Learners*. Washington, DC: National Education Association.

Volosinov, V. N. (1973) *Marxism and the Philosophy of Language* (L. Matejka and I. R. Titunik, trans.) Cambridge, MA: Harvard University Press.

West, C. (1993) The cultural politics of difference. In C. McCarthy and W. Crichlow (eds), *Race Identity and Representation in Education*. New York: Routledge, 11–23.

Willis, A. I. and Harris, V. J. (2000) Political acts: literacy learning and teaching. *Reading Research Quarterly*, 35, 72–88.

Wolfram, W., Adger, C. and Christian, D. (1998) *Dialects in Schools and Communities*. Mahwah, NJ: Lawrence Erlbaum Associates.

Wong, S. (2000) Transforming the politics of schooling in the U.S.: a model for successful academic achievement for language minority students. In J. K. Hall and W. Eggington (eds), *The Sociopolitics of English Language Teaching*. Clevedon, UK: Multilingual Matters, 117–39.

Wong, S. (2005) *Dialogic Approaches to TESOL: Where the Ginkgo Tree Grows*. Mahwah, NJ: Lawrence Erlbaum Associates.

Wong-Fillmore, L. (2000) Loss of family languages: should educators be concerned? *Theory into Practice*, 39, 203–10.

Zentella, A. C. (1997) *Growing up Bilingual*. Oxford, UK: Blackwell.

Part III

Habitus and other

Chapter 10

Tracing habitus in texts

Narratives of loss, displacement and migration in homes

Kate Pahl

Ethnographers always have trouble leaving the field. In the case of this ethnographic research study on children's meaning-making in the home, it was particularly hard. I had visited three families in their homes in an inner city area of London for over three years and shared their experiences. In some cases, children had experienced exclusion; in others, schools had been labeled as failing. All three families presented me with a complex mesh of identity and practice, bringing to the research data set migratory narratives of loss and displacement.

One June evening in 2004, five years after I began visiting, I went to Elif's home to find out what she wanted as a leaving present. Elif had been married at 14 and transported to England from her home village in Turkey. On her kitchen wall was hung a detailed map of Turkey where we both traced the outline of her home village and where she would take me if I visited her in Turkey. I asked her what she wanted as a present, to acknowledge her role in the research and its completion. Her face lit up. "A map of the world," she said. "Then I could see Turkey *and* England."

Introduction

This chapter opens up a theoretical space which argues that it is possible to trace habitus in children's texts made at home. Elif's map of the world, her acquired identity in practice, moving from Turkey to England, could be discerned sedimented within her son Fatih's outlines of maps made on the kitchen table. Habitus, as a system of acquired dispositions and structuring structures, comes to the fore as a theoretical tool for analyzing these narratives as expressed within texts. I provide a suggestive reading of Bourdieu's concept of habitus that enabled me to examine how children's texts were constructed in the home in relation to social practice and cultural identity.

Bourdieu's theoretical apparatus offers a lens for looking at social practice. As a theorist of literacy practices, I drew on the New Literacy Studies and, in particular, the insight from Street (1993) that literacy practices are ideological and culturally situated. Bourdieu's theoretical apparatus combines an ethnographic eye with a focus on social practice. The Kabyle House texts are examples of ethnographic fieldwork which then became the source of theoretical insights linking the person inside the space together with the space (Bourdieu, 1977).

I came to Bourdieu as a theorist of text making within homes. I needed to connect the settled dispositions of the everyday with the textual representations I found within the home. I needed a theorist who looked at social practice, but one which connected the agency of the text-maker with the social practices that lie beyond individual agency and are built up over time. Bourdieu's notion of habitus does exactly that, connecting the agent within a space with the practices that shape that agent (Bourdieu, 1990). By focusing on texts, and their relation to social practice, I could consider what the concept of habitus brought to the study of literacy practices.

Bourdieu's theoretical apparatus, however, needed updating in the context of increasing economic migration and social change. In order to look at shifts across diasporas, I found that the notion of *improvisation* on the habitus helped me focus on moments where the habitus was transformed through shifts in global migratory patterns. As Appadurai (1996) noted, "habitus now has to be painstakingly reinforced in the face of life-worlds that are frequently in flux" (p. 56). This focus on the improvised habitus in texts can be seen in the following instances.

Here, I will be looking at particular examples of children's text-making in which I claim that the habitus, the dispositions of the household, can be uncovered and traced back to wider structural forces. By tracing the habitus into the dispositions of the household, to the "space of play," the field where habitus is played out, narratives of migration, loss and displacement can be uncovered (Wacquant, 1992: 19). I argue that these narratives offer insights which can aid "schooled" pedagogy. Thus the method of tracing back the habitus opens out a theoretical space whereby cultural identity as embodied habitus is linked, in this case, to the field of global migratory patterns.

The study was an ethnographic study of children's communicative practices in the home. Literacy practices in homes have been the focus of a number of research studies (Barton and Hamilton, 1998; Heath, 1983), particularly in the context of the New Literacy Studies (Street, 1993). This study set out to explore literacy practices in homes in the context of new theories of multimo-dality, drawing particularly on Kress (1997). By focusing on literacy as a com-municative practice, the focus was widened to include multimodal text making in the home.

Three homes were selected for the study. The selection criteria included a focus on boys aged five to six and a disjuncture between home and school. The sites were selected in relation to an initial interest in boys and exclusion. Through networks within family literacy in two North London boroughs, Hackney and Islington, three families were recruited. Each family brought to the research complex identity narratives. As is common in North London, the area selected for the research contained a mix of Turkish, Indian subcontinent, Irish and Afro-Caribbean families. The families consisted of:

- A Turkish heritage family—Mother, Elif, and son, Fatih, 5.
- An Irish/Caribbean heritage family—Mother, Mary, and son, Edward, 5.
- A Sikh heritage family—Mother, Parmjit, and son, Sam, 6.

Two of the parents worked in education: one as a part-time teacher, the other as a learning support assistant training to be a teacher. The third parent attended English classes at her local college. At various points in the research, the parents were single parents. They lived in a densely populated urban area of North London, all in local authority public housing.

Each family exemplified the complexity of the global but also the specificity of the local (Luke and Luke, 2000). Elif, for example, was brought to England as a child bride, part of the continuing migration of Turkish rural families to find a better life in North London. She originally settled in an identifiably Turkish part of North London, but after separating from her husband, was re-housed in a multi-ethnic area of North London. Her original district was where I myself lived, an area of Hackney called Stoke Newington.

Mary moved to Stoke Newington from India where she was born. She subsequently moved to an area near where Elif lived. Her grandfather had moved to India as an Irish migrant worker to help build the Indian railways. In the post-colonial landscape, Mary was neither from London nor India, but said of herself:

> It's a strange story. My father and mother were born in India but their parents, like my grandfather from my dad's side of the family, came from Warwickshire . . . and um I think my dad's great-grandmother-in-law may have been from the West Indies. And my mums . . . both my mum and dad's grandmother and grandfather from both sides are from Ireland, so we've not found a trace of India. It's just that the two generations were born in India.
>
> (Transcript, January 2001)

Mary's description of herself reflects movements across diasporas. These, in turn, inform her habitus, as she delineates the past and then reflects on her identity in relation to these movements. This reflects a disjuncture between her original identity and her burgeoning, late-twentieth century identity in practice in a post-colonial era.

My relationship to the participants began in the context of my role as a family literacy tutor. I met Elif while teaching in the school her son, Fatih, intermittently attended. I asked for more informants for the study, and Mary, who attended a family literacy class in a school close to Fatih's, was interested in being part of the study. Finally, Parmjit was recruited with the help of a local teacher, who thought she would like to take part. Parmjit herself was a teacher.

I visited the homes for over two years, and gradually amassed a data set which led to a consideration of how practices seeped into texts. I made sense of the data by considering ways in which texts were linked to practices, following the relationship between field notes, transcripts and texts. Longitudinal work and the focus on an ethnographic perspective (Green and Bloome, 1996) enabled me to shade in details of the habitus, coming to the data with layered under-standings. After nearly three years, I stopped data collecting but continued to visit the families. I was both friend and ally, and supported them in negotiating the educational environments both adults and children found themselves in.

Data analysis and interpretation

Data was selected as a *telling case* of the relationship between texts and practices in homes (Mitchell, 1984). I also looked for moments in the data when a "gap" between two worlds or a "rich point" opened out, and then considered how the account could be traced back and my understanding deepened (Agar, 1996). The concept of the *case* was subject to consideration; for example, cross-site cases of children's text-making were considered as one case (Ragin and Becker, 1992). This enabled me to conduct cross-site research and to look at texts across sites. Interviews with respondents, parents, and children were coded by theme, and patterns were picked up which related to text-making over time. I looked for repeating patterns and, using Hymes' notion of narrative as an iterative form, considered narratives as they came up again and again within the data (Hymes, 1996).

The interpretative framework included a focus on household practices, and

Table 10.1 The data set

Family 1 (Edward, 5, and Mary, his mother)	Family 2 (Fatih, 5, and Elif, his mother)	Family 3 (Sam, 6, and Parmjit, his mother)
86 drawings collected, produced at home	207 drawings collected, produced at home	25 texts collected, produced at home
21 field visits, over 2 years	30 field visits, over 2 years	29 field visits
4 taped conversations with the child	2 taped conversations with the child	6 taped conversations
1 ethnographic interview with his mother	1 ethnographic interview with his mother	2 ethnographic interviews with his mother
15 photos taken by Mary, 15 by Edward	17 photos taken by Fatih, 18 by researcher	34 photos taken by Sam, 76 by researcher
2 drawings collected from play centre, 6 texts from school	8 texts collected from Fatih's classroom	1 observation of text making at school
1 field visit to Edward's play centre, 2 to his school	10 field visits to Fatih's classroom	4 field visits to Sam's school

the concept of *habitus* emerged from repeated coding of similar practices over time. In looking at the data, questions of identity and practices worked together to create the concept of identity in practice. Bourdieu's theory of habitus, together with Holland's work on identity and agency, developed a theoretical framework in which to set the data (Bourdieu, 1990; Holland et al., 2001). In addition, the data analysis drew on ethnographies of literacy practices as a context for the data analysis and to look at communicative practices in the home (Heath, 1983).

Attention was paid to my role as researcher in eliciting and framing data. Much of my role in the homes was as a witness to text-making and as a prompter for narrative and drawing. This eliciting role was less evident in Year 2 of the research. The data described below comes from both Years 1 and 2 of the data collection, and from two out of the three families. Checking visits enabled interpretations to be made which were more settled.

Habitus in texts

This chapter argues that habitus has a value in that it offers the opportunity of looking at the relationship between identity, texts and practices. I argue that habitus is both "heuristic and explanatory" (Bourdieu and Wacquant, 1992: 131) when applied to the relationship between texts and practices in the home. Habitus can be used to trace ways of being and doing. These "ways of being" settle into texts, as traces of social practice, and are linked to wider migratory patterns.

I argue that habitus has a value in that it links tiny moments of, for example, children's text-making, to the field of economic migration. By doing a detailed ethnography of one household, over time, the habitus of the household, its connections to wider social forces, and its relation to economic migration can be uncovered. Habitus both generates and is informed by social practices. These practices can be observed instantiated within texts.

The habitus concept is complex: poised between structure and agency, it offers, I argue, an account of the relationship between the person making, acting, narrating, and the place within which these things are enacted. It describes both spatiality and, through the concept of improvisation, it offers the possibility of change within a space. It is subject to experience and change. In his discussions with Wacquant, Bourdieu argued of habitus that, "It is durable but not eternal!" (Bourdieu and Wacquant, 1992: 133). Bourdieu's concept of habitus encompassed both the social fabric of things and the agent within the social fabric. It allowed and analyzed the way in which everyday life is taken for granted within practice.

Many theorists have seen Bourdieu's concept of habitus as theoretically generative. For example, Nash (1999), in an illuminating account of habitus, argued that habitus, and Bourdieu's concept of historically situated habitus, "points to the need for historically informed ethnographic studies" (p. 179).

Jenkins (1992) was more critical of Bourdieu's determinism and argued that Bourdieu continued to reside within the fixity of structuralism, and did not open his work out into a more fluid account of structure and agency. In the Kabyle House texts, Bourdieu's ethnographic voice describes a static oppositional world of inside/outside, resting on a vision of the world which seemed to have a deterministic overlay, describing habitus in terms of "generative structures" (Bourdieu, 1977). Bourdieu's concept of habitus from these early anthropological accounts based on the Kabyle House ethnography, outlined habitus in relation to existing, pre-determined structures, and was critiqued as being heavily structuralist (Bourdieu, 1977; Jenkins, 1992).

I focused on the concept of *improvisation* within Bourdieu's concept of habitus. The concept of "regulated improvisations" (Bourdieu, 1977: 78) suggests that habitus can be transformed or modified. As a "system of open dispositions" (Bourdieu and Wacquant, 1992: 133), habitus could be open to improvisation and change. By anticipating his improvisatory aspect, Bourdieu allowed for its modification. I argue that improvised habitus can be traced within texts. To do this, I draw on a tradition, coming from Williams (1958), which sees texts as informed by the cultural specifics of space. The relationship between Bourdieu and Williams hinged on their shared focus on a materialist theory of culture and of a cultural practice (Bourdieu and Wacquant, 1992: 80, note 24). Williams' focus was on cultural practices (Williams, 1958, 1961, 1973). His project was on relating the cultural practices of the ordinary and everyday to more public and settled cultural representations, which he saw as linked through what he termed "structure of feeling" (Williams, 1958, 1989). By linking ordinary practice with cultural production, Williams was giving voice to the idea of cultural practices within texts and their connection to life, and its felt experiences.

This focus on the ordinariness of cultural practice was shared by de Certeau who in *The Practice of Everyday Life* (1984) brought his attention to bear on popular culture and the ordinary. De Certeau's focus on everyday life and its culture informed my reading of textual practices within homes. His reading of the habitus concept in relation to his interest in cultural practice was teasing and reflective. De Certeau described the concept of habitus as a *heuristic*, as a point of departure and reflection. De Certeau was reading habitus metaphorically; he was working within the concept as a literary reader. It provided a place to construct theory, as de Certeau says, "It is indeed the dwelling, as a silent and determining memory, which is hidden in the theory under the metaphor of the habitus" (p. 58). His point was that habitus was a metaphoric chimera, which nevertheless was generative of research.

In Bourdieu's ethnography, habitus is a spatially focused term. The home becomes the habitus, the material the Kabyle House child has to learn. Habitus is learned through space and through the displacements of space; it is embodied and can be discerned in the field, which, says Wacquant (1992), acts as a "space of play." De Certeau's illuminating reading of Bourdieu focused on both the reading of habitus and the possibilities of the term, as a way of thinking, a heuristic tool. By focusing on the reading of Bourdieu, de Certeau comes to the space of habitus as a fresh entrant. Like Williams, he offers his account in the tradition of cultural studies, and it is in this interdisciplinary space that I offer my account.

Practical criticism offers a way in to fresh textual readings, from the Leavisite tradition. Here, I argue that, from a close reading of a text, the habitus can be uncovered. Bourdieu similarly described the way in which a minor event, the trying on of a stocking, triggers "resonances and echoes":

> I could mention the chapter of *Mimesis* entitled, "The Brown Stocking" in which Eric Auerbach (1953) evokes a passage of Virginia Woolf's *To the Lighthouse*, and the representations or, better, the repercussions that a minor external event triggers in Mrs Ramsay's consciousness. This event, trying on a stocking, is but a point of departure which, though it is not wholly fortuitous, takes value only through the indirect reactions it sets off. One sees well, in this case, that knowledge of stimuli does not enable us to understand much of the resonances and echoes they elicit unless one has some of the idea of the habitus that selects and amplifies them with the whole history with which it is itself pregnant.
>
> (Bourdieu and Wacquant, 1992: 124)

Bourdieu's reading of the incident in *To the Lighthouse* from *Mimesis* triggers off a description of how it is only possible to understand "resonances and echoes" in the context of "the habitus that selects and amplified them." This is suggestive reading, richly resonant of the way minor events can be pregnant with "history forgotten" (Bourdieu, 1990). Like de Certeau, Bourdieu is acting as a reader, and working with the notion of habitus as a trigger, a point of departure.

Bourdieu's theory of habitus can be applied to the New Literacy Studies, as a way of considering the space of literacy practices (Bartlett and Holland, 2002). In their analysis, Bartlett and Holland described how the modification of habitus through narratives and other artifacts of identity could be a fruitful research task. They used the habitus concept as a way of describing identity in practice within wider social forces. These readings of habitus as being a way of analyzing identity in practice, in the context of the New Literacy Studies, were helpful for my theoretical framework. In order to describe the way practices were instantiated within texts, I developed the concept of *sedimenting* to describe the way practices could be glimpsed and caught within texts. This concept is explored in the heuristic figure (Figure 10.3) at the end of this chapter, which describes how practices, instantiated within texts, enable texts to be read as traces of habitus.

Habitus cannot, Wacquant argued, be divorced from *field*. In this chapter, "field" is constructed in relation to different physical spaces—Turkey, India, Saudi Arabia, England—subject to pressures of economic migration. Bourdieu argued that "to think in terms of field is to think relationally" (Bourdieu and Wacquant, 1992: 96). Field becomes the site for struggle, and the interaction between habitus and field a way to describe the physical dislocations created through economic imperatives. I also considered field in relation to schooling. In the case of Fatih (below), I found that the habitus of the household did not operate effectively in relation to the field of schooling. Mapping the different fields within a household created a sense of the difficulties and displacement different fields created for different households.

Case study 1: the prayer bead map

Elif and her two sons, Hanif, nine, and Fatih, five, were a Turkish household. The household was situated in a new block of flats, overlooking a busy road, in an area of North London characterized by a number of different ethnic communities, and a high density of housing and shops. Elif was from a small village in central Turkey and was a devout Muslim. She wore a headscarf and dressed simply. Her home included a few images of mosques and Islamic inscriptions on the walls. In the kitchen was the Islamic calendar, with praying times printed out. There was a large television which was usually tuned to a Turkish channel. The boys, Hanif and Fatih, were often found sitting on the floor of the living room watching television or playing PlayStation. Fatih made paper models of flags, birds and boats, and often drew images of characters from children's popular culture, including Pokemon and Super Mario. Here, the habitus takes on the quality, as noted in Appadurai (1996), of improvisation. From Turkey to London, the ways of being, doing and living followed, in some cases, patterns from central Turkey. However, interlaced with this habitus were images, taken with Fatih's home video or recorded by me in field notes, of new practices such as the two boys trading Pokemon cards, and Elif surfing the internet or using chat rooms.

The data contained many references to migration. Elif had come from a village near Aksaray in Central Turkey, about three hours by coach from Ankara. The family supported the Turkish football team Galiteceri. In the summer months, Elif, Hanif and Fatih visited Turkey. Elif used Turkish textbooks to help Fatih learn to read in Turkish. These selections from field notes provided the context for my discussion of Fatih's texts and enabled me to build up the habitus.

> We talked about her visit to Turkey—two months. She is very excited about going back to see her parents—she said she would take a lot of pictures.
>
> (Field notes, May 7, 2000)

Elif has 2 sisters both in Turkey, 4 brothers, 1 in Turkey, 1 in Saudi
Arabia and 2 in England.

(Field notes, June 4, 2000)

Through numerous discussions and repeated visits, I picked up a sense of
the family's habitus, the way in which practices were generated and improvised
upon, in relation to travel to and emigration from Turkey. Every summer, if she
could afford it, Elif visited her home village in Turkey.

[to get there involved] flying for 3 and a half hours to Istanbul and then
the coach. "I like the coach," said Elif. Then a bus journey to her parent's
farmhouse. They have cows, some chickens and a dog [in the village].

(Field notes, February 28, 2000)

About halfway through the two-year study, I interviewed Elif. This was a
wide-ranging ethnographic interview exploring Elif's own schooling, her son
Fatih's schooling, and Fatih's models and drawing. She was sad because Fatih's
school progression was unsatisfactory. Fatih was excluded from school half of
the day for the entire time of the ethnography. In order to explore this further, I
asked Elif about her school days, and she told me about her primary years, and
then she started to describe her time at secondary school.

Elif: My school finish class five its finish . . . one year no school and after
         make new building secondary school for 3 years.
Kate: So you have to wait for it to be ready?
Elif: I waiting for it to finish with my friends. (laughs)
Kate: So for one year no school. What did you do? Play?
Elif: I can't remember my . . . (2) daddy my daddy he goes to Arabia, Saudi
         Arabia.
Kate: He went to Saudi Arabia. Right//
Elif: //Yeah. Long time maybe five years, six years. And . . . (3) When I start
         secondary school my daddy go to (3) Arabia, Saudi Arabia.
Kate: He went um. So he was away for five whole years?
Elif: //Yeah.

(Transcript, April 23, 2001)[1]

In this excerpt, Elif waits for her father to come home for five years, and also
waits for the building of her school to finish. To my question, "What did you
do?" she responds, "I can't remember my daddy." Here the "rich point" (Agar,
1996) opens out. Elif described a period of waiting "five years" while her
father worked abroad. This interview gives a glimpse into a sedimented practice of moving across the globe to find work. Again, following Bourdieu, the
family's movement into the field of economic migration was giving the habitus
an improvisational quality and disrupted its settled nature. Appadurai's (1996)

insight that the habitus is now constantly improvising can be seen within this bit of data. Tracing the habitus across diasporas in Fatih's texts brings to the fore the migratory shifts the family took to gain economic stability.

Following this discussion, I explored with Elif the multimodal meaning-making Fatih engaged with. We discussed together the range of objects and drawings that he made both at school and at home. I was especially interested in which objects Fatih made at home and which at school, and also in the processes of meaning-making. Elif tried to explain this to me. Fatih had previously drawn a map of his home as part of a game played by him and his brother, Hanif. I was interested in whether there were any other examples of map-making to be found in the home, and also whether these originated from home or school.

My original question was, "Are there other things he makes? School and home birds, he made, didn't he?" After some discussion about what was made at home and what at school, Elif interrupted me to say,

Elif: Do you know sometimes he ... (3) er ... (2) just er, for mine I explain ...

Kate: Show me

(She gets some prayer beads and makes a shape.)

Elif: (8) Lots of these making these ...

Kate: Fatih makes?

Elif: No!

Kate: You make?

Elif: No ... (1) *playing* this.

Kate: Beads?

Elif: After the prayer he making. (laughs) He make it like this (2) on the carpet. (See Figure 10.1.)

Kate: Yeah?

Elif: Like any//

Kate: //A shape?

Elif: Which country.

Kate: Ah I like that!

Elif: I said Ireland he make it different like how Turkey like this. I said Turkey like this I said Turkey different very different I said England, Arabia I said, he make all! (laughs)

I selected this account to discuss as it offered, in Agar's terms, "a gap ... between two worlds" (1996: 31). Elif breaks into my questioning with the word "No!" then describes how Fatih, "after prayer" made shapes in the form of countries on the carpet. This account can be related back to Elif's account of her father's experience of Saudi Arabia; her brother was also currently working in Saudi Arabia. The bead map is made within the habitus of economic migration, and its outline traces that process. The concept of texts as traces of

Figure 10.1 Fatih's prayer bead map.

the habitus is brought to the fore. If texts are seen within a context through an ethnographic eye, the habitus, and its traces, can be discerned sedimented within a text. This analysis relies on an understanding of texts in an understood and richly researched context.

Fatih had used his mother's prayer beads, which combine with the concept of *map*. For Fatih to use these freely as a representational resource (Kress, 1997) was interesting. There was a complex link between the meanings Fatih was generating, the tools he was using to make the meanings, and the context—the habitus of the family, caught between a number of different countries—which offered different conceptual possibilities. I used Bourdieu's concept of habitus to help me make that link. Data gathered during the ethnography continued to flesh out the habitus of migration. Elif showed me, for example, a video she made when visiting her relatives in Turkey, of her mother sending love to her children in the UK. Here, the narrative of migration and displacement is caught on video. The family's habitus, sutured by the experience of migration is made and remade in different contexts. In the case of Fatih's bead map, the narrative is caught as he makes and remakes the shape of the countries, playing a game which echoes his family's habitus, crossing countries to find work. Elif was 14 when she arrived in England, taken from her home village to get married. However, she later separated from her husband to live on her own with her sons.

I was interested that Fatih was learning map-making at school, and that there was a link between the texts he was creating at home and the texts he was making at school. However, the context and the meanings created by the bead map text echoed the family's habitus. It was these "rich points" in the data that I focused on, where I located texts or descriptions within the field notes linked to ways of being, or generative structures.

Repeated visits to the home enabled me to shade in details of the habitus. An earlier photograph taken three months before, which formed part of a set of photographs by the family—I gave them a disposable camera to use at home—showed him doing exactly the same thing: making a map out of beads, but with a different tool, a curtain tie. The use of the curtain tie showed how Fatih employed different "tools" to make the same set of shapes, playing at enacting the countries his family encountered. I saw Fatih's making of a map using the prayer beads as a reflection of two different social practices: prayer and the describing of countries through shape-making. It articulated two powerful social practices within the household: the regular cycle of prayer Elif participated in, and the narratives of migration described in videos, stories, and conversations which I observed and recorded as part of the ethnographic study.

Within this practice, we gain a glimpse of migratory patterns. Fatih's grandparents lived in a rural setting in Central Turkey. Most of their children moved away, the majority to the UK, looking for work. Fatih's uncle was working in Saudi Arabia. The "interest" of the child as described by his mother focused on these countries—England, Saudi Arabia, Turkey—as places overheard in conversations and etched out in the shape of a map. Markers of cultural identity, they operated as articulations of the habitus, as the identity of a Turkish child growing up in London. The gift I was to give Elif, the map of the world, opened out her worlds still further.

Bourdieu's concept of habitus as a practice-centered theory of intergenerational dispositions as expressed in daily life is a theoretical tool for looking at the bead map in the context of migratory patterns. The habitus as expressed in practices, sediments into texts, and the representations found in the household contain traces of the habitus. However, as Appadurai (1996) and others have noted, improvisation on the habitus has to be the focus, in the context of economic migration and diasporic movement. Researchers can draw on this theoretical lens to consider where the improvisation takes place. I would argue that here the tool Fatih used, the prayer beads, constitutes an improvisation as he draws on a tool imbued with the practices of Islam to delineate new, global migratory patterns. Ethnography enables the habitus to be grasped, over time, and then this understanding of the habitus can be used to "read" texts as instantiations of habitus. This was the work I did when understanding Fatih's text-making.

Case study II: the Welsh valley farm

In the second case study, I take a group of texts across a time frame of over a year. These were constructed by Mary and Edward, who lived in a block of housing not far from Elif and Fatih, although Edward attended a different school. Mary was a teaching assistant at her son's school. Mary's partner, Edward's father, was a bus driver. Edward was a late child; the two other children were grown up, one worked as a teacher. The school had suggested family literacy classes as Edward was not progressing. Mary had fought for him to be recognized as a "bright" child; she said he was slow to develop but they knew he was bright, and now he was reading and writing fluently. I asked Mary to keep Edward's drawings and explained that I was trying to understand children's literacy at home. I visited the home regularly for two years.

The flat was a two-storey maisonette with a balcony. There were tiny models of buses and cars in a series of glass cabinets which lined one wall. The carpet was thick pile, and there was a new television beside the glass cabinets. The room also contained a box of Edward's toys, mostly cars. There were also books on a coffee table which were connected to her older daughter's teaching work, a football which Edward kicked around sometimes, and piles of books, mostly school books, on the floor.

Mary explained how she grew up in India, saying, "My grandfather, . . . worked on the railways and stuff." Her mother-in-law, Edward's "nanny" (his grandmother), lived in the Welsh valleys. I learned that the family visited Edward's nanny in Wales when they could. They would have liked to move out of London but could not afford to. Mary had been brought up in India, but moved to London when she was 11. Edward visited his nanny's farm in Wales frequently.

This selection of the data will focus on how the narratives of migration, from India to London, and the pull of the Welsh valleys, were articulated in the texts and narratives which Mary and Edward presented to me in the field visits. As an ethnographic researcher, I worked with Mary to uncover meanings around the texts Edward drew. When I began visiting, he sometimes drew texts for me, partly in response to having a strange researcher in the home. As my visits became more regular, drawings were not produced in response to me but in the context of visits to his nanny in Wales or in school contexts. Again, the process of ethnography was one of painstakingly recovering the taken-for-granted habitus with the household. Texts were a focus for research, and the process of tracing back the habitus was an active part of the ethnographic project.

The data I have selected here came from a period during which I visited the family regularly. These texts, and the field notes that accompany it, were produced for a period of over a year, but belong to a longer experience of Edward's, in which he visited his nanny's farm in Wales. The visits were told and retold within the household, and framed by his mother's own stories of the farm. The texts associated with the Welsh valley farm included drawings by Edward and photographs taken by Mary. In this analysis, the visual and oral work together, side by side, are used to construct a richly patterned narrative. This narrative consists of stories as well as visual displays and photographs shaped and retold to form a wider, long-running narrative—that of the Welsh valley farm.

The first image was produced after Edward had visited his nanny's house in Wales during the Easter holidays, about two months into the field visits. It was a carefully drawn image of a farm (see Figure 10.2).

[Note: I was sitting on the family settee and Edward and Mary both described the visual image to me.]

"Nanny's house in Wales," said Mary, as an introduction. Edward described the vans: "My nan's little van." Mary supplied the details. "She has a floristry business in the week and is a special constable at weekends." Edward said, pointing to the blue car on the top left of the vehicle drawings, "My granddad's big blue car." [The blue car is the light blue car directly above the motorbike.] Mary said, "It's too big for him to ride on it." Edward said, "My uncle's motorbike." "He hasn't seen it yet," said

Figure 10.2 Edward's drawing of Nanny's farm in Wales.

Mary. Mary said that she longed to go to Wales and found it very difficult returning to London. She said that as soon as she trained as a teacher she would like to move.

(Field notes, April 6, 2000)

The Welsh valley farm drawing shows the farm, with fields of sheep behind it that look as if they had been drawn by Mary. The cars are distinguished by their colors and position. Color is salient in the image, and the image uses careful partitioning by lines to indicate area. By setting out the elements of his nanny's house in Wales, Edward was introducing us to key concepts in his world, and producing a visual image, a "display" of what he observed in Wales. However, the image fed into a longer narrative about the house in Wales. It could be set within a chain of representations connected to Nanny's farm, and welded together by the family across time and space. The chain crossed modes and drew on both adult and child to supply details. The visual text was then passed to the nanny in Wales; the picture was scanned in by his mother, and sent to her via the internet.

A month later, Mary was telling me more information about the drawing.

We went back to the Welsh valley drawing and Mary told me about the chickens—I had not mentioned or noticed that there were chickens in the drawing, "and he has to collect the eggs," she said. [The chickens are in the little hut to the right of the main house in Figure 10.2.]

(Field notes, May 4, 2000)

The exploration of nanny's farm was accompanied by Edward's repeated drawings connected to the farm, which also were linked by Mary to the photographs she took of the farm. In the summer holidays of that year, Edward visited his nanny in Wales and spent time feeding the animals on the farm. He also had an interest in pets, which was one of the family's "ruling passions" (Barton and Hamilton, 1998). This accretion of images, oral stories, and drawings to produce a narrative is a conception of narrative which is collage-like and repetitive.

During a visit the next summer, I tape-recorded the following piece of data. Mary was talking to her son Edward about the farm:

Mary: What did you do in Wales?
Edward: We went like I done all these—there's like two lambs and now they they've there's like four lambs but they can only look after two because their mother hasn't done . . . hasn't have much milk. So I had to feed the other ones.

(Transcript, June 7, 2001)

A piece of writing by Edward, produced at his nanny's house in Wales, speaks to the images and can be "read" in the context of the images.

My Nanny's Farm
    My Nanny has a little farm in Wales. She has sheep two dogs one is called Zoe; the other is named Rushie. She has a nice horse his name is Bugsy, she also has hens. I collect the eggs everyday. I feed two lambs because their mums has four lambs but has not got milk for all of them, two of the lambs are Bill and Ben. I have got a pony to ride. She is called Annie. I love my Nanny.

This writing describes the animals Edward's nanny kept, already drawn by Edward, and describes the hens, the eggs and the lambs. The visual descriptions were captured before this writing was collected, and the writing was constructed in relation to the visual image. The writing was presented to me in the summer of 2001, about a year after the "Nanny's Farm in Wales" drawing, as an example of Edward's writing when he was in Year 2. The writing retrospectively lists many elements of the visual images.

    These narratives were constructed in relation to a language of displacement and desire. Both mother and child loved visiting Wales, and the Welsh valley farm narratives were produced, mainly for the nanny but shown to me, in the context of that longing. Life in urban London was placed in contrast to the rural life on the farm. In this series of images, talk and writing, the habitus of the family is expressed through multiple texts, often jointly constructed and framed, which the family then showed to me as researcher. Both visual images and written images as well as oral conversation worked to create the overall narrative of longing (Stewart, 1993). I used Stewart's work to help me understand how in many households, objects "told a story." They often "held" the habitus of the family and were resonant with narrative. Like Mrs Ramsay's stocking, I found that a particular text could amplify the habitus, drawing out the resonances and echoes of the family's habitus, as expressed in social practices. The following example explain this concept in more detail.

Case study III: the train texts

In the last case, I draw on objects, photographs, taped narratives and drawings to present a "telling case" of the relationship between habitus and texts. These objects were models of trains which "told a story" and were used by family participants to evoke emotional links to the past, as Mrs Ramsay's story of trying on a stocking evokes past experiences.

    In this field visit, I had sat down on the family settee in their front room, and was given a picture of a train by Edward, who was then five. He said,

    "This is a Mallard train." Mary explained—"He likes trains, so we got him all of these." "These" were a collection of trains done as miniature figurines. I looked at "Little Wonder" and Edward produced for me

"The Flying Scotsman." Edward knew all their names. "They come with a book—you can send off for it." The book was called "Legendary Trains," "Edward sits and read it for hours," said Mary.

[later on in the field visit]

Mary told me a bit about herself. Her family come from "all over"— "They built the railways in India—they came from Ireland and went over there to build the railways."

(Field notes, March 23, 2000)

This episode identified a number of different themes. The "trains" interest appeared to be only an interest by Edward, expressed in the "Mallard" drawing. But then Mary provided another context, that of her family background.

A year later I conducted an extended interview with Mary about her life.

Mary: Me you know my life God it was a real struggle because I was the oldest of six and coming from India I came here in 1967 I was only 11.

Kate: So when you were in India. You said your dad built the railways.

Mary: My grandfather, no, worked on the railways and stuff. My grandfather built the train in the back there, he made it and stuff . . .

[This train was displayed at the back of the glass cabinets to the right of the room.]

Kate: You said your parents were Indian.

Mary: My . . . it's a strange story my father and mother were born in India but their parents, like my grandfather from my dad's side of the family came from Warwickshire . . . and um I think my dad's great-grand-mother-in-law may have been from the West Indies and my mums . . . both my mum and dad's grandmother and grandfather from both sides are from Ireland so we've not found a trace of India its just that the two generations were born in India.

(Transcript, January, 2001)

Mary made the connection between the trains in the cabinet and her grand-father by telling me that her grandfather made the train in the display cabinet. This story was then placed within the context of Mary's identity in practice, her acquired habitus. Both formed a wider pattern of stories alongside objects and drawings, including Edward's trains in the display cabinet.

I followed up on this with an interview with Edward, in which he took some photographs of the Indian train and the Mallard train.

Kate: This is the grandfather's train [i.e., Mary's grandfather's train].

Mary: This is my [grandfather's] one yeah he worked on the railway in India and he used to make models.

Edward: Most of the trains in there are, and actually what I got is models. Before we used to collect them now there's no more left because I got all of them so now there's only one left, and that's the one I still got. It was the one it was the one it was the Bugton P 11, and it's like this train yeah, and it's got like this where it goes and it keeps going down and like your going and like it's a bend and you going straight and you down and up.

Mary: Where was this?

Edward: In a book.

Edward: You know the side then I couldn't see that side so I just took the front now do the other side.

Kate: How old is that?

Mary: He died when he was 70-odd, he died when he was 70, 30 years ago.

Edward: My mum's dad gave me this to one year ago and its um

Mary: Can you see the whole train?

Edward: . . . 39 . . . I can't see the back.

Mary: My dad said he loves trains that much he'd appreciate it more than him keeping it so he gave it to him last year.

(Transcript, June 7, 2001)

Edward here linked the interest he had in trains and collecting with his grandfather's train. The trains were displayed in a glass cabinet in the front room. The original train, made by Mary's grandfather, operates as a memento of the family history of building the railways in India. Mary described a complex family history, involving a great-grandfather from Warwickshire and two relatives from Ireland on both sides, plus an ancestor in the West Indies. These narratives resonate with the colonial history of that period. However, the focus of the discussion was on the train, which was carried over into her grandfather's model of a train. Edward was given this partly because of his enthusiasm for trains. The family then framed the interest in trains partly through Edward's collecting passion, and partly in their focus on their family history.

Underlying this story were long-term family themes of cultural identity, and the "family stories" of the Welsh valley and the Indian trains both flow from these original themes. Mary describes her story as "strange" and talks through geographical movement, "Warwickshire . . . West Indies . . . Ireland." The names "stand for" a host of other stories, as her name, an unremarkable English name, hides a complex family history. Places, names, and languages feature in Mary's account of herself, as she circles around her identity and her sense of who she is. Part of her narrative accounts refer back to a lost world, such as the Welsh valley farm, which evokes a rural idyll from which she has since been removed. Here in a later interview, she describes being sent to the countryside when she lived in India:

Mary: Me and my sister in the holidays were sent down to the country and we had our best times here, there is a photograph of the bungalow, . . .

[she refers to the photograph and how Edward had taken it to school]
It was like mum's Welsh valley.

(Transcript, June 30, 2004)

Mary's account of her final journey back to England also traces closely the experience of migration back to the city, where her father had to start all over again:

Mary: We got a ship, an Italian ship to Genoa, best journey of my life, got on a train, went to the Swiss Alps, first time I saw snow, got to France, went across on the ferry, such a journey but we loved it such an amazing journey.

(Transcript, June 30, 2004)

Her habitus is located both in the objects she refers to—in her son's drawings of the Welsh valley farm and the train, the model of the train, the photograph of the bungalow—and in her own narratives of migration. By linking the drawings and the narrative together, a richer understanding can be made of the way the habitus constructs the text-making of the child.

The field of schooling

If these narratives are related to "school" pedagogy, where can they appear and be used within classrooms? Interestingly, Fatih did "learn" map-making the term before the bead map episodes were recorded. Drawing on observations and collection of data from his classroom, a record was kept of episodes of map-making but without the rich content described above. Fatih's maps included drawings of how to get from Red Riding Hood's house to Granny's house, or depicted a rough drawing of trees and bushes called "A Map of the Park." The concept of *map* was diluted within the class context. One of the values of the habitus concept when analyzing children's texts was that it imbued texts with meanings which were often absent in schooled settings, where the curriculum in England was strongly derived from traditional English fairy tales, again without any meaning to Fatih's home.

The field of schooling had its own tight rules and regulations. One aspect of the data here was its relationship to time. It spanned years, and many of the narratives referred to events that happened over extended time periods, richly grounded in the family's habitus. This complex accretion of meaning was difficult to duplicate within the school setting. Therefore, when I conducted classroom observations within Edward's class, his stories remained grounded more concretely within the present tense. They lacked the complexity of the jointly constructed Welsh valley farm and train narratives.

Narrative of migration and dislocation

The ethnography which situated these selections of talk, images, and writing was able to describe, and then reconstruct within a research context, the habitus. This habitus in turn informed the practices within the household, which then sedimented into texts. My work as an ethnographer was to uncover traces of the habitus within texts, to make situated meanings from the texts I found in homes. I developed a model, which operated as a heuristic for describing this process (see Figure 10.3).

Habitus *generated* practices, such as the practice of prayer. Habitus was also *informed by* practices; for example, the practice of visiting the Welsh valley farm built up the family's accustomed habitus of regularly visiting the farm. Texts *sedimented into* practices; Fatih's bead map, for example, had sedimented into the "game" of playing maps. Practices were *instantiated within* and *sedimented into* texts; the practice of prayer was caught within the prayer bead map. Texts themselves sedimented into and became part of the habitus, particularly through narrative and *iteration*, in the telling and retelling, as the Welsh valley texts have demonstrated.

My particular focus was on the way in which the concept of the habitus opened out my analysis of home texts and practices. The value for me, also, is that it was an attempt to define the way in which "life" is lived in relation both to the power structures in which households play out their lives and to the ephemera, mess, and miscellaneous piles created by family life (Pahl, 2002). Like de Certeau's celebration of everyday strategies, my work celebrates the complex, often hastily tidied up artifacts and objects that occupy home spaces (de Certeau, 1984). In this, I was interested to find Wacquant in agreement with my configuration of habitus as "mess."

> *Habitus is in cahoots with the fuzzy and the vague.* As a generative spontaneity which asserts itself in the improvised confrontation with endlessly renewed

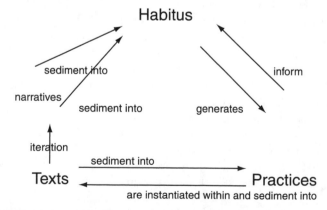

Figure 10.3 Heuristic model of how practices are sedimented into texts.

situations, it follows a practical logic, that of the fuzzy, of the more or less, which defines the ordinary relation to the world.

(Wacquant, 1992: 22)

The link between habitus as the wider social conditions and the detailed practices and strategies of everyday life was one I used when looking at the relationship between texts and practices in the home. I worked with the idea that culture is ordinary and the making of culture from embodied identity in practice was something I observed within homes (Williams, 1989). The lens of habitus helped me to trace the process back. By seeing how habitus can be improvised upon through a textual improvisation, in relation to identities-in-practice, the relationship between texts and practices can be set within the theoretical frame from Bourdieu which argues for relations of power, of the construction of the taken-for-granted, the "life," to be placed under scrutiny (Bourdieu and Wacquant, 1992). It has been argued that the New Literacy Studies need to take account of the way the French theorists, such as Bourdieu, could be applied to micro-ethnographies of texts and practices (Collins and Blot, 2003). This was what I was attempting to do here in these accounts of children's text-making in the home. This then develops the debate on issues around texts, power, and identity within the New Literacy Studies.

Note

1   Transcription conventions: . . . = pause; (1) indicates time of pause; *playing* indicates emphasis; // indicates overlapped speech. () indicates researcher's comments on gesture, or other communicative practices. [ ] indicates explanations by researcher of context. I have punctuated the text to make it easier to read.

References

Agar, M. (1996) *The Professional Stranger: An Informal Introduction to Ethnography* (2nd edn). New York: Academic Press.

Appadurai, A. (1996) *Modernity at Large: Cultural Dimensions of Globalization*. Minneapolis: University of Minnesota Press.

Collins, J. and Blot, R. K. (2003) *Literacy and Literacies: Texts, Power and Identity*. Cambridge, UK: Cambridge University Press.

Bartlett, L. and Holland, D. (2002) Theorizing the space of literacy practices. *Ways of Knowing*, 2(1), 10–22.

Barton, D. and Hamilton, M. (1998) *Local Literacies: Reading and Writing in One Community*. London: Routledge.

Bourdieu, P. (1977) *Outline of a Theory of Practice* (R. Nice, trans.). Cambridge, UK: Cambridge University Press. (Original work published 1972)

Bourdieu, P. (1990) *The Logic of Practice* (R. Nice, trans.). Cambridge, UK: Polity Press. (Original work published 1980)

Bourdieu, P. and Wacquant, L. J. D. (1992) *An Invitation to Reflexive Sociology*. Cambridge, UK: Polity Press

De Certeau, M. (1984) *The Practice of Everyday Life* (S. Rendell, trans.). Berkeley, CA: University of California Press.

Green, J. and Bloome, D. (1996) Ethnography and ethnographers of and in education: A situated perspective. In J. Flood, S. Heath, and D. Lapp (eds), *A Handbook for Literacy Educators: Research on Teaching the Communicative and Visual Arts*. New York: Macmillan, 1–12.

Heath, S. B. (1983) *Ways with Words: Language, Life and Work in Communities and Classrooms*. Cambridge, UK: Cambridge University Press.

Holland, D., Lachicotte, W., Skinner, D. and Cain, C. (2001) *Identity and Agency in Cultural Worlds*. Cambridge, MA: Harvard University Press.

Hymes, D. (ed.) (1996) *Ethnography, Linguistics, Narrative Inequality: Toward an Understanding of Voice*. London: Routledge.

Jenkins, R. (1992) *Pierre Bourdieu*. London: Routledge.

Kress, G. (1997) *Before Writing: Rethinking the Paths to Literacy*. London: Routledge.

Luke, A. and Luke C. (2000) A situated perspective on cultural globalization. In N. C. Burbules and C. A. Torres (eds), *Globalization and Education: Critical Perspectives*. London: Routledge, 275–99.

Mitchell, J. C. (1984) Typicality and the case study. In R. F. Ellen (ed.), *Ethnographic Research: A Guide to General Conduct*. London: Academic Press, 238–41.

Nash, R. (1999) Bourdieu, "habitus" and educational research: is it all worth the candle? *British Journal of the Sociology of Education*, 20, 175–87.

Pahl, K. (2002) Ephemera, mess and miscellaneous piles: texts and practices in families. *Journal of Early Childhood Literacy*, 2, 145–65.

Ragin, C. C. and Becker, H. S. (eds) (1992) *What is a Case? Exploring the Foundations of Social Inquiry*. Cambridge, UK: Cambridge University Press.

Stewart S. (1993) *On Longing: Narratives of the Miniature, the Gigantic, the Souvenir the Collection*. Durham, NC: Duke University Press.

Street, B. (ed.) (1993) *Cross-cultural Approaches to Literacy*. Cambridge, UK: Cambridge University Press.

Wacquant, L. J. D. (1992) Toward a social praxeology: the structure and logic of Bourdieu's sociology. In P. Bourdieu and L. J. D. Wacquant (eds), *An Invitation to Reflexive Sociology*. Cambridge, UK: Polity Press, 1–6.

Williams, R. (1958) *Culture and Society: 1780–1950*. London: Chatto and Windus.

Williams, R. (1961) *The Long Revolution*. London: Chatto and Windus.

Williams, R. (1973) *The Country and the City*. London: Chatto and Windus.

Williams, R. (1989) Culture is ordinary. In R. Gale (ed.), *Resources of Hope: Culture, Democracy, Socialism*. London: Verso, 3–18. (Original work published in *Conviction*, N. MacKenzie, ed., 1958, London: MacGibbon and Kee, 74–92)

Chapter 11

The capital of "attentive silence" and its impact on English language and literacy education

Tara Goldstein

Introduction

This chapter explores what happens when the notions of *linguistic capital* and *cultural capital* (Bourdieu, 1982/1991) are teamed with the notions of *peer social capital* (Valenzuela, 1999) and *attentive silence* (Cheung, 1993) to explain adolescents' language practices in a multilingual high school. Although it is not typically discussed in educational research, "silence talks" (Gerrard and Javed, 1994: 65), and I will argue that an analysis of its presence can offer something significant to research on language practices and literacy education. In making this argument, I will draw upon the findings from a four-year critical ethnographic study (1996–2000) that investigated how immigrant high-school students born in Hong Kong used Cantonese as well as English to achieve academic and social success in a Canadian school where English was the language of instruction.[1]

The chapter begins with a brief discussion of the ethnographic research methodology underlying the study. It continues with an ethnographic description of the language and literacy policies that were in place at Northside Secondary School, a pseudonym for the multilingual high school being researched. This description is followed by a Bourdieusian sociolinguistic analysis of the Cantonese-speaking students' language practices at school. As part of this analysis, I will look at the students' practice of attentive silence and the impact it had on their English language and literacy learning. The chapter concludes with a discussion of the pedagogical practices and policies that might enhance English language and literacy learning in multilingual schools.

Methodology: undertaking research on bilingual life and language choice in a multilingual school

The ethnographic research study that informs the writing of this chapter began with an investigation of how immigrant high-school students born in Hong Kong used Cantonese as well as English to achieve academic and social success in a school in Toronto, Canada, where English is the language of instruction. As will be explained in greater detail below, the findings revealed that while the use of Cantonese contributed to academic and social success in a number of ways, it also created different kinds of linguistic and academic dilemmas for teachers and students in the school.

Over the four years of the study, I worked as the principal investigator and leader of a multilingual, multicultural, multiracial research team. The team comprised a co-investigator, Cindy Lam, ten graduate and undergraduate students from two universities in Toronto, as well as some of the high-school students studying at Northside. One Cantonese-speaking Chinese parent born in Hong Kong also joined the team as a translator and transcriber for a short period of time.

The co-investigator, research assistants and I did not all work together at one time. There were a total of five research teams: one that was put together for the pilot study in the summer of 1994, and four different research teams that were put together over the four years of the project. The pilot study team conducted 78 hours of fieldwork between July 7 and August 5, 1994. The other research teams spent about 445 hours conducting fieldwork in the school during the first two years of the study (1996–98). In the third year, research assistant Gordon Pon organized and led a homework club in the school for the English as a Second or Other Language (ESOL) students who had participated in our study, while others on the team continued to transcribe and translate data. By providing assistance with English homework one day a week, Gordon, on behalf of the entire team, returned the gift of time and knowledge the students had shared with us. The fourth year was spent working with data that had not yet been transcribed and translated, discussing different ways of understanding talk by Cantonese-speaking students, and examining both the bilingual and the monolingual transcripts for important ideas and discourses.

Our fieldwork

Participant observation, interviews, audio recording, and document analysis

In Year 1 of the study, the team conducted participant observation activities in a number of different classes (art, business, computer, English, geography, history, math, physical education, and science) and at a variety of co-curricular events (such as the annual talent show, music night, parents' night, and student council election). Particular classes and events were selected as research sites because of their high enrolment of Cantonese-speaking students and/or their teachers' interest in our project. Teachers leading the classes we had observed were interviewed about their students' bilingual language practices. In Years 2 and 3 of the study, we also observed and interviewed those teachers who had identified the use of Cantonese as either a resource or an issue in their classroom. In all, 12 teachers were interviewed; all the interviews were conducted in English.

The teams audio-recorded speech in classrooms where talk in Cantonese was particularly prevalent. These included one math, one computer science, two art, and three English classrooms. At the same time, we interviewed the Cantonese-speaking students whose talk had been recorded to see if we could find out why particular language practices were in place. The bilingual research assistants on the project transcribed and translated the Cantonese and bilingual (Cantonese/English) talk that had been recorded.

The students we interviewed from the classes we observed came from a variety of language, cultural, and racial backgrounds: Anglo-Canadian, Canadian-born Chinese, Euro-Canadian, Hong Kong-born Chinese, Iranian (born both in Canada and in Iran), Taiwan-born Chinese, and South Asian (born both in and outside of Canada). While almost all the student interviews were undertaken in English, one was undertaken in Cantonese. The Cantonese interview was conducted by one of the bilingual research assistants on the team and translated by another. While I had taken a ten-week course in Cantonese at the University of Toronto in the first year of the project, so I would be able to at least understand a few words in Cantonese and more confidently distinguish the use of Cantonese from Mandarin, I am a non-speaker of Cantonese. The bilingual research assistants on the teams sat in on my interviews with Cantonese-speaking students, transcribed the interviews and provided me with their own interpretations of the students' responses to the interview questions. While working with linguistic and cultural interpreters meant working with multiple layers of interpretation, it also meant that I had access to some of the sociocultural and sociolinguistic background knowledge necessary for understanding talk by Cantonese-speaking students participating in the study. This knowledge, the importance—and complexity—of which has been discussed by sociolinguists interested in intercultural interview situations (see e.g., Belfiore and Heller, 1992; Briggs, 1986; Gumperz, 1992) was not accessible to me without linguistic and cultural interpreters. It is knowledge that I believe strengthened my analysis.

At the same time as the fieldwork in Years 1 and 2 was being conducted, some of the research assistants worked with me in a reading group. The reading group read traditional research reports on the education of Chinese immigrant students and teachers as well as a memoir and a play by two Asian-American writers.[2] Engaging with Asian-American literature led us to the work of King-Kok Cheung, whose notion of attentive silence is linked to Angela Valenzuela's notion of peer social capital in this chapter.[3] Finally, in addition to our observations, interviews and audio-recording activities, the research teams examined a number of school documents: the school board's language and literacy policies, the *Quality Assurance School Review* done the year before the study began, and the school's course calendars, newsletters, newspapers, and yearbooks.

An ethnographic description of academic programming, linguistic diversity, and the language and literacy policies at Northside

Since opening in a mostly middle- and upper-middle-class suburb north of Toronto in 1970, Northside Secondary School had established a reputation of academic excellence. At the time the study was conducted, the community was still mostly comprised of middle- and upper-middle-class families. Most Northside students were working toward college or university admission, and the school's 1995–96 *Quality Assurance School Review* reported that students identified high academic standards as a major strength of the school. The *School Review* also reported that students at Northside achieved at levels above the system average in math testing and English language literacy testing, and accumulated credits at 16 years of age.

According to the *School Review*, 86 percent of the students at Northside were immigrants to Canada, and 60 percent reported that their primary language was a language other than English. The top five primary languages spoken by students were English (by 38 percent of the students), Cantonese (35 percent), Mandarin (6 percent), and Farsi and Korean (4 percent). The large percentage of bilingual and multilingual speakers at the school meant that while English was the language of instruction, everyday talk in classrooms, hallways, and the cafeteria took place in languages other than English as well as English. This was a concern for many people at the school.

The review team, which had interviewed individual teachers, department teams, students, student groups, office staff, caretaking staff, and administrators for the 1995–96 *School Review*, reported that "all parties interviewed expressed concern about the amount of non-English spoken in both the hallways and classrooms of the school" (p. 3). The team also reported that the group of ten parents they spoke to expressed "considerable concern about language and the strong feeling was that English should not only be the language of instruction, but also the only language spoken at school" (p. 7). Although the review team did not explain the reasons behind this concern, one of the recommendations they made was that the school continue to work on the English literacy initiative it had already begun, but also include within this initiative a "major focus on oral [English] language development" (p. 10). I interpreted this recommendation as a direct response to the amount of "non-English" being spoken at school and the desire to make English the only language spoken at school. What the teaching staff was being asked to do was this: initiate a school-wide oral English development program in a multilingual school where students were already successfully using both English and other languages to conduct their academic and social lives at school.

The desire for institutional monolingualism

Why was there such concern that English be the only language spoken at the school when, overall, Northside students were achieving above the system average and successfully working toward admission to colleges and universities? Findings from a 1995 survey study (Tung et al., 1997) undertaken in Hong Kong, where many students at Northside had begun their secondary school education, provided a preliminary answer. When asked about their beliefs regarding the use of English and Chinese as languages of instruction, parents said that English instruction brought about a better standard of English than did a combination of English and Chinese instruction.[4] They also said they favored English instruction over Chinese instruction because of the socio-economic importance of English in Hong Kong. Most of the children agreed with their parents' views on English-medium instruction. However, they also supported a gradual transition from Chinese- to English-medium education, and were in favor of teachers using both English and Chinese in the same lesson. In contrast, both parents and teachers tended to believe that teachers should not teach the same lesson in both English and Chinese even though many teachers were teaching bilingually in their own classrooms. In commenting about this contradiction, sociolinguist Angel Lin (1997b) has suggested that the surveyed teachers experienced some conflict between what they believed was "officially" correct practice and what they found necessary to do in their own classrooms. She also suggested that the unfavorable attitude toward bilingual classroom practices expressed by parents and teachers in the survey might have been a result of the official, academic and media discourses, which claimed that bilingual classroom practices had negative educational effects.[5]

Returning to the question of why there was such concern that English be the only language spoken at Northside, for some respondents the answer did, indeed, seem to lie in understanding the linguistic, economic, and social privileges English held for parents, teachers and students. For others, as will be discussed below, it lay in understanding the kinds of difficulties, tensions, and dilemmas that students and teachers associated with the use of languages other than English at the school.

In discussions of the desire for English monolingualism, I have found it helpful to distinguish between the desire for a monolingual English classroom and the desire for a monolingual English school. While the *School Review* reported that there was a strong feeling at Northside that English should not only be the language of instruction, but also the only language spoken at school, not one of the 12 teachers we interviewed had any objections to the use of Cantonese for social interaction outside the classroom. Those who believed that their students' best interests were served by English monolingualism in the classroom did not call for English monolingualism in the hallways and cafeteria.

In August 1995, very shortly after the *School Review* was submitted to the principal of the school, the school board to which Northside belonged adopted a new language policy. Entitled the *Language for Learning Policy*, the policy consisted of ten "core assumptions" that administrators and teachers were to adopt as a basis for their planning around language initiatives. Four of the ten assumptions are particularly relevant for the discussions I pursue in this chapter:

> 1 Language, culture and identity are closely linked. A program that recognizes, respects, and values students' racial, cultural, and linguistic backgrounds, as well as the varieties of language, helps them to develop a positive sense of self and motivates them to learn. All students need opportunities to think critically about the social values and status assigned to different languages by various groups in our society and to explore issues of bias and stereotyping related to language and culture.
>
> 2 First-language literacy is important for second-language learning. It helps students to grasp key concepts more easily and influences general academic achievement.
>
> 3 All languages and varieties of languages are equally valid forms of thought and communication. Canadian Standard English is the language of instruction in the Board's Schools and all children in the Board's District need to develop proficiency in this language.
>
> 4 Students' first languages play an important role in the classroom, in the school program as a whole, and in communication with the home.
>
> (Toronto District School Board, 1995: 7, 8)

While the *Language for Learning Policy* explicitly named and legitimized English as the language of instruction in its schools, it also legitimized student use of languages other than English at school in several ways. First, it asserted that effective, "motivating" school programming recognized, respected, and valued students' linguistic backgrounds. Second, it asserted that first language literacy was important for second language learning. Third, it asserted that students' first languages had an important role to play in the classroom and in the school program as a whole.

The introduction of a language policy that legitimized student multilingualism at the same time as its latest *School Review* acknowledged a local desire for English monolingualism and recommended a school-wide oral English development initiative produced an extremely interesting moment in Northside's history. Teachers and administrators were being asked to respond to a set of contradictory desires: a local desire for institutional English monolingualism and a school board desire for student multilingualism that acknowledged English as the legitimate language of school instruction. In practical terms, this meant implementing a school-wide oral English development initiative designed to produce a monolingual English learning environment while recognizing that students' primary languages played an important role in learning.

It was within this schooling context of contradictions that the ESOL students at Northside were provided with a space to use their own linguistic strategies to achieve academic and social success at school. These strategies are at the center of the discussions that follow.

When several different schools' boards in the Metropolitan Toronto Area merged to form the new Toronto District School Board in January 1998, the policies that had been implemented in each school board were replaced with new policies. A new language policy for the new Toronto District School Board was adopted on May 27, 1998, after our classroom observation work had been completed. A discussion of the similarities and differences between the *Language for Learning Policy* and the new *Literacy Foundation Statement* is taken up in the conclusion. The impact that the implementation of the new policy has for critical educational practice is also discussed in the conclusion.

A Bourdieusian sociolinguistic analysis of the Cantonese-speaking students' language practices at school

Peer social capital: extending Pierre Bourdieu's ideas on capital and language choice

The preceding analysis of linguistic contradictions at Northside Secondary School sets up the possibility for extending Pierre Bourdieu's (1982/1991) ideas on capital and language choice, which have been very influential in research about language minority students and schooling.[6] Language choice research involves finding out what makes people in multilingual settings choose to use one language rather than another in different instances. Bourdieu theorized that people make choices about what languages to use in particular kinds of markets, which he defines as places where different kinds of resources or capital are distributed. Markets allow one form of capital to be converted into another. *Linguistic capital* can be cashed in for educational qualifications or *cultural capital*, which in turn can be cashed in for lucrative jobs or *economic capital*. People assess the market conditions in which their linguistic products will be received and valued by others. This assessment can constrain the way they speak or the way they think they ought to speak. Some linguistic products (e.g., English, the language of instruction at Northside) are more highly valued than others and are endowed with what Bourdieu calls a "legitimacy" that other linguistic products (e.g., Cantonese) are not. Such an analysis helps explain the results of the 1995 Hong Kong survey described above. While Bourdieu sees school policies and practices as a site of struggle in which individuals seek to maintain or alter the legitimacy of different forms of capital, he has not written about the possibilities, dilemmas, and tensions that appear in a moment of linguistic struggle or contradiction. The data collected at Northside provides me with an opportunity to do so.

In the next discussion, I look at the possibilities that might be created by linguistic struggle and contradictions at school. Specifically, I discuss the possibility of the development of "peer social capital" (Valenzuela, 1999) among linguistic minority students. A discussion of the dilemmas and tensions that appear in a moment of linguistic struggle or contradiction follows.

Developing peer social capital by using Cantonese at school

At Northside, most Cantonese-speaking students born in Hong Kong used Cantonese to speak to other Hong Kong-born students. The use of Cantonese was associated with membership in the Cantonese-speaking community at the school. It symbolized a Hong Kong-Canadian identity. The choice to use Cantonese to seek and maintain membership in the Cantonese-speaking community was related to the students' goals of academic and social success at school. To illustrate, research in both a finite math class during the pilot study in 1994 and a calculus class in 1997 revealed that the use of Cantonese allowed students to gain access to friendship and assistance that helped them achieve good marks in the course. Having friends in the classroom was related to the goal of getting a high or passing mark in several ways.

First, friends explained things you did not understand; for example, an explanation the teacher had given of a math concept or how to do math problem. This is illustrated in the following classroom interaction in which Anthony is helping Edward[7] work out a calculus problem. Both Edward and Anthony were born in Hong Kong. The interaction took place during the "classroom practice" component of a Grade 13 calculus class. The teacher had finished his lecture of the topic for the day and the students were working on problems he had assigned. In the classroom interaction that follows, the only English words uttered by the Cantonese-speaking students were words associated with the math problems they were talking about.[8]

Edward: *Let's go back to the previous question. This one has been changed. How about the last part* [of the question]? *Are you going to find the* **common denominator**?

Anthony: *It must be changing the angle, right? Because you already have a* **common angle**.

Edward: *Will that be messy and complicated?*

Anthony: *No, not that messy and complicated, though. Big brother* [Oh, man], *now you can change it again!*

Edward: *Well . . . that means* **2 cosine square times 1 over**, *doesn't it?*

Anthony: *No, yours should be in this way . . .*

(Transcript, February 6, 1997)

Second, having friends was important to academic success as it had to do with the way friends provided each other with an opportunity to discuss the marks they received on an assignment or quiz. This is illustrated in the next interaction where one of the students, Lawrence, was trying to figure out why his finite math teacher, Mrs Lo, had taken three marks off an answer he had given to one of the problems on a quiz. He did not think his answer was completely wrong and wanted to ask Mrs Lo to reconsider the mark she had given him. Eddy and Cindy were helping Lawrence figure out why his answer was not completely wrong when Cindy realized that Eddy had also correctly answered one of the questions that had been evaluated as partly incorrect. Once again, the only English words uttered by the Cantonese-speaking students were words associated with the math problems and courses they were talking about.

Lawrence: *I really don't understand it. I only have two parts wrong. How could someone take away three marks? I didn't think too lowly of her* [And I thought so highly of her].

Eddy: *She thinks lowly of you.*

Lawrence: *I don't know.*

Cindy: *How come you have half a mark for your* **bonus question***?*

Lawrence: *Yeah. That's what I don't understand. It's not that I don't know* [the right way to do the problem]. *Where did I lose nine marks? There are only two parts here, that is the* **A** *and* **B relationship** *one.* **A** *and* **B** *are wrong, but* **C** *is correct.*

Cindy: (Looking at Eddy's answer that was also evaluated as being partly incorrect) *Heh, heh, heh. Your last question should be right.*

Eddy: *Me?* [Mine?]

Cindy: *You.* [Yours.]

Eddy: *I told her. She said she's not going to talk it over with me. I don't know how to do it* [how to explain why my answer is partly right and why she should change the way she marked the answer]. *Forget it.*

Lawrence: *Never mind.* (Laughs)

Eddy: *Yesterday, I asked the* **afternoon finite** [math] *teacher. He said I should have some marks, that I shouldn't have lost a mark.*

Lawrence: *Did you find it?* [Did you find a way to explain why your answer is partly right?] *Even you can't find it?* [Even you can't find a way to explain why your answer is partly right?] *I really don't know what to do.*

(Transcript, July 20, 1994)

Negotiating a mark in a second language was not always easy for Cantonese-speaking students. As English was the legitimate language at Northside, those students who wanted Mrs Lo to consider changing a mark she had given them on a test or assignment had to submit a written statement in English as to why they should receive more marks. This meant that students needed to be able to articulate exactly why their answers were right and why they should receive more marks. Talking with friends about your case in Cantonese sometimes helped make the task of negotiating a mark easier.

The use of Cantonese to seek and maintain friendships within the Cantonese-speaking community at Northside can be understood as a strategy for developing peer social capital (Valenzuela, 1999). As explained by Angela Valenzuela, the concept of social capital is rooted partly in economic sociology. It involves the exchange of scarce resources, based on relations of trust and solidarity, which permits people to attain goals that they cannot easily attain individually. Explaining how the notion of social capital might be applied to educational goals, Stanton-Salazar (2001: 265) talks about "associations" among people that, when activated, enable them to "empower themselves" in some meaningful manner (e.g., completing a calculus problem or negotiating a higher math mark). Such associations can occur in various ways: 1) between two individuals (as in the first classroom interaction between two students); 2) between individuals in a group (as in the second interaction between several students in a classroom); and 3) between groups within a community.

Continuing his description of social capital, Stanton-Salazar suggests that it has three fundamental characteristics. First, social capital is a dynamic process based on reciprocal investments in a relationship. To have social capital is to be in a relationship where two or more parties make reciprocal investments and commitments, although not always to the same degree. The students featured in the first interaction had social capital, or more specifically peer social capital (Valenzuela, 1999), because they sat next to each other for the entire calculus course and were committed to helping each other complete the homework problems for the entire semester. Similarly, the students in the second interaction sat at the same table for the entire finite math course and were committed to completing assignments and reviewing each other's tests.

The second characteristic of peer social capital involves developing trust in the relationship. Trust is displayed in both examples of classroom interaction when Anthony demonstrates some vulnerability and asks Edward if working through the calculus problem will be "messy and complicated," and when Lawrence talks about his difficulty of discussing his math mark with his teacher (*"I really don't know what to do"*). The third characteristic of peer social capital is the capacity to generate resources. In the first interaction, the students generate knowledge of how to complete a particular kind of calculus problem and knowledge that they have the right kind of evidence to negotiate a higher math mark if they can figure out how to approach the teacher.

Understanding the students' use of Cantonese at Northside as the development of peer social capital, made possible by a space opened up by the one of the contradictory discourses of the *Language for Learning Policy*, allows us to see something important. Given a space to legitimately use Cantonese in school, ESOL students were able to capitalize on ethnic forms of solidarity for both social and academic support. Instead of using their minority language, culture, and networks to resist the dominant academic culture of the school (e.g., as reported in the educational literature by Fordham and Ogbu, 1986; Matute-Bianci, 1991; Ogbu, 1991, 1993), the students used them to negotiate and manage the development of their academic competence at school.

Importantly, the peer social capital described here, created through the use of Cantonese, was not capital that fitted closely with the mainstream or dominant language and culture of the school. Yet, it was capital that was convertible to mainstream cultural capital (good grades) and economic capital (access to university and a professional occupation). Such a finding expands on Bourdieu's understanding of capital as necessarily being associated with mainstream or dominant cultural and linguistic practices. It was the use of a minority language, Cantonese, that provided students with access to the linguistic capital of English and to the cultural and economic capital associated with English.

Developing peer social capital by not using English

While Cantonese was associated with building up peer social capital among students at Northside, the use of English was considered risky as it could jeopardize the access to friendship and assistance that was important to academic and social success in school. Cantonese-speaking students who were born in Hong Kong reported that other Hong Kong-born students told them they were "rude" if they spoke to them in English. When asked why it was rude to speak in English, one student told us that some people thought that you were trying to be "special" if you spoke English or that you liked to "show off your English abilities." In the following interview excerpt, Victor Yu, a Grade 12 student who had immigrated to Toronto from Hong Kong three years prior to the interview, explains "showing off" this way:

> For the Hong Kong people, right? We will, we will rarely use English to speak to each other except for people who are born here or have been here for a long time. If that is not the case, right? We will speak Cantonese because if we like talk English with them, right? They do think you are really, like, showing off your skill in English.
> (Victor Yu, personal communication, October 9, 1996)

To understand the reasons behind the association between the use of English and showing off, it is helpful to refer to the work undertaken by Angel Lin (2001), who talks about English as the language of power and the language of educational and socioeconomic advancement in Hong Kong. To illustrate her point, Lin writes that a student who wants to study medicine, architecture or legal studies in Hong Kong must have adequate English resources (linguistic capital), in addition to subject knowledge and skills, to enter and succeed in these English-medium professional training programs (gain cultural capital). After graduating from these programs, students also need to have adequate

English resources to earn the credentials to enter these professions, which are accredited by British-based or British-associated professional bodies (Hong Kong was a British colony until July 1997). Students' access to linguistic capital that would provide them with the mastery of English needed to enter high-income professions in Hong Kong is uneven. Only a small elite group of Cantonese speakers has had the opportunity to obtain such mastery. The elite bilingual class in Hong Kong includes people who are wealthy enough to afford high-quality, English-medium private secondary and tertiary education, and a very small number of high-achieving students who get access to such education via their high scores in public examinations. It is the association of English with membership in this elite bilingual class in Hong Kong that helps explain why Cantonese-speaking students at Northside associated speaking English with showing off. It also helps to further explain the results of the Hong Kong survey described earlier.

Back in the city of Toronto, English is also the language associated with educational and socioeconomic advancement. Students at Northside passed courses and acquired cultural capital by demonstrating what they had learned in English. Students from Hong Kong who were first-generation immigrants to Canada used English with varying levels of proficiency and mastery. This meant they had varying levels of linguistic capital at school. When Cantonese-speaking students used English with other Cantonese students, they demonstrated their proficiency or mastery and could be seen as showing off their linguistic capital and flexing their linguistic power. Students who depended on peer social capital did not want to risk being considered a show-off. This is illustrated in the following excerpts from Cathy's interview. Cathy was born in Hong Kong and came to Toronto when she was eight. She was in Grade 12 at the time of the interview.

> If you're speaking English out of the class with your friends, your friends will think that—think that—um—"Why don't you speak Cantonese to me?" Right? Um—we're—like—it's your home language. Right? So why do you speak English instead? Why don't you speak Cantonese instead of English? Right? So—like—they would think that you were not a—as—I don't know—like pretending you were very well in English and something like that. They—you wouldn't—Naturally, you'd speak Chinese.
>
> (Cathy Lee, personal communication, April 30, 1998)

A second, alternative explanation of showing off can be found in the association of English with being "too Canadianized." This is illustrated in the following interview excerpt. Max, a Grade 11 student who was born in Hong Kong, had been in Canada for two years when this interview was conducted. In answer to the question of what would happen if he were in a group of Hong Kong-born, Cantonese-speaking friends and someone started talking in English, Max replied:

They would feel that this person is very proud. It's like showing off that his English is good. Somebody may think that way.

In response to a follow-up question asking how he would feel if he discovered that this person always spoke to him in English even though he understood and spoke a lot of Chinese, Max answered:

Maybe they speak English because most of their friends are Canadian [people who are born in Canada and are English speakers]. They are used to speaking English. They may already have formed their group. At home they may speak in Chinese.

Finally, when asked if he would make friends with such a person, Max said:

Well, there's always this barrier. They're kind of too Canadianized, and there's not much difference with the Canadians compared to them.
(Max Yeung, personal communication, July 27, 1994)

To Max and other students at Northside, Cantonese-speaking students who spoke English with other Cantonese speakers were not part of the Hong Kong community at Northside. Speaking English was seen as showing off because you were trying to show that you could be or act Canadian, and/or that you were mastering the language of social and economic opportunity in Canada, which was a challenge for everybody.

In summary, while the use of Cantonese was associated with the building up of peer social capital, the use of English was associated with losing it and most students in the Hong Kong community at Northside avoided using it with each other. This linguistic strategy created several dilemmas and tensions for students, especially when it rubbed up against both the institutional and the individual desire for students to use only English at school.

Dilemmas and tensions associated with using Cantonese

Choosing to only use Cantonese with other Cantonese speakers at Northside was problematic for some of the students. These students told us that while working and socializing almost exclusively in Cantonese provided them with friends and helped them succeed in their courses, it did not provide them with many opportunities to "practice" English. These students talked about the educational and socioeconomic benefits, the cultural and economic capital, associated with being able to use English well. English was not only the legitimate language of instruction and evaluation at Northside, but also the legitimate language at the universities they wanted to attend as well. Strong proficiency in English provided students with access to a wider range of programs and courses at university. The students also suggested that strong English skills were required in many of the local labor markets and in such high-status and high-influence professions as law, politics, and upper management positions in both the private and the public sectors. These understandings reflect Kyo Maclear's (1994) discussion on the need for the Canadian school system to ensure that the English language abilities of Asian high-school students are developed on an equal basis as other students.

One particular dilemma for the Cantonese-speaking students was how to find opportunities to practice English (which would benefit them in the long term) at the same time as they used Cantonese to develop peer social capital and achieve more immediate social and academic success at school. A second dilemma, or perhaps a tension associated with using Cantonese at school, was that many of the teachers and students did not like hearing it in the classrooms and hallways of the school. Teachers who believed that students' academic success depended on English monolingualism in the classroom contested the *Language for Learning Policy*'s acceptance of student multilingualism, and promoted the use of English in a number of ways. To illustrate, some teachers experimented with classroom English-only rules or policies. One such teacher, Mrs Yee, who was a bilingual (Cantonese/English) teacher with 17 years of experience both in Hong Kong and in Toronto, explained the reason behind her English-only policy this way:

> I have a strong commitment to make sure that they speak only English in class because I think I understand the family backgrounds. Not just the Chinese kids' [backgrounds], the ESOL kids' [backgrounds]. I mean they don't speak English at home. Their parents don't usually speak English with them and their parents very often expect them to be able to retain their mother tongue. So, these kids, if we don't force them to speak English at school, they'd have no chance of speaking the target language or the language that they need to acquire. And if we cannot provide such an environment for them, I think we are doing them a disservice. Secondly, time is short. If we don't enforce an English-only environment, I am sure that when they get to universities, no one is going to do that. And since Canada is an English-speaking country, for the sake of the future of the students, I think we have to make them speak English.
>
> (Anne Yee, personal communication, May 27, 1998)

While Mrs Yee used an English-only policy to promote English monolingualism, other teachers discussed their preferences with students at the beginning of their courses and reminded them to "Speak English, please" whenever they heard another language being used. Often, these teachers' preference for English was related to the fact that some students in their class reported that they felt excluded or "left out" when other students used languages they did not understand, especially when they were working in small groups. Students also reported that they were worried that others were talking negatively about them in languages they could not understand. These feelings of being excluded and talked about often reflected the teachers' own feelings. These reports of feelings of exclusion help explain the desire for English monolingualism at Northside.

Students who spoke Cantonese (or other languages) in classrooms where teachers had made their preference for English clear risked their teachers' displeasure and disapproval. Students overheard using Cantonese in classrooms with English-only rules or policies risked being punished or disciplined. In all classrooms, students who spoke Cantonese risked the anger and resentment of classmates who felt excluded from their conversation. Yet, as discussed earlier, using English with Cantonese speakers was also costly. In the following interview excerpt, Grade 11 student Frank Li, who had immigrated from Hong Kong two and half years before, puts it this way:

Tara: So is it correct to say you use both English and Cantonese during the day, here at Northside?

Frank: Well, mostly I use English, 'cause even though [I am] with Chinese people, I, I sort of avoid talking in Cantonese because most of the time I'm, I'm with some Chinese people and then around there's someone who cannot speak, couldn't understand Cantonese. I, I always think it's not nice, to, to, to speak Cantonese in front of people that don't understand it. That's why. But [when] I, I talk with some Chinese people I still use Can—English in [some cases], but if they don't understand English that's another story.

Tara: Okay, then you'll use Cantonese.

Frank: Yeah.

Tara: Let me ask you about teachers in Northside. Do you have any teachers who have rules about using Cantonese in the classroom?

Frank: Well, me, I don't, but I've heard of other people that have [teachers who have rules] . . . [One teacher] says, a nickel or a dime [thus, imposing a fine for speaking Cantonese], every time that you speak Chinese and, but, for me I think, well, I try my best not to speak Chinese in class . . . But, you know, sometimes it's really hard because when my Chinese friends are talking in Chinese, you know, that, that's, it's not polite [to speak in English]. 'Cause like, okay, [it's like] I was trying to show off or whatever. That, that, you know, in that case, I'll, I will speak in Cantonese, but maybe just a few words . . . Well, you know, trying my best not to [speak in Cantonese]. Sometimes it just happens. Okay, [if] they ask, they ask me a question in Chinese, [then] I should answer in Chinese, that's what I should do.

(Frank Li, personal communication, February 19, 1997)

There were a number of ways Cantonese-speaking students tried to work through this linguistic dilemma at Northside. Some, like Frank, tried to accommodate the language preferences of their English-speaking classmates and teachers whenever it was possible, censoring their use of Cantonese when necessary. Others chose to use Cantonese despite the anger of other students. A few code-switched from Cantonese to English and from English to Cantonese in an effort to accommodate both English and Cantonese speakers and work across linguistic differences in their classrooms (see Goldstein, 2003 for further discussion of this last strategy). Importantly, some students chose a strategy of silence to avoid the risks associated with speaking either English or Cantonese. In the next section, I analyze this strategy by working with King-Kok Cheung's (1993) notion of *attentive silence*.

The capital of attentive silence

As an applied sociolinguist interested in questions of multilingualism and schooling, I have been trained to listen to and analyze multilingual talk. I have not been trained to listen to and analyze what I call "the practice of silence." However, when I realized that silence was being used as a strategy to manage academic life at Northside, it became important to layer my Bourdieusian analysis of language practices with an analysis of the practice of silence.

As discussed above, students used silence to avoid the risks of losing peer social capital by speaking English in front of Cantonese-speakers and Cantonese in front of English-speakers. Another way Cantonese-speaking students used silence in the classroom had to do with the cultural convention of not answering their teachers' questions in class. In the following interview excerpt, Victor Yu, who spoke about the cost of "showing off" earlier, discusses the risks of answering teachers' questions in the classroom.

Tara: Tell me some of the differences between going to school in Hong Kong and going to high school here in Toronto.

Victor: Oh, there's a big difference. In Hong Kong, right? The teachers are really dominating, like, they, they, want everything under their control because there are 40 people at least in one class, even in Grade 7. So, there are many people, right? If one student gets, like, out of control, right? Everyone will be out of control. So that teacher wants absolute control. And in this case, the good students will have no questions. They will always follow the teacher instruction. So, in here, right? Maybe the teacher, teacher will say that, "This guy is doing really good in, in his task, in his, his, work. How come he doesn't answer any questions?" Or "How come he doesn't answer any of my, how he come didn't answer my questions?" Because this is a different culture.

Tara: Right. Tell me more about that. You were telling me before I turned on the tape [recorder] about that. You were telling me this is something I should tell my [pre-service teacher education] students.

Victor: Yeah. If, if you see a student, right? Like especially from Hong Kong or from Asia. Like, they, they do their work really good. But they're quiet, right? Don't blame them because this is like what they used to be in the school in Hong Kong, or in, in their country. Because they, they think that, "If I don't have any problems for the teacher, the teacher will think I am good." So they keep quiet. They don't know that if they don't, like, answer questions, then they are not really participating in the class. Right? It's, it's, they will, like, the teachers will see them as not really good students. So this is, this would be a difference from the school in Hong Kong and here.

Tara: Let me ask you [this]. Was it very hard for you when you first came to Toronto to get used to the presentations and the group work and the speaking out in class?

Victor: Yeah. It was really, really hard. 'Cause, okay, 'cause I, when I want to answer some questions I was thinking about, "If I answer," right? "What will other Cantonese students or students from Hong Kong think about me?" If I, like, they may be thinking about how I am showing off my knowledge. I mean, yeah, I know the [answers to the] questions, right? I know it. That's, that's good. I can keep it in my heart. But then, if I put my hand up and then say, "Sir, I understand," and then answer the question, right? They will, they may think, think I am showing off. So it is really hard.

(Victor Yu, personal communication, October 9, 1999)

As Victor explained, Cantonese-speaking students used silence as a strategy to avoid answering their teachers' questions and being perceived as showing off. This grounded theoretical notion of showing off can be further theorized through the work undertaken by literary scholar King-Kok Cheung (1993).

In her book *Articulate Silences*, Cheung raises important questions about the negative social assessment the practice of silence receives in the West. Analyzing the use of silence in the literary works of Asian-American writers Hisaye Yamamoto, Maxine Hong Kingston, and Asian-Canadian writer Joy Kogawa, Cheung critiques the ways in which contemporary Anglo-American feminists have valorized voice and speech indiscriminately and dismissed all practices of silence as a sign of passivity. Cheung also critiques Asian-American male writers who attempt to refute Western stereotypes of the devious, timid, inscrutable, and shrewd Asian in their work by renouncing silence entirely. She argues that silence can carry a variety of functions and meanings that vary with individuals and cultures. There are a variety of modalities of silence, which need to be differentiated from each other. Cheung is interested in the "resources as well as the hazards" of silence: "While the importance of voice is indisputable, pronouncing silence as the converse of speech or as its subordinate can be oppressively univocal" (p. 6). To analyse the ways in which silence is practiced by the characters portrayed in the works of Yamamoto, Kingston, and Kogawa, Cheung proposes at least five differing, and often overlapping, modes or tonalities of silences: attentive, inhibitive, oppressive, protective, and stoic. Of these five modes of silence, two are relevant to an analysis of students' practice of silence in Northside classrooms: *attentive silence* and *inhibitive silence*.

Attentive silence is a form of silence in which there is acute listening, empathy for others, and awareness of even the subtlest signs from a speaker. In essence, attentive silence is a quiet understanding. Such a mode of silence, argues Cheung, is empowering and thus the antithesis of passivity with which it is often associated. For students at Northside, this practice of quiet understanding was associated with the accumulation and maintenance of peer social capital. Importantly, Cheung argues that all modes of silences can fluctuate between being enabling or debilitating. For this reason, she warns against romanticizing or eroticizing silences. While the practice of attentive silence enabled students at Northside to avoid "showing off" and to access peer social capital, it was also inhibitive. Cantonese-speaking students who chose to keep knowledge in their hearts to avoid drawing negative reactions from their Hong Kong-born friends were placed in another linguistic dilemma. While the capital of attentive silence allowed students to accumulate and maintain peer social capital, it also jeopardized their accumulation of mainstream linguistic and cultural capital. Students who did not speak English or answer questions in class lost grades and opportunities to develop their English language and literacy skills. One of the challenges for teachers at Northside, then, was to find ways of working with their students' practice of attentive-inhibitive silence. This involved providing students with opportunities to develop their English language and literacy skills without assuming the social and academic risks associated with breaking the sociocultural, sociolinguistic norms of their linguistic community. A discussion of how these opportunities were provided for students follows.

English language and literacy education in multilingual schools

It is beyond the scope of this chapter to include a discussion of all the innovative pedagogical approaches that took place within Northside classrooms. However, the work undertaken by English teacher Leonard Robertson is particularly helpful in thinking about how to respond to the linguistic tensions, dilemmas, and practices of silence outlined in this chapter.

Although small group work and co-operative learning activities were popular in many Northside classrooms, they also became sites of linguistic tension when students used Cantonese in linguistically mixed groups. Linguistic tensions were particularly high when the groups had to complete tasks (both oral and written) that were to be graded as a group assignment. In response to these tensions, many students chose to practice attentive silence and did not talk at all during small group work, creating additional tension between students. In response to these tensions, Mr Robertson, an English teacher with 33 years of teaching experience, did two things. First, he lowered the stakes of group work by reserving the use of small group work in his classroom for activities that were not graded, but that were designed to help students prepare for individually graded assignments. Second, he provided students with an opportunity to work in a language other than English if they desired. To illustrate, here is a small group activity that Mr Robertson designed to help his Grade 11 students prepare an essay on William Shakespeare's play *Macbeth*.

Many of the students in Mr Robertson's class were Cantonese-speaking ESOL students, and their task was to develop arguments to support one of eight different statements about the play. An example of such a statement was: "Lady Macbeth has sometimes been called the Fourth Witch. Construct a thesis that argues that she should be regarded as the fourth witch, and support it in an organized essay." A contrasting statement asked students to argue that Lady Macbeth should not be regarded as the fourth witch. Students were placed in eight different linguistically mixed groups and each group was asked to create a flipchart (poster) which provided a thesis statement and supporting evidence for one of the eight statements. The linguistic tensions typically associated with such group work diminished as the work being done by the group was not going to be graded. After each group had finished working on their flipchart, they were hung up on the walls of the classroom. The students then worked individually on a plan for the essay they had each chosen to write. Just before the students were scheduled to write their in-class essay, Mr Robertson gave them a class period to talk to any one of their classmates about their plan and consult the flipcharts on the wall one more time to improve their plans. During this class period, students were encouraged to use whatever language they wanted, and I observed that a number of students worked together in Cantonese as well as English. A lot of students used the period to talk to Mr Robertson about their plan as well as with other students, and many students consulted the flipcharts on the wall. Here, small group work was planned to provide students with an opportunity to use both English and languages other than English to produce strong, individually assessed written work in English. As Mr Robertson explained,

> I was trying to structure the learning for all students in order to ensure that students had good examples of a solid argument of which the teacher approved, and which they could use with full confidence that they would be rewarded.
> (Leonard Robertson, personal communication, June 12, 2001)

What Mr Robertson provided the students in his class were opportunities and pressures to use English conversationally with non-Cantonese-speaking students. He also provided students with opportunities to use their preferred language (Cantonese) and peer social capital in the service of their English literacy development. The flipcharts, with examples of thesis statements and supporting evidence for each of the essay questions, provided all students with model outlines of the essay they were expected to produce individually.

In addition to carefully planning his group work activities, Mr Robertson also alternated small group work with whole group work. Examples of such work included reciting poetry or prose in chorus and asking students to answer questions in unison. When observing these activities, I noticed that several Cantonese-speaking students who were usually silent when asked to individually respond to a question in English (a practice which inhibited their English language and literacy development) responded to a question that was posed to the group.

Linking Mr Robertson's pedagogy to the linguistic struggle between the desire for English monolingualism reported in the *School Review* and the desire for student multilingualism allowed for in the *Language for Learning Policy*, we can see that it is the legitimization of student multilingualism that best supports the Cantonese-speaking students' chances for academic and social success at Northside. As mentioned earlier, a new language policy for the new Toronto District School Board was adopted in May 1998. The 1998 *Literacy Foundation Policy* was similar to the 1995 *Language for Learning Statement* in that it articulates the belief that "all languages and varieties of languages are equally valid forms of thought and communication" (p. 2). It also states that "first language literacy is important for second-language learning and for achieving academic success in the second language" (p. 2). However, the new policy does not include the statement that "students' first languages play an important role in the classroom, in the school program as a whole, and in communication with the home" that was contained in the 1995 policy. As discussed earlier, it was this statement that legitimized student multilingualism at Northside. Replacing this statement was a more general one about valuing and respecting diversity:

> Valuing and respecting diversity requires an inclusive curriculum which recognizes and affirms the life experiences of all learners, regardless of gender, place of origin, religion, ethnicity and race, cultural and linguistic background, social and economic status, sexual orientation, age and ability/disability.
>
> (p. 7)

While such a statement keeps a space open for the acceptance of student multilingualism at school—accepting student multilingualism is a way of recognizing the linguistic life experiences of learners at school—it is not as powerful a statement as the 1995 statement which explicitly discussed students' first languages as playing an important role in the classroom and school program.

Conclusion

In conclusion, I have argued that by investing in and developing peer social capital—often through the practice of attentive silence—Canadian Cantonese-speaking students capitalized on ethnic forms of solidarity to negotiate and manage the development of their academic competence in an English-speaking school. In doing so, I have been able to expand Bourdieu's understanding of capital as necessarily being associated with mainstream or dominant cultural and linguistic practices. At Northside, it was the use of a minority language, Cantonese, and the practice of attentive silence that provided students with access to peer social capital. In turn, the accumulation of peer social capital provided them with access to cultural capital associated with and acquired by the dominant language, English.

The attention I have paid to the practice of attentive–inhibitive silence in classroom interactions is important for Western-educated linguistic and language education researchers. Our training has taught us to privilege the analysis of speech over the analysis of silence, and to view silence as the absence and the subordinate of speech. King-Kok Cheung's work, which names a variety of modalities of silence—each of which can be either enabling or debilitating—is extremely helpful to future analysis of the practice of silence in a multilingual and multicultural setting where silence can carry a variety of meanings and functions.

Finally, I have argued that students at Northside were only able to accumulate and maintain peer social capital because there existed a space to legitimately use Cantonese in school. The willingness of teachers such as Mr Robertson to legitimize their students' bilingual language practices had a positive impact on their English language and literacy education. Such teachers need a literacy policy that legitimizes student multilingualism to support their work. In Canada, as well as in many other English-speaking countries, immigrant elementary and secondary school students are growing up with several languages and cultures. They are living in more than one community and building different kinds of capital in more than one language. Learning to work effectively with students who have strong affiliations in more than one community is critical to good teaching. Teachers in multilingual schools today need to develop new understandings about the lives, language, and literacy needs of our immigrant students. In a small way, this chapter attempts to begin a discussion about what such an understanding entails.

Notes

1   I would like to acknowledge and thank the Social Sciences and Humanities Research Council of Canada (SSHRCC) for funding this study (1996–99). For a fuller report of the findings, see Goldstein, 2003.
2   The research reports we read included works by McKay and Wong (1996), Lee (1996), and Lam (1996). The memoir and play we read were *The Woman Warrior:*

Memoirs of a Girlhood Among Ghosts by Maxine Hong Kingston (1989) and *FOB* by David Henry Hwang (1990) respectively.

3   I would like to acknowledge research assistant Gordon Pon who introduced me to the work of King-Kok Cheung. Gordon and I have co-written two previous pieces on attentive silence (Goldstein and Pon, 2003; Pon et al., 2002), which have informed my writing of this chapter.

4   As Lin (2001) explains, "Chinese" in the Hong Kong context is often taken to mean Cantonese in its spoken form and Modern Standard Chinese in its written form.

5   See Lin (1997a) for a critical analysis of these official, academic, and media discourses.

6   Researchers of language minority students and schooling who draw upon Bourdieu's notions of capital, social fields, markets, and legitimacy include Heller (2001), Heller and Martin-Jones (2001), Lin (2001), and Martin Jones and Saxena (2001).

7   The names of all the students and teachers used in this chapter are pseudonyms.

8   In examples of classroom interactions, each Cantonese speaker's original Cantonese utterances have been translated into English and appear in *italics*. Any additional information needed to make the meaning of the speaker's words clear to the readers appears in brackets [ ] within or right after the translated or English utterance. Non-verbal communication such as laughter is indicated in parentheses ( ). Words that appear in **boldface** are words that were originally spoken in English.

References

Belfiore, M. E. and Heller, M. (1992) Cross-cultural interviews: participation and decision-making. In B. Burnaby and A. Cumming (eds), *Sociopolitical Aspects of ESL*. Toronto, Ontario, Canada: OISE Press/Stoughton, 233–40.

Bourdieu, P. (1991) *Language and Symbolic Power* (G. Raymond and M. Adamson, trans.) Cambridge, UK: Polity Press. (Original work published 1982)

Briggs, C. (1986) *Learning How to Ask: A Sociolinguistic Appraisal of the Role of the Interview in Social Science Research*. Cambridge, UK: Cambridge University Press.

Cheung, K.-K. (1993) *Articulate Silences: Hisaye Yamamoto, Maxine Hong Kingston, Joy Kogawa*. New York: Cornell University Press.

Fordham, S. and Ogbu, J. (1986) Black students' school success: coping with the "burden of acting white". *Urban Review*, 18, 176–206.

Gerrard, N. and Javed, N. (1994) A dialogue about racism and silence: Personal and political perspectives. *Canadian Woman Studies*, 14(2), 64–7.

Goldstein, T. (2003) *Teaching and Learning in a Multilingual School: Choices, Risks and Dilemmas*. Mahwah, NJ: Lawrence Erlbaum Associates.

Goldstein, T. and Pon, G. (2003) Responding to silence. In T. Goldstein (ed.), *Teaching and Learning in a Multilingual School: Choices, Risks and Dilemmas*. Mahwah, NJ: Lawrence Erlbaum Associates, 58–80.

Gumperz, J. (1992) Interviewing in intercultural situations. In P. Drew and J. Heritage (eds), *Talk at Work: Interaction in Institutional Settings*. Cambridge, UK: Cambridge University Press, 302–27.

Heller, M. (2001) Legitimate language in a multilingual school. In M. Heller and M. Martin Jones (eds), *Voices of Authority: Education and Linguistic Differences*, Westport, CT: Ablex, 381–402.

Heller, M. and Martin-Jones, M. (2001) Introduction: symbolic domination, education and linguistic differences. In M. Heller and M. Martin Jones (eds), *Voices of Authority: Education and Linguistic Differences*. Westport, CT: Ablex, 1–28.

Hwang, D. H. (1990) *FOB and Other Plays*. New York: Plume.

Kingston, M. H. (1989) *Woman Warrior: Memoirs of a Girlhood Among Ghosts*. New York: Vintage International.

Lam, C. S. M. (1996) The green teacher. In D. Thiessen, N. Bascia, and I. Goodson (eds), *Making a Difference About Difference: The Lives and Careers of Racial Minority Immigrant Teachers*. Toronto, Ontario, Canada: Garamond Press, 15–50.

Lee, S. J. (1996) *Unraveling the "Model Minority" Stereotype: Listening to Asian American Youth*. New York: Teachers College Press.

Lin, A. (1997a) Analyzing the "language problem" discourses in Hong Kong: how official, academic, and media discourses construct and perpetuate dominant models of language, learning and education. *Journal of Pragmatics*, 28, 427–40.

Lin, A. (1997b) Bilingual education in Hong Kong. In J. Cummins and D. Corson (eds), *Encyclopedia of Language and Education (Vol. 5): Bilingual Education*. Dordrecht, Netherlands: Kluwer, 281–9.

Lin, A. (2001) Symbolic domination and bilingual classroom practices in Hong Kong schools. In M. Heller and M. Martin Jones (eds), *Voices of Authority: Education and Linguistic Differences*. Westport, CT: Ablex, 139–68.

Maclear, K. (1994) The myth of the "model minority": rethinking the education of Asian Canadians. *Our Schools/Our Selves*, 5(3), 54–76.

Martin-Jones, M. and Saxena, M. (2001) Turn-taking and the positioning of bilingual participants in classroom discourse: insights from primary schools in England. In M. Heller and M. Martin-Jones (eds), *Voices of Authority: Education and Linguistic Differences*. Westport, CT: Ablex, 117–138.

Matute-Bianchi, M. (1991) Situational ethnicity and patterns of school performance among immigrant and nonimmigrant Mexican-descent students. In M. Gibson and J. Ogbu (eds), *Minority Status and Schooling: A Comparative Study of Immigrant and Involuntary Minorities*. New York: Garland, 205–47.

McKay, S. L. and Wong, S. C. (1996) Multiple discourses, multiple identities: investment and agency in second-language learning among Chinese adolescent immigrant students. *Harvard Educational Review*, 6, 577–608.

Ogbu, J. (1991) Immigrant and involuntary minorities in comparative perspective. In M. Gibson and J. Ogbu (eds), *Minority Status and Schooling: A Comparative Study of Immigrant and Involuntary Minorities*. New York: Garland, 3–33.

Ogbu, J. U. (1993) Frameworks-variability in minority school performance: a problem in search of an explanation. In E. Jacob and C. Jordan (eds), *Minority Education: Anthropological Perspectives*. Norwood, NJ: Ablex, 83–111.

Pon, G., Goldstein, T. and Schecter, S. (2003) Interrupted by silences: the contemporary education of Hong Kong-born Chinese-Canadian adolescents. In R. Bayley and S. Schecter (eds), *Language Socialization and Bi-multilingual Societies*. New York: Multilingual Matters, 114–27.

Stanton-Salazar, R. (2001) *Manufacturing Hope and Despair: The School and Kin Support Networks of U.S.-Mexican Youth*. New York: Teachers College Press.

Toronto District School Board. (1995) *Language for Learning Policy*. Ontario, Canada: Author.

Toronto District School Board. (1998) *Literacy Foundation Statement*. Ontario, Canada: Author.

Tung, P., Lam, R. and Tsang, W. K. (1997) English as a medium of instruction in post-1997 Hong Kong: what students, teachers, and parents think. *Journal of Pragmatics*, 28, 441–59.

Valenzuela, A. (1999) *Substratice Schooling: U.S.-Mexican Youth and the Politics of Caring*. New York: State University of New York Press.

Chapter 12

Improvising on artistic habitus

Sedimenting identity into art

Jennifer Rowsell

Content, the internal part of a semiotic domain, gets made in history by real people and their social interactions. They build that content—in part, not wholly—in certain ways because of the people they are (socially, historically, culturally). That content comes to define one of their important identities in the world. As those identities develop their further social interactions, they come to affect the on-going development and transformation of the content of the semiotic domain in yet new ways. *The relationship between the internal and external world is reciprocal* [italics added].

(Gee, 2003: 29)

Introduction

Art is a symbolic representation of one's internal world made external. Artifacts sediment moments as an expression of how an artist feels or thinks at a moment in time. Art and artistic creation thereby trace social practices used to express how one feels within a social context or social space. In this chapter, I reflect on art created by three artists-turned-teachers to demonstrate how they actively embed parts of themselves, an event, their beliefs, into artifacts they produce. The study is framed within my lens as a teacher educator. The three case studies derive from ethnographic research with three Bachelor of Education (B.Ed.) students I worked with over the course of their teacher preparation year.

These artists—Taiga, Anjani, and Henry—have taken up an aesthetic over time, yet they remain three individuals born into a specific set of dispositions which indirectly and at times directly impact their aesthetic production and consumption. All three of the participants in the research study came into a teacher education program to make life changes, and each one has used artistic production to objectify their repositioning in art. What is more, these three participants negotiate identity shifts and represent habitus across several intersecting fields—art and design, student teaching, immigration to Canada, parenthood. In Bourdieu's terms, the cultural capital—"as an embodiment of distinctive and distinguishable sensibilities" (Calhoun, 1993: 70)—they share is aesthetic production. They are equally involved in a world of art and design that informs their teaching, their values and beliefs, and their epistemologies. Their instantiation and manipulation of art as cultural capital transform their practice and critically frame their pedagogy. I therefore read cultural capital not in relation to Bourdieu's sociological enterprise, but in relation to Bourdieu's theory of aesthetics.

Bourdieu refers to the unconscious appropriation of rules, values and dispositions as *the habitus*, defining it as "the durably installed generative principle of regulated improvisations which produce practices" (1991: 12). Habitus derives from our cultural history, which stays with us and impinges on our actions and reactions. In interviewing three artists who had consistently imbued their cultural history into artifacts they create, it was clear to me and to them that they were *consciously* doing so.

In this chapter, I consider Bourdieu's theories on cultural production and his notion of habitus to explore how each individual actively reconstructs themselves through their art. I will be looking at particular moments of cultural production, and I claim that artifacts which grow out of these moments "sediment" (Pahl, 2004) habitus *and* cement shifts in their identity. In my analysis of interview and artifactual data, I trace their stories within their art, thereby tying them to habitus (and the act of modifying habitus).

By considering ways of understanding the world through cultural production at a particular time, in a particular place, and even at a particular stage in life, I take on board a concept of creative work as a means of materializing or objectifying shifts in identity. James Gee's quotation as a segue to the chapter captures well a complex and continuing dialogue between structure and agency that transpires when we work within a semiotic domain of any kind—written narratives, art, interface design. In particular, Gee's emphasis on "the relationship between the internal and external world" as reciprocal ushers us well into an analysis of how these three B.Ed. students use their art to come to terms with their external world. Clearly, what fuels our production—creative or otherwise—are the internal and external parts of us.

A question that grows out of exploring "sedimented subjectivities in art" is: How does cultural production modify habitus, and is it a conscious or unconscious act? Bourdieu's enduring dialogue with objectivism and subjectivism is helpful in discussing how three case studies engage with aspects of their habitus (consciously or unconsciously) and the outside world in artifacts they create. Bourdieu's definition of practice in *The Logic of Practice* (1980/1990) invites us to think more about how internal and external worlds collide:

> Informed by a kind of objective finality without being consciously organised in relation to any explicitly constituted end; intelligible and coherent without springing from an intention of coherence and a deliberate decision; adjusted to the future without being a product of a project or plan.
>
> (pp. 50, 51)

Bourdieu's description of practice draws precisely on the concept that producers of texts have to operate within their habitus and to creatively produce beyond its rules (that is when the creative and cultural part comes in). In works such as *Distinction* (1979/1984), Bourdieu considers our propensity to engage with the game of culture by examining the relationship between artistic taste and social background. In the case studies, I present three individuals who choose to objectify their enduring dialogue with changes in their lives and vocations in art. According to them, they "sediment" these changes in art because it gives them greater voice and greater freedom of expression.

However, in Bourdieusian terms, there is a key difference between parts of one's habitus tied to an artistic habitus that we have acquired over time, and parts of habitus inextricably tied to our past, present, and future as "durable dispositions of our character" (Bourdieu, 1991: 12).

Habitus and cultural production

What I have frequently noted in my work in classrooms and in sessions with B.Ed. students is: it is not only the language of face-to-face interaction that shapes our understandings, but also our viewing and creating of artifacts that significantly impacts meaning-making. In particular, analyzing cultural production in the light of Bourdieu's habitus allows us to see the interface between what we feel–believe–carry with us, and how it is expressed and manifests itself to others or the outside world. Cultural production, and the ability to do so, becomes symbolic capital. Working with three artists who actively embed their habitus in art and, by extension, use this reflective improvisation in their teaching, they become examples of embodied cultural capital. In Bourdieu's words: "I have analyzed the peculiarity of cultural capital, which we should call *informational capital* to give the notion its full generality, and which itself exists in three forms, *embodied* [italics added], objectified, or institutionalized" (Bourdieu and Wacquant, 1992: 119).

The three participants in my study represent case studies of embodied cultural capital. When we view or produce a text, we bring our dispositions alongside the structures within which texts are viewed or produced (e.g., a classroom or an art gallery). The value of habitus is that it mediates between our social condition—Guyanese-Canadian-designer-turned-teacher, or Russian-Canadian-artist-and-semiotician-turned-mother-and-then-teacher —*and* our everyday life, practices, and decisions. By naming habitus in this way, albeit essentialist, we see that Anjani and Taiga respectively are born into specific situations that impinge on their decision making, but their decision making is also mediated by events that take place or epiphanies they experience. We see later in the data that all three participants negotiate innate dispositions versus moments of discovery wherein they challenge norms, which are then improvised in their art.

In Bourdieu's writings on Martin Heidegger (1988), he attributes Heidegger's academic success predominantly to his conscious opposition to the field. I harness my definition of social condition to Bourdieu's notion of field, defined by Fowler (1997) as "a force operating within a field over time exerting either positive or negative effects upon the trajectories of the groups within it" (p. 41). As the son of rural craftspeople, Heidegger's social condition as part of a certain social class at a particular period of time seemingly constrained his social power. However, he entered the field of professional philosophy and used the field or structure in which he grew up to support his philosophical opposition of the period; he "reproduces into the domain of academically acceptable philosophical thought … topics and modes of expression … which were previously confined to those sects encamped on the margins of the field" (Fowler, 1997: 35). Within my study, field operates in a similar way, as participants move from corporate settings such as advertising firms or video game developers, to a B.Ed. program at a particular university in a specific city during a certain academic year.

Bourdieu's work speaks of cultural production as pivoting on the dictates of our habitus or, the way I like to think of it, our second nature *within* the cultural fields in which artifacts are made. The dialectic between habitus and field, or in other terms between agent and structure, is central to looking at how artistic practice or cultural production operates in a social context. Tied to Bourdieu's theories on cultural production are his discussions about an artistic habitus as a response to social class—that is, artistic creation is driven by a rejection and even repudiation of the upper or ruling class—in particular, his analysis of the Impressionist movement.

The traditional notion of "the starving artist" as an interloper—creating art in reaction to a governing structure or class—has become a common perception as choosing, practically and ideologically, the life of an artist. In short, being subversive is innate to the artist's persona. This aspect of Bourdieu's work comes out most strongly in works such as *The Field of Cultural Production* (1993) and *In Other Words* (1994). Bourdieu's work on the artist and improvising on artistic habitus is particularly germane to the chapter in that the three participants in my study *chose* a lifestyle for themselves that defied a familial pattern. Being an artist and a teacher was not an obvious, or easy, trajectory for their lives. Their choices often went at odds with expectations from society and at times from their families. But for them, being an artist and a teacher fit them ideologically.

Improvising on artistic habitus

If we accept that we embed or sediment our habitus (which I will later illustrate) into artifacts, then the question remains: Do we have choice or conscious control over doing so? Bartlett and Holland (2002) draw on Bourdieu's habitus as a way of describing a process of being—dispositions that fall into succeeding generations and miraculously find themselves in artifacts. However, they address an underplay of modifying habitus in artifacts.

As Bartlett and Holland note in their article, "Theorizing the space of literacy practice," "Bourdieu's theory remains limited by a tendency to underplay the importance of culturally produced narratives, images and other artifacts in modifying habitus" (p. 12). Invoking Bourdieu's notion of habitus as unconsciously structuring our words and deeds helps pave the way in analyzing the degree of conscious awareness and agency involved in meaning-making through art or words. The chapter thereby takes up Bartlett and Holland's challenge to invoke Bourdieu's notion of habitus to show how individuals change their situations and their positions within particular contexts and specific circumstances by producing artifacts.

Taiga, Anjani, and Henry seek to objectify distance from shifts that take in their identity, and they do so in their creative production of works of art. Their artifacts, profiled later in the chapter, sediment shifts in their identities and their active renegotiation of these shifts in art. In *Pascalian Meditations* Bourdieu accounts for our habit of taking on a disposition or habitus:

> The agent engaged in practice knows the world . . . too well, without objectifying distance, takes it for granted, precisely because he is caught up in it, bound up with it; he inhabits it like a garment . . . he feels at home in the world because the world is also in him, in the form of the habitus.
>
> (2000: 42, 43)

Bourdieu claims that practice is always informed by our ability to control or understand our actions. Through our dispositions and values, we respond to situations or contexts in different ways—largely because of a second-nature response, that is, our habitus. But what if we actively set out to change our cultural conditions? We are naturally inclined to a disposition, but what if we make an effort to subvert, negotiate, and reposition ourselves in the face of it? It is with this question in mind that I set out to interview three B.Ed. students who have been and continue to be artists.

All three participants come from immigrant families who came to Canada for more opportunities in life (Henry is the second-generation of an immigrant family). Hence, as with the families in Pahl's study, they had experience with migration and induction into a new language and new culture. In some ways, this "rootlessness" is indicative of Bourdieu's artistic habitus. What differentiates them and at the same time conjoins their experience is a re-enactment of identity shifts in artifacts that they create.

Taiga uses photography in her work; she creates three-dimensional and smaller two-dimensional works. Anjani has been a landscape architect and graphic designer for years, and her aesthetic is composed of images from her cultural heritage set in a digital medium. Henry is a graphic artist committed to environmental issues and manifests his convictions about preserving the environment by using materials from the environment and more traditional artistic practices such as woodcutting in his work. In my teaching, supervising, and interviews with each one, we discussed their personal and professional histories always in light of their body of work.

As I analyzed the data, it was evident that the visual and their aesthetic invited growth and changes in their lives and their identities. It is a twist on Bourdieu's writings on artistic habitus as rootless and repudiating ruling class in that all three tried, to varying degrees, to eclipse and move beyond what Holland terms their "history-in-person" (Holland et al., 1998). Their stories of migration, their struggles in a new culture, and indeed their attempts to escape a mold, all resonate with Bourdieu's discussions about Impressionist artists and their rejection of a more elite conception of what art is and should be.

Background to study

Over the course of my B.Ed. teaching, I have encountered students from diverse backgrounds and eclectic experiences. Of particular note, several artists enter the profession to pursue a love of art and design in their teaching. I interviewed a sample of students to consider their decision to become teachers and how this decision impinged on their design/artistic background.

Taiga, Anjani, and Henry were three students I taught and supervised over the course of a B.Ed. year, who had formerly been artists and were training to be teachers. At the conclusion of their B.Ed. program, I interviewed them to explore the role of creative production in their personal and professional lives.[1]

To conduct the research, I used ethnographic methods to interview participants about their art, by observing their teaching and by analyzing semiotic mediation of identity in their texts. The interviews were informal but were framed by a set of questions: What is your personal history before the B.Ed. program? What is your professional history? How and when did you become an artist? To what extent does your experience—past and present—affect your art? Has teaching changed your artwork at all? Are there other factors that have influenced your art? Much of the interview talk revolved around personal histories and their relationship to their art.

Each participant created artifacts as a response to habitus and as a means to modify their own habitus given the constraints and affordances of their circumstances. For some, it was entering teacher's college, while for others it was becoming a parent, and still others it was mediating their own culture with a North American one. The induction into a new "space of practice" (Bartlett and Holland, 2002) supplied new discourses and invoked new practices.

During the interviews, what emerged was that the practices each one performed in creating art were tied to their own dispositions and values. Taiga, for example, creates three-dimensional objects because, to her, they are far more "authentic, concrete, and a real picture of life." Taiga believes art mirrors life and she hopes to have art as a cynosural force in her teaching. Each interviewee created images manifesting their identities and their ongoing dialogue with their identities. For Taiga, becoming a mother strongly affected her art, not only because it represented a new stage in her life, but also because it changed the space in which she created her images. Previously she worked in studios, but with the birth of her daughter she worked in her home and created smaller, "more intimate works of art."

For Anjani, she had an artistic epiphany while creating an interface for a video game, when she fused East Indian images, colors, and shapes from her culture within a digital form or medium, and it gradually became her signature and her aesthetic. Bringing the two together made it more meaningful for her because they were fundamental parts of her identity. For Henry, he felt disillusioned with the commercial nature of graphic design in larger firms and as a result became committed to privileging environmental art over other, digitally governed art. What is more, he adopted more traditional methods of design such as woodcutting to get back to basics in art. Woodcuts provided a simplicity he desired. I remarked how these identity negotiations and mediations were thrown into relief in works of art.

What also became apparent in the interviews was the degree to which motivation resides in the *process* of making an artifact over the product itself. That is, it was actually *making* the work of art that caused the identity shifts. In Bourdieu's analysis of art and artist, he underplayed the role of art and the habitus. Instead, he tended to play on art and social class, who decides what is fine art and what is not. Culturally produced artifacts bring together social fields (context, institutions, and so on). I would add, in light of a modest survey of art and artists, that cultural production changes habitus, and this change is deliberate and active.

Case studies of improvising on artistic habitus

The individuals featured in this chapter had all worked in the field of art or design in some capacity. I chose these participants because they were artists and as such more inclined to reflect on cultural production.

Webb and colleagues (2002) speak of the artistic habitus having particular features: "particular ways of dressing, for instance (colourful and eccentric clothing); a commitment to the inner life and to a personal vision . . . having an attitude of disinterest in 'normal' measures of success (like bank balances, or a large mortgage)" (p. 175). We tend in our minds to have a picture of what an artist is and thinks. Such a depiction does not necessarily correspond with the interviewees, who were quite different in their own right, combining practicality with an interest in measures of success; yet what they seemed to share was a reflective nature about their identities.

In the interviews, much of our conversation revolved around shifts in their aesthetic and practices they employ in creating cultural artifacts. Throughout each interviewee's life experiences, they have consistently turned to the visual to express their feelings, their beliefs, and their negotiation with contexts and situations. It is for this reason that I juxtapose interview excerpts and artifacts to enrich our understanding of participants in the study.

Case study 1: Taiga Ultera—appropriating reality in three dimensions

Taiga and her family came to Canada from Russia when she was a child. They fled communist Russia to have a "better" life. They initially fled to Prague and later the International Rescue Committee posted them in Canada. Taiga found her induction into a new schooling system relatively easy because of what she considered to be a rigorous schooling system in Russia. She recalls, "Russian schools were very strong," so she did not have any real problems academically. She did, however, have some difficulty adapting socially to a new culture.

According to Taiga, in Russia, life is regarded as fairly "black and white," and from very early on she fought against that mentality. By "black and white," Taiga was referring to a dogmatic yet on the whole practical and decisive view on most things and issues. Although, eventually, she appreciated the malleability of the Canadian sensibility, she found herself sitting between two worlds. She was "pulled by the past," yet eschewed a perceived negativity of the Russian community in Toronto. Bartlett and Holland (2002) point out that it is when habitus encounters a foreign structure that changes in identity take place:

> The key moment in Bourdieu's theory occurs in practice, in the encounter between structures (history brought to the present in institutions) and habitus (history brought to the present in person) (Holland and Lave, 2001). Bourdieu's theory suggests that we analyze literacy events with an eye to the ways in which historical and social forces have shaped a person's linguistic habitus and thus impinge upon that person's actions in the moment.
>
> (p. 3)

It was only once Taiga attended art school in Toronto that she found a voice and inspiration in her learning. Although she had good grades in high school and the first year of university, she did not feel tied to her learning. After completing a degree at the Ontario College of Art in Toronto, Taiga began theorizing her technical skill by looking at theory in semiotics, linguistics, and visual design and communication as part of a Master's in Visual Arts at York University. Her graduate experience put a theoretical overlay (i.e., semiotics of art, critical theory on design and visual communication, and so on) on her work.

With theory and practice in unison, she taught courses on theorizing art and visual communication *as* she created art herself. For instance, positioning herself as a mother, as a daughter, as a lecturer, *next* to her femininity in

Figure 12.1, in which she personifies her ambivalence about her gender and her roles. The program she took at York was centered on defining works of art around theoretical principles, which is what Taiga did by instinct. A key part of completing the program was teaching a course at the undergraduate level. Taiga realized that she was not only a natural teacher, but also that her love of art and the aesthetic permeated her philosophy of teaching.

From that point forward there was a recursive cycle of art–theory–practice–art–theory–practice. In her work as a freelance artist and teacher, Taiga continues to sediment her art into her teaching of adults and of children. Over the course of the B.Ed. program, she discovered that art is an ideal medium for teaching children with special needs. Taiga believes that special needs students have a more acute sense of touch in the face of their struggle with cognitive activities. These epiphanies inform her present teaching and dictate her future teaching.

Figure 12.1 Installation of burning dress.

Before entering the B.Ed. program, Taiga opened an art school in her home with a Russian colleague. The art school was based on many of the principles she derived from her technical training in art, and enhanced by a theoretical understanding of space, texture, dimensions, semiotics, and how all of these ideas and ideologies impinge on visual artifacts.

Taiga dwells in a world that stresses the real and the concrete. In her pursuit to appropriate reality, she encourages both children and adults to let things happen—let their instinct (their senses of smell, touch, sound, visual perception) preside over cultural production. Taiga does not like to live by set rules and, indeed, in line with our discussion of artistic habitus, she expresses this clearly in her art.

Taiga has had exhibitions of large installations composed of eclectic objects which collectively represent an idea or concept—family strife, struggles with stereotypes, and so on. In Figure 12.1, Taiga is capturing a moment in time in a particular space; as she expresses it, "When I create something, you know, I could be thinking of the smell or just very vague memories of feelings, you know, from the past, I think definitely, in that way, it is like an exercise." You see pastiches of Taiga in the dress with the fire around it "emblematic of her struggles with female stereotypes." Children creating artifacts in Taiga's classroom will inherit her belief in manifesting reality through artwork that will in turn transform their own artwork.

Taiga's burgeoning philosophy of art resides in a belief in working in three dimensions. She opts for three-dimensionality over other modes because it "feels more real and tangible than other modes." Taiga believes that people are not necessarily clear about what she is creating and three-dimensionality gives her a "more real and more concrete voice" in which to speak to her audience.

Case study 2: Anjani Mistry—invoking digital media to find culture

Anjani, born in Guyana and raised in Toronto, has always been artistic and expressed herself visually. She has fond memories of her experiences at an inner-city elementary school in Toronto, but had less of a positive experience in high school. In an assignment on "Language as a construction of social identity," Anjani described herself as follows:

> I am Anjani Mistry, a displaced East Indian and Guyanese Canadian in her early thirties. I am a self-described somewhat neurotic artsy-techie and will soon be an educator. My first language is English, as the dialect spoken in Guyana. I immigrated to Canada when I was three and a half and quickly lost my Guyanese dialect.

She has always been aware of her East Indian heritage and how it impacts her integration (or lack of integration) into new settings and situations. Anjani initially pursued a career in landscape architecture, and it was during the five-year program that she found her aesthetic in art and design.

There are certain artifacts that stand out in her mind as seminal works in manifesting her sense of identity and articulating her often-felt sense of marginalization next to other students in the program. As she expresses it, "I was aware that I was treated a little bit differently by all of my class . . . but I had a serious denial of my past. I do this as a protection mechanism." We see traces of artistic habitus here emerging, eschewing a past to find her way in a different culture. At a certain point near the end of Anjani's landscape architecture degree, she found ways of defying a social positioning she often resented. Bartlett and Holland describe this type of shift in identity in their article:

> Particular persons are figured collectively in practice as fitting certain social identities and thereby positioned in power relations. Over time actors grow into such worlds, figuring themselves as actors in those worlds and gaining a sense of their position, their standing, in the relations of power that characterize the particular community of practice.
>
> (2002: 14)

After completing a degree in landscape architecture, Anjani worked in a variety of jobs and one in which she designed video games for children and adults. It was in this particular capacity that Anjani was able to combine her love of East Indian design within a digital medium; we see this in her description of a program that she designed:

> The program was judgement-free and it was graphic and it allowed room for bells and whistles and that really wasn't part of my design previously and so I remember I was really cognizant of how I came about that idea. I wanted to take old images and the first time it was totally an identity issue, I was cognizant that I was Indian, and there was this old sculpture and old images but in a very new medium with new colours, bright orange and blue and faded insects and sculpture.

In Figure 12.2, we see how Anjani strongly responded to the capacity of new technologies in making old things look new. It was an epiphany in that through programming and using "all of the bells and whistles" of new technology, she could come to terms with her heritage and negotiate a relationship with it and her design aesthetic.

In Anjani's work, as described earlier, she fuses East Indian images in a digital medium and uses this aesthetic in her artwork and embeds it in her graphics. Just as people find a voice in writing, Anjani suddenly found her voice in the visual. As she describes it, "I am not sure which came first, the freedom allowed me to embrace this heritage or the heritage gave the freedom to

Figure 12.2 Making old look new.

express myself visually." She could thereby use all the trappings of technology to embrace an aesthetic which was otherwise silenced: "Now, this is where the technology helped me see something that I didn't know I wanted; but it's something that when you see it you know it . . . it is obviously cultural and we are talking about language, skin tone, and even economics, because I did come from a humble upbringing."

With digital media, Anjani was able to reconfigure herself and mediate her art with her culture within a particular type of space. It clearly affected the way she perceived her world and her relationship to it. Like Taiga, Anjani would embed her aesthetic into her teaching, and it informs the way she regards the learning process.

Case study 3: Henry Theroux—reacting to a medium to find identity

Born and raised in Toronto, Henry had been a graphic designer for 12 years before entering teacher's college. Henry always felt an affinity with art and drawing. After completing a degree in graphic design, he worked for a number of large advertising firms and did some freelance work. Although he enjoyed the business, he turned to freelance work because he found there was too much emphasis on sales and marketing within the corporate world. As a freelancer, Henry had a few contracts that mirrored his own philosophy of design and life (i.e., focused on environmentalism). We spoke at length about his dispositions to practice, and he spoke of opting for an arts and crafts approach over a web-based approach:

> I hate designing for the web. I get quite bored designing for the Web because I found it to be very—well, it wasn't my medium . . . I am a tactile creator, I need to have a pencil and react to the medium that I'm using. This is not to say that I don't do most of my work on the computer, but the thinking process—to me, working on the web doesn't lend itself to it. Now, having said that, I love looking at web sites, I love looking at web designs, web materials; it is fantastic stuff.

What Henry enjoyed most was researching designs, conjuring up images based on research, and playing with the medium. As he notes: "Working within web design is not as tactile as I would like. I think of web design as architecture." Interestingly, in my interview with Anjani, she said precisely the same thing: "Suddenly I had this medium where I could put me and parts of myself as if it was an architectural form." Both interviewees speak of the architectural nature of digital design, but where one enjoys the odd juxtaposition of conflating older images with new technology, the other opts for using traditional methods of design (e.g., woodcuts) and only at the end of the process manifesting them in an electronic form.

Henry spoke of the "unpredictable" nature of web design in that you do not know how the user will use it. He prefers to have some degree of control over how his artifacts might be used and, to a great extent, you cannot pre-empt web use: "It [a web site] is not as concrete [as printed text] and you are not sure how people are going to go through it . . . it is about going through a space." In "going through a space" you are governed by the whims of the user, and Henry would prefer to navigate (as much as he can) how a reader interprets his visuals.

At one time, he conceived of a web page where "instead of creating a web site where you moved up and down, you moved into the site. As you clicked on a button, you move up and down within your web site, you navigate through it, and the web site would come at you." In other words, Henry likes to play with the conventions of a medium to control more of the reading of text, whereas Taiga and Anjani leave interpretation open to the reader. In my interview with Henry, he alluded to "improvising on his habitus" by "going back to basics" and "back to nature," which he consistently mentioned in our discussions relating back to his unconscious dispositions. The "objective structure" or, in Bourdieusian terms, field of the corporate world made him appreciate that it did not fit with his life and his life philosophy. What is more, where his colleagues would take advantage of the affordances of technology—in terms of visuals and programming—he went against accepted and ruling digital practices of design by taking an arts and crafts approach to his design.

We spoke briefly about an image Henry created for the B.Ed. class as an icon for their Annual Dance and Drama Conference. Given that Henry was the "tech guy" for the class, he volunteered to create an image to celebrate the day. The theme of the Dance and Drama Day was Shakespeare's "All the world's a stage." With this phrase in mind, Henry created an image of a person enveloped by a globe-like stage:

> All of a sudden I got the image in my head. I knew the style; I knew pretty much what to look for. And, in this case, because I volunteered to do it, I am going to give it my best shot, I am going to be quite free about it, they could take it or leave it. I didn't have a lot of time, and I just basically, did just that; I spent a couple of hours one morning, like before the March break and just played with an image until it was what I wanted it to be.

He saw a stage and he saw a world and he "imagined an amphitheatre, and the text being the amphitheatre and the globe being the stage, and being in a very African style" (see Figure 12.3).

Figure 12.3 African-style woodcut of All the World's a Stage.

Although Henry has consistently had a certain aesthetic in his work, resembling woodcuts, his aesthetic has changed over the years, sparked by different phases in his life. Again, we return to Bourdieu's habitus and shifts in habitus in the face of structural or systemic changes. Prominent among these stages was becoming a father. In Figure 12.4, we see how fatherhood impacts his images, compared to the Dance and Drama icon (a later icon).

In Figure 12.4, Henry expresses his tie to fatherhood as the focal point of his life, "as a driving force of his work." In light of this image and others done over the past couple of years, Henry discovered that for him, his love of art and producing images derives from process and not necessarily product: "I really have become more sensitive to the process, being more important than the product, it may be cliché but it is about the journey." The phrase "it is about a journey" came up in some guise in each interview. One of the recurring themes was that art helped the interviewees through stages in their lives.

What became a common strand in the three interviews was how space dictated given sets of practices. This brings us back to Bartlett and Holland's discussion of the space of practice. For both Taiga and Henry, having a child

Figure 12.4 Fatherhood.

shifted the nature of their artistic space. Where formerly they might have had more liberty working in different and perhaps larger spaces, such as a studio, with a child they spent more time at home, which constricted their space and time devoted to images. For Taiga, when her daughter was a baby, she would create smaller and more personal images: "When I was working at home the baby may cry, and I produced smaller things that were more personal." For Henry, he had to work more in his apartment and this shifted the way he conceived art: "I wanted to work with oil paint but with a child it is more difficult." Henry is now teaching in an inner-city primary school and arts integration lies at the heart of his program.

Conclusion: texts as traces of modified habitus

As individuals, we establish our identities and history-in-person in the manner in which we make meaning. People establish their identities and their differences through the diverse ways in which they produce and interpret texts and more generally incorporate them into their own practice. What became apparent after the first interview was the degree to which identity—past, present, and future—encroached on text-making. It was clear from the first few minutes of each interview that texts provided a means to engrave habitus and, to my surprise, express shifts in habitus. An account of micro practices used to create artifacts also revealed important differences and similarities among the three participants.

Through semiotic mediation each participant came to terms with shifts in their identity. Where Taiga used installations and three-dimensional art improvising on artistic habitus, Anjani found her medium interweaving East Indian images with digital forms. Through insights such as these, I derived a far richer understanding of how my interviewees make meaning. Their production of artifacts allows them to negotiate a relationship with their identity in practice (Holland et al., 1998). The interplay between agent and structure, or habitus and field, during production brings them closer to mastering their own behavior and understanding their habitus in new circumstances. In this way, "habitus is a social construction" (Calhoun et al., 2002: 74), and mobilizing discourses and practice is key to social mediation. Interestingly, with each interviewee, their practices fit within a different, more marginalized paradigm of learning. The mixing and melding together of different modalities offered each interviewee more latitude of expression than written prose.

The key point here is that their acceptance and instantiation of art becomes cultural capital in their teaching. Their manipulation of the cultural capital of artistic production rendered them more reflective and, what is more, far more original and contemporary in their planning and teaching. Literacy is increasingly premised on a notion or an epistemology of design (Cope and Kalantzis, 2000), which makes Taiga, Anjani, and Henry more contemporary and meaningful literacy educators, wielding the symbolic power of their artistic and design background in the field of their classrooms. We see this in Taiga's response to visual theory during her Master of Visual Arts Degree and Anjani's response to digital media when she completed her final project for a degree in landscape architecture. For these participants, culturally produced artifacts provide a vehicle and a space to modify their relationship to their identity/habitus. Figure 12.5 highlights the process of improvising on habitus within the field of creative production.

What the diagram below depicts is the act of habitus being inscribed through semiotic mediation *as an embodiment of cultural capital into a mediating artifact*. This in turn modifies the habitus of the artist (Pahl, 2002). Artifacts foregrounded in the chapter show a clear and conscious tie to a stage—to a feeling—a reaction to the external world. Invoking Bourdieu's notion of cultural capital, habitus, and field enabled me to recognize and theorize how three artists-turned-teachers refigure and reposition themselves through art. Within the framework of the book, Bourdieu's work helps to evoke the process of meaning-making for three individuals, bringing us that much closer to understanding the way our internal worlds function within a highly diversified external one.

Identities are always forming, always in a state of flux, and always sedimenting themselves in artifacts. Clearly, in light of the interviews, each interviewee was driven by an internal cultural logic (i.e., habitus) but, at the same time, aware of an external cultural logic impinging upon them and objectified in their art. With each interviewee, art or the visual helped them come to terms with the trajectory of their lives, both as child and as adult producers. It is as if life experiences were objectified in their art (Bourdieu's structuring of structure) and with each artifact they sensed a shift in their personality. Hence, the process is both generative and iterative. Identities move in and out of situations and with each new phase, there are contestations, subversions, and negotiations.

What does it mean when we travel across intersecting fields? Are there homologies and, if so, how do they relate to artistic habitus? What all three participants share is a clear and presiding belief in design and arts-infused teaching and programming. All three participants were exemplary students in our program and went on to create exceptional programs with art and design as a centerpiece of their teaching. I attribute the efficacy of their teaching to their ability to reflect on themselves and use the symbolic capital of their art in their teaching.

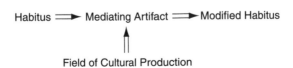

Figure 12.5 The process of improvising on habitus in the field of creative production.

Each participant in my study crossed fields and figured these crossings within the visual narrative (Kress and Leeuwen, 1996) of their art and within their artistic practice (e.g., Henry's woodcuts). Bourdieu understood and theorized crossing fields as an internalization of structure, but importantly as an *incorporation* of that structure. It is as if we carry each crossing within us. For Taiga, Anjani, and Henry, they felt compelled to objectify these crossings within their art and, to my mind, the act of materialization made them conscious of their habitus. Habitus provides a set of actions and impressions within which improvisation occurs. Crossing fields requires a change in habitus but also an exchange of capitals. The capitals of one field are not easily exchanged to another. As a result, people transform or reproduce their social structures, but they do so within specific social conditions, including social conditions within which they exist. The point in the chapter is to demonstrate how Taiga, Anjani, and Henry used their art to come to terms with and move in different directions. Each one did not want to be fettered to a social condition, but they wanted mobility in their personal lives, in their art, and in their teaching. Capitals at contest within a field are intertwined with the particular logics of that field. For example, art and education traditionally do not accept the value of the other.

Within the scope of this book, with valuable studies that invoke dimensions of Bourdieu's work to explain or elucidate studies within literacy education, where does this study fit? Literacy within the framework of this book is viewed as making meaning with texts within a structure or field. Artistic creation and cultural production is a somewhat neglected form of meaning-making that students take within their already full course of study. Yet, through their extensive exposure to modern forms of communication, art and design dominate our students' worlds. Indeed, tensions highlighted in this chapter demonstrate the powerful potential of art and design as central and abiding meaning-making tools in classrooms and as signifiers of student habitus and, equally, as a means of using artistic capital to shift their social conditions. For example, children creating a website can contrive a field for themselves that complements or contrasts their own field. There are certainly homologies within art and literacy education that need to be explored and mobilized in classrooms. Mistaking the value of art within literacy education is not a question of how or if they are related, but instead, a firmly established common sense about literacy and what it is or should be.

Note

1 I have used pseudonyms to protect their identities, and they have read each draft of the paper.

References

Bartlett, L. and Holland, D. (2002) Theorizing the space of literacy practices. *Ways of Knowing*, 2(1), 10–22.

Bourdieu, P. (1988) *The Political Ontology of Martin Heidegger*. Cambridge, UK: Polity Press.

Bourdieu, P. (1990) *The Logic of Practice*. Cambridge, UK: Polity Press. (Original work published 1980)

Bourdieu, P. (1991) *Language and Symbolic Power* (G. Raymond and M. Adamson, trans.) Cambridge, UK: Polity Press. (Original work published 1982)

Bourdieu, P. (1993) *The Field of Cultural Production*. Cambridge, UK: Polity Press.

Bourdieu, P. (1994) *In Other Words: Essays Toward a Reflexive Sociology*. Cambridge, UK: Polity Press.

Bourdieu, P. (2000) *Pascalian Meditations*. Cambridge, UK: Polity Press.

Bourdieu, P. and Wacquant, L. J. D. (1992) *An Invitation to Reflexive Sociology*. Chicago: University of Chicago Press.

Calhoun, C. (1993) Habitus, field, and capital: the question of historical specificity. In C. Calhoun, E. LiPuma and M. Postone (eds) *Bourdieu: Critical Perspectives*. Chicago: University of Chicago Press, 61–88.

Calhoun, C., LiPuma, E. and Postone, M. (2002) *Bourdieu Critical Perspectives*. Chicago: University of Chicago Press.

Cope, B. and Kalantzis, M. (eds) (2000) *Multiliteracies: Literacy Learning and the Design of Social Futures*. London: Routledge.

Fowler, B. (1997) *Pierre Bourdieu and Cultural Theory: Critical Investigations*. London: Sage.

Gee, J. P. (2003) *What Video Games have to Teach us About Learning and Literacy*. New York: Palgrave Macmillan.

Kress, G. and Van Leeuwen, T. (1996) *Reading Images: The Grammar of Visual Design*. London: Routledge.

Holland, D. and Lave, J. (eds) (2001) *History in Person: Enduring Struggles, Contentious Practice, Intimate Identities*. Santa Fe, NM: School of American Research Press.

Holland, D., Lachicotte, W., Skinner, D. and Cain, C. (1998) *Identity and Agency in Cultural Worlds*. Cambridge, MA: Harvard University Press.

Pahl, K. (2002) Habitus and the home: texts and practices in families. *Ways of Knowing*, 2(1), 45–53.

Pahl, K. (2004) Narrative spaces and multiple identities: children's textual explorations of console games in home settings. In J. Marsh (ed.), *Popular Culture, Media and Digital Literacies in Early Childhood*. London: RoutledgeFalmer, 126–45.

Webb, J., Schirato, T. and Danaher, G. (2002) *Understanding Bourdieu*. London: Sage.

Chapter 13

Social hierarchies and identity politics

Jessica Zacher

Introduction: struggles for representation in the fifth grade classroom

The value of multicultural curricula has long been accepted, but the consequences of their implementation on children's identity work, the ways children identify themselves as certain kinds of people, have seldom been looked at through a Bourdieusian social reproduction frame, with an emphasis on how children's positioning intersects with official curricula. To this end, this chapter focuses on what fifth grade students in a racially and linguistically diverse classroom *did* with discursive practices for talking about difference that they gleaned from assigned multicultural texts.

The ways that the students framed difference in their identity struggles were often at odds with the official school goal of honoring all diversity equally while recognizing humanity's past mistakes. I suggest that these "struggles in which agents clash[ed] over the meaning of the social world and their position within it," as well as "the meaning of their social identit[ies]" (Bourdieu, 1985: 729), were intimately tied not to explicit school goals for valuing difference, but to students' social hierarchies, their perceptions of what counted about difference, and the ways that they learned about and through texts.

Using this frame, I found that students in this urban California classroom took notions and terms from the literacy curriculum and used them in strikingly innovative ways as tools with which to build and maintain a stable social hierarchy. For example, some students explicitly converted their racial, linguistic, and religious identities into symbolic capital when it suited their social maneuvering. The bulk of this chapter is devoted to an analysis of their hierarchy as a whole and descriptions of some students' struggles for representation within it. Ultimately, I discuss possible implications of those struggles for the ways that students perceived of themselves as social agents who could "*determine themselves*" (Bourdieu and Wacquant, 1992: 136) in the classroom at the moment of struggle *and* in their unfolding life pathways.

At stake in these struggles was "the very representation of the social world" (Bourdieu, 1985: 723); students negotiated the right to categorize themselves and others, as well as the right to claim membership in different categories and identify themselves with certain groups of people, based on the weight and volume of their symbolic capital in a variety of school contexts. These were undertaken as students and teachers jointly constructed definitions of otherness, of difference, drawing on ideas and ideologies from the school's multicultural curriculum. Indeed, as I explain below, otherness was negotiated and interpreted by students and adults in both school-based and out-of-school contexts. As students conducted this work with and through the school curriculum, they simultaneously jockeyed for positions in the status hierarchy. They did so in teacher-led literacy events, on their own in small groups, on the playground, in after-school programs, on the bus, and at home.

In the classroom literacy events that are the focus of this chapter, students were exposed to a wide variety of texts that they used to mediate their affiliations and position themselves vis-à-vis their peers in particular ways. Where Bourdieu looked at entire social structures and practices—from the Kabyle in Algeria to the French education system to French society's tastes in food—to evolve his theory of social reproduction, I use a microanalysis of a year's worth of literacy events to attend to the ways in which *children's* social relationships were as contested and as full of struggles as those of adults. Bourdieu's sociological data (see Bourdieu, 1977, 1984) shed light on larger societal issues and trends; my ethnographic data show in minute detail how youth use, create, and weight capital in their daily lives. The following analysis extends his work to the heretofore unexamined realms of identity politics and agency in children's lives, offering concrete examples of the high stakes of representational politics in their worlds. These stakes, I argue, imply varied gains for children's symbolic and economic capital in the present as well as the future. I expand on these issues and explicate the use of Bourdieu's ideas in combination with some sociocultural perspectives on literacy theory in the sections below.

The purpose of a microanalysis of identity positioning

Social spaces, capital, habitus, and reproduction

As Bourdieu has noted, "to speak of a social space means that one cannot group just *anyone* with *anyone* while ignoring the fundamental differences" (1985: 726). Although Bourdieu referred in this passage and in many of his works to larger social groups—his diagram of the "space of social positions" in French society, in which he used differences in economic and cultural capital to show how social space was affected and formed by various groups, is an example (1984: 128, 129)—the same holds true for children's social hierarchies. At Gonzales Elementary,[1] where "fundamental differences" themselves were often open for negotiation, charting the social space required close attention to differences as they were defined by students. To accomplish this, I relied upon

Bourdieu's notions of capital, habitus, and reproduction; below I offer a brief description of these terms in the service of furthering my own research and analysis.

As with the Algerian Kabyle, on whose social worlds Bourdieu extended his theories of practice, the children in Room 126 had little first-hand access to economic capital (although *not* because the children were not members of a literate society, as was the case with the Kabyle). For the majority of this analysis, I use the term *symbolic capital* purposefully. In various exchanges, an "economic circulation" that could not "be seen purely in terms of material goods" (1977: 181) was in play; in many cases, students' current symbolic capital was related to their parents' economic capital. However, the representational rights at stake, the "*recognition*, institutionalized or not" that students received (Bourdieu, 1982/1991: 72, emphasis in original), was almost entirely symbolic and pertained more to "legitimate . . . prestige, [and] reputation" (1985: 724) than the actual accrual of economic resources. At Gonzales, funds of symbolic capital included, depending on the market and field, religious affiliation, language abilities, skin color, neighborhood, and so forth.

The children in this study derived notions of what counted as such symbolic capital in various markets of the school field from two sources. First, these understandings of what counted as capital grew from the dispositions that constitute the habitus, a "set of relatively permanent and largely unconscious ideas about one's chances of success and how society works" (Swartz, 1997: 197). Second, they were developed by students out of their unconscious or taken-for-granted understandings about the workings of the classroom social hierarchy. My analysis takes place at the intersection of habitus, "that product of history [that] produces individual and collective practices" (Bourdieu, 1977: 82), and social space, where such practices are formed and reformed. The children were social agents, "*product[s] of history*" who "*actively* determine[d], on the basis of socially and historically constituted categories of perception and appreciation, the situation that determine[d] them" (Bourdieu and Wacquant, 1992: 136, emphasis in original). In this sense, students' identity and affiliation choices were mediated by both their habitus-histories and their sense of what kinds of identity claims were permitted to them by their position in the classroom social hierarchy.

In their politics, the children in Room 126 attempted to represent the social world as they saw it and as they envisioned their roles in it. The "deep-rooted choices of the habitus" (Bourdieu, 1984: 454), which is itself both a "structuring structure" and a "structured structure" (p. 170), undergirded many of the students' identifications, but an analysis of social hierarchies necessarily addresses students' more overt political actions. Cyclically, an analysis of their identifications requires that we understand their social hierarchy because students' maneuvers, like the ones described in the latter half of this chapter, indicate "the more or less explicit and systematic representation[s] an agent has of the social world, of his position within it and of the position he 'ought' to occupy" (Bourdieu, 1984: 170). Along the same lines, I frame identities here as individuals' stated and unconscious perceptions of their positions as actors and participants in a variety of fields, and argue that they are "always in part a narrative, always in part a kind of representation," and are "not something which is formed outside and then we tell stories about it" (Hall, 1997: 49). These identities, which can be viewed as affiliations that people choose to make in their social worlds, may be temporary or more permanent in duration, and are supported to varying degrees by the "structures" of the habitus itself.

Indeed, as Hall notes, identities are "narrated within one's own self" (1997: 49), and they necessarily draw upon and reflect the habitus. These identities can also be written and performed. Regardless of the mode of representation, the main point here is that identities are narrated or performed *for others*, and it is in the act of representation of self to any audience that we can capture slices of students' identity politics. Such politics—how students position themselves socially in different contexts through narration, writing, and performance, and how those positionings affect others in local and broader social spaces—are enacted at the intersection of deep-rooted choices and moment-to-moment positionings. Researchers can see these intersections in literacy events, and highlight the theoretical and practical tensions between students' efforts at meaning negotiation (from a sociocultural perspective) and their struggles for representational rights (from a Bourdieusian perspective). The tensions at these intersections are the subject of the following section.

The place of identity politics in literacy theory

Bourdieu's work on social exchanges has a contested relationship to socio-cultural perspectives on literacy development (see Dyson, 1997; Finders, 1997). In one sense they go hand in hand: the social—interactions between people—are at the heart of both theoretical frameworks. However, his ideas about social reproduction—how those with the most symbolic power in any society strive (consciously and unconsciously) to maintain that power, to develop into predisposed places in the social hierarchy over time—are at odds with the developmental perspective of most literacy theorists. From a sociocultural per-spective, individuals' literacy practices and ideologies about the world develop over time through their interactions with others around texts, and less attention is given to the role of reproductive social structures. For example, Dyson's (1997) sociocultural examination of popular culture texts in an elementary school classroom draws on Bourdieu's definitions of taste and distinction to describe the relative cultural capital associated with such texts, but her analysis of children's literacy practices in the "interplay of textual and social spaces" is Bakhtinian (1981, 1986), or dialogic, in nature. As mentioned above, my examination of how children identified themselves, how they valued their own and others' capital in the various markets of the school field, and how these identifications played out and were enacted in literacy events, requires using both frameworks, despite the tensions between them.

On the other hand, literacy practices—what people do with texts on their own and in interactions with others (Street, 1995)—are always about habitus and identity. Each time a child reads (or chooses not to read) a book, each time she scribbles a note to a friend, each time she conducts an online search for song lyrics, that child is constituting and maintaining some identification. In order to understand the relationship of literacy practices to identity politics and social hierarchies, I look at the ways these children positioned themselves in their classroom social hierarchy, with the understanding that some of their maneuvers were conducted in literacy events, through literacy practices. From this broader perspective, we can gain a greater understanding of how the ideas and topics that children take up from literacy curricula (as well as particular literacy practices) influence their identity politics. In addition, we can make some conclusions about how such small and large choices may influence children's life pathways (Luke, 2004). To get to this point, I will first introduce Gonzales Elementary, the students of Room 126, and their social world.

Constructing the social world: introducing Room 126 and Gonzales Elementary

Teaching about difference: the official curriculum

Gonzales Elementary was a small public kindergarten through fifth grade school with approximately 250 students; about one-third were African-American, one-third Latino/a, one-sixth White, and one-sixth Asian. Over the past seven years, the principal had endeavored to draw neighborhood middle-class (mostly White) families to the school as she maintained the interest and support of existing African-American and Latino families (who tended to be working-class and poor, and who usually lived in other, more distant, neighborhoods). Teachers were encouraged to talk explicitly about diversity with children whose before-, during- and after-school lives varied by the economic and cultural capital of their parents as well as by their own social positions in the classroom hierarchy.

In this setting, a central curricular question that underlay book choices, holiday celebrations, writing assignments, and class skits was one of balancing competing pressures. The school, its teachers, and its students attempted to teach and learn about historical and present inequities while recognizing and honoring differences. One of the school's answers to the curricular dilemmas brought on by the increasing diversity of their student population was a language arts and social studies curriculum with an overt and carefully planned "civil rights" agenda. In Room 126, most of the nine- and ten-year-old children had spent the past five years at Gonzales surrounded by the school's particular approach to difference. As an ethnographer interested in the social foundations of children's literacy practices, I attended to the ways that children organized themselves and the practices through which they signified their affiliation with the groups they had created. Over the year, I realized that the children's identity work—the words they spoke, actions they took, and texts they wrote in service of the construction of particular identities in and out of school—could only be understood and explained in the context of both their classroom curriculum and their social world.

In the multicultural literacy and social studies curriculum, students read texts like *Sojourner Truth: Ain't I a Woman?* (McKissack and McKissack, 1992) and *Number the Stars* (Lowry, 1989). They also discussed racism, sexism, homophobia, nationalism, lookism, and other -isms in a semester-long study of the "Cycle of Oppression." They learned how to historicize and label injustices and differences, how to empathize with victims of injustice, and were provided with several methods for dealing with injustice on a day-to-day basis; for instance, they learned ways to stand up to racist and sexist comments in role-playing scenarios. Students took up and deployed these discursive practices in teacher-directed literacy events across the year. Additionally, they signified their affiliations with multiple peers in various "social groups," in Bourdieu's terms, or friendship groups, along a variety of "axes of difference" (Bordo, 1993) in and out of the social field of the classroom. These axes of difference were sometimes immediately visible (i.e., gender, race), but were often less clear (cultural interests such as sports participation, musical knowledge, language preferences).

Taking difference as social capital: friendship groups

From open coding of the data to the final analysis, I struggled to find a way to explain how children used identity politics to operate, maintain, and regulate the social hierarchy. I began to see that this work was done almost entirely in inter- and intra-group social work, which led to my focus on friendship groups. Data for this project was gathered mostly through fieldwork, which consisted of twice-weekly visits with attendant field notes, and audio- and video-taped data. I also interviewed half of the students (focal students and some of their friends), collected literacy artifacts, and had several students make maps of the friendship groupings in the room. I checked the validity of the friendship groups listed on these maps with at least one person from each group, and I use one such map here to explain the social hierarchy from one group's perspective.

My analysis of these groups, including both intrinsic and relational hierarchies, is based in part on an understanding of the context-dependent weight and volume of symbolic capital that students bring to social relationships. In this classroom, where notions of difference were jointly constructed with the teacher around multicultural texts, the children usually formed friendship groups with peers who held similar amounts and types of capital. Differences were overtly valued at Gonzales; however, the "specific logic of the field" dictates that social capital "only exists and only produces its effects in the field in which it is produced and reproduced" (Bourdieu, 1979/1984: 113). In other words, the "social rank and specific power" (p. 113) of certain students enabled them to weight their own and others' social capital (in the form of ethnicities, socioeconomic classes, and religious affiliations) in ways that benefited their own rankings in the classroom hierarchy. The school curriculum, with its focus on the value of difference, set the stage for these rankings and for students' capital-based struggles for representational rights.

In this context, although we may be aware that "the social world can be uttered and constructed in different ways" (Bourdieu, 1985: 727), we must circle back to identity, and be sure to "take account of the contribution that agents make toward constructing the view of the social world . . . by means of the *work of representation*" (p. 727). If identity is "always within representation" (Hall, 1997: 49), children's identity politics—how they distribute and value capital based on self-representations—are central to their struggles for representation of the social world. In Room 126, children with more social capital, and higher rankings through which they could maintain the value of their capital, were more able to construct the social world as they saw fit, and more likely to erase or undermine other students' attempts to change the world.

In the subsequent section, I introduce the social hierarchies in Room 126 from the perspective of two key informants as well as from my own vantage point as an outside observer. I outline the general attributes of symbolic capital in the classroom, and focus on how certain types of identities were valued over others and the ways that such valuing was linked to the multicultural curriculum. To this end, I concentrate on one particular group that I call the "Three Amigas," a group whose palpable symbolic power was on display in literacy events across the year. One student in the Three Amigas, a girl labeled by the school as White, claimed a Latina identity. As part of my argument about how these children claimed identities in this classroom hierarchy, I will detail her habitus formation, her accrual of social and cultural capital, and the role she had in constructing and maintaining a particular social order in the classroom. I end the chapter with an analysis of a struggle for "the very representation" of the social world in a literacy event. In it, she and two of her peers negotiate identity rights and their places in the social hierarchy using language and ideologies about difference that they also used when they talked about multicultural texts in teacher-driven literacy events.

"He has no friends": mapping the social hierarchy

Thus, agents are distributed within [the social world], in the first dimension, according to the overall volume of the capital they possess and, in the second dimension, according to the composition of their capital—i.e., according to the relative weight of the different kinds of assets within their total assets.

(Bourdieu, 1985: 724)

Each group in Room 126 constructed their relationship to the others in ways that left students with relative understandings of their group's position in the between-group hierarchy of the classroom. The groups were hierarchized externally in relation to one another, through students' subtle (and not-so-subtle) affiliation choices, some of which we will witness below. They were also hierarchized internally; for example, in the Three Amigas group, the girls negotiated the weight of their social and cultural capital as they vied for symbolic power and claimed identities that mattered to each other, other peers, and themselves. In Bourdieu's outline of the formation and logistics of social fields, including his perspective on how people form groups based on capital distribution, he does not focus on any particular form of capital—in fact he wrote that the types and "overall volume" of capital that people hold grant "relative" weight to participants in groups—but he does argue that we could map inter- and intra-group hierarchies for specific agents and for groups depending on the "overall volume of capital they possess, and . . . the composition of their capital" (1985: 724).

To begin, I turn to a friendship map drawn by Christina and Vanessa, two of the Three Amigas. Because of their combined social, cultural, and symbolic capital, and its weight in relation to that of others' capital in the classroom, Christina and Vanessa had the "capacity to make entities exist in the explicit state, to publish, to make public (i.e., render objectified, visible, and even official) what had not previously attained objective and collective existence" (Bourdieu, 1985: 729). In other words, they had the symbolic power, partially because of how they were structurally located in this classroom in terms of their available capital, "to make groups by *making* the common sense, the explicit consensus, of the whole group" (p. 729).

Early in the school year, I asked Christina and Vanessa to draw me a map of "who sits where" (see Figure 13.1). They sketched out the classroom's six tables as circles, labeled who sat where, and proceeded—on their own initiative—to add color-coded stars by each student's name to indicate the friendship group(s) to which each person belonged. Afterwards, they handed me the map and made a few quick assessments: Bettina was not really their friend—"She's nice," one said, but the other added, "She's too quiet." Dylan, a White boy who had cerebral palsy, got no star because, as Vanessa said, "He has no friends." Christina said that that assessment was "harsh," and Vanessa replied, "But it's true!"

As their map illustrates, there were several distinct groups of girls and boys who were friends in this class. To stress the usefulness of a Bourdieusian analysis, I focus on the Three Amigas in relation to other groups (and not on the equally labyrinthine relationships within other groups). The influence of

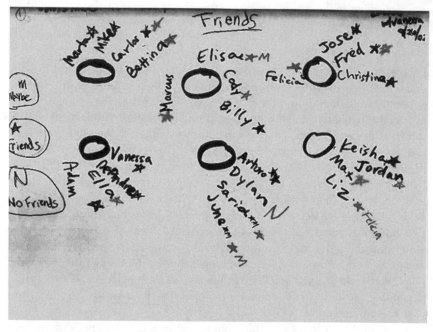

Figure 13.1 Christina and Vanessa's map of friendship groups in Room 126.

Note: The [x] indicates cross-listings, that is, someone the girls believed crossed between two friendship groups:

★ Christina, Vanessa, Marta
★ Bettina, Felicia, Saria, Keisha [x]
★ M: Elisa, June
★ Felicia with Liz
★ Cody, Jordan, Ella
★ DeAndre, Mike, Arturo [x], Keisha [x]
★ Adam, José, Billy, Fred, Carlos [x], Arturo [x] (Billy left the classroom halfway through the year)
★ Marcus, Max, Fred [x], Carlos [x]
  N: Dylan

friendship groups in each child's life was visible throughout the year, as much for the few children with no specific friends (Dylan, Liz, and sometimes Elisa) as for those who were enmeshed in particular groups. The Three Amigas' power base was undergirded by each girl's individual capital, and Christina's contributions included: her status as a "gifted and talented" student (a school district classification based on high third grade test scores); her relationship with an African-American boy named DeAndre; her knowledge of hip-hop culture, music, and dance steps; and her basketball playing.

Other groups had different sorts of power in the class—Cody and Jordan's parents ran the parent association for the most part, and made choices about what sorts of extra-curricular activities and field trips they could fund—and weighted their capital accordingly. For instance, Christina's extensive knowledge of hip-hop lyrics was integral to her relationship with DeAndre, but the all-boy group of Adam, José, Billy, and Fred paid little attention to popular music, valuing instead their peers' computer gaming skills.

As it turned out, Christina and Vanessa were fairly accurate with their lists and assumptions. My own "classroom friendship map," based on interviews with eight focal students, the teacher, and observations over the year, varied only slightly. Because I made it from a particular point of view, it (like the girls' map) may have errors, but I checked my groupings with at least one student in each group for accuracy (see Table 13.1).

There were three major differences between my own map and the one the girls made, changes that instantiate the notion of how social structures can be "uttered and constructed in different ways" (Bourdieu, 1985: 726) depending on who does the uttering. Christina and Vanessa cross-listed Keisha with the female group of Bettina, Felicia, and Saria, *and* with the otherwise male group of DeAndre, Mike, and Arturo; but in my observations, Keisha spent about half of her school time with the all-female group of Cody, Jordan, and Ella, and very little time with Saria, Bettina, and Felicia. The girls also listed Marcus as a friend of Carlos, Max, and Fred, but although he occasionally played with Carlos, he seldom spoke to Max and Fred; he mostly "hung out" with DeAndre, Mike, and Arturo. Finally, the girls cross-listed Liz with Felicia, who was in another group, but granted her neither a list of other friends nor an N for no friends.

These subtle variations are telling about between-group hierarchy issues of the classroom. First, Christina and her friends often jockeyed for positions of favor with the teacher (e.g., to get special privileges, to be recognized for doing good or quick work) in something of a competition with Cody's group. Leaving Keisha out of that group may or may not have been a doubly purposeful move, to both slight Keisha and appear as if the authors of the map had little knowledge of the other girls' group. Second, as the year went on, I watched Marcus' status slip in DeAndre, Mike, and Arturo's group; it is possible to read

Table 13.1 My own list of friendship groups in Room 126

Christina	DeAndre	Cody	Adam	Liz (solo)
Vanessa	Arturo	Jordan	José	
Marta	Mike	Ella	Fred	Dylan (solo)
	Marcus	~Keisha	Max	
Saria	~Carlos		~Elisa (solo)	
Bettina				
Felicia				

Note: The ~ symbol next to a student's name indicates their partial or peripheral membership in the group (e.g., Elisa was usually solo but occasionally affiliated with José's group).

the girls' deletion of Marcus from the group with whom *he* most identified as an insult to him, as well as an accession to DeAndre's group's growing denial of Marcus' membership. Finally, leaving Liz in a no-kids'-land of semi-belonging placed her status, and her feelings about it, at or near the bottom of their version of the social order.

Senses of place: the Three Amigas (and Liz)

Although African-American and Latino/a students—such as the Three Amigas, and DeAndre and his friends—held most of the symbolic power, the place of race in classroom identity politics shifted according to context. In Room 126, the "work of categorization, i.e., of making-explicit and of classification, [was] performed incessantly, at every moment of ordinary existence" (Bourdieu, 1985: 729). Some groups of students, including Adam and his mixed-race group of friends and, on occasion, the middle-class White girls Cody, Jordan, and Ella (who was born in Mexico of Mexican parents and adopted by a White middle-class family), simply elected to remove themselves from certain negotiations, but, as I will show, no one could escape the ongoing classification. Whether they were actively asserting a certain identity or denying any racial categorization, students were engaged in representational acts, telling stories about themselves, and making identity claims.

In this section, I focus on the Three Amigas because they held the symbolic power to name and label—to structure the social space of the classroom—and because they exercised that power in countless moments, including the creation of the map. Almost all of the students' identity work in Room 126 was done through their membership in particular friendship groups. Each child's actions, words, and literacy practices could thus be viewed through, explained by, or understood through an observer's recognition of the students' need to participate in the maintenance of or struggle against the social hierarchy. In seemingly mundane literacy events, struggles took place, "struggles in which agents clash[ed] over the meaning of the social world and their position within it, the meaning of their social identity" (Bourdieu, 1985: 729).

For example, Liz, a poor White student with blond hair and blue eyes, felt "weird" calling herself "White," and she, like Christina in her own way, struggled for a place, a category, in this multiracial classroom. Liz's sense of place was also a "sense of limits," but, unlike Bourdieu's theoretical subjects, she often pushed at the "distances" that others might have marked and kept (p. 728). At the end of this chapter, I present an interaction between Liz and Christina that highlights their individual struggles for representational rights, the different ways they as social actors manipulated the "space of relationships" (p. 725), negotiating the right to choose and deny labels.

Race, friendship, and representation: positioning Christina in the Three Amigas

I call this group of girls—Christina, Marta, and Vanessa—the Three Amigas to represent their bilingual English-Spanish Latina identities, and to highlight their "group-ness." The other main reason that I focus on them here is that the identity politics of the classroom were writ large in their group, especially around race, gender, and social class fault lines. Christina was White (the school recorded her ethnicity as "W" for White in kindergarten, on a form filled out by her parents), and her parents both identified as White, with her father also claiming a Jewish heritage. However, she most often identified, or *labeled*, herself as "Latina." She also dissociated herself from other White girls in the class who were, she said in an interview, "edgy" and "got mad easier." At the same time, Christina declared that it was "not the color of their skin" that bothered her, but that "certain kids that just happen to be White" just got on her "nerves." She herself had fair white skin and long, dark brown hair; unlike her two darker skinned friends, or Liz, she could pass for either White or Latina.

Christina lived with her artist mother and reporter father in a rented house in a racially mixed urban neighborhood that was continually undergoing gentrification. Marta and Vanessa both lived in a city neighborhood that was a mix of Spanish-speaking immigrants, established Latino and Chicano families, and young urban (White) professionals. Christina told me that she liked her neighborhood because "It's cool. It's kinda half-ghetto." Describing her own street corner, aligning it with Vanessa and Marta's more well-known Latino neighborhood, Christina once noted that, "We got people by my house and Vanessa's, too, named Vato, Chico, Cruiser" all typical Latino gangster nicknames. Christina took several dance classes a week—flamenco, salsa, and hip-hop among them—and had weekly cello lessons. She also read a book or two a week at home, and wrote in a journal occasionally. At the beginning of the fifth grade, she started teaching herself Spanish; she was already a fluent speaker of African-American Vernacular English.

Marta, a Salvadoreña, and Vanessa, who had a Venezuelan mother and Salvadoran father, both identified as "Latina." The girls often played with Kathy, a Latina from the other fourth/fifth grade class who was DeAndre's girlfriend, but since she was not in Room 126, she did not get included in the Three Amigas' everyday hierarchy-maintenance practices. Marta and Vanessa were "cousins"—their parents were distantly related—and they spent time together almost every weekend. That pair also spoke fluent Spanish. Vanessa was perpetually obsessed with the story of Anne Frank, and peripherally curious about all things and people Jewish—one strong link between the girls was Vanessa's awareness of Christina's father's Jewishness. In this sense, the Anne Frank stories, books sanctioned if not provided by the teacher, were textual mediators of the girls' relationship. Vanessa reported that she had read *Anne*

Frank: The Diary of a Young Girl (Frank, 1993) at least ten times, seen a children's television movie production based on the book several times, and read assorted biographies of Anne Frank on her own.[2]

Although Vanessa was generally loyal and kind to her two close friends, she was capable of being charming and rude at almost the same moment to anyone in the class. Despite these traits, the teacher believed Vanessa was the "nicest" of the triad of girls, and that she might flourish if she were removed from the joint orbit of Christina and Marta. These girls were often framed by school adults and other students—including Cody, Jordan, and Ella, the "edgy" White girls—as being troublesome, snotty, or cliquish, and they did little to dispel that image. When they worked together, Christina and Marta tended to do more of the work, while Vanessa played or teased others in the class. When separated, each girl had a tendency to search out the other's gaze, occasionally making gestures or getting up to whisper messages. The teacher said that sometimes she found it easier in terms of classroom management to let them work together, rather than bother to separate them.

Christina and DeAndre, an African-American boy and head of the boy group parallel to the Three Amigas in symbolic and social capital, were the only "gifted and talented" students in the room. Christina also counted DeAndre as a close friend after Vanessa and Marta. Romance issues, common to a few boy–girl relationships in the school, were not an impediment to their friendship because they had spent years backgrounding romance. With the help of Christina's mother, who had fostered the friendship over the years, they had foregrounded a mutual interest in amassing social capital in the form of popular culture knowledge, good test scores and good grades, and an ability to flaunt the rules and get away with it. This social capital led to increased symbolic capital and power for each of them and their groups of friends. This relationship added significant weight to Christina's position in the Three Amigas, and may have even been the insurance that allowed her friends to at least tolerate her claim to a Latina identity; from their perspective, her solid link to DeAndre may have been worth believing a sometimes questionable identity claim.

Even if usually unspoken, racial politics undergirded much of the students' identity work in Room 126. Christina told her parents that one reason she preferred to be known as a Latina was that Marta and Vanessa "made fun of" White people. In December, before her eleventh birthday party, Christina's mother reported to me that her daughter had asked, very seriously, that her mom *not* tell the other girls that she was "not a Latina." Christina said she knew her mom objected to lying, but she was concerned that her friends did not like White girls. Her friends knew that her dad was Jewish, but in that conversation, Christina asked her mother how much of a stretch it would be to think of someone who was Portuguese as "Latin" (Christina's maternal grandmother, Linda, was from Portugal). However, as we will see, Christina was not above invoking her father's Jewishness, whether to make a point with Vanessa, a self-styled specialist on the life of Anne Frank, or with Liz, who tried to make identity claims beyond her "place."

Christina's identification as a Latina was tenuously constituted in time, instituted in an exterior space (the school community) through a repetition of acts that were themselves "produced through the stylization of the body" (Butler, 1999: 179). We can see this in the "mundane way in which bodily gestures, movements, and styles of various kinds constitute the illusion of an abiding gendered self" for Christina (p. 179). Her identity work included the stylization of her body to look Latina: long hair done in hairdos like those of her friends, particular clothes bought at the stores her friends frequented, classes in hip-hop and salsa dancing. Her neighborhood's "Vatos, Chicos, and Cruisers" were corralled into this process as well, enabling her to suggest that she lived in a neighborhood populated with certain types of Latinos whose presence added to the "half-ghetto" effect.

Bourdieu thought that the "categories of perception and appreciation"— such as "half-ghetto"—that provided agents with the "principle of . . . (self-) determination," were "themselves largely determined by the social and economic conditions of their constitution" (Bourdieu and Wacquant, 1992: 136). In an analysis of children's everyday life, this argument—what is valued is what is determined to be valuable by socioeconomic conditions, which are in turn dependent on the value allotted to *them,* and so on—helps us to understand why a Latina identity might be attractive to Christina (Hall, 1996). What to adults or outsiders might seem an outlandish claim becomes, from the perspective of a White student at Gonzales, reasonable and even necessary. Christina's multiple acts of signification, the varied ways she enacted her claim, were not "*founding act[s], but rather a regulated process of repetition*"; we can locate agency "in the possibility of a variation on that repetition" (Butler, 1999: 185, emphasis in original). At Gonzales, coming from a "half-ghetto" neighborhood granted Christina's claims legitimacy, and her repeated acts of signification, like the ones I discuss below, maintained and regulated her identity in the classroom.

Christina writes a Latina identity

Christina's identity choice was more than the performance of an available identity category. Indeed, her work was situated in, fueled by, and served the particular identity politics of the classroom, which were visible in literacy performances across the year. Many students, including Christina, used texts to bolster their identity claims and to represent themselves as certain kinds of people. In the classroom writing center, where students chose from a list of teacher-provided prompts, Christina once began an in-class essay with the lead-in: "Which member of your family understands you the best, and why?" As I watched, she began to write about her "Tía Tamara" in an overt political maneuver, both representing the social world and narrating her identity (see Figure 13.2).

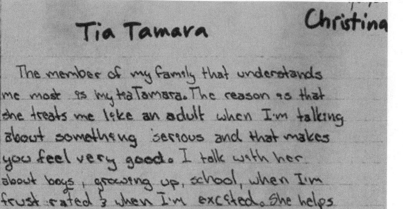

Figure 13.2 Christina's "Tía Tamara."

I was taking notes, and I asked Christina what her aunt was "called." She said that she herself called her "my Tía Ta*ma*ra," but that people who did not know her called her "Tamara," "American English" style. I had met Tamara, and she was White, with strawberry-blond hair; in fact, when we met, she introduced herself to me as "*Ta*mara." This essay would eventually be read by her friends and typed up on the computer, for later "publication" on a classroom wall.

Another day, in the after-school program, I visited a table populated by the Three Amigas and two African-American girlfriends from the other fifth grade classroom. As usual, my notebook was in hand. At a break in the conversation, I asked Vanessa and Marta, who had told me that they were related, about their family connection. Vanessa said they were "cousins," and Marta said, "No, no, no!" Vanessa went on, saying that her "mom's cousin has a sister, and her sister had a baby, and—" once again, Marta cut her off. Marta turned to me and said, "My dad's cousin is her mom." Christina, who had seen me write Marta's answer down, asked me, "Want to know about my *abuela*?" She drew a picture explaining how her maternal grandparents, including her "abuela"[3] Linda from Portugal, had married other people and then married each other. She repeated the name "Linda" with a Spanish accent (as *Lean-dah*) three times and referred to her as her "abuela" twice. She also said her grandfather David's name with a Spanish accent—*Dah-veed*—despite the fact that he was a White American (I had met him, as well as Tamara and Linda, on different occasions). She wrote the complicated triangle out, labeling Linda as "abuela" and showing with a straight line how her mother descended from the pair.

White privilege, passing, and wanting to be "ghetto": Christina in context

> It is no accident that the verb *kategoresthai*, which gives us our "categories" and "categoremes," means to accuse publicly.
>
> (Bourdieu, 1985: 729)

These momentary events, in which Christina literally wrote her identity as she drew out and relabeled her relatives, underscore her ability to work and rework events to her advantage. She had the flexibility to quickly reposition herself as someone with family connections to Latinos, connections not unlike those discussed by Vanessa and Marta a moment before. She literally wrote her grandmother as an *abuela*, and capitalized (in the Bourdieusian sense of the word) instantaneously on the way that Linda could become *Lean-dah* and David could become *Dah-veed* in writing, with no spelling changes. As with most of Christina's other performative moments, neither Vanessa nor Marta stopped her from re-pronouncing her family's names. Only once, in a year of observations, did I hear Vanessa counter Christina's identity work, calling her "White" in a discussion about who would be a slave if slavery still existed; in my sight, she was never corrected for claiming a Latina identity. In other words, Christina was never "accuse[d] publicly" of creating a false identity, or of choosing the wrong *category*, although her choice was not a simple one to make or maintain.

Within her social group, Christina constantly struggled, I argue, to claim a Latina identity and membership in the group. She brought certain social capital to the group—her extensive popular culture knowledge, her hip-hop and salsa dance moves, her close friendship with DeAndre, her ability to do school-work well and quickly—but she lived, in a sense, on the edge. Not only were her other options—including the "edgy" White girls, the other group of "too quiet" Latinas, or being a loner—unpalatable, but the Three Amigas had the symbolic power to represent the social order as they willed it, to label others, and Christina may not have wanted to give up her position in this powerful group. The school's emphasis on diversity, and on the equity of all racial groups, was not lost on these girls; Christina adopted some of that language to explain her friendship choices, as when she noted that it was "not the color of their skin" that made the other White girls unattractive friends. This curriculum, which I have touched on only briefly throughout the chapter, was, I argue, partially responsible for the seeming inevitability of Christina's choices.

As a White girl, Christina had the ability to pass as Latina, to look Latina enough to be considered as one; Vanessa was roughly the same color, with darker hair, and might have tried to pass as White, but Marta had much darker skin and could not have passed for White. This privilege, Christina's ability to switch, is of course not fair. It is, however, indicative of her power in the classroom and her keen sense of the subject positions that were available, and attractive, to her. Attempting to explain Christina's friendship choices to me, her teacher once said, "She just wants to be ghetto," implying that she did not want to be Latina or White, but an amorphous, probably non-White "ghetto." Cody and Jordan were both blond, as are some Latinas, yet they never claimed to be anything other than White; Liz, on the other hand, felt uncomfortable calling herself White, but did not have sufficient capital in the classroom, or support from any friendship group, to construct and maintain any other racial identity. As we will see below, Christina accused Liz publicly of lying, of transgressing, of over-reaching herself, when she tried to claim a Portuguese ancestor.

Who has the right to name and label: "your mom does not look part"

Jessica: What ethnicity are you, Liz?

Liz: Uh, I'm a lot of things. I just call myself "Other Asian," and, 'cause, like I want to say "Asian," "Other Asian," I just put "Other Asian."

Jessica: You don't say White?

Liz: I say everything I am, I say I'm Irish, I'm German, I'm Russian. (laughs)

Jessica: How come you don't say you're White? You don't like that word?

Liz: No, I don't. When I say, "I'm White," it doesn't feel right. If I say "I'm White," it feels weird to say that.

Bourdieu thought that, with adequate knowledge of agents' histories and capital, it would be possible to "construct a simplified model of the social field as a whole" in which we could "conceptualize, for each agent, his or her position in all possible spaces of competition" (1985: 724). For Liz, a relative loner with limited social capital—partly because of her parents' class status, which was visible in her second-hand clothing, her known lack of stable housing—being White was problematic, felt "weird," in this diverse classroom. She had lived for a time as a foster child with Jordan (see Figure 13.1), while her mother found housing for the family, but had never been accepted into Jordan's mostly White friendship group.

As we will see below, while they engaged in the joint construction of otherness, students such as Christina and Liz sometimes attempted to identify along racial lines that were not "theirs" to claim (with varying degrees of success). Other students, such as Adam, sometimes refused to be labeled by ethnicity or race at all. In the interview excerpt above, Liz tried to explain—relying on her feelings—why she did not like to "say" she was "White." In the diverse setting of Room 126, neither Liz's socioeconomic status nor her Whiteness granted her social capital; in contrast, Jordan and Cody, the two middle-class White girls, claimed the label White without accompanying feelings of "weird-ness." As Bourdieu has noted, the verb *kategoresthai* means both to categorize and to accuse publicly; Liz was often excluded from groups and was not, in a sense, categorized by and with other peers.

Adam, another White student in the class, whom we will meet below, looked White—like Liz, he had blond hair and blue eyes—but he was Jewish, too. As noted on Christina and Vanessa's map, he was friends with José, a recent immigrant from Mexico, Max, a boy of mixed African-American and White parentage, and Freddie, a Chinese-American student. When asked about their racial identities, Adam and José declared that they were "vampires" and "monkeys," refusing to own "White," "Jewish," or "Latino." Unlike Christina, who bolstered her Latina identity at every turn, Adam and his diverse group of friends often preferred to leave their racial identities undefined.

The friendship groups that made up these social spaces were not merely for play. Indeed, as I have shown, scratch the surface of any innocent-seeming trio of friends, and you would find a seething mass of sometimes contradictory motives embedded in the realm of identity politics. Students and adults at Gonzales engaged in a joint process that I call the "construction of otherness"; the practices involved in this constant interpretation of difference were "code-velop[ed]" because they embody the "linked development of people, cultural forms, and social positions in particular historical worlds" (Holland et al., 1998: 33). In other words, the identity work that students such as the Three Amigas did at this school was situated in a particular "codeveloped" context that fostered certain identity politics, the maintenance of friendship groups and group hierarchies, and drew on the school's multicultural curriculum for discursive tools with which to construct and maintain those groups.

As noted above, Jordan and Cody, both from upper-middle-class families, easily labeled themselves as White, although they, too, used national qualifications (German, Irish, Russian) in their descriptions. In this classroom, where "the categories of perception and appreciation which provide the principle of . . . [self-]determination" were "themselves largely determined by the social and economic conditions of their constitution" (Bourdieu and Wacquant, 1992: 136), Liz and her peers struggled to make sense of the official discourse on difference and their personal relationship to the multicultural ethos. The following vignette reveals the complex political maneuvering of Liz, Christina, and Adam, three "White" yet "not White" students, as they prepare to read a teacher-assigned book. This vignette and analysis offers a final review of how students were able to convert their differences into capital, and how they used their resulting symbolic power to influence representations of the social world in ways that were advantageous to their social work and, perhaps, their educational trajectories.

Number the Stars reading groups are assigned: "this is very ironic"

At the start of a literature study unit on the book *Number the Stars* (Lowry, 1989), Liz was put into a randomly assigned group with Adam and Christina. The threesome sat at a table, discussing their group's name for the duration of the study unit. In different ways, both Adam and Christina's racial identities were linked to their social groups, and those in turn were linked to the external hierarchization of the groups in the classroom, in which Christina's group was more likely to make racialized identity claims, while Adam's was more likely to discuss their online *Neopet* projects.[4] Teacher-sanctioned literacy events, in which students were "artificially" grouped outside of their friendship comfort zone, afforded insights into how each student worked to either maintain or disrupt some aspect of the classroom hierarchy. In the instance below, Liz, who had no friendship group to support her and little in the way of symbolic capital, struggled—in vain, it might initially seem—against the ways that others represented her in the classroom. This representational struggle—symbolic, yet visceral—centers on identity politics and positionality; it also highlights Liz's sense of her "place" and the contradictory ways in which she attempted to circumvent the established hierarchy.

Number the Stars tells the story of how a Danish family helped a ten-year-old Jewish girl escape the Nazi "relocation" of Jews to Sweden in the midst of the Nazi occupation in 1943. One subtext of the conversation below was the label of Jewishness, including the history the label implies and the present "relative weight" of Jewishness—relative to other identity claims and the current positions of each child in their friendship groups—in the identity politics of Room 126.

> The threesome sat at a rectangular table, Christina facing Liz, Adam at one end of the table. Adam had just said that his mom was half Jewish, and his dad was too; his mom's mom was Jewish, so she [his mother] is too. He said, "Since my mom's mom is Jewish, she counts as Jewish." He went on to say, "I don't understand all the . . . I don't pay attention," referring to his knowledge of Jewish heritage rules. Christina, looking at him, said, "That's the way." Liz said "I'm German," and Adam said, with one of his small smiles, "This is very ironic." Liz, not seeming to pick up on the irony of two Jews and a German together discussing this particular book, added, "and Russian."

The class had already been through a month-long lesson on the "Cycle of Oppression," in which they built on what they already knew about racism, sexism, homophobia, religious persecution, and other "isms." Liz often spoke up in those sessions and others about such issues, and in later classroom discussions about the Nazis she would present facts about their atrocities, but she seemed to miss Adam's wry comment.

Liz went on to add Polish and Portuguese to her list of ethnicities. Christina, hearing this addition, said in a firm voice, "No, you're not." Liz replied "Yes, I am!" and Christina repeated, more annoyance in her voice, "No, you're not." Liz said again, "Yes, I am." Christina said that she herself was part Portuguese, and then said, "Part, maybe part French or something." Liz said, "I think my mom is part Portuguese." Christina said, "What kind of Portuguese?" Liz said, "I dunno."

At first, this appeared to be just a friendly, or at least civil, discussion about ancestry. Liz was often told—by Christina, Vanessa, and Marta, as well as their male friends DeAndre and Mike—that she could "not" do something, that she was not allowed to join, to play, to work with them. She was accused by many different students of lying outright; this general treatment of Liz did not excuse Christina for acting the same way, but it shows that there was a pattern in existence for the denigration of Liz. It initially appeared that Christina was just engaging in this nearly acceptable behavior; Liz often seemed to accede to other students' rights to terrorize her, to relegate her to a particular low place on the social ladder. Christina was able to exercise her symbolic power, her power to deny Liz's claim of Portuguese ancestry, because Liz recognized Christina's power. These girls and their classmates had together defined Christina's power in and through their relationships, and had learned to work the balance between "those who exercise power and those who submit to it" (Bourdieu, 1982/1991: 170).

After a pause, Liz added, "English and German" to her list of ethnicities/ nationalities. Adam, one eyebrow raised, asked, "And Irish?" Liz said, "Yes, and Irish." Christina said to Adam, not addressing Liz directly, "She's like, probably a *centimeter* Portuguese." Liz said nothing; Christina continued, "Your mom does not look part. If you saw my family you'd see [what a Portuguese family looks like]." Liz just looked at Christina, without changing her claim, and Christina said, "Okay, if you're gonna go on like this, I am *so* gonna ask for another group."

Christina's tone of voice was so clearly insulting that even I, as an observer, was taken aback—"I am *so* gonna ask for another group"—yet Liz said nothing. The two suddenly explicit tensions were over a label (Liz saying she was Portuguese and Christina not allowing Liz to claim Christina's "own" ethnicity) and a threat (Christina saying she would move groups if Liz continued to "go on like this" about her ancestry). In fact, Christina talked as much about her family as did Liz, yet only Christina had enough symbolic power to claim a Portuguese ancestor, and only she could use the weight of her symbolic capital to maintain her position in this group, in the Three Amigas, and in the classroom as a whole.

After Christina's comment, Liz stood up and went and got a spiral note-book, without saying a word. She wrote a message on it to Adam; apparently Liz had decided, in response to Christina's threat, that she wasn't allowed to talk. Christina, ignoring or not commenting on Liz's actions and written words, asked, "Can you guys read fast?" Adam said, "Slightly." Liz said, "No," breaking her vow of silence. Adam, reminding Liz of her plan, said, "You said you wouldn't talk." Christina looked at Liz, who had written a second message to Adam, and asked, "Do you guys have, like, a secret language? You guys should go out."

Christina's final comment, ignored by Adam and Liz, was tossed out casually, but it revealed some of her peer group's key internal rules about how dating comments could be below-the-belt insults. Her tone and words were in line with the "alternative aggression" of female bullies the world over (Simmons, 2002), with the cruelty perhaps made worse by its casualness. The ultimate insult— "You guys should go out"—was preceded by Liz's small act of compliance/resistance (writing notes instead of talking, so that Christina would stay), but engendered, I argue, by Liz's claim to Portuguese ancestry. That Christina should insult Adam so cavalierly—suggesting that two ten-year-olds "go out" is almost always an insult, regardless of classroom status—hinted again at Christina's "sense of place," her understanding that she was able to insult Adam without fear of retaliation.

Conclusion and discussion: social group hierarchies, literacy practices, and multicultural curricula

Liz's sense of place in and out of Gonzales elementary

Liz's claim may have been her attempt to make an "immediate, de facto gain" (Scott, 1985: 33) in her own identity/status campaign, but as she did so, she overreached and forgot her "position occupied in social space"; Christina's comments, on the other hand, revealed her "practical mastery of the social structure as a whole" (Bourdieu, 1985: 728). Bourdieu argues that agents who have such a "sense of one's place, as a sense of what one can or cannot 'permit oneself,' " tacitly accept their "place, a sense of limits ('that's not for the likes of us,' etc.), or, which amounts to the same thing, a sense of distances, to be marked and kept, respected or expected" (p. 728). Christina, at the top of the hierarchy of this particular work group and a master of the classroom social structure, was able to accept these distances, and she often enforced them in scenes such as the one above. In their own ways, she and Liz, as agents who were the *"products of history,"* each attempted to "actively determine . . . the situation that determine[d] them" (Bourdieu and Wacquant, 1992: 136). In the context of this diverse classroom, where discussions about multicultural texts offered particular "situations," jockeying for positions in this way was common.

As this analysis shows, deceptively straightforward literacy events can, in fact, showcase students' identification choices, and exemplify how even such brief performances contain and can reproduce elements of the social order. For Liz, this performative moment, a "dramatic event or period in social relationships during which the enactment of self is foregrounded or intensified" (Hull and Zacher, 2007), could have been a pivotal one in which her position in the larger classroom hierarchy was solidified, or it could have been one in which she felt she had stood up for herself and made a stand against her peers' judgments. Such literacy performances—and their attendant exposure of taken-for-granted social hierarchies—occurred throughout the day, and students' ideologies about otherness, difference, and identity categories were constantly being reworked in them.

However, these students' maneuvering went beyond Liz's use of a label to momentarily reposition herself. Liz was subject to this kind of treatment on more than one occasion; I saw her slighted or excluded from classroom activities and games by her peers on more than one occasion. For Liz, and for other classroom members, this event was just one in a series of their performances that (re)accustomed them all to Liz's particular position. Liz was not always the one who came out at the bottom—there was space for negotiation, and in different situations she occasionally had more capital with which to work—but she frequently found the status quo reinforced to her detriment. Liz's identity work, which here involved pushing the boundaries of Whiteness and finding them more solid for herself than for Christina, was often embedded in literacy events, where "social change" was slow to happen for her.

As with any social relations, the power balance in this field was not set. The "work of categorization, i.e., of making-explicit and of classification," which these children "performed incessantly, at every moment of ordinary existence," was visible in just such "struggles in which agents clash over the meaning of the social world and their position within it" (Bourdieu, 1985: 729). Each day, Liz and other students would engage in these struggles, but Liz often did so from a position of less power, with less freedom to categorize, label, or name herself or others. There was always tension in this dynamic because although Liz and other students helped sustain the legitimacy of the power of Christina and her friends, they also continued the struggle against that group's power over them.

Because it was a relatively small school, with an emphasis on community participation and attention to the details of students' lives, social fields at Gonzales were not entirely distinct, and it seemed that students such as Liz could never fully escape other people's categorizations. When Christina and Vanessa wrote Liz into the bottom of the social hierarchy in their map, they were echoing perceptions and judgments from other fields—the staffroom, where Liz's case was occasionally discussed, and parent nights, to which Liz's mother rarely came—as they constructed their own social hierarchy. Christina, too, was well known for her association with Vanessa and Marta, and as noted above, her identity claims went largely unchallenged at Gonzales. However, in other social fields, students such as Liz and Christina had opportunities to remake themselves, to (re)present themselves as cello players (Christina) or as mainstream rock enthusiasts (Liz), categories that they downplayed in the social field of the school.

Mapping out Liz's place in this classroom requires that we remember that "while each field has its own logic and its own hierarchy, the hierarchy that prevails among the different kinds of capital and the statistical link between the different types of assets tends to impose its own logic on the other fields" (Bourdieu, 1985: 724). Despite Liz's struggles against them, she could not avoid the hierarchies of the classroom in almost all markets of the school field. At Gonzales, students and teachers always knew about her social status vis-à-vis other individuals and groups. Although they talked about larger societal influences on students' socioeconomic class and housing patterns, and even discussed the unfairness of "classism," the students' often unspoken hierarchy of social and cultural capital continued to "impose its own logic" on other fields in which Liz found herself.

The "properties . . . which are attached to agents are not all simultaneously operative" (Bourdieu, 1979/1984: 113) in any field, but Liz had few resources on which to fall back in each market of each field in which she found herself. Charting the volume and composition of capital held by Liz, as well as the "change in these two properties over time (manifested by past and potential trajectories in social space)" (p. 114), we find that Liz's potential trajectory, her ability to build up her capital in this and other fields, might not change very much over time. This is not to say that there is no chance that Liz could change her status in this classroom's hierarchy or in future settings; she doubtless will continue to struggle over the "meaning of the social world" (Bourdieu, 1985: 729) and her place within it. As mentioned above, a Bourdieusian analysis suggests that agents such as Liz "*actively* determine, on the basis of socially and historically constituted categories of perception and appreciation, the situation that determines them" (Bourdieu and Wacquant, 1992: 136, emphasis in original). Over time, in middle and high school, for example, the categories of perception and appreciation through which Liz filters her social and cultural capital will change, and she and other students from Gonzales may find new ways to "determine" themselves.

Implications for multicultural education

> Multiculturalism is inherently contradictory with respect to the redefinition of cultural capital.
>
> (Olneck, 2000: 325)

Christina used her symbolic power to legitimize her identity claims and Liz's status in the classroom hierarchy, but she did so in a classroom and a world where the value of identities and products was shifting more rapidly than Bourdieu might have thought possible. We are living in a time of flux, and children around the world increasingly identify—purposefully and subconsciously—along multiple axes of difference. Multicultural curricula have provided many children with some tools to deal with racism, sexism, and other "isms" (Olneck, 2000), but the policies underlying multicultural education date from segregation-era notions of equity and difference that are insufficient in our multilingual and multiethnic schools (Luke, 2003). However, we still do not have a better way to grasp or teach or get a handle on the "how to" of teaching about diversity, about the multiplicity of urban, suburban, and rural life to and with kids, in such a way that it resonates with what they already do in terms of their affiliation strategies, the ways they form social groups, grant "relative" weight to social, cultural, and symbolic capital, and, in short, conduct ongoing identity work in and out of the literacy classroom.

The paradox of multicultural education to which Olneck refers, the difficulty of teaching about difference while trying to change "current cultural hierarchies and . . . redefine or replace existing symbolic boundaries" (2000: 234), often against the underlying wishes of those who hold the most cultural capital, lurked forbiddingly at the edges of students' identity work at Gonzales. Efforts to teach students to honor diversity were taken up and subverted by these students, sometimes in the same moments. Christina, for example, could honor Jewish peoples' suffering at the hands of Germans, empathize with them by claiming a personal link—her father's Judaism—and then use her symbolic power to deny Liz, another "White" student, any claim to a non-White, part-German identity.

One reading of these students' work would be that Christina simply subverted the multicultural curriculum, making it "contradictory" to any redefinition of cultural capital on a local or more global scale. However, the issue is indeed more complex. At Gonzales, the curriculum that aimed to celebrate diversity and arm students with critical understandings of past injustices did influence Christina's choices, but it also informed her consciousness of diversity in many of the ways that the teacher would have wished, providing us with a different kind of paradox. While it was successful at giving students sophisticated ways of talking about difference, it was often co-opted by the same students in the service of increasing their symbolic capital. As diversity was officially honored, difference—in the case of Christina and Liz, non-White identities—was granted more weight in some markets of this elementary school field. The students' representational work, their struggles to be even "half-ghetto," for example, were battles for the power to order their social world and secure their places within it. Although the stakes may seem small to observers—what, after all, does a "centimeter" of Portuguese ancestry get one?—they were quite high to these students.

Issues of difference reared their heads continually in this school, but neither symbolic power nor the "value accorded to different products" (Thompson,

1991: 24) were fixed. Children such as Liz, who had little symbolic power, and Christina, who held much more, continued to negotiate their positions through their changing interpretations of what counted as different at Gonzales. As they grappled with the multicultural curriculum, these students made choices about their own ethnic affiliations, choices that positioned them in specific ways in the classroom hierarchy. The Bourdieusian frame presented here allows us to view children's actions, words, and literacy artifacts as products directly related to larger social fields and particular markets in the classroom as we begin to think about reconstructing our notions of multicultural education in a "glocalized" age.

Classroom and pedagogical implications

In the same way that skills acquired in the "[artificial] social field called the school" are "reconstituted and remediated in relation to variable fields of power and practice in the larger community" (Luke, 2003: 140), the values—the composition—of social, cultural, and symbolic capital in any given elementary classroom are themselves tied to fields of power and practice in children's larger communities. Every day, as teachers conduct literacy programs of various stripes, and students (usually) follow directions, write papers, take tests, and turn in homework, classrooms are the sites of symbolic struggles "where what is at stake is the very representation [in all senses of the word, Bourdieu later says] of the social world and, in particular, the hierarchy within each of the fields and among the different fields" (Bourdieu, 1985: 723).

When we analyze events such as the ones above, we can trace both how students do this work and how we might offer them ways to think about the links between their hierarchies and larger societal inequalities. We can also remember to view all students as agents, as resourceful and intelligent people who make meaning out of their lives based on their experiences. It is, after all, no surprise that Liz, with her ill-fitting clothes, unsteady housing situation, and lack of capital in this classroom, was often pushed to the bottom rungs of the social ladder. Adults who are more conscious of the inequalities that are in part responsible for Liz's "place" and Christina and Liz's identification choices in the political arena of the classroom can help students link local classroom actions and discussions with global issues.

As children around the world are faced with increasing choices about how and with whom to identify, literacy educators need to investigate curricula that can help children begin to wrestle with these intertwined issues of symbolic capital, identity politics, and social hierarchies. One future direction to go with findings such as these is to ask how curricula could be developed that asks children to examine notions of difference in relation to capital, with a push toward social change. Such curricula would entail a constant awareness that children as social agents are always struggling to figure out their positions in social space, to represent themselves, and to utter their social worlds.

Notes

1 Names of all participants and the school have been changed to protect the confidentiality of the research subjects.
2 From January to March, Vanessa carried *Anne Frank: Beyond the Diary: A Photographic Remembrance* (Van Der Rol et al., 1995) with her wherever she went, and I often saw her read it while she was supposed to be doing something else.
3 "Grandmother" in Spanish, although some speakers might say "abuelita" to be less formal.
4 Adam and his friends spent a great deal of time playing video games (on PlayStation 2 and XBox as well as computers); they also went online at home (for Adam and Max) and at school (José and Carlos) to invent, maintain, and care for free Neopets, digital pets that they accessed and cared for online. See www.neopets.com for more information.

References

Bakhtin, M. M. (1981) *The Dialogic Imagination: Four Essays*. Austin, TX: University of Texas Press.

Bakhtin, M. M. (1986) The problem of speech genres. In C. Emerson and M. Holquist (eds) and V. W. McGee (trans.), *Speech Genres and Other Late Essays*. Austin, TX: University of Texas Press, 60–102.

Bordo, S. (1993) *Unbearable Weight: Feminism, Western Culture, and the Body*. Berkeley, CA: University of California Press.

Bourdieu, P. (1977) *Outline of a Theory of Practice*. Cambridge, UK: Cambridge University Press.

Bourdieu: (1984) *Distinction: A Social Critique of the Judgement of Taste* (R. Nice, trans.). Cambridge, MA: Harvard University Press. (Original work published 1979)

Bourdieu: (1985) The social space and the genesis of groups. *Theory and Society*, 14, 724–44.

Bourdieu: (1991) *Language and Symbolic Power* (G. Raymond and M. Adamson, trans.) Cambridge, UK: Polity Press. (Original work published 1982)

Bourdieu: and Wacquant, L. J. D. (1992) *An Invitation to Reflexive Sociology*. Chicago: University of Chicago Press.

Butler, J. (1999) *Gender Trouble: Feminism and the Subversion of Identity*. New York: Routledge.

Dyson, A. H. (1997) *Writing Superheroes: Contemporary Childhood, Popular Culture, and Classroom Literacy*. New York and London: Teachers College Press.

Finders, M. J. (1997) *Just Girls: Hidden Literacies and Life in Junior High*. New York: Teachers College Press.

Frank, A. (1993) *Anne Frank: The Diary of a Young Girl* (B. M. Mooyart, trans.). New York: Prentice Hall.

Hall, S. (1997b) Old and new identities, old and new ethnicities. In A. D. King (ed.), *Culture, Globalization, and the World-System*. Minneapolis: University of Minnesota Press, 41–68.

Holland, D., Lachicotte, W. J., Skinner, D. and Cain, C. (1998) *Identity and Agency in Cultural Worlds*. Cambridge, MA: Harvard University Press.

Hull, G. and Zacher, J. (2007) Enacting identities: an ethnography of a job training program. *Identity: An International Journal of Theory and Research* 7(1), 71–102.

Lowry, L. (1989) *Number the Stars*. New York: Dell Publications.

Luke, A. (2003) Literacy and the other: a sociological approach to literacy research and policy in multilingual societies. *Reading Research Quarterly*, *38*, 132–43.

Luke, A. (2004) On the material consequences of literacy. *Language and Education*, *18*(4), 331–5.

McKissack: and McKissack, F. (1992) *Sojourner Truth: Ain't I a Woman?* New York: Scholastic.

Olneck, M. (2000) Can multicultural education change what counts as cultural capital? *American Educational Research Journal*, *37*(2), 317–48.

Scott, J. C. (1985) *Weapons of the Weak: Everyday Forms of Peasant Resistance*. New Haven, CT: Yale University Press.

Simmons, R. (2002) *Odd Girl Out: The Hidden Culture of Aggression in Girls*. New York: Harcourt.

Street, B. (1995) *Social Literacies: Critical Approaches to Literacy in Development, Ethnography, and Education*. New York: Longman.

Swartz, D. (1997) *Culture and Power: The Sociology of Pierre Bourdieu*. Chicago: University of Chicago Press.

Thompson, J. B. (1991) Editor's Introduction. In P. Bourdieu, *Language and Symbolic Power*. Cambridge, MA: Harvard University Press.

Van Der Rol, R., Verhoeven, R. and Quindlen, A. (eds) (1995) *Anne Frank: Beyond the Diary: A Photographic Remembrance*. New York: Scott Foresman.

Chapter 14

A "head start and a credit"

Analyzing cultural capital in the basic writing/ESOL classroom

Mary Jane Curry

I just wondered, some foreigners study, they just come here to learn English, they probably don't speak English that well. How come they able to pass those [university] degrees?

(Saky, 24, Laotian immigrant)

This quotation from Saky, a community college student, highlights a key question for the education of immigrants in American institutions of higher education: Why do some English language learners (ELLs) arrive to study in the United States and do quite well, while others struggle and drop out? Simply evaluating students on the basis of their language proficiency, or even on their academic English, does not explain this discrepancy. Instead, Saky's question points to the types of knowledge about academic practices that immigrants who arrive with high educational levels may possess, while others with lower levels of formal education may not.

This question has become increasingly salient, as in the past 25 years immigration to the United States has risen steeply—and continues to climb, with the foreign-born population now comprising 12 percent of the US population (US Census Bureau, 2004). No longer able to find manufacturing jobs that do not require high levels of English language and literacy, many immigrants are now turning to community colleges for courses in English and other subjects (Hull, 1997). The contemporary English (and writing) classroom is a "contact zone" (Pratt, 1991) of immigrants, political refugees, and international students and their relatives, whose diversity falls along the familiar lines of nationality, ethnicity, race, class, gender, age, and religion.

In this chapter I focus on another important dimension of immigrant students' backgrounds: their previous educational experiences. I argue that students who arrive with high educational attainment levels benefit from bringing the cultural capital (Bourdieu, 1990, 1998) that can help them negotiate the practices of the community college. In contrast, students without such cultural capital may become bewildered, like Saky, and discouraged.

This chapter explores the ways in which certain students enrolled in a Basic Writing 3 (BW3) course at Midwestern Community College (MCC)[1] were able to succeed, while others were not. Specifically, those who arrived with high educational levels were most likely to make their way through and beyond the Adult Learning Division (ALD), while students with less education struggled to continue. I aim to demonstrate how the students' various types of competence comprised the cultural capital that enabled those with higher educational attainment to pursue their goals. Through this analysis I hope to contribute an understanding of how these competences, as manifestations of cultural capital, were at work in classroom interactions.

I propose that students' cultural capital encompassed the following competences for "being doing" a student at the community college (Gee, 1996): 1) *spatial competence*—choosing to physically inhabit classroom spaces that afford greater access to the instructor; 2) *participation competence*—beneficial ways to engage with the instructor and the curriculum; 3) *curricular competence*—grasping both the implicit larger pedagogical purposes behind decontextualized classroom activities and how current coursework is related to the broader contexts of the educational field; and 4) *institutional competence*—knowing how to draw on resources and negotiate restrictions.

Finally, I will explore the issue of whether teachers can transmit to students aspects of cultural capital they may not have acquired through family environments and experiences. This chapter contributes to the growing number of studies on "international" and "US resident" college students (e.g., Harklau et al., 1999; Reid, 1997; Vandrick, 1995), especially those focusing on the increasing diversity of community college students (e.g., Goen and Gillotte, 2000; Goto, 1999; Harklau, 2000; Losey, 1997; Sternglass, 1997).

Background to the study

This chapter draws on data from a larger classroom ethnographic study of the free, non-credit BW3 course. I began the study trying to understand the experiences of ELLs as they studied academic literacies, the valued communication practices of higher education (Curry, 2004; Lea and Street, 1998; Lillis, 2001). The BW3 course included high-school graduates hoping to enter vocational or academic programs, bachelor's degree holders preparing for further study, and retirees simply wanting to improve their English to function more easily in the United States. Its curriculum was designed to prepare students for academic writing by covering descriptive, narrative, and argumentative modes of writing (Connors, 1981). However, BW3 "was not a success," as the instructor admitted; indeed, its dropout rate reached 80 percent. Because little that I observed in BW3 related to learning academic literacies, the focus of my study shifted to trying to understand reasons for the course's high dropout rate (Curry, 2001, 2002, 2003).

Variation in students' education levels emerged as a powerful index to their experiences in BW3 and after: while one-third of the students had a high school diploma or less—educational attainment levels typically associated with immigrants—two-thirds of the class already had bachelor's, master's, medical, or doctoral degrees from their native countries. This chapter uses the notion of *cultural capital* to understand an important phenomenon that, I argue, contributed to BW3's high dropout rate: that classroom interactions between the instructor and the highly educated students sustained their investment in the course, while many students with low education levels were marginalized. I contend that the cultural capital of the well-educated students underpinned this phenomenon, as my analyses of my data suggest.

Elsewhere I have examined other factors contributing to the course's high attrition rate, and I will summarize these findings as background to this chapter. First, the material conditions of the community college played a key role: the ALD, which housed the English as a Second Language (ESL) and basic education programs, depended mainly on grant funding, relied heavily on part-time adjunct faculty yet offered them little training and support, and served a broad range of students but offered inadequate advising and counseling. Second, and resulting from the foregoing material conditions, the course instructor, George Cleary, was an adjunct faculty member who was inexperienced in and under-prepared for teaching second-language academic writing; his writing pedagogy focused on sentence and paragraph skills, which under-challenged the well-educated students and confused those with less explicit meta-knowledge of grammar (Curry, 2003). A third factor in the high dropout rate was the mismatch between the competing cultural models (Gee, 1996) that the students and instructor held of each other and the course (Curry, 2002). Fourth, despite being enrolled in Basic Writing, a course not officially categorized as an ESL course, the students were labeled "ESL." This ESL identity stigmatized students within the institution while obscuring their past achievements and future goals. Finally, the hidden curriculum of the course rewarded docile students who complied with the instructor's skills pedagogy, notably by ratifying his shift of the curriculum from writing to grammar (Curry, 2001).

Exploring cultural capital

Cultural capital is one of the forms of capital that carry exchange value in "fields of cultural production" (Bourdieu, 1998: 139). Fields such as the scholastic are, to Bourdieu, "social universes" that create and regulate their own rules and practices. One aspect of the "practical sense" (1990: 66) that enables people to participate in a given field is cultural capital, which derives primarily from the family.[2] To Bourdieu, "families are corporate bodies [with] a tendency to perpetuate their social being, with all its power and privileges, which is at the basis of reproductive strategies" (1998: 19), especially educational strategies. The forms of cultural capital of the middle and upper classes generally carry the most value and are transmitted to the next generation alongside economic capital (McDonough, 1998). Cultural capital that one receives from the family provides the benefits of early and unconscious induction into the valued practices of the social class, as Bourdieu elaborates:

> The embodied cultural capital of the previous generations functions as a sort of advance (both a head-start and a credit) which, by providing from the outset the example of culture incarnated in familiar models, enables the newcomer to start acquiring the basic elements of the legitimate culture, from the beginning, that is, in the most unconscious and impalpable way—and to dispense with the labor of deculturation, correction, and retraining that is needed to undo the effects of inappropriate learning.
>
> (1990: 70–1)

While Bourdieu generally focused on high cultural forms such as the arts, cultural capital also includes the intuitive understanding, or feel for the rules of the game, of the practices and procedures of the educational field, where official interpretations of high cultural forms are developed and disseminated. People must also be prepared to grasp, understand, and deploy the various forms of capital. Bourdieu's concept of *habitus* provides a way to examine this process:

> The conditionings associated with a particular class of conditions of existence produce habitus, systems of durable, transposable dispositions, structured structures predisposed to function as structuring structures, that is, as principles which generate and organize practices and representations.
>
> (1990: 53)

The constructs of cultural capital and habitus are particularly useful for understanding the issues facing globally mobile students, who must often leave behind the structural benefits of their social class position to enter new contexts. At the same time, as this chapter demonstrates, those who have acquired cultural capital in their native countries retain some of its advantages when they come to US college classrooms. For example, college graduates bring a "command of valued cultural knowledge" (Olneck, 2000: 319) such as familiarity with reading academic texts (in any language), participating in classroom activities, and navigating institutional structures.

This aspect of cultural capital relates to the social knowledge explored in studies of the use of home and school languages (e.g., Cook-Gumperz, 1986; Heath, 1983), that is, what Gee (1996) calls "primary Discourses" and "secondary Discourses." Secondary, or school, discourses encompass knowledge not only of the social languages used within educational settings, but also of the particular practices and conventions that enable students to engage in and be rewarded for locally sanctioned behaviors such as, for example, typing their homework. Also highly relevant here is Gee's notion of discourses and Discourses, that is, situational ways of using language—"little-d discourses"—as opposed to "big-D Discourses," which are sets of habits, practices, and ways of using language, similar to habitus. For immigrant students in a new educational context, while the local language of schooling (e.g., English) may be new, the previous educational attainment of some students represents a mobile form of cultural capital. This capital can be revalidated within the new educational system, acting as a Discourse that may encompass old practices with new labels. In the case of BW3, besides previously acquired knowledge of disciplinary content and English language, those students with higher education experience held a crucial type of knowledge: how to be a student, that is, how to participate in the practices of the course and to draw on the resources of the college.

Data collection and participants

The larger ethnographic study took place during a semester of BW3, during which I made observations and took field notes of the twice-weekly course meetings, and recorded the classroom discourse. I conducted interviews with the course instructor, the ALD lead teacher and dean, and six focal students whom I chose to represent a range of features such as national/ethnic background, age, and gender. I also wanted to focus on students who planned to continue in higher education after basic writing. They included three students who left BW3 (Saky, Ahmad, and Katarina), and three who stayed in the course (Minji and sisters Rana and Leila). Second interviews with the focal students took place one and two years after the initial study to explore their subsequent experiences. I gathered supplemental data such as student demographic questionnaires, the course textbook (McWhorter, 1997), instructional materials, student essays, and institutional documents, publications, and reports. I analyzed the themes and categories emerging from the data with critical educational (Apple, 1990, 1995, 1996; Bernstein, 1990, 1996; Bourdieu, 1990, 1998) and discourse analytic theories (Fairclough, 1992; Gee, 1996).

The BW3 instructor, George Cleary, was a White, middle-aged man who had taught English in Mexico for many years. Like many adjunct faculty, he held multiple jobs: he was teaching writing part-time in MCC's Arts and Sciences Division and English to Mexican migrant workers, worked half-time as a Spanish medical interpreter, and had childcare responsibilities. Cleary was hired three weeks into the semester by ALD lead teacher Maureen Powell, a White, middle-aged woman. She has worked at MCC since 1976 and was assigned to be Cleary's mentor, although the two rarely met.

The 20 students in BW3 included 12 immigrants/refugees[3] and six spouses of international students or researchers at the local university. Twelve students held at least bachelor's degrees; five of these students also had graduate degrees. Three of the advanced degree holders—Olga, Irina, and Boris—were retired Russians who had previously taken English courses at MCC, including BW3. A younger Russian, Petra, held a PhD in philosophy and was married to an

American. All of the international student spouses held at least bachelor's degrees. Students' levels of oral and written English proficiency were roughly comparable according to my observations and reading of their essays. However, they had acquired English in quite different ways, with the more-educated students having had much more classroom language instruction, whereas the refugees had learned as much English informally as formally. Students' social class backgrounds and educational experiences also varied widely. I will next give brief profiles of the six focal students, then discuss their classroom participation.

Focal student profiles

Katarina was a young Russian with a bachelor's degree in shipbuilding engineering who had arrived in the city with her six-year-old son a month before the course began. She had just married an American accountant, whom she had met while he was in St Petersburg on business. They then conducted an email correspondence, during which she taught herself English. She felt that her previous study of Swedish and German had made learning English relatively easy. Katarina planned to become a tax preparer so she could work at home part-time. She stayed in BW3 for ten weeks both to socialize with the other Russians and "to study English, proper English." In the two semesters after BW3, Katarina took courses at MCC to learn to become a tax preparer, a goal she achieved with support from her husband as well as her cultural capital. In the third year she had a baby with her American husband.

Minji, a Korean piano teacher, had a bachelor's degree in design and had worked as a shoe designer. She came to the city when her husband began a PhD at the local university, where he now worked as a research sociologist. Minji had the academic, financial, and emotional support of her husband who actively helped with raising their two daughters when Minji entered MCC. She stayed in the BW3 class almost to the end of the semester, when her mother visited from Korea. By then she had been accepted to the flagship campus of the state university to begin a second bachelor's degree and teacher certification program in music education, which she was on track to receive in 2004.

Leila and Rana Hasan (as well as their older brother Ali), young Palestinians from the United Arab Emirates (UAE), were applying to state universities. They had finished high school in the UAE, where their father worked for an oil company and their mother was a housewife. Their grandmother lived nearby in the city. The Hasans stayed in BW3 the longest. They had been accepted to a state university campus near their uncle's place and entered undergraduate programs the following September. They planned to graduate in 2004.

Ahmad, a young man who fled Sierra Leone's civil war, was alone in the city. He worked full time at a bakery and sometimes drove a taxi. He was attempting to pass the General Education Development (GED) high school equivalency diploma tests and wanted eventually to become a lawyer. In Sierra Leone

Ahmad had attended high school and was fluent in English, an official language of the former British colony. He left BW3 after seven weeks. One year after the study, Ahmad had not returned to the college, although he planned to re-enroll. Two years later he returned and enrolled in first-year courses but again dropped out, troubled by psychological difficulties and persistent impressions that racism was hindering him.

Saky, a young Laotian man, had lived in refugee camps until the age of 14, including seven months in a Philippine refugee camp, learning English before he emigrated to Texas. He attended high school there, then in California, Montana, and finally in the Midwest, where he graduated. Saky worked full time (with much overtime) as a machine operator for a plastics manufacturing company and wanted to become a police officer. Saky and his young son lived with his family; his parents spoke little English and his brother had dropped out of high school. Saky stayed in the course through the ninth week. He returned to MCC the next year, enrolling in Basic Writing 2 and Basic Reading 2. Despite feeling more comfortable, Saky dropped out again, citing overwork, stress from a new supervisor, and lack of time for homework. Yet in an interview two years after the original study, his attitude had changed: "Last spring, between the year before, it's a lot different. I think I know what I'm doing now. I just don't have the time to do it." Saky planned to re-enroll at MCC in the future.

As mentioned, the course had a 80 percent dropout rate.[4] Table 14.1 shows the attendance over the semester and summaries of student backgrounds and goals. Attendance peaked at 15 students in Weeks 3 and 4 and ended with four students in the last week. By the ninth week, all of the students with lower educational attainment levels had left the course, citing their frustration at not understanding what was going on in class or the instructor's expectations of them, and a lack of support. At the same time, many of the well-educated students left throughout the semester because of boredom and their perception that the course was irrelevant to their needs.

Cultural capital as spatial competence

The cultural capital of the students with higher levels of educational attainment included a number of aspects of Bourdieu's "practical sense," ranging from their physical orientation within the classroom to their ability to draw on cultural knowledge to participate in classroom discussions. From my vantage point at the back of the classroom I usually observed the well-educated students such as Minji, Katarina, Irina, and Petra sitting at the front of the room. This manifestation of "embodied cultural capital" (Carrington and Luke, 1997: 102) is what I term *spatial competence*, that is, an intuitive sense of which classroom spaces to occupy in order to "be-do" a good student.

In BW3, such spatial competence meshed well with the instructor's preference for initiation–response–evaluation (IRE) interactional patterns. Typically, the classroom was teacher-fronted, with students and instructor rarely

Table 14.1 Profile of BW3 students (week in the semester they left, their educational
backgrounds, reasons for leaving, and goals for the future)

Week	Student	Student Background/Goals
Week 4	Hong	No information available.
Week 5	Murat	Less than BA. Went back to Turkey for extended visit. Planned to retake course.
Week 6	Rosa	Less than BA. Stayed in MCC physics course.
Week 7	Sik-yu	BA in political science. Goal: graduate degree.
	Ahmad	Less than high school. Goal: law degree. Returned to MCC 2 years later.
	Sylvia	BA. Goal: graduate study.
	Hye-Ra	Graduate degree. Goal: another degree in music.
Week 8	Petra	PhD in philosophy. No goal given. Moved to another state.
Week 9	Saky	High school diploma. Goal: to be a police officer. Returned to MCC but dropped out.
	Susie	Graduate degree in special education. Goal: to be a special education teacher in the US.
Week 10	Katarina	BA in mechanical engineering. Goal: to be a tax preparer. Took MCC courses the following semester.
Week 12	Jessica	No information available.
	Olga	MD/PhD. Retired. Left on vacation.
	Irina	PhD in mineralogy. Retired.
Week 13	Minji	BA in design. Goal: to be a music teacher. Entered university next semester in music education.
Week 14	Boris	BA in engineering. Retired. Left to care for ill wife.
Week 15 (last week)	Ali	Some college courses. Goal: BA in business. Entered university next semester.
	Leila	High school diploma. Goal: BA in information technology. Entered university next semester.
	Rana	High school diploma. Goal: BA in information technology. Entered university next semester.
	Atsuko	BA. Goal: to be a teacher in Japan.

moving around. The interactional patterns resulting from this physical arrangement advantaged students who chose to sit up front, as Cleary was more likely to hear their questions and involve them in classroom discussions, compared with those who sat in the middle such as the Hasan siblings, and at the back such as Ahmad and Saky. The students sitting at the front thus tended to use the strategy of "position[ing] themselves spatially" in institutionally sanctioned ways (Carrington and Luke, 1997: 107). Occasionally this positioning also supported efforts to regulate the classroom behavior of others. For instance, for a number of weeks when Rosa, a young Dominican student, attended the class, she and the Hasan sisters frequently chatted during class activities. More than once, Minji turned around in her seat to quiet the younger women. This behavior displayed to the teacher and her peers that Minji took seriously the role of "being-doing" a student, and was aligned with her plans to become a teacher herself.

Cultural capital as classroom participation competence

Some well-educated students' familiarity with academic discourse also resulted in the ability to draw on what I call *classroom participation competence* in order to interact with the instructor and each other. These students more comfortably and quickly volunteered to participate in activities such as saying out loud their answers to the textbook exercises. They also responded more quickly and enthusiastically to teacher-initiated discussions, while students with less education often struggled to understand how specific activities in the class functioned. In general, the students with lower educational attainment participated less than the other students, whether in being called on and responding less frequently or in volunteering less often to participate publicly; for example, by reading aloud from their own essays or the textbook.

Likewise, the frequency and quality of the instructor's responses to student questions and comments varied markedly. The verbal contributions of the less-educated students were ratified less frequently by the instructor than those of the well-educated students. For example, although Cleary had first explained the concepts of metaphor and simile on January 26, when the class did a textbook exercise on analyzing topic sentences on February 2, Saky was taken aback by one example:

Saky: By the way, I have a question about that, "World hunger is a crime." How does a crime get involved in hunger? I thought a crime gotta, somebody, you know, [somebody murder someone.

Cleary: [Ah, yes.

Before Cleary could acknowledge Saky's central question, Petra and Minji jumped in to discuss the implications of the example, fully grasping its metaphorical nature:

Petra: I think this is a crime because they have so many rich countries and they have extra resources . . .

Minji: Yeah.

Petra: We have a computer, we have so much so many technology and so much achievements in many areas.

In her contribution immediately following, Minji responded directly to Saky:

Minji: In the current political situation like that the hunger, that there is a problem in the North Korean situation, is that they have a very bad condition about the hunger. But the political leaders, they don't think about other things, so it's a kind of crime.

When he tried to answer Saky, Cleary did not address Saky's original question. Rather than explaining metaphor, he repeated the example:

Cleary: I would say this, just to start over again. "World hunger is a crime." Isn't that a metaphor? So it's not really a crime where they're going to arrest someone and put them in jail. They don't mean it that way. They mean it like a metaphor.

This exchange exemplifies how the better-educated students drew on their cultural capital gained from previous educational experiences to understand the textbook example. For these students, Cleary's earlier discussion of metaphor had served as review of a literary concept they knew from previous study of literature as well as speech. In addition, the instructor allowed them to take the floor although they cut off his explanation of metaphor to Saky. After the other students jumped in for four conversational turns, when Cleary returned to Saky's question he did not check whether Saky understood the idea of metaphor, although he answered the second part of Saky's question. Saky did not respond to Cleary and withdrew from the conversation, which continued for seven more turns taken by Petra, Irina, Minji, and Cleary. This example of classroom discourse supports the findings of Hall's (1998) study of a high school Spanish class in which the teacher's different ratification of student contributions gradually—and unconsciously—shifted students' participation patterns, leading some students to become completely disengaged in the class without understanding why.

Another demonstration of the well-educated students' use of classroom participation competence came in their use of English grammar to take the floor. I was particularly struck by the ways in which many of the students, such as Katarina and Minji, who had formally studied English or other languages drew on their knowledge of the metalanguage of grammar and language learning as another strategy to participate in the course. At times these students initiated grammar discussions both to distract the instructor from what they perceived as his tedious instructional style and to gain something from the course (e.g., Katarina wanted to learn "proper English"). As a former teacher of English as a foreign language, Cleary was more comfortable discussing grammar than writing. He rewarded students for questions on grammar, quickly ratifying such queries and allowing considerable class time for discussing them. For example, a textbook exercise asked students to identify whether this example was a sentence fragment: "Leaving the room, she turned and smiled." This example generated considerable discussion about possible variations, once Cleary confirmed that the sentence was indeed grammatical.

While Saky and other lesser educated students sat bewildered, the well-educated students used the example as raw material for trying out various hypotheses about English usage:

Minji: So how about "When she left the room."
Cleary: Sure, you could do it that way. "When she left the room, she turned and smiled. As she left the room, she turned and smiled."
Murat: "While she left the room."

Cleary sustained the topic by offering an alternative phrasing:

Cleary: "Before she left the room . . ."
Petra: I have a question . . . Does it mean that while she was leaving the room in this time she turned and smiled or because I think if you say "She left the room and she turned and smiled" this says she already left.
Katarina: ["And then
Petra: ["And then she turned and smiled." Does it mean that?
Cleary: No, it means that she is leaving the room right now and then she turned and smiled, yeah.
Petra: It means like this action, turned and smiled was while she was leaving the room?
Cleary: Yes, that forces that, in fact modifies the meaning of the sentence. It changes the meaning.

This discussion continued for 44 exchanges about the exact temporal and spatial meaning of the phrase, until Cleary seemed to reach the end of his explanatory abilities and told the class:

Cleary: You must realize that most of language is like that, spontaneous, and so you say it very fast. And you just have an impression. And we have about the same impression.

However, as my observations showed, not all students equally "just have an impression" of the use of a second language. Those students who knew meta-linguistic grammatical terms learned in previous formal study were more attuned to fine shades of meaning and better equipped to examine language in such detail than their peers who lacked such learning.

As this example occurred early in the semester when attendance was high, it is notable that the questions about the precise meaning of the example came mainly from three Russian students and Minji. The rest of the class remained quiet and disengaged during this discussion, and it took quite a while for Cleary to return to his main point about topic sentences. Similarly, Hall's study included a primary group of students that she characterized as enjoying "high participatory status" and a "secondary participation status group . . . act[ing] as supportive audience to the other group's talk" (1998: 301). As a result, students in the secondary group began to doubt their ability to learn Spanish without realizing that they had been left out of discussions. In contrast, BW3 students such as Saky and Ahmad quickly became aware that they were being marginalized.

Cultural capital as curricular competence

Another form of cultural capital is the understanding of the ways classroom activities fit into a larger picture of pedagogical work and, indeed, into broader contexts of the educational field. The more educated students in BW3 were familiar with course requirements and understood the specialized language of the textbook and the demands of its decontextualized exercises, which Cleary did not always explain. On the other hand, Saky and Ahmad were often puzzled by the assignments. For example, Saky became confused about Cleary's expectations for a homework assignment to write static and then dynamic descriptions:

Cleary: We're going to do two different kinds of descriptions. One's a static, static doesn't move, okay. A static description is the same as a photo. . . . Now next time, I want you to write for me next Tuesday, a dynamic description. Now that's the same as a movie. . . . It will have movement in it. . . . Yes?
Saky: Can you start over?

In response, Cleary summarized the distinction between static and dynamic descriptions.

Cleary: Sure, yeah. A static description is like a photograph. It doesn't move.
Saky: Yeah, but what we doing?
Cleary: We're going to do a dynamic description for next time. One paragraph, okay?

Saky later explained his frustration with not knowing what was going on: "He kept giving me homework, that week we have to do that, that paper we have to do that. It's really making me crazy. . . . Not really too much [work]. I just don't know what to do." Here Saky makes a point of distinguishing the amount of homework from the inadequate explanations he received. A year later, he raised the issue again in another interview:

Saky: I think it's the, well, first of all, I didn't go on the right track, you know. So that's why it's too hard for me. Maybe the teacher not co-operate, not explain me the writing paper.

Saky's confusion illustrates what can happen when students lack certain types of knowledge, in this case, an understanding of the purpose and meaning of writing an isolated, decontextualized paragraph. Activities such as practicing abstract types of writing for their own sake rather than for a clear objective constitute traditional practices of the educational field, with usually unarticulated justifications for such activities. However, these reasons are hardly self-evident to students coming new to the field. For example, Ahmad needed to take the GED tests but was stumped by the multiple-choice format, which he felt prevented him from learning from his mistakes. Nor did he see the basic education courses as helping him learn subject-specific content needed for these tests, apart from mathematics. Ahmad felt that students from other cultures are disadvantaged in testing by not knowing specific bits of information:

Ahmad: It's the small things, you need a lot of studies, you see. But here . . . they [the tests] don't go according to the syllabus, they just bring anything from wherever. And if you are not from here it's difficult. It's very difficult.

Although Ahmad identified his frustration as stemming from the need to know the specific content that the GED tests examine, his lack of experience with the practice of test-taking, especially multiple-choice tests, also disadvantaged him. His comments also point to the difficulty that foreign-born students encounter in trying to acquire a lifetime's worth of cultural knowledge that is often necessary to decipher standardized test items. Their experiences exemplify how "one of the principal means by which this disenfranchisement [of students] occurs in traditional and progressivist pedagogies alike is by the invisibility of classroom rules and criteria governing worth and value of specific texts, procedures and moral identities" (Luke, 1996: 318). While Saky and Ahmad attempted to participate in the practices inherent in gaining an education, it was their unfamiliarity with institutional practices as much as the academic content or English language that held them back.

In contrast, the well-educated students drew on their previous experiences as students who had been conditioned to feel comfortable in fulfilling decontextualized requirements. Along the way these students had developed not only intuitions and understandings about how fragmented educational practices such as textbook exercises are meant to build to larger concepts, but also the faith that classroom instruction would lead them somewhere they wanted to go. Cleary spoke about his understanding of this phenomenon after the semester:

Curry: Which were some of the students that you thought had notable, good progress?

Cleary: A Russian student, Boris, was excellent. Because he is very proud, *very educated, and he already had systems of learning incorporated into his learning style. He knows how to go to any course and learn from that course.* (emphasis added)

Although Cleary articulated that Boris's previous education (in engineering; see Table 14.1) had prepared him well for MCC courses, Cleary did not generally translate this intuitive understanding into his teaching, nor did he seem to consider that, to the contrary, less-educated students such as Ahmad and Saky would need help in developing "systems of learning" to achieve their goals.

Cultural capital as institutional competence

One form of what I call *institutional competence*, or knowing how to draw on institutional resources, is students' understanding of the vagaries of the requirements of different faculty members, that is, that what particular instructors require may contradict more broadly accepted guidelines. In another discussion of topic sentences, Minji demonstrates her understanding of the vagaries of writing for different instructors and her willingness to apply this understanding strategically. In this instance Cleary is eliciting students' ideas on structuring a paragraph:

Cleary: Then should I put my best idea first? Or last?
Minji: Some teachers actually, they put it first thing in the assignment, or they put it the last.

It is interesting here that Minji's reply is not situated in an understanding of text rhetorical differences related to audience or purpose, but in the politics of being a student. Her nuanced understanding that prescriptive rules may come into conflict with teachers' preferences seems to be another instance of her cultural capital. Not only had Minji completed her Bachelor of Arts in Korea, gaining "institutional capital" (Carrington and Luke, 1997: 102), but she had also previously taken other ALD courses including another BW3 course with a different instructor (in which she felt she learned more about writing than in Cleary's course). Further, her sociologist husband often helped her complete course assignments, including doing library research at the local university.

Another form of institutional competence relates to the "systems of learning" that the engineer Boris brought with him to BW3, that is, an understanding of how their current courses fit into the bigger picture. Those well-educated students heading immediately from MCC's Adult Learning Division to local four-year universities displayed their understanding of the broader educational field, including where the BW3 course was meant to lead. For instance, Leila, one of the siblings from the UAE, had strategically changed her intended major from computer science to management information systems "because of the TOEFL score. They need 550 [to do] computer science. I did it twice but I only did 500, not 550. So they need over 500 for the management information systems." Leila's keen awareness of such subtle variations in prerequisites illustrates her cultural capital, which enabled her to research, then apply to the university program whose requirements she would meet, even if it was not her first choice. Although Leila had just graduated from high school, her middle-class family had endowed her with the ability to navigate the educational system in a new country. She also had the immediate support of her brother and sister, both students, and support from other family members.

In contrast, Saky and Ahmad had only foggy notions of the requisite paths to their goals of becoming a police officer and a lawyer, respectively. One year after the study, Saky had started investigating MCC's law enforcement program. He was put off, however, by his lack of confidence about the quality of his education in four high schools across the country and ignorance about his academic record:

Saky: [The law enforcement program takes] two year, I think. I don't know [my] average from high school diploma. That's a problem right there. . . . 'Cuz I just graduate but I don't really know much, you know, so I probably have a lot of bad grades in there.

Not only did Saky not know his grade point average, he had no idea of how to obtain a copy of his high school transcript. In the quotation that opens this chapter, he displays a clear sense that he was missing some important knowledge possessed by foreign students at the local university:

Saky: I just wondered, some foreigners study, they just come here to learn English, they probably don't speak English that well. How come they able to pass those [university] degrees?

Saky's question emblemizes the gulf between him and students such as the Hasans or Minji as well as students at the university. Like many people, he conflates the distinction between academic preparation (in any language) and knowledge of the English language. While the international university students he wonders about may need to take several English courses, their typically middle- and upper-class backgrounds have often prepared them well for the content and practices of academic work at US universities (Vandrick, 1995).

Supplying cultural capital?

The classroom discourse extracts included here represent common kinds of interactions that took place in the BW3 classroom and demonstrate the deployment of the various competences I have explored above. As the profiles of the focal students show, what remains important is that the well-educated students subsequently made progress toward their stated goals in the community college or four-year universities, despite nearly universal negative experiences in BW3. In contrast, the students with less education dropped out of BW3 and then found it difficult to return to the college or to complete subsequent courses. As Hall points out, "participation structures constructed in different educational practices can lead to academic stratification" (1998: 288). In BW3, the classroom participation structures re-inscribed the social class trajectories of most of the students, ratifying the cultural capital of the well-educated students rather than supplying cultural capital to those without it.

This analysis then raises the question of whether teachers and schools can supply cultural capital, or help students construct cultural capital, or if "the acquisition of cultural capital in the schools of dominant cultures depends on prior acquisition of particular forms of habitus," as Carrington and Luke (1997: 110) paraphrase Bourdieu and Passeron (1990). While the evidence from this chapter may support their claim, I continue to resist the implied determinism of this notion. In my view, its circularity appears to leave little space for those without valued forms of capital to acquire it in order to engage successfully in valued and rewarded social practices. Clearly many non-traditional students, including ELLs, have managed to acquire the requisite forms of cultural capital to succeed academically.

Although I do agree that many subtle and highly valuable forms of cultural capital are mostly likely to be transmitted by the family, constituting, as Bourdieu says, "a head-start and a credit" (1990: 70), I would argue that some aspects of cultural capital can be acquired in other ways. While appropriately considering the ways that novices learn the practices of a particular group, social practice approaches to literacy and learning (e.g., Barton, 1994; Gee, 1996; Lave and Wenger, 1991) do not exclude the possibility that students can also be explicitly taught the "rules of the game." The competences used by the well-educated students in this study provide concrete examples of ways to achieve greater success in BW3 for some students compared with others. While some of these competences may be entirely tacit, others can be explicitly discussed with students. For example, students who inhabit classroom spaces near the teacher are rewarded because of the underlying social value of active student participation. Teachers can encourage students to sit near the front of the room; or, more usefully, they could explicitly discuss with students the premium placed on participation in most US classrooms and explore the underlying values that contribute to this premium.

Explicit discussions about other conventions and demands of higher education such as the practices of academic work, classroom behavior, homework, and particular activities could also take place. While it may be more difficult to explain to students how academic politics works, exploring their own experiences with the fact that different teachers have different standards could lead to discussions of how conventions develop, how practices can change over time and across contexts, and that knowledge is not fixed but constantly evolving. These discussions also could support giving students the bigger picture about why they may be asked to do certain activities in class. The teacher can thus crucially mediate and transform what students bring to the classroom. Indeed, Rose (1989), Gilyard (1991), and others have attested to the power of individual teachers to motivate and support students from outside the American middle class.

Nonetheless, it is unrealistic and unfair to put responsibility on the shoulders of one instructor to equalize the effects of students' life histories. The demands of the global economy have affected staffing, with contingent part-time faculty comprising the majority of the instructional staff at many community colleges, particularly in the areas of language and composition (Brill, 1999). To teach students with a wide range of educational levels and career and educational objectives first requires an understanding of students' backgrounds and goals. Such knowledge could provide the foundation for a range of curricular responses to these challenges, beginning with a collaborative, learner-centered curriculum grounded in students' competence rather than perceived deficits, recognizing their life experience as well as intellectual and academic potential (Kutz, 1991; Kutz et al., 1993). Rather than building on skills as exemplified in the grammar exercises Cleary favored, a practice approach would engage students in writing texts for real purposes, both inside and outside academia. Students may then understand the ways in which literacy is enmeshed in larger social practices. For the students in BW3, for instance, a pedagogy could be built on their backgrounds, their future goals or other interests; that is, students could engage in research related to their individual interests, such as Saky's goal of becoming a police officer, in both academic and practical terms.

Services such as academic advising should also support teachers in providing knowledge of institutional practices. For students to reach their educational goals, they must understand what these practices entail in terms of education, credentials, and other factors. Students who cannot gain this idea from personal and family connections should be able to receive it from teachers or guidance or placement counselors. Among the focal students in the study, Minji and Katarina had the clearest goals and best sense of what they needed to do to meet them. Minji's husband's academic profession contributed to her ability to maneuver in higher education. Likewise, in becoming a tax preparer, Katarina was helped by sharing her American husband's occupation. Similarly, Leila and Rana held a clear sense of how to enter the university. Although Ahmad and Saky held definite goals, they did not know how to achieve them, and lacked family networks to support them.[5] They would have also benefited from counseling, in Ahmad's case for lingering trauma from the civil war in Sierra Leone. Saky, too, had deep emotional responses to his situation: he had left the course partly because he had "no time for homework . . . and feel ashamed [of] myself, and work, you know, too much pressure."

By examining the aspects of cultural capital that were at work in the BW3 classroom, I have explored the advantages that high previous educational attainment levels confer on some adult immigrant learners. In this study, although most students had negative experiences in BW3, those who arrived with high educational levels were most likely to make their way through and beyond the ALD, while students with less education struggled to continue. In many ESL and basic education programs, students' language competence rather than educational attainment levels are used in placing students in courses. While I do not advocate segregating students on the basis of educational attainment, ignoring this information serves no end. Instead, with increasing numbers of well-educated immigrant students making their way to community college classrooms, we need to learn about and build on students' prior experiences. At the same time, we need to examine and discuss with students the practices of the academy, so that they can become open doors rather than barriers.

Notes

1   The institution and the participants in this study are referred to here with pseudonyms.
2   Cultural capital builds on economic capital but is not completely tethered to it. Although it may seem obvious, economic capital is an important factor in college students' difficulties, particularly those of adult students. The possession or lack of economic capital often translates directly into a student's ability to use academic and other services of educational institutions as well as to have sufficient time and space to study.
3   The distinction between immigrants and refugees is difficult to make without knowing why people migrate. For example, the retired Russians were Jews who had fled anti-Semitism in the Soviet Union and so could be called refugees. However, the two younger Russian women were married to Americans and thus could be considered immigrants. Ahmad and Saky were refugees from the political situations in Sierra Leone and the Lao People's Democratic Republic, respectively. The Hasan family—Leila, Rana, and Ali—had left the United Arab Emirates both to seek educational opportunities and to escape the discrimination against Palestinians in the UAE.
4   Although information on attrition in adult education is difficult to obtain, this rate compares unfavorably to the 50 percent of ESOL students surveyed nationally who persisted into the fifteenth week of their first year of adult education (National Evaluation of Adult Education Programs; Development Associates, 1994).
5   BW3 students' need for advising accords with the findings of the National Evaluation of Adult Education Programs (NEAEP) that students "enrolled in programs that reported providing a large number of support services logged, on average, far more hours [in class] than those enrolled in programs that provided fewer support services" (Development Associates, 1994: 2). However, the NEAEP also found that ELLs were the least likely to use such support services, with only 15 percent of those surveyed using them.

References

Apple, M. W. (1990) *Ideology and Curriculum* (2nd edn). New York: Routledge.

Apple, M. W. (1995) *Education and Power* (2nd edn). New York: Routledge.

Apple, M. W. (1996) *Cultural Politics and Education*. New York: Teachers College Press.

Barton, D. (1994) *Literacy: An Introduction to the Ecology of Written Language*. Oxford, UK: Blackwell.

Bernstein, B. (1990) *The Structuring of Pedagogic Discourse: Class, Codes and Control* (Vol. 4). London: Routledge.

Bernstein, B. (1996) *Pedagogy, Symbolic Control, and Identity: Theory, Research, Critique*. London: Taylor and Francis.

Bourdieu: (1990) *The Logic of Practice*. Palo Alto, CA: Stanford University Press.

Bourdieu: (1998) *Practical Reason: On the Theory of Action*. Palo Alto, CA: Stanford University Press.

Bourdieu: and Passeron, J. C. (1990) *Reproduction in Education, Society, and Culture* (2nd edn, R. Nice, trans.). London: Sage.

Brill, H. (1999) False promises of higher education: more graduates, fewer jobs. *Against the Current*, 35, 34–9.

Carrington, V. and Luke, A. (1997) Literacy and Bourdieu's sociological theory: a reframing. *Language and Education*, 11, 96–112.

Connors, R. (1981) The rise and fall of the modes of discourse. *College Composition and Communication*, 32, 444–55.

Cook-Gumperz, J. (ed.) (1986) *The Social Construction of Literacy*. Cambridge, UK: Cambridge University Press.

Curry, M. J. (2001) Preparing to be privatized: the hidden curriculum of a community college ESL writing class. In E. Margolis (ed.), *The Hidden Curriculum in Higher Education*. New York: Routledge, 175–92.

Curry, M. J. (2002) Cultural models in the US writing classroom: matches and mismatches. In M. Graal and R. Clark (eds), *Writing Development in Higher Education: Changing Contexts for Teaching and Learning*. Leicester, UK: University of Leicester, 45–61.

Curry, M. J. (2003) Skills, access, and "basic writing": a community college case study from the United States. *Studies in the Education of Adults*, 35(1), 5–18.

Curry, M. J. (2004) Academic literacy for English language learners. *Community College Review*, 32(2), 51–68.

Development Associates (1994) *National Evaluation of Adult Education Programs: Preview of the Third Interim Report* (Bulletin No. 5, January). Arlington, VA: Author.

Fairclough, N. (1992) *Discourse and Social Change*. Cambridge, UK: Polity Press.

Gee, J. P. (1996) *Social Linguistics and Literacies: Ideology in Discourses* (2nd edn). London: Taylor and Francis.

Gilyard, K. (1991) *Voices of the Self: A Study in Language Competence*. Detroit, MI: Wayne State University Press.

Goen, S. and Gillotte, H. (2000) Transforming remediation: the San Francisco State University post-secondary reading and writing program pilot project, 1999–2000. Paper presented at the annual meeting of the American Educational Research Association, New Orleans, LA.

Goto, S. (1999) The struggle for mobility in the contact zone of basic writing. In K. M. Shaw, J. R. Valadez and R. A. Rhoads (eds), *Community Colleges as Cultural Texts:*

Qualitative Explorations of Organizational and Student Culture. Albany: State University of New York Press, 39–57.

Hall, J. K. (1998) Differential teacher attention to student utterances: the construction of different opportunities for learning in the IRF. *Linguistics and Education,* 9, 287–311.

Harklau, L. (2000) From the "good kids" to the "worst": representations of English language learners across educational settings. *TESOL Quarterly,* 24, 35–67.

Harklau, L., Losey, K. M. and Siegal, M. (eds) (1999) *Generation 1.5 Meets College Composition: Issues in the Teaching of Writing to U.S.-Educated Learners of ESL.* Mahwah, NJ: Lawrence Erlbaum Associates.

Heath, S. B. (1983) *Ways with Words: Language, Life, and Work in Communities and Classrooms.* New York: Cambridge University Press.

Hull, G. (ed.) (1997) *Changing Work, Changing Workers: Critical Perspectives on Language, Literacy, and Skills.* Albany: State University of New York Press.

Kutz, E. (1991) *An Unquiet Pedagogy: Transforming Practice in the English Classroom.* Portsmouth, NH: Boynton/Cook Heinemann.

Kutz, E., Groden, S. and Zamel, V. (1993) *The Discovery of Competence: Teaching Diverse Learners.* Portsmouth, NH: Heinemann.

Lave, J., and Wenger, E. (1991) *Situated Learning: Legitimate Peripheral Participation.* Cambridge, UK: Cambridge University Press.

Lea, M. and Street, B. (1998) Student writing in higher education: an academic literacies approach. *Studies in Higher Education,* 23, 157–72.

Lillis, T. M. (2001) *Student Writing: Access, Regulation and Desire.* London: Routledge.

Losey, K. (1997) *Listen to the Silences: Mexican American Interaction in the Composition Classroom and the Community.* Norwood, NJ: Ablex.

Luke, A. (1996) Genres of power? Literacy education and the production of capital. In R. Hasan and G. Williams (eds), *Literacy in Society.* London: Longman, 308–38.

McDonough, M. (1998) Structuring college opportunities: a cross-case analysis of organizational cultures, climates, and habiti. In C. A. Torres and T. R. Mitchell (eds), *Sociology of Education: Emerging Perspectives.* Albany: State University of New York Press, 181–210.

McWhorter, K. (1997) *The Writer's Express: A Paragraph and Essay Text with Readings* (2nd edn). Boston: Houghton Mifflin.

Olneck, M. (2000) Can multicultural education change what counts as cultural capital? *American Educational Research Journal,* 37, 317–48.

Pratt, M. L. (1991) Arts of the contact zone. *Profession,* 33–40.

Reid, J. (1997) Which non-native speaker? Differences between international students and US resident (language minority) students. *New Directions for Teaching and Learning,* 70, 17–27.

Rose, M. (1989) *Lives on the Boundary.* New York: Penguin.

Sternglass, M. (1997) *Time to Know Them: A Longitudinal Study of Writing and Learning at the College Level.* Mahwah, NJ: Lawrence Erlbaum Associates.

US Census Bureau (2004) Foreign-born population reaches 33 million; most from Latin America, Census Bureau estimates (Press release August 5). Retrieved February 22, 2005, from www.census.gov/Press-Release/www/releases/archives/foreignborn_population/002.

Vandrick, S. (1995) Privileged ESL university students. *TESOL Quarterly,* 29, 375–81.

Chapter 15

Implications of practice, activity, and semiotic theory for cognitive constructs of writing

Robert J. Bracewell and Stephen P. Witte[1]

In this chapter, we treat the relationship between practice, activity, and semiotic theory on one hand, and cognitive theories of writing on the other hand, by examining correspondences between the constructs of these two areas of research.[2] These correspondences provide a common ground that argues against any inherent opposition between a sociocultural perspective versus a cognitive perspective on writing; and at the same time indicate ways in which the sociocultural perspective can become better grounded in what individuals do, and the cognitive perspective can be more realistically related to the everyday and commonplace exigencies involved in writing that serve communicative purposes.

It is clear to all who study writing for any length of time that writing, in that it serves communicative functions, is both social and material. The social aspect is perhaps seen most obviously in the writer's concern for the reader—a concern that in a distorted fashion occupies even the bored middle-school student penning an arid exercise to be graded by the teacher. The social nature of writing can also be seen in the other direction, as it were, by looking at the circumstances that lead to writing. Just as the writer attempts to predict and evaluate the reader's response, the act of writing is at least in part a response in itself to a request or need that comes from others. At the same time, writing is grounded in the material world in at least three ways: the writer communicates using material objects (letters, pen, paper, word processor, internet), which in turn shape the writing;[3] the product of writing, that is the text, is a material object in itself; and the text also often influences events in the material world.

It is also clear that writing is cultural. This is seen most obviously in the high value that our culture, and indeed most cultures, places on literacy and the mastery of reading and writing. It is seen perhaps less obviously in the assumption that cultural factors operate in part through history, and that these histories occur for individuals. To the extent that individuals experience the world differently, cultural effects are not deterministic but are part of a dialectic in which individual characteristics interact with cultural characteristics to influence writing. This assumption both motivates a cognitive perspective of writing and requires an integrated account of the relation between cultural and cognitive factors in writing. A writer's history is seen in the individual and idiosyncratic knowledge and processes that are brought to bear as the writer composes for particular readers, selects content for text, structures the text, and evaluates and modifies it. Such knowledge and processes are often subject to the writer's volitional control, and although writers rarely consider "cultural" factors in an explicit manner, they certainly consider characteristics of their intended readership, and publicly honored characteristics of language (e.g., genre and register) that indicate an awareness of cultural constraints. At the same time a sophisticated cognitive perspective sees other knowledge and processes operating in an automatic manner in appropriate situations. These, too, may be influenced by both cultural and idiosyncratic factors.

Thus to acknowledge that writing is social and cultural opens up the issue of how social, material, and cultural factors exert their influence on individual writing activity and practice. In part this is an issue of mechanisms. For example, by what means does a writer's past interaction with an audience come to influence word choice when composing? In part this issue is also one of theoretical elaboration. For example, in considering how authority is established and maintained through writing, in what sense are we dealing with a sociocultural factor, and in what sense are we dealing with an individual factor such as unique knowledge in a domain? The current challenge for those of us who study writing and its development is to integrate social, material, and cultural factors that bear on writing with cognitive factors that underlie planning, writing, and revising text. An examination of the correspondences among principal theoretical constructs of sociocultural and cognitive approaches is a starting point for this integration.

Correspondences

Habitus/habits and expertise

The first correspondence is between the constructs of *habitus* (Bourdieu) and *habit* (Peirce) in sociocultural perspectives and *expertise* in the cognitive perspective. Both Bourdieu (1990) and Peirce (1934) see their respective constructs as determining performance, and as being the result of prior experience with the world, especially one's communicative or social world.

Bourdieu (1990) proposed the construct of habitus to account for regularities in performance, or, as Bourdieu would call it, the practices of activity:

> The conditionings associated with a particular class of conditions of existence produce habitus, systems of durable, transposable dispositions, structured structures predisposed to function as structuring structures, that is as principles which generate and organize practices and representations that can be objectively adapted to their outcomes.

(p. 53)

In order to relate Bourdieu's perspective with cognitive approaches, it is relevant to examine how Bourdieu accounts for the creation of habitus, and how he sees habitus as having its effects. With respect to how habitus arises, Bourdieu places heavy emphasis on the process of embodiment or incorporation:

> The process of acquisition—a practical mimesis (or mimeticism) which implies an overall relation of identification and has nothing in common with imitation that would presuppose a conscious effort to reproduce a gesture, an utterance or an object explicitly constituted as a model . . . tend[s] to take place below the level of consciousness, expression and the reflexive distance which these presuppose . . . the essential part of the modus operandi that defines practical mastery is transmitted through practice, in the practical state, without rising to the level of discourse. The child mimics other people's actions rather than "models."
>
> (pp. 73, 74)

The contrast Bourdieu is making here is between a process of incorporation that is on the whole not verbally explicit as compared with a process that is verbal and public (i.e., "constituted as a model"). Bourdieu reinforces this contrast by citing Havelock's analysis of the shift from a corporeal to an external representation that accompanied the introduction of writing as a general skill and practice in classical Greece:

> As Eric Havelock (1963), from whom this argument is borrowed, points out, the body is thus constantly mingled with all the knowledge it reproduces, and this knowledge never has the objectivity it derives from object-ification in writing and the consequent freedom with respect to the body.
>
> (p. 73)

With respect to the way in which it affects performance, as indicated above, the habitus provides the principles for the generation and organization of the practices of activity. Moreover, Bourdieu views this process as being unconscious:

> Objectively "regulated" and "regular" without being in any way the product of obedience to rules they [practices and representations] can be collectively orchestrated without being the product of the organizing action of a conductor.
>
> (1990: 53)

As will be seen later in this section, this characterization parallels those cognitive processes that are assumed to underlie expertise.

Peirce (1931–58, vol. 5) proposed his construct of *habit* to account for regularities in performance in similar situations early in his philosophical writings;

and throughout his scholarly work, it maintained its place as a central construct. Compare the following two quotes from essays written in 1868 and 1906, respectively:

> A habit arises, when, having had the sensation of performing a certain act, m, on several occasions, a, b, c, we come to do it on every occurrence of the general event, l, of which a, b and c are special cases. . . . Thus the formation of a habit is an induction, and is therefore necessarily connected with attention or abstraction. Voluntary actions result from the sensations produced by habits, as instinctive actions result from our original nature.
>
> (5.297)[4]

> Multiple reiterated behaviour of the same kind, under similar combinations of percepts and fancies, produces a tendency—the habit—actually to behave in a similar way under similar circumstances in the future.
>
> (5.487)

Two aspects of Peirce's habit construct are noteworthy as they tie in with aspects of at least some recent cognitive theories. The first of these is indicated in the initial quote above: habits arise through one's paying attention to an experience—"No new association, no entirely new habit, can be created by involuntary experiences" (5.478). The second aspect of Peirce's construct of habit, comparable to Bourdieu, that ties in with cognitive theory is that habits exercise their effect without conscious awareness of their origins or their presence:

> If the interpreter be already familiar with the logical interpretant . . . it will then be recalled to his mind by a process which affords no hint of how it was originally produced.
>
> (5.489)

> Habits in themselves are entirely unconscious, though feelings may be symptoms of them.
>
> (5.492)

In cognitive theory the construct of expertise has been the principal one used to account for the acquisition of regular and skilled performance or, if you will, habits of mind that distinguish particular pursuits or knowledge domains. Expertise comes from a long and motivated experience in a domain, an experience that produces a large and complex knowledge base that one uses in the course of activity (Ericsson and Smith, 1991). The nature of this experience and of the knowledge base were revealed in initial studies of expertise in chess (Chase and Simon, 1973). In rule-of-thumb values, expertise in chess is achieved only after about ten years of dedicated study, and it results in a knowledge base that is made up of 50,000 to 100,000 patterns of board arrangements of chess pieces plus at least an equivalent number of patterns of strategies for using these arrangements (Richmond et al., 1996). These ballpark figures for duration and amount of content have held up for other domains of expertise that have been investigated both historically and empirically, such as musical performance, medical diagnosis, athletics, and scientific research (Hayes, 1989).

The psychological mechanisms underlying the acquisition of knowledge that contributes to expertise remain speculative. This may seem surprising for a discipline that takes learning as one of its major domains of study. It is clear, however, that once one moves from artificial laboratory tasks to the study of change in performance over substantial time periods and in real environments, then mechanisms of learning must be articulated with effects of development, individual difference, and motivation, to name just three. As Pylyshyn (1996) has stated, "The study of learning has been a sad chapter in the history of psychology, with the ironic consequence that the most studied problem in psychology remains the least understood" (p. 63).

Psychological research has demonstrated that learning can come about from agents attending to phenomena and consciously rehearsing them (see Broadbent, 1975). Briefly, the theoretical mechanism consists of two parts: 1) storage in memory of the encoding representation of the perceptual stimuli that constitute the phenomenon (this occurs by the agent paying attention to the phenomenon); and 2) easier access to the representation as a function of how many other elements the agent is attending to (in rehearsal, the agent attends repeatedly to the same encoding thereby creating easier access on subsequent occurrences of the same perceptual stimuli).[5]

An important issue raised by the sociocultural perspective and by research on expertise is whether this mechanism is sufficient to account for the types of learning that lead to skilled performance and practice in everyday life. Certainly it would appear adequate for Peirce, but it might not be adequate for Bourdieu. The Soar model of cognitive architecture (Newell, 1990) posits a different learning mechanism that is not directly dependent on an attentional component. This model is of course more than simply a learning mechanism; the attempt by Newell and his colleagues to provide a general architecture for cognition also addresses issues of the actual time-based constraints on performance, skill acquisition, and goal-based activity, among others. This comprehensiveness makes characteristics of the model, such as its learning mechanism, germane to our consideration of the relation between constructs of sociocultural and cognitive theories.

In the Soar model, learning is a by-product of one's acts. Cognition is viewed as an active process of dealing with the environment—which could be social, material, or mental—based on a goal that one is attempting to achieve. To achieve a goal one acts on the immediate environment, changing it in some way, and then one evaluates whether this changed environment realizes the goal one was seeking. (Note that there is no commitment in this formulation to the environment being "out there" as opposed to the "in here" of cognition; the goal can be something that is mindful, such as achieving an understanding of what an eigenvalue is in factor analysis.) Learning occurs when an action achieves a goal: the representation of the prior environment and the action are encoded as a pair and stored in memory, so that if the representation occurs subsequently, the action will be carried out automatically. Newell (1990) calls this process *chunking* (pp. 185–193). In this "bare-bones" characterization, learning is still closely dependent on attention in that one is attending to the immediate environment and to the goal which is realized in a single action.

Learning that is less dependent on attention is found in Soar in two mechanisms. The first arises with *subgoaling*. Where a single action does not achieve a goal directly, one creates a subgoal of finding an action that can be applied to the environment—in the worst case, the action will simply change the environment in a way that *may* allow an action that will achieve the goal (this process is usually called a trial-and-error strategy); in the best case, the action will change the environment so that the goal can be achieved with only *one more* action. Between the worst and the best cases lie a number and range of subgoal elaborations and actions (e.g., strategies called difference reduction, hill climbing, and means-end analysis) that can lead to the achievement of a goal. In the instance in which one of these strategies does achieve a goal, the sequence of representations and actions are chunked together and stored in memory. Thus representations attended to at a prior time are subsequently stored. The second mechanism arises through chunking itself. Once representations and actions are chunked, they are available as a unit and can be embedded in subsequently realized larger chunks of learned actions.

It is important to recognize the kind of learning that is modeled in recent cognitive theories such as ACT-R and Soar is not simply a static mastering of concepts; rather it is learning that occurs in the course of one's acting on the world and, hence, is closely linked to subsequent performance and acting, especially as this performance becomes proceduralized through repeated use. Thus these models of learning bridge the gap between "knowing that" and "knowing how."

In summary, the constructs of habit and habitus developed in sociocultural approaches correspond to the knowledge construct that has emerged from the study of expertise in the cognitive approach. It might be more accurate, however, to view the sociocultural and cognitive constructs as complementing each other—the nature of habit and habitus and how they may arise are accounted for by the knowledge and learning constructs outlined above.

The role of signs in activity

The second correspondence concerns the role of signs in activity. Especially for activity and semiotic theory (e.g., Leontyev, 1959/1981; Peirce, 1935; Vygotsky, 1986), the use of signs to mediate interaction with the social and physical worlds is a central construct. In the cultural/historical tradition of psychology, the activity triangle was proposed initially by Vygotsky as one of two hypotheses (the other being internalization) required to account for the effects of culture and society on the development of an individual's consciousness. As Leontyev (1959/1981) explained:

> According to the first of these hypotheses, the specifically human characteristics of mind arise as a consequence of previously direct, "natural" processes being converted into indirect ones through the inclusion of an intermediate link in behaviour ("stimulus-means"). As a result, simple elements were combined into a new "unit" in the brain. An integrated process described as in the schematic triangle [Figure 15.1]:

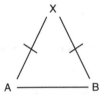

Figure 15.1 Leontyev's schematic triangle

> in which A–B symbolizes the developed indirect [sic] process, while A–X and X–B are elementary connections formed through the closure of ordinary conditioned reflexes. In mediated memory, for example, the elementary associations formed are combined structurally by means of a mnemo-technical sign X; in other cases this role is played by a word.
>
> Thus, Vygotsky saw the distinctive nature of man's psychic activity compared with the activity of animals not only in its quantitative complexity, and not only in the objective content reflected by it itself being altered but primarily in a change in its structure.

> (pp. 281, 282)

In its initial formulation, the sign X was viewed as bringing together and mediating two concepts such as events experienced by an individual. A concrete example would be the request by one's spouse to buy a loaf of bread on the way home (Event 1) and the act of purchasing the bread (Event 2); the request and the action might be mediated by the mnemonic device of one's moving a ring to another finger (see Kozulin's essay "Vygotsky in context," which forms a preface to his translation of Vygotsky's *Thought and Language*,

1986: xxv). A number of implications of the triangle are worth further comment. First, the mediation of the sign provides for a new linkage of concepts that might either: a) already exist as a pair (e.g., immediately purchasing bread upon the request being made), or b) not be previously paired. Second, mediation is general with respect to what it mediates—social situations (as in negotiation between people), the material world (as in using a special lure to catch fish), or a combination of social and material (as in the above example).

In later formulations all three nodes of the triangle were elaborated in order to deal with the complexity of interacting with the world. The following activity triangle (in Figure 15.2) is taken from Cole and Engeström (1993), who drew on Luria (1928):

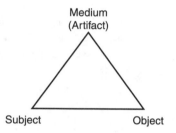

Medium
(Artifact)

Subject   Object

Figure 15.2 The activity triangle. (Reprinted with permission of Cambridge University Press.)

The sign at the apex of the triangle became a medium or artifact, which comprised both sign and tool, thus carrying implications for how it is used in activity. The left-hand base was conventionally designated as the Subject, and the right-hand base as the Object. In brief, the triangle became a schematic for the mediating role that signs and tools play in allowing a person to interact with the social and material world.

This elaboration of the triangle makes a more useful theoretical construct for those of us who wish to investigate realistic activity. However, it also produces a theoretical problem, which has been treated by a number of researchers (Bracewell and Witte, 2003: 519–22; Davydov and Radzikhovskii, 1985: 60; Kozulin, 1990: 253, 254). This problem concerns the issue of whether treating the apex of the triangle as a tool introduces a tautology into the activity construct such that activity in general is to be explained by the activity associated with the tool. That is, in the initial formulation the sign serves as a mediating device, and as such can mediate actions (as is illustrated in the example above), thereby creating from them a coherent structure. The additional characterization of the mediating device as an artifact or tool presupposes a way of using the tool in order to effect the mediation, thereby introducing the category of activity in order to characterize the activity triangle as a coherent structure.

Part of the problem presented by the activity triangle can be illuminated and partially resolved by considering what Peirce had to say about sign relationships some years earlier than the activity theorists. For Peirce, our knowledge of the world was mediated entirely by signs. His structure for the sign relationship was also a triad, and corresponds in a number of ways to the elaborated triangle of the activity theorists. According to Peirce, a sign (called a *representamen*) stands in relation to an object such that it determines a second sign (called an *interpretant*) in the mind. This relation is commonly represented as the semiotic triangle (Witte, 1992) in Figure 15.3:

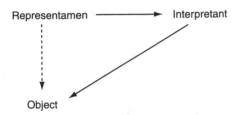

Figure 15.3 The semiotic triangle.

As with the activity triangle, Peirce presents constructs for both object and sign/representamen. And, as will be seen below, Peirce's construct of interpretant elaborates in an important way the activity theory construct of subject in that it begins to specify the nature and role of the subject's knowledge in activity.

Four aspects of Peirce's formulation are noteworthy because they permit his semiotic triangle to act as the basic unit for a generalized approach to cognition and learning. First, what constitutes a representamen is broadly construed. A representamen does not "point to" an object; rather it "stands for" or "represents" its object. Thus, as well as traditional symbols such as words, natural phenomena can also stand as representama; for example, a thundercloud can be a sign of rain. Second, the interpretant of a triangle can itself function as a representamen, with its object being the initial representamen/object relation. This allows the realization of elaborated sign structures that include multiple and prior interpretants. Third (really a corollary of the second), objects can be real (e.g., my computer as I write this) or ideal (e.g., the argument that I am attempting to realize in writing this), allowing semiosis to go beyond immediate contingencies for realizing a sign–object–interpretant structure. Fourth, the basis of habit formation, and thus of learning in general, is the interpretant:

> Yet this does not quite tell us just what the nature is of the essential effect upon the interpreter, brought about by the semiosis of the sign, which constitutes the logical interpretant. . . . [T]he definition does not require the logical interpretant . . . to be a modification of consciousness, yet our lack of experience of any semiosis in which this is not the case leaves us no alternative to beginning our inquiry into its general nature with a

provisional assumption that the interpretant is, at least, in all cases, a sufficiently close analogue of a modification of consciousness to keep our conclusion pretty near to the general truth. . . . [T]he logical interpretant is general in its possibilities of reference . . . [but] there remains only habit, as the essence of the logical interpretant.

(5.484–6)

Taken together, these aspects imply that a material object such as a tool serves as a mediator because of appropriate knowledge that the subject is able to apply, leading to the proposition that there cannot be effective tool use without accompanying semiosis.[6]

For cognitive theory, signs are encountered under the label of *symbols*, and their definition and role have arisen within the treatment of knowledge as representation. What symbols are and how they function has been presented in some detail by Simon and Newell (see Newell, 1990; Simon, 1996; Vera and Simon, 1993), partly in response to challenges by researchers who take a situated view of cognition that rejects an essential role for signs in performance (see, e.g., Greeno et al., 1993). Simon (1996) begins by defining a symbol as a special type of pattern, namely, one that denotes something else (a pattern is defined as an arrangement of elements, and is illustrated by examples such as letter strings, schematic drawings, and even wallpaper). A symbol is thus one member of a dyad, and the Simon formulation resembles Saussure's sign-object pair (Saussure, 1969). The adequacy of Saussure's definition for the application and use of signs in actual activity has been criticized by Witte (1992), and that criticism would apply also to this cognitive definition of symbols. However, Simon (and Newell and their colleagues) are interested not in symbols per se, but in using their dyad as part of a processing system (usually termed by them as a physical symbol system) that is capable of storing patterns and acting on them.

The properties of this system considerably elaborate the bare-bones definition of a symbol presented above. First, symbols themselves can be denoted by other symbols, given that a mapping relationship exists between elements of the pattern that constitutes the symbol; in this characteristic the cognitive approach resembles Peirce's. Second, symbols are the building blocks of the process of representation. This process is cryptically notated by Newell (1990: 59) as the *representation law*:

$$\text{decode}[\text{encode}(T)(\text{encode}(X))] = T(X)$$

where X is an external object and T is a transformation that is being applied to it (a simple example would be one's rolling a ball along a surface). Unpacked, this law consists of the following operations:

1 the symbol system encodes the object X as a symbol (this is the inner encode operation in the law);

2 the symbol system encodes the transformation T as another symbol;
3 the symbol system applies the internal transformation to the internal object encoding to produce a transformed object encoding (in the case of rolling the ball, this transformed encoding would be that the ball has changed location);
4 the symbol system compares the transformed internal object encoding with the current encoding of the external object (this is the decode operation).

Where the symbol system finds a match (in the example of rolling the ball this would be a match for the changed location), then the symbol system's processing (encoding, application, comparison) has achieved a successful representation.

Parallels to the constructs of activity theory are obvious: the object X corresponds to the object of activity theory; the transformation T to the medium; and the sum of the encoding, decoding, and comparison activities (i.e., applying the encoded transformation to the encoded object) correspond to the subjective or ideal object (i.e., the representation achieved). The significant point to note here is that the use of symbols for representation is inherently embedded within actions that one takes. Even the seemingly straightforward and simple act of recognizing an object without acting on it requires the application of an identity transformation in order to maintain the "sameness" of the object over time.

The "sense of playing the game" and performance under the constraint of bounded rationality

The way in which Bourdieu and Peirce view their constructs as affecting immediate performance has been mentioned above—for both, the effects do not require conscious thought although they do require semiosis, explicitly so for Peirce and implicitly for Bourdieu.

For Bourdieu especially, this unconscious operation of the habitus is important in accounting for how people carry out activities in the face of both knowledge and real-time constraints on performance. In discussing the basis of skill at issuing and replying to challenges, Bourdieu (1990) states:

> The motor of the whole dialectic of challenge and riposte . . . is not an abstract axiomatics but the sense of honour, a disposition inculcated by all early education and constantly demanded and reinforced by the group, and inscribed in the postures and gestures of the body . . . as in the automatisms of language and thought . . . This practical sense, which does not burden itself with rules or principles . . . still lesss [sic] with calculations or deductions, which are in any case excluded by the urgency of action "which brooks no delay", is what makes it possible to appreciate the meaning of the situation instantly, at a glance, in the heat of the action,

and to produce at once an opportune response. Only this kind of acquired mastery, functioning with the automatic reliability of an instinct, can make it possible to respond instantaneously to all the uncertain and ambiguous situations of practice.

(pp. 103, 104)

Bourdieu emphasizes the remarkable nature of being able to respond in an appropriate manner in situations where reflective thought is not possible, with sports providing an accessible domain for illustration. He prefers rugby, and makes the case that participation as a player is probably necessary in order to achieve an appropriate "read" of a game and an appropriate response to the actions on the field (Bourdieu, 1993: 124, 125). The choice of rugby as an illustration is a particularly apt one for those of us who reside in North America. For most of us, the activity on the field appears chaotic and incomprehensible; we certainly do not have a "feel for the game," yet it is clear even to the uninitiated that the players are conducting themselves at high speed and in relation to the many other players in some sort of skillful manner.

In both activity theory and cognitive approaches, constructs have been elaborated that provide mechanisms for the effect of dispositions on skilled activity. One of these is Simon's construct of *satisficing*, that is, acting on the basis of limited knowledge using rules-of-thumb (more formally known as *heuristics*) in order to achieve goals. This type of bounded rationality (as opposed to a rational process that accesses all pertinent information and seeks to optimize action) characterizes most decision making in the real world (Simon, 1982). It is certainly familiar to activity theorists. Consider the following example from Leontyev (1959/1981):

> Let us take the case of a human being's activity that is motivated by food. The food is the motive. However, in order to satisfy his/her need for food, he/she must carry out actions that are not immediately directed toward obtaining food. For example, his/her goal may be to make a tool for hunting. Does he/she subsequently use the weapon he/she made, or does she give it to others and receive part of the total catch?

(p. 60)

This vignette is as fine an example of one of the major heuristic strategies, means-end analysis, that one is likely to find. Bourdieu also acknowledges the construct of satisficing as a factor in skilled performance, referring in a footnote attached to the quote cited above, to Simon's early (1954) publication on economic decision making (see Bourdieu, 1990: 297, 298, footnote 9).

Bourdieu (at least implicitly) criticizes Simon, however, for not appreciating an important effect of a satisficing process, which is to allow decisions to be made quickly within the time constraints of the situation. In fact, the mechanism for this process has been addressed by both activity and cognitive approaches in terms of the *proceduralization* of knowledge and action. For example, Leontyev's tri-level characterization of activity (activity/motive, action/goal, operations/conditions) provides the framework for his analysis of how actions, which initially are subordinated to achieving a (conscious) goal, can become operations that depend on conditions (i.e., external or internal states) for their execution (Leontyev, 1959/1981: 63–5). Leontyev illustrates the transition with the example of shifting gears in learning how to drive a car. Initially the manipulation of moving the shift lever is an action that realizes the beginning driver's goal of changing gears. Subsequently, the manipulation becomes part of the driver's action of increasing (or decreasing) the speed of the car. At this point the manipulation is an operation, with no direct goal, but rather a set of conditions that are required for its execution. What appears to happen is that once a goal and the actions for realizing it become routinized, then they become absorbed, part of the "feel for the game" that requires no further conscious attention.

Similar constructs can be found in cognitive approaches. Both the ACT-R model (Anderson, 1993) and the Soar model (Newell, 1990) include processes that produce proceduralization. In the ACT-R model, sequences of encodings (declarative representations) and the transformations carried out on them can be stored in memory as a unified composed procedure or production. This production is then available and will execute its actions if the conditions of the initial encoding are encountered again. In the Soar model (as is implied in the outline of the representation law presented above), all representation is fundamentally procedural in that an encoding is always paired with a transformation. The process of chunking serves to put together sequences of productions that have been successful in achieving a goal. As with the ACT-R model, these "chunks" of productions are stored in memory and will execute if the initial conditions arise again. An important feature of the Soar model is that productions, whether elementary or in chunks, execute automatically if the perceptual inputs that satisfy their conditions occur. Another way of putting this is that recognition in the Soar model does not require attention or consciousness. Such a capability would appear to be a necessary component of a general cognitive model of performance since, although we are not able to attend to all constraints of the environment, we nevertheless regulate our behavior appropriately (e.g., I maintain my balance in my chair as I type this without paying attention to either the chair or the process of balancing). Finally, an important characteristic of both the ACT-R and Soar models is that, because of the proceduralization processes, the conditions on procedures can be successively elaborated, providing an encoding that allows one "to appreciate the meaning of the situation instantly, at a glance."

The overarching process that is realized by the constructs of satisficing and proceduralization is an instance of semiosis in the Peircean sense. Both encodings and transformations constitute signs for representing objects and acts that one can observe or perform, respectively. But the encoding/sign pairs do not stand alone; rather they stand in relation to a goal that is part of one's ongoing task in dealing with the world. This latter aspect realizes the interpretant that completes the Peircean semiotic triangle. Moreover, the creation of subgoals that occurs with the use of heuristics in the construct of satisficing, and the incorporation of knowledge into other active knowledge structures that occur with proceduralization, realizes Peirce's unlimited semiosis—that is, the idea that the interpretant in any triadic sign relation can itself become a sign in another triadic sign relation. Thus these constructs stand as candidates for the semiotic mechanisms that underlie complex skilled performance.

The role of dialectic and the significance of ill-structured tasks

This is perhaps the least obvious area of correspondence between the socio-cultural and cognitive approaches. Activity theory most explicitly, but also Bourdieu and Peirce, focus on the importance of the social/communicative aspect of human experience for the development of individual competence. Constructs such as the zone of proximal development, the internalization of activity, and even mediation by tools assume a social and material dialectic that underlies and supports the realization of the constructs in particular situations. The challenge for the cognitive approach is to develop constructs that are capable of managing this dialectic. At least one of these is the construct of the ill-structured task.

The defining characteristic of an ill-structured task is that part of the task itself is to define what the task is. Another way of putting this is in terms of goals: What one does in an ill-structured task, in addition to trying to achieve the goal, is to define what the goal is (Simon, 1978). This is not to say that there is no goal with an ill-structured task; rather for these types of tasks the goal is defined initially at a high level of abstraction (e.g., "write a paper on the relation between sociocultural and cognitive constructs in writing"), which does not connect readily with the constraints, such as time limitations; or resources, such as one's knowledge; or tools, such as lexical and semantic signs which work across knowledge domains, that constitute the immediate context for the task. In order to make this connection, one must elaborate the nature of the task from the initial abstract characterization.

This construct is significant for a number of reasons. First, most of the interesting things that one does, both in the classroom and beyond, have the characteristic of the ill-structured task. Second, because one must elaborate the goal of an ill-structured task, the task context (which also includes one's current knowledge, see p. 579) necessarily changes in the course of doing it—these changes occurring because of the dialectic that occurs between one's agency, including one's knowledge, and the evolving task definition. This out-come addresses a criticism made by activity theorists of Western psychological perspectives that assume a fixed external environment (say society) to which the individual must adapt. For activity theorists, activity changes context and altered context changes activity. More specifically, the criticism is that the Western perspective does not admit the influence of the context in terms of bringing goals to the individual, nor does it admit a dialectic which consists of activity between oneself and the social, material, and ideal worlds of performance (see, e.g., Leont'ev, 1981: 47, 48). Third, ill-structured tasks provide a vehicle for determining the task definition through interactive social means. Although other cognitive constructs are probably required, the construct of the ill-structured task will remain a central one for the adequate treatment of dialectic.

Implications for how writing is construed

The above analysis of correspondences between sociocultural and cognitive constructs that account for complex performances such as writing shows that there is no inherent opposition of the constructs of the two theoretical domains. For some correspondences the differences either are simply terminological—as in the role of signs in activity—or are differences of elaboration in what at this time ought to be taken as equivalent constructs—as in the correspondence of habit/habitus compared with expertise. For other correspondences the differences are ones of complementary levels of analysis—as in the phenomenological sense of "playing the game," which is realized by means of the construct of proceduralization—and as in dialectical processes, which are based on the doing of ill-structured tasks.

These correspondences indicate the possibility of an integrated and comprehensive theoretical treatment of writing (and indeed literate competence generally) that ranges from Bourdieu's constructs of different types of field and capital to the cognitive process involved in knowledge retrieval and transformation into sentences. Such a treatment would end pointless arguments about whether writing is cognitive, social, or cultural—it is, of course, all of these. It would also serve to support adequate and viable pedagogical practices for students' mastery of writing, practices which are primarily based on traditions of monolingual British and North American education, and which cannot serve students in the multilingual and multiethnic environment that is emerging with increasing globalization (Luke, 2004).

Realizing the promise of an integrated treatment will, of course, require substantial theoretical analysis and empirical research. In the cognitive area an important project concerns what we may call the semiosis of writing. Early cognitive work on writing was concerned primarily with specifying the control processes for writing (e.g., the Hayes and Flower model, 1980); very little work was done on what the control processes operated on.[7] The constructs of unlimited semiosis, habit(us), proceduralization, tool mediation, and task definition highlight the need to specify in much greater detail the "content" of the writing act. This content lies in at least two domains. One concerns the knowledge that the writer brings to bear in creating both task and text. It is not clear that the traditional methods of a priori task definition (see Ericsson and Simon, 1993) are adequate to the demands of analyzing the knowledge one applies in ill-structured tasks such as writing, particularly since expertise in writing appears to consist in large part of increasing the complexity of a given writing task (Scardamalia and Bereiter, 1991). Further research is required on the issue of how one retrieves, transforms, and constructs knowledge in the course of writing (e.g., Bracewell and Breuleux, 1994; Chenowyth and Hayes, 2003). A second domain concerns the material contingencies of writing. This would include empirical studies of the nature of writing tools and how these affect writing (e.g., Haas, 1996), and of the role that writing plays in the shaping of the world (e.g., Haas and Witte, 2001; Medway, 1996). Such studies would also include theoretical analyses of the way in which one overlays language (and hence writing) upon "natural" semiotic systems, whether social or material in nature.

Acknowledgments

Preparation of this chapter was supported by the Partnership for Leadership in Learning, Faculty of Education, McGill University, funded by Scotiabank, and by the Center for Research on Workplace Literacy, Kent State University, funded by the Ohio Board of Regents. We thank Tina Newman and Vicky Tung for their assistance with editorial matters.

Notes

1   Steve died from brain cancer in April 2004. We wrote most of the text of this chapter prior to his illness.
2   We are treating activity, practice, and semiotic theories as a general approach without dealing with important theoretical differences that exist both between these theories and within versions of each. For the purpose of examining a fit with cognitive constructs, we think that this "broad brush" approach is justified in that it presents the major correspondences.
3   As a form of communication, writing does not stand alone in being material. The material basis of oral communication is seen in its necessary use of deictics and proxemics.
4   Citation sources for Peirce refer the volumes of his *Collected Papers* (1931–58). The numbers recorded in the parentheses indicate first the volume number and second the paragraph number(s) of the quotation. The present quotation comes from volume 5, paragraph 297.
5   See Anderson's discussion of learning mechanisms in his ACT-R theory of cognition (Anderson, 1993: 25–7, 69–91) for an elaboration of this sketch.
6   Certainly there is obvious evidence for the contrapositive case. Although younger folk recognize societally abandoned objects such as slide rules to be tools, they cannot use them because they do not know what their parts and notations signify.
7   Flower and Hayes (1984) presented a sketch of knowledge structures involved in writing, but unfortunately there has been minimal subsequent development of their outline.

References

Anderson, J. R. (1993) *Rules of the Mind*. Hillsdale, NJ: Erlbaum.

Bourdieu: (1990) *The Logic of Practice* (R. Nice, trans.) Stanford, CA: Stanford University Press. (Original work published 1980)

Bourdieu: (1993) *Sociology in Question* (R. Nice, trans.) London: Sage. (Original work published 1984)

Bracewell, R. J. and Breuleux, A. (1994) Substance and romance in the analysis of think-aloud protocols. In P. Smagorinsky (ed.), *Speaking About Writing: Reflections on Research Methodology*. Newbury Park, CA: Sage, 55–88.

Bracewell, R. J. and Witte, S. P. (2003) Tasks, ensembles, and activity: linkages between text production and situation of use in the workplace. *Written Communication*, 20, 511–59.

Broadbent, D. E. (1975) The magical number seven after fifteen years. In R. A. Kennedy and A. Wilkes (eds), *Studies in Long-Term Memory*. New York: Wiley, 3–18.

Chase, W. G. and Simon, H. A. (1973) Perception in chess. *Cognitive Psychology*, 4, 55–81.

Chenoweth, N. A. and Hayes, J. R. (2003) The inner voice in writing. *Written Communication*, 20, 99–118.

Cole, M., and Engeström, Y. (1993) A cultural-historical approach to distributed cognition. In G. Salomon (ed.), *Distributed Cognitions: Psychological and Educational Considerations*. Cambridge, UK: Cambridge University Press, 1–46.

Davydov, V. V. and Radzikhovskii, L. A. (1985) Vygotsky's theory and the activity-oriented approach in psychology. In J. V. Wertsch (ed.), *Culture, Communication, and Cognition*. Cambridge, UK: Cambridge University Press, 35–65.

Ericsson, K. A. and Simon, H. A. (1993) *Protocol Analysis: Verbal Reports as Data* (rev. edn). Cambridge, MA: MIT Press.

Ericsson, K. A. and Smith, J. (1991) *Toward a General Theory of Expertise: Prospects and Limits*. Cambridge, UK: Cambridge University Press.

Flower, L. and Hayes, J. R. (1984) Images, plans, and prose: the representation of meaning in writing. *Written Communication*, 1, 120–60.

Greeno, J. G., Smith, D. R. and Moore, J. L. (1993) Transfer of situated learning. In D. K. Detterman and R. J. Sternberg (eds), *Transfer on Trial: Intelligence, Cognition, and Instruction*. Norwood, NJ: Ablex, 99–167.

Haas, C. (1996) *Writing Technology: Studies on the Materiality of Literacy*. Mahwah, NJ: Lawrence Erlbaum Associates.

Haas, C. and Witte, S. P. (2001) Writing as an embodied practice: a case of engineering standards. *Journal of Business and Technical Communication*, 15, 413–57.

Havelock, E. A. (1963) *Preface to Plato*. Cambridge, MA: Harvard University Press.

Hayes, J. R. (1989) *The Complete Problem Solver* (2nd edn). Hillsdale, NJ: Erlbaum.

Hayes, J. R. and Flower, L. (1980) Identifying the organization of writing processes. In L. Gregg and E. Steinberg (eds), *Cognitive Processes in Writing*. Hillsdale, NJ: Erlbaum, 31–50.

Kozulin, A. (1990) *Vygotsky's Psychology: A Biography of Ideas*. New York: Harvester Wheatsheaf.

Leontyev, A. N. (1981) The problem of activity in psychology. In J. V. Wertsch (ed. and trans.), *The Concept of Activity in Soviet Psychology*. Armonk, NY: M. E. Sharpe, 37–71.

Leontyev, A. N. (1981) Problems of the development of the mind (M. Kopylova, trans.) Moscow: Progress. (Original work published 1959)

Luke, A. (2004) The trouble with English. *Research in the Teaching of English*, 39, 85–95.

Luria, A. R. (1928) The problem of the cultural development of the child. *Journal of Genetic Psychology*, 35, 493–506.

Medway: (1996) Virtual and material buildings: construction and constructivism in architecture and writing. *Written Communication*, 13(4), 473–514.

Newell, A. (1990) *Unified Theories of Cognition*. Cambridge, MA: Harvard University Press.

Peirce, C. S. (1931–1958) *Collected Papers of Charles Sanders Peirce* (8 vols). C. Hartshorne: Weiss and A. Burks (eds). Cambridge, MA: Harvard University Press.

Pylyshyn, Z. W. (1996) The study of cognitive architecture. In D. Steier and T. M. Mitchell (eds), *Mind Matters: A Tribute to Allen Newell*. Mahwah, NJ: Lawrence Erlbaum Associates, 51–74.

Richmond, H. B., Gobet, F., Staszewski, J. J. and Simon, H. A. (1996) Perceptual and memory processes in the acquisition of expert performance: the EPAM model. In K. A. Ericsson (ed.), *The Road to Excellence: The Acquisition of Expert Performance in the Arts and Sciences, Sports, and Games*. Mahwah, NJ: Lawrence Erlbaum Associates, 167–87.

Saussure, F. de (1969) *Course in General Linguistics* (W. Baskin, trans.) New York: McGraw-Hill. (Original work published 1916)

Scardamalia, M. and Bereiter, C. (1991) Literate expertise. In K. A. Ericsson and J. Smith (eds), *Toward a General Theory of Expertise: Prospects and Limits*. Cambridge, UK: Cambridge University Press, 172–94.

Simon, H. A. (1954) A behavioral theory of rational choice. *Quarterly Journal of Economics*, 69, 99–118.

Simon, H. A. (1978) Information-processing theory of problem solving. In W. K. Estes (ed.), *Handbook of Learning and Cognitive Processes: Human Information Processing* (Vol. 5). Hillsdale, NJ: Erlbaum, 271–95.

Simon, H. A. (1982) *Models of Bounded Rationality*. Cambridge, MA: MIT Press.

Simon, H. A. (1996) The patterned matter that is mind. In D. Steier and T. M. Mitchell (eds), *Mind Matters: A Tribute to Allen Newel*. Mahwah, NJ: Lawrence Erlbaum Associates, 407–31.

Vera, A. H. and Simon, H. A. (1993) Situated action: a symbolic interpretation. *Cognitive Science*, 17, 7–48.

Vygotsky, L. (1986) *Thought and Language* (A. Kozulin, trans.). Cambridge, MA: MIT Press. (Original work published 1934)

Witte, S. P. (1992) Context, text, intertext: toward a constructivist semiotic of writing. *Written Communication*, 9(2), 155–207.

Part IV

Remaking the field

Chapter 16

Learning from our failures

James Albright

Early in his second administration, United States Democratic President Bill Clinton introduced the *Reading Excellence Act*. Unlike what some have argued, this legislation was not the first that linked education explicitly to the promotion of economic growth and competitiveness (see Edmondson and Shannon, 1998). This policy initiative confirmed that "the locus of control" of US education was no longer with the states (see Astuto and Clark, 1988). With bipartisan support, the legislation proposed that reading pedagogy be based on systematic, scientifically based instruction. Most American lawgivers, Republicans and Democrats, agreed that this legislation would restore order to reading education and research (Dunn and Woodard, 2003). The Reading Excellence Act, enacted on October 21, 1998, apportioned US$260–280 million to states with low performance in literacy education on standardized assessments (Roller and Long, 2001). Many states followed the federal policy lead. At this time, the National Research Council (NRC) published a "consensus document," the *Preventing Reading Difficulties in Young Children* report (Snow et al., 1998), which was criticized for not specifying how reading ought to be taught (National Institute of Child Health and Human Development [NICHD], 2000: 1).

In response, the American Congress commissioned the National Reading Panel (NRP) to review existing research on early reading development and instruction to determine how best to make it available for "effective" change in classroom instructional practices. The NRP's report, *Teaching Children to Read: An Evidence-Based Assessment of the Scientific Research Literature on Reading and Its Implications for Reading Instruction* (NICHD, 2000), became the basis for the newly elected Republican administration's *Reading First* initiative. Underscoring the NRP's support of "scientific" reading research, which stressed phonemic awareness, phonics, vocabulary development, reading fluency, and reading comprehension, this bill once again focused on states, districts and schools with failing standardized reading test scores (Manzo, 2002). The Reading Excellence Act, the Preventing Reading Difficulties report, and the National Reading Panel report purportedly gave educators and researchers specific criteria to determine best reading practices. President George W. Bush's Reading First initiative and the *No Child Left Behind (NCLB) Act of* 2001 set strict guidelines for poor performing (often impoverished) schools across the United States to make yearly progress in order to get and retain needed federal money.

Bourdieu's reflexive sociology may assist in understanding what to many seems a dramatic shift in US education policy. Yet, the current Bush administration's NCLB-related initiatives may be understood as a part of an ongoing development in the American policy field over the past 30 years. As Ladwig (1994) argues, "the 1980s' educational policy reforms [in the US] reveal the maturation of the historically rooted social field of education policy . . . [and American] educational policy has historically developed its own relative autonomy and carries its own rewards" (p. 342). And contrary to the hopes of many who have attempted to influence policy from the outside, since policy initiatives are rarely, if ever, declared successful in terms of effectively changing educational practice, policy effectiveness would be better described in terms of contests within the policy field itself. I argue that Ladwig's (1996, 1998) Bourdieusian analysis may help account for how progressive and radical literacy education researchers and practitioners have had so little influence over current American literacy education policies. Weaker linkages between policy and practice than many of them have generally assumed may explain why they have over the past 30 years failed to influence the American education policy field in general. Also, progressive and radical literacy education researchers and practitioners' strategies to affect policy may have exacerbated literacy education's weakening relative autonomy vis-à-vis the policy field. Outside the US, inter- and intra-field relations of the social fields of practice and policy in literacy education may be quite different. My analysis might resonate with similar contentious relations between literacy education policymakers and researchers and practitioners in other countries.

A Bourdieusian understanding of inter- and intra-field relations inaugurates my re-reading of McCollum-Clark's (1995) recount of the National Council of Teachers of English (NCTE) Executive Committee's failure to affect the burgeoning standards movement in American education in the 1990s. My re-reading also illustrates the generally misrecognized limitations of progressive and radical literacy education researchers and practitioners to enact internally effective politics within their own field of practice as well as to effect changes in the policy field. McCollum-Clark's narrative seemingly confirms Ladwig's (1994) 1980s' analysis. Bringing this story into the present, this chapter reviews the current controversies associated with the current Bush administration's NCLB Act and the NRP's report. With specific reference to "epistic" representatives of progressive and radical responses to the legislation and documents associated with these initiatives, I hope to suggest the limitations and, perhaps, some possibilities for these researchers and practitioners in the future to engage more effectively within and without the US literacy education field. My re-reading of Ladwig's (1994) and McCollum-Clark's recounts and my analysis of the extensive literature associated with NCLB/NRP seem to confirm Ladwig's (1996, 1998) contention that what success (and that has been limited) progressive and radical researchers and practitioners have had in the academic field is a result of the extent to which they have conformed the fields' own logics, while they have at the same time struggled over those very regimes of truth. Inquiry into their inability to influence the literacy education field to a greater extent and, perhaps as a consequence, their failure to influence legislation affecting educational practice or defend the relative autonomy to conduct recognized and valued forms of research from increasing encroachment of policy field, may reveal a crucial misrecognition about what counts in terms of habitus and capital in both fields. Bourdieusian analysis may be a corrective that could lead to a future realist politics for conducting research and practice in literacy education and more effectively influencing policy.

Ladwig's case

Employing Bourdieu's notion of *epistic* individuals to identify holders of specific positions in the policy field, Ladwig (1994) maps out some agents' and institutions' objective structures of positions and relations in the field of American educational policy in the mid-1980s. To study any field, enduring connections between the social and identities, discourses, practices and products, found in positions and dispositions across the field, need to be mapped (Bourdieu and Wacquant, 1992). Ladwig identifies the Public Education Information Network (PEIN); the National Coalition of Advocates for Students (NCAS); National Governor's Association (NGA); and the presidential commission, the National Commission on Excellence in Education. He recounts a particular historical contest. In it, PEIN occupied a dominated position within the field. As an outside group of progressive academics, its intervention revealed the difficulty in leveraging the kinds of capital recognized in the policy field by more dominant players. NCAS had a proposal similar to PEIN's, emphasizing democracy and a broader humanistic rationale for literacy education. Yet, NCAS recognized existing federal, state and local policy structures and framed its recommendations within economic discourses. Ladwig's tracking of NCAS reveals it also occupied a marginal position in the field. Its unsuccessful struggle to gain a more powerful position within the education policy field, he argues, may be measured by how its recommendations were not taken up by the more dominant players. Further, Ladwig observes, as the economic rationale for education pushed the debate outside the realm of female teachers and into that of male policymakers, progressive discourses of nurturance and equity evaporated. None of the players in the field positioned parents as holding much capital in the field. While nominated by the NGA, teachers and teachers' unions do not fare well either in this contest.

At this time, most interpreters of US educational policy placed "the locus of control" with the states (Astuto and Clark, 1988). Contrary to these analyses, Ladwig's study suggests that the NGA was not the strongest player in the policy field. The governors clearly were struggling to establish hegemony in the field but they did this "obliquely" through deference to the federal government and the courts. The US federal government held and still holds, Ladwig posits, the dominant position in educational policy, as evidenced then in the commissioning of *A Nation at Risk* (National Commission on Excellence, 1983), which monopolized the rhetoric of economic and technological justifications for educational reform.

Given the public's growing lack of confidence in schooling, in part manufactured by the dominant players in the field, Ladwig argues that the federal government's proposal of devolving or divesting power to the states may seem counterintuitive to the logic of the policy field. Yet, Ladwig asserts that the consequence for educational reform within what was a collapsing market of education policy solidified overall federal control while mitigating any failure in the implementation of any reform. With emerging opposition to NCLB among the policymakers and others at the state level, this strategy was no longer as effective as it once was (see CNN, 2005). Ladwig notes, "For educational policy then, investments of policy capital would be made to the extent that profits could be made" (1994: 356). His reading is rather broad but it helps to identify the relative power of the players in future contests over the direction of US education policy.

Methodologically, Ladwig suggests that investigating the inter-subjectively recognized positions of important individuals within dominant policy organizations may be helpful in future policy research, arguing:

> Certainly such accounts, however difficult to obtain, could reveal social networks indicating the social capitals current in the field of educational policy. It is possible, of course, that the social capital may be quite significant in determining who holds dominant positions in educational policy; but it may also be that these social capitals are capitals outside the field of educational policy. . . . [A] survey of the relative prestige or power of relevant institutions would prove vital in mapping out the structural relations of the field and would provide necessary measures of relative values for some of the elemental capitals, which constitute the overall educational policy capital. . . . [A]n analysis of their reception as such constitutes a complementary and necessary line of analysis in the overall project of building a cultural sociology of educational policy.

> (pp. 353, 358)

Illustrating the critical capacity of Bourdieu's conceptual framework for a cultural sociology of educational policy, Ladwig contends that progressives may mount a more effective influence in the course of educational practice and policy. Field analysis may assist our thinking relationally about social action in all its multiple, complex, and contradictory meanings. The significance of Bourdieu's sociology is that it conceives social relations as "objective to the extent they are inter-subjectively recognized" (p. 344). Ladwig's analysis of the field of educational policy illustrates the relative and constrained autonomy of action agents may have in struggles over different forms of capital. Agents' strategies for distinction in the educational policy field may have unintended, secondary or unappreciated consequences in educational practice. "The notion of field as a set of lived objective relations asks us," Ladwig observes, "to acknowledge external constraints and the explicit lived experiences, the strategies of players in the field" (p. 348). This orientation to social life can help formulate a politics through answering four important questions:

> To what degree are our actions governed by the logic of the field and our struggles to maintain a position therein? What about our actions can be attributed to our position in a field? To what degree are our actions guided by our positions in the "larger" social structure? And what about our actions can be attributed to our positions in the social structure?
>
> (p. 348)

McCollum-Clark's case

A Bourdieusian reading of McCollum-Clark's recount of what happened when the National Council of Teachers of English (NCTE) leadership attempted to appropriate authority in the policy field in the 1990s to promote a progressive agenda within English language arts recapitulates Ladwig's history of their failed attempt to affect policy in the 1980s. McCollum-Clark (1995) writes:

> In part, [my] study seeks to tell the story of the participation of the National Council of Teachers of English in the national standards movement of the 1990s to affect the future curriculum of English. Although many within the Council viewed the national standards movement with concern and alarm, its Executive Committee committed to the creation of standards in English/Language Arts so that its progressive views of the language and literacy would be the most influential ones across the nation. This study describes the decisions made by the Council in establishing the numerous panels, boards, task forces and other structures for collaboration in the standards-setting endeavor and attempts to reconstruct a timeline detailing the outcomes and consequences of the Council's involvement from the beginning of the process.
>
> (p. 9)

McCollum-Clark recounts how progressive and radical players in US literacy education attempting to call on the field of power, with its statist capital, to improve their positions within their field illustrates how linkages between policy and practice are underdetermined. As an endgame strategy to finally settle the contest for capitals within English in their favor, it failed. Interestingly,

McCollum-Clark's history reveals that other endgame strategies being enacted within English language arts by players which, upon analysis, were more closely allied to corporate philanthropic policy foundations within the economic field, and thus better positioned in social space to pursue their goal to redress their perceived loss of ground in the field to progressives and radicals. This is certainly echoed in Kenneth Goodman's lament that within the field of power, an intersection of conservative political and economic groups positioned themselves to contest educational policy as part of a concerted try at significantly and permanently altering the social organization of the US (Goodman, 1998: 13, 14).

Analyzing NCTE documents, interviews, and "insider accounts" of what happened, as opposed to public announcements broadcast to its membership, McCollum-Clark reveals how ineffective the NCTE leadership was in its attempt to speak for the whole field. Her recount reveals how the NCTE did little early on to contest the discursive strategies employed by the standards movement to construct a public crisis in the field of education. This "meek" response was in part a consequence of the NCTE leadership's under-theorized notion of literacy as political and its inability to conceive English language arts as a sociological field. For example, progressive elements of the NCTE construct literacy through particular capitals mediated by personal choice of texts and text practices that value individual meaning-making. This notion slips over social and critical literacies and, thus, makes effective political action difficult (Church, 1992).

McCollum-Clark's analysis shares similarities with Ladwig's earlier study. She notes the policy field focused on technical and economic rationales (1995: 22). Ladwig's study indicates that these are the historically recognized capitals at play within educational policy. And, while McCollum-Clark provides a detailed history from the turn of this century of the connection of the economic to the education policy field (pp. 57–62), she argues it is "in the absence of federal structures [that] coalitions of groups struggle to influence education policy" (p. 22). Yet, Ladwig contends that these kinds of struggles are what structure educational policy, and that federal players have historically been successful in holding dominance within the education policy field. McCollum-Clark's recount points to such a conclusion, too. She traces the effectiveness of standards movement, naming epistic individuals and groups (p. 28). But without a sociological framework, she makes only allusions to structural linkages that would be necessary in providing a fuller account of the standards movement's trajectory in the field of power or in positing how it could so effectively blunt progressives' and radicals' strategies, or how progressives and radicals might have succeeded in responding to such a powerful assault on their relative autonomy.

A more extensive mapping of the social field might reveal some interesting cultural and class patterns in this contest. McCollum-Clark's analysis offers data about the habitus of epistic individuals in the conflict. For example, she provides information about the location of important players such as Governor Hunt of North Carolina (p. 63), and important groups such as America 2000 (p. 73). She also illustrates how, within the field of education policy, distinctions and positions were staked out and defended within the standards movement itself (pp. 78 and 79). Thus, McCollum-Clark presents highly suggestive data on how the standards movement was able to successfully "broker a consensus" for the employment of statist power to enact legislation within the educational field:

> Content and performance standards are only two in a dizzying list that grew from the original impetus of *A Nation at Risk*; others included delivery standards, skill standards, opportunity-to-learn standards, standards for teacher preparation and certification, standards for school plants, and school administration and management standards. The terms have dispersed widely across the educational landscape, and as testimony to the success of the advocates of "excellence," one can hardly pick up a mainstream education newsletter or journal without some reference to standards. Creating and mandating content and performance standards as well as establishing potentially nationwide assessment tools to determine the degree to which American children "measure up" to such standards represent logical conclusions to the coalition's arguments supporting the connections between education and the economy and the inevitability of the unequal distribution of society's resources according to "merit."
>
> (p. 53)

Turning her attention to the history of the NCTE, McCollum-Clark notes the issue of standards has been present since the beginning of the organization (p. 92). The history reveals that a number of endgames, "to settle the English curriculum for once and for all" (p. 85) had been played since NCTE's inception in the nineteenth century. The recent standards movement distinguishes itself in representing itself as "new and revolutionary." Bourdieusian field analysis regards this as a common strategy, in this case used to construct distinction among humanist, scientific management, child-centeredness and social reconstructionist positions contesting established field capitals and borders in English language arts. McCollum-Clark contends that previous struggles "to define the discipline were conducted without the spectre of federal intervention, national curricula and examinations, and manipulation from outside of English language arts education" (p. 86). She presents a stark analysis of this endgame strategy.

> It is important to consider the history of other "standards-setting" endeavors in English for a number of reasons. First, the originators of the contemporary standards movement refuse to recognize that the steps they advocate taking to reform the discipline have historical antecedents and

have been attempted before. Secondly, a look at previous attempts to rationalize and systematize English reveals struggles of the opposing curriculum interest groups that have contended for the power to define the discipline from its inception. Periodically, one group or another achieves momentary preeminence only to lose impetus as the clamor of competing views drown out what appeared to be a final consensus. Today's increasing federal intervention into the clamor changes the entire terrain of the battle irretrievably.

(p. 87)

Her assessment that this move may have "irretrievable" consequences for English language arts education is questionable. First, English language arts may be able to retain its relative autonomy as a field because of the inherent *doxic* effect of all players' belief in the importance of the field, or their realization that a successful endgame strategy would collapse the field and diminish the possibility of constructing distinctions and capitals in it. This could be one interpretation of the commissioning of the National Research Council committee's report, *Scientific Research in Education* (SRE) (Shavelson and Towne, 2002), which greatly expanded and modified the NRP's definition of valued forms of educational research. Second, a Bourdieusian analysis of the field would place it within social space. As part of the intellectual field, any such analysis would demonstrate ongoing weak and/or strong historical linkages between the field of power and English language arts practice in the habitus of epistic individuals and groups. Such an analysis may look at past interventions in the field that may or may not have had direct statist capital to legislate in English but had the effect of statist capital in English. The history of selection of textbooks by governmental agencies comes to mind. Third, the conservative forces that have intervened in English practice seem to have a better sense of the sociological importance, within the field of power and social space in general, of the field in sites other than schools and universities. As McCollum-Clark observes, the stances in the field linked texts and text practices to politics, the economy and the society. Earlier projects of epistic positions in the field "intended to set the vision of English, to inspire teacher education, commercial curriculum development, and everyday practice of the discipline" (1995: 93). Recent proposals for reconceptualizing English do not move much beyond what has been the historic contest in the field (Albright, 1999). Further, conservatives' endgame strategies in the US may provide impetus for progressives to re-examine English language arts in order to mount a more effective campaign against this conservative "putsch." Nor is it reasonable, given the logic of distinction, to consider conservative positions within literacy education, or the policy field for that matter, to be monolithic. Any apparent "collapse" of the field would be mitigated by ongoing struggles for dominance.

McCollum-Clark argues that literacy education has been particularly "bedeviled with a troublesome lack of definition." But her contention that,

"Unlike science or math, literacy education does not present a unified, relational framework for study, leaving the discipline open to attacks that as a subject, it is not sufficiently systematized" (1995: 93) is open to question. Such a charge could be made against many disciplines. For example, Lee's (1996) study outlines the similar conflicts within geography. While McCollum-Clark provides an interesting overview of strategies various positions in literacy education have employed to gain dominance in the field, her historicism prevents her from seeing these conflicts as structuring the field (1995: 93–116). For her, they are cyclical patterns and signs of instability. Examining the play of humanist, scientific management, child-centeredness and social reconstructionist positions in this contest, McCollum-Clark argues some were:

> effectively silenced . . . shutting down the lively tensions between groups and reestablishing hierarchies within the field that were beginning to shift. If current descriptions of different standards projects are any indication, educators with ties to the humanist and scientific management aspects of English education are finding their positions strengthened by powerful links to national standards. Individuals and groups who favor child-centered and social reconstructionist visions of English and instruction, however, find their voices to be weakened, if not silenced, in the debate.
>
> (p. 92)

She concludes that this was the unhappy consequence of the NCTE Executive Committee's activism and reform on behalf of moderate child-centered and more progressive and radical factions, effectively leaving both the NCTE and progressives weakened in English language arts.

The Council's decision to participate in the standards movement, McCollum-Clark contends, was an attempt to promote "one discourse of English and [secure] the Council's role as the most influential and important national group dealing with the discipline of English. . . . Unfortunately, in focusing attention exclusively on the Council's own political problems and desires for influence and authority, Council officers failed to account for the political desires and assumptions underlying the standards movement itself" (p. 119). McCollum-Clark tracks the role of the Executive Director, Miles Myers, as an epistic individual in this struggle. She notes how Council presidents have historically used the NCTE to influence the issues and concerns of the field. The NCTE was uncomfortable in taking political stances toward literacy education in general, and was growing more disparate as a confederation of assemblies, conferences, and affiliates. Council documents reflected middle-of-the-road perspectives. McCollum-Clark argues many in leadership roles worried that the NCTE was not effective in convincing the public it was "the definitive voice of the profession," but that "its members have only created surface changes in the way English is taught in most schools" (p. 127). She observes:

> NCTE's decision to become involved with federal projects to create content standards, then, was politically motivated. It did not occur in response to a congruence between the deeply held educational beliefs of the Council and those of the US Department of Education . . . But because Council officials were struggling with their internal political issues of authority in the process of nailing down issues of what English is to be and who is to decide. The consequences of turning one's back on this movement were more than the Council wished to contemplate—further loss of authority and the mantle of expertise in the field. Participation in the standards-setting process would require an activism the likes of which the Council officials had not yet attempted, and cooperation with groups with whom the Council differed on important philosophical points. Public intolerance of philosophical divisions within the field, however, was part of the problem facing NCTE as it made its proposals for English curriculum in the past. In order to have a voice in the process at all, the NCTE would have to compromise not only these philosophical differences, but its own representations of its role with its members.
>
> (pp. 128, 129)

The seduction of statist power led to compromises with the long-standing inclusive practices within the organization. McCollum-Clark outlines how Council deliberations and decisions became less public. Official stories of events to the membership did not reflect what was happening behind the scenes. Those radicals who dissented with Council decisions were rebuked and ignored. In the end, the compromises made by NCTE leadership could satisfy neither the standards movement nor much of its membership (pp. 164–76). The NCTE's agenda to affect and support a vision of public schooling failed against better organized and strategized economic and political positions whose agenda was to diminish public education. The failure of the NCTE to mount an effective politics in the face of this challenge left the field more vulnerable to unwelcome interventions than it had previously been. McCollum-Clark notes, "in accepting the chief propositions of the standards movement—that students, parents, and teachers are responsible for the failure of schools, and by implication, of American competitiveness abroad—the NCTE has limited the possibilities that it may have some influence on these material conditions in the future" (p. 171). This was one of the most serious compromises made by the NCTE leadership.

In the intervening period, various progressive and radical elements in the field have attempted to make sense of what happened (Berliner and Biddle, 1995; Goodman, 1998; Vine, 1997). Their analysis points to Bourdieusian-like observations that those closest in the field to sources of economic capital and sharing those class and other faction locations in social space (habitus), and often associated with empiricist stances toward literacy research or cultural heritage stances to literacy education, have benefited from this struggle.

They are "in bed with the Far Right" (Goodman, 1998). In their eyes, literacy education became "politicized." Goodman writes:

> In imposing on teachers explicit constraints on how and what they teach, however, promoters like Adams [(Adams, 1990) Distar and Open Court] run a strong risk of alienating teachers from the views they are trying to get them to accept. They are playing another dangerous game as well. No doubt they believe that because their views are "scientific" they will be persuasive in the power plays of the far right in the current political scene. But the far right is upping the ante, broadening its attack and the demands it is making on mainstream politicians.
>
> (1998: 23)

In part, his analysis agrees with McCollum-Clark's position that what is at stake is not so much progressive or radical positions in English language arts but universal public education. As a consequence, Goodman proposes a program to win back the relative autonomy from statist interventions that was lost to the field (pp. 32–5). Although his agenda is framed in the negative—to oppose the state from legislating in English—its effect is to establish the state as the guarantor for the relative autonomy of literacy education researchers and practitioners. Similarly, Carole Edelsky (1998) and Bess Altwerger (1998) sketch a history of the goals and tactics employed by the Far Right to undermine public education. Yet, neither they, nor Goodman, relate the complicity of the NCTE as analyzed in McCollum-Clark's history. This is troublesome. While Edelsky and Altwerger offer what may be effective strategies for engaging opponents of public education within the field of power—educating pre-service teachers, mobilizing teacher activists in public policy debates and elections, forming coalitions, exposing hypocrisy, addressing the public, and so forth—theirs is not a reflexive response. Rarely do those who have addressed the recent failures examine in a fundamental way their positions in the literacy education field. Some may have been politicized through this experience. Yet, these failures have not changed how research and practice in literacy education is normatively conceived (Albright, 1999, 2006).

Ladwig's and McCollum-Clark's histories point up the significant limitations of progressive and radical positions in mounting an internal and external field politics to affect educational policy in support of particular forms of research and practice in American education. The NCLB Act and NRP report can be read as an extension of Ladwig's and McCollum-Clark's accounts. Ladwig (1996, 1998) contends that progressive and radical researchers' and practitioners' ties to perspectives inspired by the no longer "new" sociology of school knowledge helps explains why they have not produced a revolution in mainstream educational theorizing. Later in this chapter, I reprise Ladwig's argument for a more persuasive normative grounding for progressive positions in literacy education following the Bush administration's NCLB legislation.

I will suggest a Bourdieusian-inspired politics for rethinking the literacy education field and the course of educational policy in the US.

The National Reading Panel and No Child Left Behind

> To what degree are our actions governed by the logic of the field and our struggles to maintain a position therein? What about our actions can be attributed to our position in a field? To what degree are our actions guided by our positions in the "larger" social structure? And what about our actions can be attributed to our positions in the social structure?
>
> (Ladwig, 1996: 348)

Ladwig's questions are important when attempting to make sense of how the NRP—charged to ascertain the best knowledge available to the field on early reading development and instruction, and to consider how to disseminate it to the nation's schools and classrooms—focused on scientific, replicable research as the sole legitimate form of educational inquiry. Studies from other research perspectives were set aside as not being valid. The NRP's report had a significant bearing on the current Bush administration's NCLB policy with its emphasis on phonemic awareness, phonics, vocabulary development, reading fluency, and reading comprehension. Briefly, the program legislates the adoption of scientifically based reading programs for kindergarten to Grade 3 students, and makes provision for the training teachers and the increased surveillance of their work. Schools and districts are mandated to demonstrate adequate yearly progress in improving reading scores subject to sanctions for failure.

While the American literacy education field may be beleaguered, it certainly showed surprising vitality in the speed and severity of its critical response to NRP/NCLB reports and policies. Significantly, the focus of address of much of what teachers and researchers have published since 2000/1 has been directed toward the field itself. Progressive and radical elements opposed to NRP/NCLB have been most active in positioning themselves within the field against those factions allied to the current Bush administration's policies. This labor has seemingly done little to affect the penetration of these policies into the literacy education field and American schools in general. The intensification of the struggle, as may be seen from the preceding battles against standardization in the 1980s and 1990s, seems to show the magnitude of what is at stake—the possible further marginalization of progressive forces in the field and the field's increasing loss of autonomy to the policy field.

Critique has come from varying positions within the literacy education field. These can be seen as struggles for distinction even among progressive and radical opponents to the NRP/NCLB. Edmondson (2004b), citing Goodnough (2003) and Yatvin and colleagues (2003), characterizes those responses that "express dissatisfaction with limiting schools to particular forms of research and reading programs" or "debate the merits of particular programs and the quality of the science employed in determining a program's worth" as pejoratively liberal. Others, including Edmondson, position themselves in more radically social, philosophic, moral, and epistemological opposition to the NRP/NCLB. To cover the full extent of publishing about the NRP/NCLB is not possible within the limitations or intent of this chapter; nor can the array of progressive responses to this legislation be neatly categorized as liberal or radical, as Edmondson implies. Yet such distinctions appear to construct essentialist, yet heuristically workable, ontologies of competing epistemological stances. But "epistemological rules are nothing other than the social rules and regularities inscribed in structures and/or in habitus, particularly as regards the way of conducting a discussion (the rules of argumentation) and settling a conflict" (Bourdieu, 2004: 71). Edmondson's dismissive distinctions are a social product of her field.

While, as noted above, some promote various accommodations to this legislation—"Knowledgeable, caring teachers are key to implementing NCLB in ways that help children experience learning success and become lifelong learners who choose to read and write in their daily lives", and "Knowledgeable teachers—armed with understandings gleaned from research that is scientifically based, rigorous, and pertinent . . . can implement instruction tailored to their specific students in order to accomplish the NCLB mandates" (Stewart, 2004: 740, 735)—most progressive literacy teachers and researchers have attacked it on a variety of fronts. Coles (2000) was one of the first to challenge the NRP's claims about the scientific merit of skills-emphasis programs and approaches, arguing that progressive approaches such as whole language are more effective in teaching children to read. Coles (2003) elaborates his case with specific reference to NCLB. His questioning of what constitutes "good science" and "good practice" is repeated in many subsequent critiques. In what has become a familiar target for analysis, Goran (2002) critically reviews the NRP report to contest the science used to support the commercial reading programs, seemingly approved by the NRP; and Camilli and colleagues (2003) independently review the NRP's meta-analysis of the 38 studies cited in the report to "reconstruct their findings," concluding that instructional policies flowing out from the report are "misdirected." Gee's (1999) early analysis of the National Academy of Sciences report on the prevention of reading difficulties in young children (Snow et al., 1998) is exemplary.

Other studies focus on the consequences of the NRP/NCLB. Mathis (2003) reviewed ten studies on the financial costs and presumed benefits of NCLB. He concluded that substantial additional funds are necessary in excess of existing federal educational spending to meet its goals. Further, he argued that NCLB mandates will have unintended consequences of narrowing curriculum, increased dropout rates and widening "achievement gaps" for at-risk populations. These themes are repeated in Fusarelli's (2004) review of state-level, systemic-based accountability initiatives associated with NCLB, and in Meier and Wood's (2004) indictment of NCLB's "undermining" of American public schooling. Peterson and West's (2004) edited volume explores the political and social histories associated with standards and accountability manifest in NCLB, and again Altwerger and colleagues (2004) discuss the implications of these and other consequences of NRP/NCLB for teachers and teacher educators.

While many contest NRP/NCLB's merits and implementation, more radical factions in the literacy education field have engaged in forms of critical policy analysis, epistemological deconstruction, and political appraisal. Often informed by postmodern, poststructuralist, neo-Marxist, Foucauldian, and/or feminist orientations, these arguments can become so contentious that opponents have positioned some of these critiques as unfair *ad hominem* attacks (Snow, 2000; Spear-Swerling, 2000). Critical policy analysis undertakes historical development and discourse analysis of shifts in policy language about literacy education "to explore how the policies influence cultural models and social arrangement" (Woodside-Joron, 2003: 533). Epistemological deconstruction revisits many of the problems associated with the concepts of reliability, objectivity, validity, and so on in the philosophy of science to make the case that, "practicing scientists of reading should be embarrassed by the simplistic, old-fashioned, and generally discredited verificationism of the National Reading Panel," and it is likely to have "chilling effects on funding, publication and influence on all reading research that fails to follow the positivist methodological standards for our field" (Cunningham, 2001: 328, 329). Researchers and teachers engaged in political appraisal focus on what is seen as an ongoing conservative attack on public education as an anti-democratic and possibly unconstitutional power-grab by the federal government to dominate educational policy in the US (Allington, 2002; Shannon, 1998). As with much of what has been written in radical opposition to NRP/NCLB, critical policy analysis and epistemological deconstruction frequently mix elements of political appraisal in their arguments (see Altwerger, 2005).

Edmondson's (2000, 2002, 2004a, 2004b) work in critical policy analysis of the NRP/NCLB is exemplary. She employs a form of critical discourse analysis to "demystify" how policy is developed for teachers who "lack a critical understanding of government, political parties, politics, and political ideology" (Edmondson, 2000: 4). While some have argued that her methodology is unclear (Woodside-Joron, 2003), working from a neo-Marxist perspective, she traces the ideological positions of important individuals associated with the America Reads initiative against the shifting political landscape of the Clinton administration in the late 1990s to elaborate its "neo-liberal" values. In response to the NRP, Edmondson and Shannon (2002) analyze the verbatim transcripts of all the public meetings and town halls associated with the deliberative process in writing the report. They conclude, "The panel used ideological means in an attempt to legitimize itself and its work" (p. 6). They contend that the process was highly idiosyncratic, yet the panel worked to make "their values natural and self-evident" (p. 7) Distinctions were made "between the 'experts' on the panel, and those who were considered 'scientists' " (p. 10). Edmondson and Shannon observe that the language of scientific consensus on reading research belie the process of these deliberations, and the transcripts' language reveals a dangerously undemocratic "fear of diversity that would challenge the values of control and predictability" (p. 17). In her more recent work, Edmondson (2004b) urges teachers to take up critical policy study as part of their professional development while organizing citizen groups to effectively resist neo-liberal and conservative educational initiatives associated with NCLB.

Epistemological deconstruction of the NRP's philosophy of science is also a radical response. Cunningham (2001) asks, "What are we to make of a report that so boldly lays claim to what science, rigor, and objectivity are in reading research, and first denigrates, then ignores, the preponderance of research literature in our field?" (p. 327). In her Egon Guba Invited Lecture at the 2003 American Educational Research Association conference in Chicago, later published in *Qualitative Inquiry*, radical poststructuralist and feminist researcher Patti Lather argues that the US federal government's incursion into educational research is "marked by the anxieties, rhetorics, and practices of a decentered masculinist and imperialist regime of truth" (2004a: 27). In her AERA address, she advocates obdurate refusal of any possibility of compromise with NRP/NCLB "as the very way toward producing different knowledge and producing knowledge differently" (p. 28). Elsewhere, Lather reiterates her case that NRP/NCLB represents "a backlash against the proliferation of research approaches of the last 20 years out of cultural studies, feminist research, radical environmentalists and social studies of science" (2004b: 760). But, in this more recent article, she proposes an alternative response to "this new form of coercive and authoritarian governmentality" (p. 763). She advises that critical theory be put to work in a principled manner to engage with policy evaluation in order to overcome rigid "lines between empirical research, politics and the philosophical renewal of public deliberation" (p. 767).

Among other possible influences, this apparent shift in Lather's radical feminist politics of refusal to engage with neo-liberal and conservative research perspectives and agendas may be understood in part as a response to her reading of Danish urban developer Bent Flyvbjerg's (2001) argument for rich and strategic methodological diversity in social science research. And, in co-editing a recent issue of *Teachers College Record* with feminist and Bourdieusian scholar Pamela Moss, which focused on the National Research Council committee's report, *Scientific Research in Education* (SRE) (Shavelson and Towne, 2002), Lather writes of hoping to encourage discussion within the field about how to "address the complexity and the messiness of practice-in-context which call in to question the adequacy of conventional methods, the desirability of generally applicable research and policy standards, and the philosophies of science that prescribe, narrow views of these issues" (Lather and Moss, 2005: 2). Falling on the heels of the NRP and NCLB, the US Department of Education's National Education and Policy and Priorities Board commissioned the report to review the current literature on what may count as scientific research in education. While some holding to Lather's earlier politics of refusal have rejected the report's findings as "wrong," "dangerous," and "vague" (see Erickson, 2005; Gee, 2005), her co-editor Moss's Bourdieusian reading offers both critique and praise for the report. She concludes, "That the committee members and NRC staff have been willing, repeatedly, to engage in public dialogue about the document . . . only reinforces the positive potential of SRE to provoke critical reflection as long as we join its authors in treating the document as a turn of talk in an on-going dialogue" (Moss, 2005: 27).

Why the politics of refusal fails

Bourdieusian readings of inter- and intra-accounts of the relations American educational policy and literacy education fields from the mid-1980s to the present, I have argued, narrate the inability of progressive and radical literacy education researchers and practitioners to enact an internally effective politics within their own field of practice and to effect desired changes in educational policy. Lather is not alone among important radical researchers and theorists in the field to address this problem. Apple (2000) calls for "an unromantic appraisal of the material and discursive terrain" (p. 12) presently facing critical pedagogy. He suggests:

> The rhetorical flourishes of the discourses of critical pedagogy—a trad-
> ition that continues to play a role in challenging parts of the neo-liberal
> and neo-conservative policies in education—need to come to grips with
> these changing material and ideological conditions. Critical pedagogy
> cannot and will not occur in a vacuum. Unless we honestly face these
> profound rightist transformations and think tactically about them, we will
> have little effect either on the creation of a counter-hegemonic common
> sense or on the building of a counter-hegemonic alliance.
>
> (p. 13)

Yet, in his thorough review of the substantive of these recent developments in educational policy critiques (Ball, 2003; Lauder and Hughes, 1999; Whitty, 1997, to name a few), he does not reflexively come to terms with his own epistic position in the field. He calls for more effective tactics in opposition to neo-liberal and neo-conservative policies but offers little in explaining why critical pedagogues' responses to them have to change and how that may happen.

Ladwig (1996, 1998) contends that the failure of progressives and radicals to affect educational policy mirrors their failure to mount an effective research agenda over the last three or four decades within education. In his analysis of radical school sociology, he argues that, as players in a contest in the intellectual field constructing particular dispositions and habitus, they have had limited success in struggles over what counts as research:

> Current radical educational research limits its own potential in such ways that it cannot meet the basic tenets of conventional science, and it will not be persuasive to anyone not already in agreement with the basic tenets of radical theories of education. In this light, the stances of radical educational research have been very effective for opening and defending non-conventional positions in academic space. However, if the initial agenda of the New Sociology is to be met, and if a wider audience of educational scholars is to be persuaded by radical educational analysis, an alternative research agenda clearly is needed.
>
> (1996: 3)

In the course of his argument, Ladwig traces the historical antecedents of the Radical Sociology of School Knowledge (RSSK) in British sociology of education, demonstrating that the neo-Marxist/structuralist position RSSK initially adopted, and later poststructuralist and feminist research that followed from it, were self-contradictory and unable to speak to conventional empirical science. Within Bourdieu's logic of distinctions, Ladwig contends that:

> These "partially equivalent" dispositions can be seen as elements of a radical educational research social identity. In this view, the theoretical debates in the field can be seen as strategies of social differentiation within one very small academic field that is reflective of debates rehearsed in many academic subfields throughout the 1980s (particularly in the social science and humanities).
>
> (p. 4)

Ladwig posits that their critique of positivism is the core strategic distinction for these dispositions. His Bourdieusian stance, wary of the dualisms inherent in objectivism and subjectivism, permits him to question this move in the field. He is not questioning the philosophical validity of the critique but problematizing how the critique was played out strategically within the field. He argues that the relationship of positions in the field, to see science as rhetoric, "demonstrates how radical sociology of school knowledge fails to meet conventional canons of science in such a way that its basic persuasiveness can be seen as problematized" (p. 5). While defenders of RSSK may reject the critiques of conventional social science, Ladwig contends that they should not so easily dismiss his argument because it addresses their position and trajectory in the field. He offers his readers an alternative proposal as an attempt to reinvigorate critical theorizing and research in a politics for the field. Consequently, he makes a compelling argument—proposing a

Bourdieusian corrective to assist the theoretical and methodological inheritors of RSSK to connect with "mainstream sociological analysis of educational inequality, social–psychological explanations of social identity formation, institutional analyses of schooling as a global world culture, and post-colonial theories of racism." He sees this as "an agenda that is at once reflexive and . . . profoundly expansive" (p. 5).

Ladwig contends that RSSK was initially constructed around Michael Apple's Parallelist Position (Apple, 1988; Apple and Weis, 1983) but has now stagnated because its "line of research is caught within a logic whose consequent claims and conclusions are as predictable as they are limited" and faces "recurrent conceptual dilemmas which it seemingly cannot escape," and "no signs have been given that this tradition has moved beyond its initial concerns and intellectual frame" (Ladwig, 1996: 14, 15). Ladwig demonstrates that the failure of RSSK to advance its agenda in the field is related to its reliance on the conceptually limiting binarism of objectivity and subjectivity. This binary differentiation has been repeatedly raised in slightly altered homologous forms, such as "structure versus agency" (p. 22) terminology. Further, RSSK's rejection of studies such as Bourdieu and Passeron's (1977) and Bowles and Gintis' (1976) as "deterministic" signaled a move away from quantitative work in the field. Ladwig comments on the inherit logic of this trend: "Seeing possibilities for change seems to hold an inverse relationship with the scope of one's vision. The larger the context one examines, the less change one sees" (p. 29). The initially favorable reception of Willis' (1977) study strengthened the objectivist/subjectivist binarism. Ladwig summarizes the early history of RSSK as a theoretical cycle:

> Where the sociology of school knowledge had initially advanced a "subjective" phenomenological agenda, and then in opposition taken a turn to more "objective" structural accounts, it had returned once again to "subjective" case approaches. And, homologously, where it had begun with a relatively optimistic political volunteerism, and had turned decidedly pessimistic with the structural accounts, it had once again found political hopes of transformation through possible cultural politics.
>
> (p. 30)

RSSK articulated a conceptual framework, such as the relative autonomy and irreducibility of fields in social space, for analyzing the reproductive and transformational aspects of schooling. Ladwig contends, "one might have expected something of an equal sided dual focus" based on "the strengths of both 'structural' and 'interpretive' positions" (p. 34). That was not the case, he argues, because determining Marxist categories persisted in the "subjectivist" interpretations of studies in the field. Ladwig illustrates this point with regard to studies in the hidden curriculum. He argues that examples such as these demonstrate a problematic in reasoning:

Interpretation though such a lens [the reproduction versus resistance binarism] would undoubtedly always find empirical verification. If something wasn't seen as reproductive, it could be labeled resistance . . . Speaking in terms of contradictions may have provided more subtlety to the US New Sociology's theory but it also provided a theory, which could never be wrong.

(p. 40)

RSSK made "a descriptive effort to generate a comprehensive theory" in including as categories of analysis race, gender, and other theoretical formulations along with class. Ladwig notes:

The homologous logic of inclusion these conceptual maneuvers represent was rather straightforward: what was not disclosed in any economic focus had been addressed through an examination of culture; and what was not disclosed by focusing on economic class could be disclosed by examining other social relations.

(p. 41)

This move was propelled by a logic of political activism that can be questioned on two counts. First, these inclusions can be read as ad hoc theorizing. Referring to Popper's (1968) work on finding falsifiable scientific reasoning, such attempts to account for evidentiary examples, for which the original theorizing could not account, did not logically strengthen the position because there was no systematic explanation as to which other categories should be added to the analytic framework—why race and not religion, why gender and not language, and so forth? Second, as a political move within the field, the inclusion of race and gender was a response to a concern for resistance and political action. Ladwig proposes that this can be read as, on the one hand, a laudable move to be sensitive and open to critique and, on the other hand, a rational tactic RSSK employed to position itself in the vanguard of the identity politics of the Left. "Thus," Ladwig concludes, "in its descriptive endeavor, the Parallelist Position stands as a set of mutually exclusive conceptual presumptions woven into a logically inconsistent theoretical framework" (p. 45). The New Sociology's dual interests in proposing a theory that is both descriptive and "emancipatory" contains an insupportable trade-off. "The more one holds for a consistent descriptive theory, the less one can maintain transformative appeal. And the more one pushes for transformative appeal, the less one can maintain a consistent descriptive theory" (p. 49).

These tensions at the heart of RSSK, though, Ladwig argues, did enable a tremendous amount of productive research in the 1980s. Forms of qualitative analysis expanded and more theoretical voices were heard in the field. Ladwig traces how these developments led to a "fracturing" and "dispersion" in the field with the rise of various forms of feminism and poststructuralism (pp. 55–81).

Ladwig argues that this fracturing of the field is symptomatic of the times where "the world has broken into its political and cultural parts . . . as a matter of *fact*, not of theory" (p. 169).

Ladwig's analysis shifts from textual reasoning to a more sociological stance, adopting Bourdieu's general methodological concerns. Again, it is a process of relating the field in question to the broader field of power, investigating structured relations between positions taken up by individuals and groups as they contest for legitimization in the field, describing the forms of economic and cultural capital that are contested and the distribution of capitals within the field, outlining dominant and subordinate positions within the field, and identifying the class habitus and social trajectories that individuals bring to the positions they take up in the field. While Ladwig's field analysis is partial, it is sufficiently elaborated to ground the work represented in this volume. Its very partialness also suggests an opportunity for charting regions of future research.

Ladwig argues such an agenda based on a materialist analysis in new literacy studies in educational research:

> [F]ollowing Bourdieu, that, academic struggles are primarily to be understood within the "specificity of the scientific field." In this logic, analyzing the social spaces in which educational intellectuals work is a task of understanding the correspondences among intellectual positions/stances and relations of power within specific socio-historical contexts. Here I take intellectual arguments as manifest expressions of cultural struggles with multiple social spaces, within habitus and fields.
>
> (Ladwig, 1996: 87)

Pointing to a homology of reasoning and positioning within and intersecting the field by the factions in RSSK and their shared commitments in the field, Ladwig contests their persuasive effectiveness. While, philosophically, these theorists have struggled over naming reality, sociologically, they have employed strategies for creating distinction and earning capitals in intellectual fields. But, "when focusing on the conceptual categories of these discourses, it seems they present arguments designed for their own marginality" (p. 88). Ladwig presents epistic evidence that "three partially equivalent theoretical dispositions are widely shared across these discourses [neo-Marxism, feminism(s) and post-structuralism(s)]: each casts its critique within the framework of an 'alternative' ('new' or 'oppositional') theoretical agenda, each relates its own knowledge claims to specific social positions, and each holds a skepticism or all out rejection of scientific objectivity" (p. 94). Differences between these discourses are not to be ignored nor are their projects entirely the same. His argument is that, "if these theoretical arguments pose such difficulties for (some) audiences, what are the rhetorical consequences? To whom would these arguments be persuasive?" (p. 92)

In Bourdieusian logic, RSSK represents a series of "choices of necessity" illustrating its dominated position in the field. RSSK's project may work to change the world but it is not a world of their making, Ladwig reminds us:

> If one is attempting to open an alternative agenda within a scientific community, which consecrates its highest social value on "discoveries" or "originality," it is no surprise to find radical scholars, continually presenting their work as "new." Consider also the field's disposition toward claiming epistemic privilege. If one is attempting to challenge and transform relations of domination or unequal power relations, and if one is in the business of creating knowledge claims, it makes some sense that this project would entail privileging knowledge that is seen to be disadvantaged, dominated, marginalized, or oppositional. Consider the rejection of objective science. If one is self-defined as radical, and thereby seeks to cut to the root of the problem, to the root of the status quo, it makes sense that in a field dominated by scientific objectivity the radicals would attempt to undermine the basis of the field.
>
> (pp. 100, 101)

Consequently, while as a subversive strategy RSSK in its various forms was partially successful in constructing distinctions and space in its field, as a rhetorical strategy these choices may not be as effective as he (or I) would hope.

In its many forms, RSSK, Ladwig argues, has normatively grounded itself against other "dominant" positions in the field with three claims: first, that dominant educational social science confirms existing social inequalities and injustice; second, this support of the status quo is legitimated by the epistemological privileging of neutrality, objectivity, and empirical validity; and third, the epistemological claims it makes are incommensurate with those of RSSK because they represent different, competing paradigms (pp. 106–23). The scholarly marshalling of this philosophical critique of the legitimacy of dominant positions in the field of the sociology of school knowledge had the sociological effect of limiting dialogue with mainstream educators. Further, it legitimated a privileging of radical school knowledge because, as Ladwig argues, the critique works, "if and only if 1) they took their view to represent the view of the dominated; and 2) they thought their view to be less distorted (or more 'objective') than the dominant positivist view" (p. 180). He notes, "it is difficult to see how one could generally advance charges of false or unjust legitimacy without implying that an alternative view offers a less distorted understanding of the basis of legitimacy in question" (p. 109). Finally, the philosophical correlation of incommensurability posits that one paradigm is unable to fully address the issues and language of another. If the established paradigms of the field had addressed the issues taken up in RSSK, a new paradigm would not have been needed. Yet, Ladwig observes, "in demonstrating that two paradigms are untranslatable, we are in fact making translatable claims" (p. 124).

Ladwig continues this line of reasoning, assessing the philosophical claims to RSSK's normative legitimacy:

> The notion of epistic privilege encounters a similar logic when it is connected with the idea of relative knowledge claims. Here relativist ideas are seen as self-refuting because some sort of nonrelative claim seems to have been made and the instate relativity was proclaimed. . . . The notion that positivistic science simply supports the status quo and is oppressive when applied to conditions of social oppression (such as in contemporary schooling) becomes questionable for the view that considers social science to be value neutral once it reaches the stage of verifying propositions and hypotheses. . . . [N]either the notion of incommensurability, nor the position of "epistic privilege," nor the idea of interest laden forms of oppressive knowledge hold up to philosophical scrutiny—unless, of course, you radically alter your notion of what philosophy is in the first place.
>
> (p. 124)

Read as sociologically grounded normative claims, though, RSSK's arguments about dominant social science are more supportable. Ladwig points to evidence that "within trenchant capitalistic societies where science has been used by powerful corporate interests, I have no doubt that empirical/analytical knowledge has oppressed people" (p. 125). RSSK, Ladwig contends, has employed a rhetoric of sociological observation, making "empirical claims," within a philosophical rhetoric of demonstration.

Within a Bourdieusian analysis this form of rhetoric must be viewed in terms of moves within the relations or politics of the field. Ladwig asserts that the methodologies he describes are, on the one hand, philosophically problematic and, on the other, sociologically problematic, and have led to the present situation of stagnation in the field. They have led to moves of inclusion, especially during the early years of RSSK's entry into the field, and then later strategies of self-isolation.

As a strategy in the academy, RSSK's reliance on philosophical critique has as much to do with earning capital in the field as with aligning itself with dominated groups in social space. The academic disposition toward theorizing became conflated with taking an oppositional stance in the field which allowed RSSK to leap over mainstream science in constructing regimes of truth in the field, while permitting those aligned with it to earn cultural capital to speak for dominated others. Ladwig observes, "In its use of philosophy and theory, RSSK has employed the very hierarchical relations of power in the academy and science that Positivism has celebrated" (p. 138). Philosophy and theory became the normalizing basis for position and the strategy of its trajectory in the intellectual field. The irony of this is that "the presupposition that social theorizing and research could make positive claims about how society ought to change, is precisely the goal sought in that educational theory which partially owes its identity to its rejection of 'Positivism'." (p. 139)

Concluding arguments

Ladwig's (1996, 1998) assessment underscores my readings of these recent failures of progressive and radical researchers and practitioners to affect policy. The argument addresses all progressive and radical literacy education researchers. Following Bourdieu, the accounts I have reviewed in this chapter suggest research and practice as socially constructed reasoned inquiry, *a science with an attitude* which acknowledges that "US educational research is indeed a field in which there is a struggle over scientific authority." Ladwig concludes, "if the critique [of scientific authority] was mistaken, it was in part mistaken in the miscalculation of the marginal return on its investment in philosophic discourse. . . . [I]t seems odd for a field of inquiry so concerned with understanding, and perhaps altering, unequal power relations to have left one of the most persuasive rhetorics in the hands of those against whom it struggles" (Ladwig, 1996: 160).

Bourdieusian field analysis recognizes three sets of choices facing researchers and practitioners in literacy education. The first involves what methods to employ. Methods should be chosen to fit the kind of claim that is being made. There is a cost in choosing methods that are not valued by various communities within (and without the field, especially with the field of power, as we have seen). Methods should reflect the intended audiences of the research and the calculated effect they are to have on them. The second concerns the origin of these methodological choices. Ladwig suggests "poaching" mainstream issues, for "there is ample space for a more publicly recognized range of radical research to develop" (1996: 165). Mainstream methodological tools can also be "poached." Ladwig argues that "the technical refinement process of disconfirming or confirming past theoretical claims can only aid in the process of specifying and clarifying one's research agenda . . . in a language that has broad appeal can only aid the process of expanding the persuasive capacity of RSSK." He admonishes, "the perception of methodological violence is only plausible if one presupposes radical social science is somehow pure" (p. 166). The third addresses procedures. He suggests that some conventional formalism would be helpful. Also, building collective productions of research, sharing the labor of research, could be very effective. While Ladwig is explicit in his advocacy of Bourdieu's framework and methodology available and viable for the field, he posits four basic requirements that any "science with an attitude" should entertain:

1 a broad frame of cultural difference in which schools are seen as institutional cultural "filtering" and "transmission" devices, with

2 a central focus on power as a basic medium though which social identities are formed and contested, and

3   a conceptual apparatus that examines "multi-level" relations, connecting the micro-, mezzo- and macro-"levels" with

4   a central focus on the relation between social and "mental" structures (Ladwig, 1996: 169).

Bourdieusian field analysis is instructive both as a methodology and as a way of theorizing about these intersecting fields and proposing alternative ways of acting in each. Grenfell and James (2004) argue how Bourdieusian reflexive sociology can provide for effective and critical discourse with practical effects. (See Bourdieu and Haacke, 1995, for a detailed discussion of available and principled tactics.)

Since his death, Bourdieu's later theoretically and methodologically informative papers and studies continue to be translated and published in English (Bourdieu, 2004, 2005). Recent works by Bourdieusian scholars have highlighted how he has bequeathed to us a critical social science available to literacy education researchers and practitioners (Browitt and Nelson, 2004; Schinkel, 2003; Swartz, 2003; Reed-Danahay, 2005; Wacquant, 2005).

In this chapter I have presented three studies bearing on literacy education research and practice. More elaborated arguments for the case I have presented here can be found in Johannesson (1998), Maton, (2000), and Grenfell and James (2004). Johannesson provides examples from his own research in Iceland to illustrate how progressive and radical scholars and educational reformers have misrecognized the contradictions that lay at the heart of the "emancipatory" discourses (1998: 278, 279). Maton provides a compelling discussion from a Bourdieusian perspective of how knowledge becomes legitimated. Citing another paper (Moore and Maton, 2000), he reiterates Ladwig's analysis that the sociology of education is marginalized and this "position is related to the tendency to substitute sociology for epistemology" (Maton, 2000: 147). He writes,

> Conceiving of educational knowledge in terms of modes of legitimation also enables one to see where social scientific debates that appear to differ in the level of ideas, actors and intellectual positions are recurrent forms of the same underlying principles (e.g. phenomenology, post-structuralism and post-modernism as anti-knowledge modes). This may facilitate a means of engaging with the underlying issues structuring such debates, rather than with their surface features, and enable social science to move beyond such cyclical recurrences.
>
> (p. 164)

References

Adams, M. J. (1990). *Beginning to Read: Thinking and Learning about Print*. Cambridge, MA: MIT Press.

Albright, J. (1999) Rethinking English. Unpublished doctoral dissertation, Pennsylvania State University, PA.

Albright J. (2006) Literacy education after Bourdieu. *The American Journal of Semiotics*, 22(1–4): 107–28.

Allington, R. I. (2002) *Big Brother and the National Reading Curriculum: How Ideology Trumped Evidence*. Portsmouth, NH: Heinemann.

Altwerger, B. (1998) Whole language as decoy: the real agenda behind the attacks. In K. S. Goodman (ed.), *In Defense of Good Teaching: What Teachers Need to Know about the "Reading Wars."* York, ME: Stenhouse, 175–82.

Altwerger, B. (2005) *Reading for Profit: How the Bottom Line Leaves Kids Behind*. Portsmouth, NH: Heinemann.

Altwerger, B., Arya:, Jin, L., Jordan, N. L., Laster, B., Martens: et al. (2004) When research and mandates collide: the challenges and dilemmas of teacher education in the era of NCLB. *English Education*, 36(2), 110–33.

Apple, M. (1988) Facing the complexities of power: for a parallelist position in critical educational studies. In M. Cole (ed.), *Bowles and Gintis Revisited: Correspondence and Contradiction in Educational Theory*. London: Falmer Press, 112–30.

Apple, M. W. (2000) Can critical pedagogies interrupt rightist policies? *Educational Theory*, 50(2), 229–54.

Apple, M. and Weis, L. (1983) *Ideology and Practice in Schooling*. Philadelphia, PA: Temple University Press.

Astuto, T. and Clark, D. (1988) State responses to the new federalism in education. *Education Policy*, 2, 361–76.

Ball, S. (2003) *Class Strategies and the Education Market*. London: Routledge.

Berliner, D. C. and Biddle. B. J. (1995) *The Manufactured Crisis: Myths, Fraud, and the Attack on America's Public Schools*. Reading, MA: Addison-Wesley.

Bernstein, B. (1990) *The Structuring of Pedagogic Discourse: Class, Codes, and Control* (Vol. 4). London: Routledge.

Bourdieu: (2004) *Science of Science and Reflexivity*. Chicago: University of Chicago Press.

Bourdieu: (2005) *The Social Structures of the Economy*. Cambridge, UK: Polity Press.

Bourdieu, P. and Haacke, H. (1995) *Free Exchange*. Stanford, CA: Stanford University Press.

Bourdieu: and Passeron, J. (1977) *Reproduction in Education, Society and Culture*. London: Sage.

Bourdieu: and Wacquant, J. (1992) *An Invitation to Reflexive Sociology*. Chicago: University of Chicago Press.

Bowles, S. and Gintis H. (1976) *Schooling in Capitalist America*. New York: Basic Books.

Browitt, J. and Nelson, B. (eds) (2004) *Practising Theory: Pierre Bourdieu and the Field of Cultural Production*. Cranbury, NJ: Associated University Presses.

Camilli, G., Vargas, S. and Yurenko, M. (2003) Teaching children to read: the fragile link between science and federal education policy. *Education Policy Analysis Archives*, 11(15). Retrieved February 20, 2004 from http://epaa.asu.edu/epaa/v11n15/

Church, S. (1992) Rethinking whole language: the politics of educational change. In P. Shannon (ed.), *Becoming Political*. Portsmouth, NH: Heinemann, 238–49.

CNN (2005) Bush faces growing revolt over education policy. *CNN* (September 5). Retrieved November 11, 2005 from www.cnn.com/2005/EDUCATION/09/05/education.reform.reut/index.html

Coles, G. (2000) *Misreading Reading: The Bad Science that Hurts Children*. Westport, CT: Heinemann.

Coles, G. (2003) *Reading the Naked Truth: Literacy, Legislation and Lies*. Portsmouth, NH: Heinemann.

Cunningham, J. W. (2001) The National Reading Panel Report. *Reading Research Quarterly*, 36(2), 326–35.

Dunn, C. and Woodard, J. D. (2003) *The Conservative Tradition in America*. Boulder, CO: Rowman and Littlefield.

Edmondson, J. (2000) *America Reads: A Critical Policy Analysis*. Newark, DE: International Reading Association.

Edmondson, J. (2002) The politics of literacy. In B. Guzzetti (ed.), *Literacy in America: An Encyclopedia of History, Theory and Practice*. New York: ABL-CIO, pp. 437–40.

Edmondson, J. (2004a) *Understanding and Applying Critical Policy Study: Reading Educators Advocating for Change*. Newark, DE: International Reading Association.

Edmondson, J. (2004b) Reading policies: ideologies and strategies for political engagement. *The Reading Teacher*, 57, 418–28.

Edmondson, J. and Shannon: (1998) Reading poverty and education: questioning the reading success equation. *The Peabody Journal of Education*, 23, 104–26.

Edmondson, J. and Shannon: (2002) Expressions of ideology and power in the National Reading Panel. Paper presented at the American Educational Research Association Annual Conference, New Orleans, LA.

Edelsky, C. (1998) It's a long story—and it's not done yet. In K. S. Goodman (ed.), *In Defense of Good Teaching: What Teachers Need to Know about the "Reading Wars."* York, ME: Stenhouse, 39–56.

Erickson, F. (2005) Arts, humanities, and sciences in educational research and social engineering in federal education policy. *Teachers College Record*, 107(1), 4–9.

Fusarelli, L. D. (2004) The potential impact of the No Child Left Behind Act on equity and diversity in American education. *Educational Policy*, 18, 71–94.

Flyvbjerg, B. (2001) *Making Social Science Matter: Why Social Inquiry Fails and How it can Succeed Again*. Cambridge, UK: Cambridge University Press.

Gee, J. P. (1999) Reading and New Literacies Studies: reframing the National Academy of Sciences report on reading. *Journal of Literacy Research*, 31, 355–74.

Gee, J. P. (2005) It's theories all the way down: a response to scientific research in education. *Teachers College Press*, 107(1), 10–18.

Goodman, K. S. (ed.) (1998) *In Defense of Good Teaching: What Teachers Need to Know about the "Reading Wars."* York, ME: Stenhouse.

Goodnough, A. (2003) Bush adviser casts doubt on benefits of phonics program. *New York Times*, January 24, 1B.

Goran, E. M. (2002) *Resisting Reading Mandates: How to Triumph with the Truth Written*. Westport, CT: Heinemann.

Grenfell, M. and James, D. (2004) Change in the field—changing the field: Bourdieu and the methodological practice of educational research. *British Journal of Sociology of Education*, 25, 507–23.

Johannesson, A. I. (1998) Genealogy and progressive politics: reflections on the notion of usefulness. In T. Popkewitz and M. Bennan (eds), *Foucault's Challenge: Discourse, Knowledge, and Power in Education*. New York: Teachers College Press, 297–315.

Ladwig, J. (1994) For whom this reform? Outlining educational reform policy as a social field. *British Journal of Sociology of Education*, 15, 341–63.

Ladwig, J. (1996) *Academic Distinctions: Theory and Methodology in the Sociology of School Knowledge*. New York: Routledge.

Ladwig, J. (1998) Looks are deceptive, distinctions are real: meta-commentary on academic distinctions. *Educational Researcher*, 27(3), 34–7.

Lather: (2004a) This IS your father's paradigm: government intrusion and the case of qualitative research in education. *Qualitative Inquiry*, 10, 15–24.

Lather: (2004b) Scientific research in education: a critical perspective. *British Educational Research Journal*, 30, 759–72.

Lauder, H. and Hughes, G. (1999) *Trading in Futures*. Philadelphia, PA: Open University Press.

Lather, P. and Moss, P. (2005) Introduction: implications of scientific research in education report for qualitative inquiry, *Teachers College Record*, 107(1), 1–3.

Lee, A. (1996) *Gender, Literacy, Curriculum: Rewriting School Geography*. Cambridge, UK: Cambridge University Press.

Manzo, K. (2002) Department of Education to hike oversight of reading grants. *Education Week*, November 13. Retrieved September 2, 2005 from www.edweek.org/ew/articles/2002/11/13/11read.h22.html?querystring=department%20education%20to%20hike

Maton, K. (2000) Languages of legitimation: the structuring significance for intellectual fields of strategic knowledge claims. *British Journal of Sociology of Education*, 21, 147–67.

Mathis, W. (2003) No Child Left Behind: costs and benefits. *Phi Delta Kappan*, 84, 679–86.

McCollum-Clark, K. M. (1995) National Council of Teachers of English, corporate philanthropy, and national education standards: Challenging the ideologies of English education reform. Unpublished doctoral dissertation, Pennsylvania State University, PA.

Meier, D. and Wood, G. (eds) (2004) *Many Children Left Behind: How the No Child Left Behind Act is Damaging Our Children and Our Schools*. Boston: Beacon Press.

Moore, R. and Maton, K. (2000) Realizing potential: Basil Bernstein, intellectual fields and the epistemic device. Paper presented at symposium on Toward a Sociology of Pedagogy: The contribution of Basil Bernstein to Research, University of Lisbon, Portugal.

Moss: (2005) Toward "epistemic reflexivity" in educational research: a response to scientific research in education. *Teachers College Record*, 107(1), 19–29.

National Commission on Excellence in Education. (1983) *A Nation at Risk: The Imperative for Educational Reform*. Washington, DC: US Government Printing Office.

National Institute of Child Health and Human Development. (2000) *Report of the National Reading Panel: Teaching Children to Read: An Evidence-based Assessment of the Scientific Research Literature on Reading and Its Implications for Reading Instruction*. Washington, DC: US Government Printing Office.

No Child Left Behind Act of 2001 (2002) Available from US Department of Education website: www.ed.gov/policy/elsec/leg/esea02/index.html

Peterson: E. and West, M. R. (eds) (2004) *No Child Left Behind? The Politics and Practice of School Accountability*. Washington, DC: Brookings Institution Press.

Popper, K. R. (1968) Epistemology without a knowing subject. In B. van Rootselaar and J. E. Staal (eds), *Logic, Methodology, and Philosophy of Sciences* (Vol. 3). Amsterdam: North-Holland, 333–73.

Reed-Danahay, D. (2005) *Locating Bourdieu*. Bloomington: Indiana University Press.

Roller, C. and Long, R. (2001) Critical issues: sounding like more than background noise to policy makers: qualitative researchers in the policy arena. *Journal of Literacy Research*, 33, 707–25.

Schinkel, W. (2003) Pierre Bourdieu's political turn. *Theory, Culture and Society*, 20(6), 69–93.

Shannon: (1998) *Reading Poverty*. Portsmouth, NH: Heinemann.

Shavelson, R. J. and Towne, L. (eds) (2002) *Scientific Research in Education*. Washington, DC: National Academies Press.

Snow, C. E. (2000) On the limits of reframing: rereading the National Academy of Sciences report on reading. *Journal of Literacy Research*, 32, 113–20.

Snow, C., Burns, M. and Griffin: (eds) (1998) *Preventing Reading Difficulties in Young Children*. Washington, DC: National Academies Press.

Spear-Swerling, L. (2000) Straw men and very misleading reading: a review of Misreading Reading. Retrieved November 11, 2005 from www.ldonline.org/ld_store/reviews/swerling_coles.html

Stewart, M. T. (2004) Early literacy instruction in the climate of No Child Left Behind. *The Reading Teacher*, 57, 732–42.

Swartz, D. (2003) From critical sociology to public intellectual: Pierre Bourdieu and politics. *Theory and Society*, 32, 791–823.

Vine: (1997) To market, to market . . . The school business sells kids short. *The Nation*, 265(7), 8–15.

Wacquant, L. (ed.) (2005) *Pierre Bourdieu and Democratic Politics: The Mystery of Ministry*. Cambridge, UK: Polity Press.

Willis: (1977) *Learning to Labour*. Lexington, MA: DC Heath.

Whitty, G. (1997) Creating quasi-markets in education. In M. Apple. M. (ed.), *Review of Research in Education* (Vol. 22). Washington, DC: American Educational Research Association, 30–47.

Woodside-Joron, H. (2003) Critical policy analysis: researching the roles of cultural models power, and expertise in reading policy. *Reading Research Quarterly*, 38, 530–36.

Yatvin, J., Weaver, C. and Garan, E. (2003) The Reading First initiative: cautions and recommendations. Retrieved November 11, 2005 from www.EdResearch.info/reading_first/index.htm

Chapter 17

Using Bourdieu to make policy
Mobilizing community capital and literacy

Allan Luke

How can literacy count?

Researchers are now assessing the educational and community impacts of the monolingual, one-size-fits-all approach to basic skills that characterizes current US federal legislation (Abedi, 2004; Evans and Hornberger, 2005). In indigenous and multicultural education in Australia, New Zealand, and Canada, there is ongoing policy debate over the contingent factors in the achievement of indigenous and multilingual students in socioeconomically marginal communities. Innovative and productive approaches begin from the building of supportive links between community language ideologies and the choice and implementation of medium of instruction and approach to literacy in the school, and a reciprocal link between teachers' understandings of the sociolinguistic patterns and language functions in the community (Au, 1998; Durgunoglu and Verhoeven, 1998; McNaughton, 2002). However, the inclusion of these elements in a language education plan may be necessary but not sufficient for transforming material conditions and life pathways in equitable ways. Increased and improved literacy via school can only make a difference if it enables access and engagement in social fields where that capital can be gainfully and fairly exchanged.

Many literacy educators and researchers, however unintentionally, have bought into the "literacy myth" (Graff, 1979): that schools and, more precisely, literacy education have the power to redress social and economic problems that have their contextual locations in the structural inequalities and forces of broader and more complex community, regional, and national fields. Graff traces this legacy to the Reformation, where "reading for oneself" was seen as pivotal in moral formation. He goes on to show how eighteenth- and nineteenth-century school reformers in Canada and the United States translated the moral power of literacy into an agenda that was affiliated with the amelioration of poverty, criminality, poor mental hygiene, and so on. This in turn formed the assumption underlying twentieth-century literacy campaigns in postcolonial sites and current models of human capital development in emergent economies, that improved literacy is an intrinsic driver of individual, social, and economic development. Graff's point is not that literacy does not matter—but that literacy in and of itself does not necessarily have such effects, even where it can empirically be demonstrated as a contributing and coexisting sociodemographic factor in social mobility, growth of GDP, the attraction of capital and so on. While not always acknowledged as such, it was this and other revisionist social history and social anthropology (e.g., Street, 1984)—empirically based critique of the onto-phylogenetic assumptions about the effects of literacy on social and human development—that set the tenor for what now are called the "new" literacy studies.

That many educators subscribe to variations of the literacy myth is not surprising. This is partly because of the motivation of those committed to educational equity and justice: to use whatever pedagogic power to shift educational outcomes and, thereby, to alter the material consequences for those students from marginalized communities. It is also supported by empirical studies showing how and in what ways literacy shaped in the classroom can make a difference. This includes the large-scale census and life pathway data on reading failure and "poor" literacy achievement, variously measured, as a strong predictor of low educational achievement, lesser occupational and income outcomes, and, indeed, criminality and cultural alienation (e.g., Lucas, 1999). By backward mapping from the predictive power of early literacy failure on subsequent life outcomes, we can infer a potential hypodermic effect of early interventions. School reform data further suggests that pedagogy can make a statistically significant difference in the performance of students from marginalized groups (e.g., Newmann and Associates, 1996). Hence, there is both normative political justification and empirical warrant for an ongoing policy pursuit of adjustments to school culture, textual practice, cultural resources and schemata, and interactional scripts that might better improve the performance of "non-mainstream" students on "mainstream" indicators.

The power of literacy education to make lived and material difference in the experiences, lives, and pathways of students strikes every teacher as self-evident when they read students' writing, talk to them about their lives and their own "readings" of the world (e.g., Vasquez, 2004). Without a belief in it, we might as well pack our bags and quit. But there is a continual risk that we promise too much—that, like the founders of state schooling in the West, we have inherited a Protestant zeal for the unparalleled capacity of literacy to reshape lives. There is, further, a very real danger that stratified social systems and discriminatory institutional practices, whatever the intentions of politicians, senior bureaucrats and public intellectuals, actually rely upon teachers' good faith in this promise as an ideological palliative to the hard social facts of inequality and structurally unequal life chances.

Arguments about the intrinsic cognitive "bias" or effects of literacy to the side, let us begin from a simple set of linked premises: that literacy education can and does make a difference; that how it is taught, shaped and constructed has longitudinal intellectual, cognitive and social effects, whether for individuals, communities, or civic society. This amounts to a social construction hypothesis: that literacy has variable linguistic and semiotic shapes, resources, and practices and, not surprisingly, differential payoffs for communities of students. This is the focus of many of the chapters in this volume, where there is ample demonstration of the variable institutional uptake and reformation of the literate habitus and its affiliated but patterned forms of practice, identity, and agency. But a Bourdieusian view of literacy education would focus not just on which pedagogic practices might make a difference in the formation of habitus, their systems of objectification, logics of practice and so on, but which differences make a difference in social fields of use.

The last decade of literacy research has done a great deal to re-situate learned literacy, school-acquired cultural capital, in institutional contexts-of-use (e.g., Barton et al., 1999). The sociological argument is that the consequences and "effects" of this capital are always mediated and re-mediated by other structural, material, and social relational forces within the social fields outside of the school—those very social and intellectual fields where literacy is locally used, reshaped, and deployed. Such a view enables us to avoid narrow "hypodermic models" (Luke and Luke, 2001) of cognitive and cultural, social and linguistic effects that, in instances, are embraced as the rationale for everything from phonics to reading comprehension to critical pedagogy. Graff's work anticipated the belief that literacy per se, that an internalized set of psychological skills and/or socially coherent textual practices, has universal effects—whether intellectual or "emancipatory," psychological or social—and that these effects apply regardless of the rules of recognition, use and exchange in complex and overlapping, equitable and inequitable social fields beyond the immediate control of teachers or curriculum developers or education ministers.

This is not to say that the historical emergence of print as human techne might not have been closely linked with the development of particular forms of economic exchange (e.g., mercantile capitalism) and state formation: hence, Benedict Anderson's (1992) important argument that the European nation-state, particular forms of civic society and nationalism, were contingent upon the emergence of "print capitalism." There is little doubt that digital communications and multimediated modalities today are providing the means for new modes of statism and governmentality, work and representation, their emergent forms still in transition (Graham, 2005; Kellner, 1995). But the relationship between state formation, economy, and technology is a sociologically contingent one—not the simple result of technological determinism by medium or mode.

This chapter presents an alternative approach to literacy education policy formation. Using Bourdieu (1992), I define literacy broadly as *a form of habitus/ capital/disposition*, arguing that the internal dynamics of curriculum, teaching, and pedagogy are bids to enable the equitable conversion of *embodied capital* (e.g., skill, disposition) into *material capital* (e.g., cognitive artifacts) for translation into *institutional capital* (e.g., credentials, diplomas, degrees) (Luke, 1996). In this regard, teachers and schools have the capacity to both set up fair and equitable, transparent and accessible systems of exchange, even as they engage in the variable and somewhat idiosyncratic social constructions of textual and literacy practice that they inevitably do.

My first point is that these forms of cultural capital have no necessary or intrinsic salience and purchase unless there are enabling conditions and other available combinatory forms of capital (e.g., social, economic, cultural, symbolic, libidinal, ecological) in those adjacent and overlapping social fields where student–literates live and practice. Improved or altered student capacity for literate practice per se in its variable shapes may be necessary but not sufficient for "success," "empowerment," "agency" or the general educational amelioration of those conditions of economic and cultural marginalization. It all depends.

My second point, focal here, is that literacy education policy can be made differently. The power of literacy, in all of its variable forms, is contingent. It is contingent upon the availability and mobilization of other forms of capital for and by students, and their passage into equitable, transparent rules of exchange in civic society, workplaces, government, corporation and other forms of life. By this view, current neoliberal attempts to "fix" literacy policy are by definition futile in shifting the patterns of achievement and failure, work and unemployment, advantage and disadvantage that they might genuinely target—unless they are lodged within a broader set of social, economic, and civic policies and reforms that mobilize and enable other forms of capital and, potentially, alter existing patterns and rules of exchange in communities and institutions, social, and intellectual fields.

This is not an easy task for any ministry or department of education. But my case here is to situate literacy and education policy (see Kaplan and Baldauf, 2003) as a subset of a broader social and economic strategy that optimizes mobility and exchange for marginalized students and communities. Such policies can be made—and they can make a difference. I here offer brief descriptions of current strategies for Aboriginal community education in Cape York, Queensland, as cases in point.

The neoliberal fix

The social facts of the new economic order of cultural and economic globalization are at hand. Cultural and linguistic diversity as a norm not just in urban school districts but wherever the pull of capital, culture, "home," and identity is mobilizing families; knowledge and epistemological standpoint are in rapid transition in the face of new technologies, new texts, and new ways of thinking; and there is compelling data that the gaps between rich and poor, between social classes is increasing—even in those contexts where GDP is trending upward, economic growth and employment levels are high. One might ask whether the general deterioration of the resources and political commitment to universal, free public schooling is a further ideological feature of the transnational, corporate state.

As the local differentials in material conditions, in access to capital of all types, and in lived experiences between dominant and non-dominant, powerful and marginal classes have been exacerbated by economic globalization (Cohen, 2006), schools become "social shock absorbers" par excellence. In many settings, curricula and teachers trained to deal with monocultural, monolingual populaces must contend with new norms of diversity, differing behavioral and epistemic responses of children, transient populations and, indeed, new curriculum demands. In many countries East/West, North/South, teachers are being asked not just to keep up with, but to ameliorate, compensate for and, indeed, "fix" structural socioeconomic and cultural disparities that are contingent upon and have their genesis in other, more complex overlapping social fields—from those of the state and multinational corporation, to community cultures and local institutions and businesses. The responses are by now built into pre- and in-service programs, ministry bureaucratic structures and, indeed, policy: marketize schools as competitive business entities, put more and more curriculum outcomes on the table, commodify curriculum and increase the density of testing and ubiquity of surveillance. This constitutes a managerial fix to what is an immediate pedagogical problem—at the level of the classroom construction of literacy—and, moreover, a complex social and economic policy issue: how to remotivate a workforce and populace around a technology in transition, where the social fields of use also are shifting.

With the global spread of neoliberal and corporate models of government that Bourdieu (1998) so adamantly critiques in *Acts of Resistance*, there is broad consensus amongst critical sociologists and educationists around the ideological bases of current educational policy. Its characteristics as political discourse have been the subject of wide-ranging critiques, and there are now broad empirical as well as social theoretic analyses of the effects of a decade-plus of neoliberal reform in the United States, United Kingdom, New Zealand and Australia (e.g., Apple, 2001; Weis et al., 2006).

In terms of literacy education, the new wave of policy is epitomized in the US *No Child Left Behind* initiatives, with similar moves toward increased standardized testing and performance monitoring, the tying of state funding to performance on these measures, with bids by the state to standardize teacher–student interaction, instructional approach and, with this, to centrally circumscribe and control as best as possible the particular constructions of literacy negotiated by teachers and students in face-to-face instruction. In some states, this has moved well beyond archetypal neoliberal "steering from a distance" into a panoptic surveillance of classroom implementation of mandated approaches to literacy. There are extensive critical commentaries on effects on pedagogy, on methodological approaches to literacy, and on the measurable performance of students (e.g., Allington, 2002; Cooper, 2005).

Many legislators and planners, educational psychologists, and assessment experts promote such reforms as in the interests of disenfranchised communities and providing better educational provision and outcomes. Yet the logic underlying "high" neoliberal policy of this order is indicative of a two-decade-long push to turn education into a measurable, training model through market competition. The syllogism goes roughly like this:

- devolved school management and a business model of education at the local level, monitored through new standards for institutional performativity; gauged through,
- universal standardized norm-referenced achievement testing; accompanied by,
- rapid and often untrained usage of other standardized measures in schools and classrooms; and,
- a rapid and ad hoc proliferation of compensatory "pull out" programs for dealing with the aforementioned cultural, linguistic, and epistemological diversity; relatedly,
- a universal and growing expenditure on behavior management programs; in the context of,
- the slow-cycle implementation of outcomes-based curricula, with voluminous print-based documentation and infrastructure in place in all states; one affiliated total effect of which is,
- increased usage of packaged and commodified instruction, reinforcing "worksheet" pedagogic practices; which in turn supports a political economy of text production, which combines the efforts of multinational publishers, university and freelance "outsourced" consultants; with universities subjected to declining state funding developing into
- research and development operations bidding to develop, market-test and scientifically validate curriculum commodities, "methods" and reading textbook series.

Policy responses to the new configurations of student diversity and exacerbated differential patterns of achievement have been marketization and an agglomerative approach to compensatory programs. These range from classical remediation to mainstreaming, often part of legislatively "tied" funding with powerful constituency lobby support (e.g., special education, behavior management, speech pathology, English as a Second Language programs, Reading Recovery, counseling and educational psychology). These "add on" approaches are accompanied by moves to further standardize and "tighten" curriculum to deal with variation. This is done in part through the focus on measurable performance, which has the effect of atomizing literacy into smaller and smaller constituent skill components. It is achieved through the development of scripted approaches to pedagogy that attempt to write out less controllable variables of teacher professional knowledge and competence, local curriculum variation, face-to-face interactional and curricular response to community diversity and variation and so on. In this way, while the rhetoric of school reform and marketization is to increase "choice," the de facto effect is less choice and more standardization, particularly amongst those communities and student bodies at the bottom end of the socioeconomic scale. It is ironic that the model of this approach, *No Child Left Behind*, was based upon an application of scientific studies of English-speaking students that excluded the growing migrant, second-language population (National Institute of Child Health and Human Development, 2000).

This combination of "science," policy, and corporatism is the new political economy of literacy. That economic field is based on rules of exchange with structural incentives for expanded multinational corporate production of textbooks and multimedia learning aids; for academics to engage in product development, testing, and trialing; and for teachers to act as commodity consumers, supported by a multimillion-dollar market of outsourced and freelance educational consultants and a growing industry of private, augmenting, out-of-school tutors and support centers (Larson, 2001). But whether and how this approach will redefine the performance and learning of those communities most at risk remains an empirical and theoretical sociological question.

Remaking educational policy

To understand how we might approach the task differently requires some preliminary definitions and reframing of educational policy. Educational policy is intrinsically normative, entailing three moves:

1   *Narrative function*: the establishment of a state ideological narrative with problems, protagonists, attempts, and outcomes—an overt objectification of the purposes and outcomes of schoolings.
2   *Resource flow*: the purposive regulation of flows of human resources (e.g., teachers, students), discourse resources (e.g., policies, syllabi, curricular materials, classroom talk) and fiscal resources (e.g., infrastructure, materials, artifacts and convertible capital) in an expository logic of practice aimed at the realization of narrative goals and aims.
3   *Pedagogical alignment*: local bids to focus the resources via alignment (and/or disalignment) of systems of practice (curriculum, instruction and assessment) in the social fields of schools and classrooms.

While at the ideological and teleological level (1) educational policy is about socially and culturally consequential narratives, in bureaucratic practice (2) it entails the selective regulation of flows of material and human resources, knowledge, and discourse. These flows, in turn, are translated by schools and teachers (3) into an enacted curriculum, versions of skill and practice, knowledge and competence, with material consequences for students and communities. This translation of policy into practice, therefore, cannot be explained or driven by principles of scientific causation (Cohen et al., 2003), precisely because of the sociological contingency of the institutional fields of schools and classrooms.

In this regard, literacy policy lands us right back where we need be: at a foundational argument about which developmental meta-narratives, which material practices, which official discourses actually should count in the reshaping of literacy for new cultures and economies. Second, it asks the practical administrative and systemic questions about which centrally and locally governed flows of resources (including tests, curriculum commodities, and teachers) might realize these and other goals. And third, it asks which local (and often idiosyncratic) alignments of educational discourse make a difference, which actually have material effects and outcomes in the construction of the literate habitus. While there is no clear causal effect from narrative to practice, the model does follow a general theoretical frame. Social discourses and larger-scale state ideologies in narrative form are reconstituted into an expository logic of practice—ostensibly based upon some kind of scientific or quasi-scientific objectification of the field. These in turn moderate and set the conditions of available capital in inter-subjective exchanges in classrooms by teachers and students.

Certainly the neoliberal model outlined above operates under principles of corporate performativity and output. That is, in itself it remains silent about the philosophic and ideological questions about what should count as knowledge and practice, for whom and with what effects, a constituent reason for its functionality in secular, plural, multi-party state systems. Policy grand narratives can remain just that, overall sets of chained events that operate at a level of discursive generality as to be both heteroglossic (appearing to voice and represent "everybody's" interests) and, ultimately, meaningless (sufficiently polysemic to justify each and any "flow" in question). In the case of Australian Aboriginal and Torres Strait Islander policy, for example, particular policy goals (e.g., the improvement of the lot of Aboriginal and Islander communities) are to be achieved through government agency and action. The government is positioned as a "heroic agent" (Luke, 1997), who will use funding and policy to raise living standards, achieve reconciliation and, thereby, realize Australia's national interests. However intentional, the policy situates indigenous peoples as passive recipients of ameliorative action initiated by dominant cultural groups and the state.

While this species of policy might purport to or appear to have a technocratic objectification underlying it—that is, to be driven by fine-grained quantitative indicators of resource utilisation and institutional performance, but in actual operation it is as likely to be the product of complex and competing discourses and institutional forces: institutional precedent, political pressure or, simply, folk wisdom and arbitrary experience of a small group of senior bureaucrats (Luke, 2005). In this way, the potentially arbitrary and idiosyncratic mediations of grand narratives into regimes of practice occur not just at the level of teacher–student classroom fields that systems seem so concerned about controlling, but they are also entailed in the discussions and decision-making cultures of bureaucrats, legislators, and other key stakeholders in the social fields of policy.

At its best in many systems, policy is made on the basis of partial, incomplete evidence or evidence taken without careful critical scrutiny of the epistemic or methodological limits. At its worst, evidence is agglomerated and used for post hoc justification. Returning to literacy education, current policy approaches are constrained both by the limits of the available evidence, and by their very narrowness as literacy and language education curriculum or testing policy. But how might we do policy differently?

Policy and capital: an aboriginal community school

One of the central features of government educational policy in the West is that it often operates independently of related social, economic, and cultural policy and legislation. This is in part because different arms of government tend to operate semi-autonomously, competitively bidding against each other for precious annual funding. In state and provincial centralized systems, such as those of Canada and Australia, for example, the two largest expenditures for state government are education and health, with each taking around a quarter of overall government budgets. Yet annual planning of strategic directions for each area—while coordinated at a premier's office (i.e., a state governor's office)—usually proceeds in camera with government branches often holding their budget strategies as confidential until annual cabinet meetings. Whatever the actual cultural processes, the resultant coordination of the provision of health care and education tends to be limited. In practice, this means that the planning and provision of schooling and, say, hospital/nursing/medical infrastructure even for a relatively small and homogeneous Aboriginal or Torres Strait Islander community, may be developed independently.

The history of government involvement and intervention in Aboriginal and Islander communities across Australia is a case in point (Luke et al., 2002). The common complaint of successive Labor and Liberal federal governments is that 20 years of substantial state and federal government funding have failed to substantially improve health and life expectancy, economic capacity, community cohesiveness and sustainability (Department of Education, Training and Youth Affairs, 2000). On all indices of relative social advantage and disadvantage, Aboriginal and Torres Strait Islanders stand well below other Australians (Altman, 2000). This is the single most significant social and cultural failure of Australian government and society.

As noted at the onset, there is a tenable but potentially misleading case that early literacy achievement and school underperformance more generally are at the core of sustained poverty, and economic and social disenfranchisement. As for indigenous education in the US and Canada, the policy question for Australian Aboriginal and Torres Strait Islander education is what to do about it. Certainly, the patterns of poor indigenous achievement in school language arts, English, and literacy persist. Over a ten-year period, from the mid-1980s to mid-1990s, the gap between the reading comprehension levels of Aboriginal and Torres Strait adolescents and "mainstream" Australian adolescents with English as a first language nominally closed (Marks and Ainley, 1997). Federal government data shows that the Years 3 and 5 test score achievement in literacy among Queensland Aboriginal and Torres Strait Islander children has improved marginally. Further, despite having a lower level of exclusions than other states and territories, this same data provides very rough comparative evidence that the overall performance of Queensland Aboriginal and Islander children in Year 3 reading is marginally better than in other states with large indigenous populations (Department of Education, Science and Technology, 2001). But none of this even approaches a satisfactory situation.

On the Year 2 state developmental assessment, urban indigenous students are roughly two times more likely to be identified as requiring developmental assistance in basic reading and writing; this ratio increases to three or four times for rural and remote indigenous students. For the Years 3, 5 and 7 tests, rural and remote indigenous students are roughly twice as likely to be below state averages on all four aspects of literacy measured (reading, viewing, writing, and spelling) than their urban indigenous peers (Luke et al., 2000). Nor does the data show noticeable upward trends across time. While the gap between indigenous and non-indigenous performance in Queensland is less than the national average gap at Year 3, it has worsened to fall below that average by Year 5 (Luke et al., 2002). While there have been some improvements to these patterns for urban indigenous students in recent years, perhaps reflecting the emergence of a larger cohort of middle-class indigenous students, there is little apparent improvement for indigenous students in most rural and remote community contexts.

A sociological explanation of pathways to and through school in these communities raises a number of larger questions about schools and communities as intersecting fields of exchange. For example, an Aboriginal girl might enter Hopevale Primary School (in a remote community on Australia's northern-most peninsula, Cape York, approximately three hours from Cairns overland) with trilingual/dialectal linguistic competence (an indigenous language, plus Aboriginal English and English) but limited early print knowledge (embodied capital), access to family networks and community infrastructure (social capital), and limited family material wealth (economic capital). The state school, as a "mainstream" social field, has the capacity to exchange and transform her capital into other forms of cultural capital. This can be done by:

- setting up optimal interactional zones and linguistic environments for the conversion of her existing linguistic competence, cultural scripts and knowledges into English literacy and oracy;
- enabling the transformation of that cultural capital into a visible portfolio of artifacts of writing, speech, performance, and multimodality (objectified capital); and

- degrees/diplomas/grades (institutional capital) with exchange value in community life and mainstream institutions and social fields.

Forms of educationally acquired cultural capital are in turn represented, re-mediated, and exchanged in other institutional settings (other educational organizations, communities local and "global," face-to-face and virtual, workplaces) with differential field-specific cache. The missing key to effective language-in-education policy and practice is the degree to which it can be dovetailed into a larger community strategy for enhancing the availability and exchange of capital. It is not just the remediation of the classroom as social field that is at issue, but the reconstitution of relations of exchange within communities and regions.

In the case of Hopevale School, the Cape York Partnership strategy aims to situate school and curriculum reform within such a larger approach. The strategy was established in 1999 by an independent community organization with government and private sector support. Its target is whole-scale community development across a range of North Queensland remote Aboriginal communities (see www.capeyorkpartnerships.com), including Coen, Aurukun, and Hopevale. Led by Aboriginal lawyer and community activist Noel Pearson, the Cape York Institute of Policy and Research promotes a comprehensive approach to community development that coordinates and mobilizes partnerships between government agencies and ministries, business and philanthropic organizations, and community elders and families. A key element of the strategy is the search for sustainable development, through what have been termed "hybrid economies" (Altman, 2001).

The aim of the Cape York Partnership is to work simultaneously to move families off of what Pearson (2006) terms "the gammon economy" of welfare into local employment, an ethics of "reciprocity and care," and economic participation. According to Pearson, both traditional indigenous economies and contemporary market economies operate on principles of exchange and "social reciprocity." The building of new relations of exchange involves the establishment of government and private sector employment projects, the community redirection of funds previously set aside for welfare payments, and the provision of planning and infrastructure resources to manage local projects and funds. Targeted strategies include working with families in income management, community-wide approaches to substance abuse and health improvement. Its aim is to develop and open pathways to and through school into productive employment and community engagement.

Various curriculum reforms are underway in several Cape York schools. These include the implementation of one-to-one basic literacy instruction to enhance early print knowledge, including but not restricted to a strong graphophonemics awareness component. There is an across the board effort to develop local projects which engage youth with digital technologies around projects of oral and cultural history, ecological sustainability, and intercultural communication. A strong emphasis of these programs is using the technology to communicate with indigenous and non-indigenous youth nationally and internationally.

Hopevale School formally trialed the Queensland *New Basics* approach (Luke et al., 1999), an integrated approach to curriculum and pedagogy that engages students in the completion of "rich tasks" focused on community-based projects. New Basics sets out to reduce overall curriculum "outcomes" and move teaching and learning toward purposive, integrated projects that are formally assessed by state-wide panels and groups. These projects focus both curriculum organization and timetabling, attempting to construct cultural and social zones for the interactive production of artifacts. Thematically, "multi-literacies," "active citizenship," "environments and technologies," and "life pathways" are used as curriculum organizers, rather than traditional quasi-disciplinary subjects or "key learning areas." The "Computer Culture Project," part of Hopevale's participation in the New Basics trial, focused primary students' rich tasks on the collection and digital archiving of elders' stories, community histories, and narratives. Hopevale students recorded and distributed their own music to local and commercial radio stations. This has been linked to the production of design artwork, a marketing website, and a business plan to support local musicians and organize tours. School projects and student work in multiliteracies are profiled and distributed online.

Approaches such as this are not new. We find the grounds for such moves not just in contemporary debates over the mobilization of social capital (Fine, 2001), but also in the educational philosophies of Dewey and Freire. While it has generated heated political debate among Aboriginal leaders over its critique of social welfare, one feature of the Cape York strategy is that it attempts to re-situate the improvement of language and literacy, the reform of curriculum and pedagogy within an overall strategy of community mobilization. During the New Basics trial, several Aboriginal and Torres Strait Islander schools, including Hopevale, that had adopted the New Basics and a community partnership model reported improved attendance, higher levels of student engagement and community support, and no deterioration of basic skills levels as measured by standardized tests (for summaries, see Matters et al., 2004)

A Bourdieusian approach to communities as social fields with available sources and practices for the exchange of capital offers a sociological analysis for the use of governments, communities, and, indeed, business interests. It provides different grounds for "evidence" and "accountability" as the basis for social policy. That evidence would require comprehensive community profiles and audits of available capital, and their combinatory potentials, rather than just relying upon a single "thermometer" approach of test scores. Educational accountability could be redefined to gauge the institutional capacity and effectiveness of schools for the setting out of equitable and productive systems for the exchange and enhancement of capital.

A more sophisticated sociological and economic analysis would shape educational policy as a subset of larger policies of social justice and economic independence. The effect is to place a caveat under the "myth" that the improvement of pedagogy, curriculum, and student performance on a range of measures in and of themselves can have sustainable and meaningful consequences in people's trajectories across highly unstable and volatile, structurally unequal and asymmetrical social fields of exchange.

Literacy education and the realignment of capital

The scenario of disalignment of educational, social, and community services is a common one. Government may put a strong push on local nursing, health care, and hospital access, while at the same time failing to provide experienced teachers, relevant and quality learning materials, and innovative instructional approaches. Alternatively, health care might improve, but without an economic strategy for jobs and improved capital flows into the community, that care would largely go to mopping up the effects of difficult cultural and material conditions. Where and when effective coordination within the social fields of the community occurs, it tends to happen at the local level, through exchanges and negotiations between community elders, local service providers, families and so on. In this way, community empowerment and development suffers from a series of disalignments of capital that can be abetted by the uncoordinated and unprincipled investment of government and non-government money. At best this has the effect of balkanizing and compartmentalizing community development. Worse, it can lead to successive government "interventions," including the efforts of schools and teachers, with little visible synergistic impact on material conditions and cultural sustainability. At worst, it can lead to a cycle of victim-blaming where communities and families are blamed for their inability to capitalize upon projects and funding.

To assume that the problems of English language and literacy can be solved between the four walls of the classroom or school is another iteration of the literacy myth. If there were a theoretical and empirical flaw to current educational policy approaches, it was a strong belief that the finding of the right curriculum or pedagogical approach had the potential to "solve" the dilemmas of indigenous achievement. The logic of this argument both misrecognizes the problem as one of "achievement," rather than improved material, bodily, and cultural conditions, and misplaces the solution in "pedagogy" per se, rather than in the overlapping fields of capital exchange where pedagogy, schooling, and language use occur. With all good intentions, this approach has been consistently reproduced over the last decade in the introduction of "stand alone" educational interventions for Aboriginal children ranging from Reading Recovery to THRASS phonics programs to, most recently, functional communicative approaches to English as a Second Language/Dialect.

Basil Bernstein's (1972) controversial claim 30 years ago—that "education cannot compensate for society"—is a reminder that other kinds of economic, social, cultural, and symbolic capital need to be put into play before the full value of educationally acquired capital can be realized. Schools have the power to open access to dominant cultural capital through the curriculum and languages that they offer. It is established that particular forms of pedagogy that recognize difference and systematically bridge students' existing cultural capital with the mainstream forms of English language and literacy can indeed improve the acquisition of institutional capital, narrowly or broadly defined (McNaughton, 2002). In the case of Aboriginal education, the long-standing "two-way schooling" model recognized that these complex relationships between school and community, English and vernacular, Anglo/European and indigenous cultures were absolutely essential (Malcolm et al., 1999). Yet in many cases, there was little capacity for schools or teachers to effect an overall community coordination of the availability and exchange of different kinds of school-acquired capital.

Acquired literacy is one form of capital—contingent upon the availability of other forms of capital. The lesson for current policy is that early intervention in phonemic awareness and "alphabetics" in itself will not suffice. Direct and explicit instruction in the code in itself won't suffice. Literacy-in-education, language-in-education, and curriculum policies designed to ameliorate or modify the socioeconomic, cultural and social disadvantage experienced by those students, need to extend beyond the school to ensure that the viable conditions for the use and exchange of that capital is possible and probable. This was a prototypical lesson in late-twentieth century "third world" literacy campaigns, that educationally acquired habitus will, indeed, atrophy without gainful exchanges, or powerful and meaningful contexts of use (Arnove and Graff, 1987). Social, economic, and literacy education policies must work synergistically. They must go beyond "fixing classrooms" and focus co-equally on mobilizing and changing the social fields of community and institutional use.

References

Abedi, J. (2004) The No Child Left Behind Act and English language learners: assessment and accountability issues. *Educational Researcher*, 33, 4–14.

Allington, R. (2002) *Big Brother and the National Reading Curriculum: How Ideology Trumped Evidence*. New York: Heinemann.

Altman, J. C. (2000) *The Economic Status of Indigenous Australians* (Centre for Aboriginal Economic Policy Research Report 193). Canberra: Australian National University.

Altman, J. C. (2001) *Sustainable Development Options on Aboriginal Land: The Hybrid Economy in the Twenty-first Century* (Centre for Aboriginal Economic Policy Research Report 226). Canberra: Australian National University.

Anderson, B. (1992) *Imagined Communities*. London: Verso.

Apple, M. W. (2001) *Educating the "Right" Way*. London: RoutledgeFalmer.

Arnove, R. F. and Graff, H. J. (eds) (1987) *National Literacy Campaigns*. New York: Plenum.

Au, K. H. (1998) Social constructivism and the school literacy learning of students of diverse backgrounds. *Journal of Literacy Research*, 30, 297–319.

Barton, D., Ivanic, R. and Hamilton, M. (eds) (1999) *Situated Literacies*. London: Routledge.

Bernstein, B. (1972) A critique of the concept of compensatory education. In C. Cazden, V. John and D. Hymes (eds), *Functions of Language in the Classroom*. New York: Teachers College Press, 131–51.

Bourdieu: (1992) *Language and Symbolic Power* (J. Thompson, ed., G. Raymond and M. Adamson, trans.). Palo Alto, CA: Stanford University Press.

Bourdieu: (1998) *Acts of Resistance: Against the Tyranny of the Market* (R. Nice, trans.). Cambridge, UK: Polity Press.

Cohen, D. (2006) *Globalization and Its Enemies* (J. B. Baker, trans.). Boston: MIT Press.

Cohen, D. K., Raudenbush, S. W. and Ball, D. L. (2003) Resources, instruction and research. *Educational Evaluation and Policy Analysis*, 25, 119–42.

Cooper, H. (2005) Reading between the lines: observations on the report of the national reading panel and its critics. *Phi Delta Kappan*, 86, 456–60.

Department of Education, Training and Youth Affairs (2000) *The National Indigenous English Literacy and Numeracy Strategy (2000–2004)*. Canberra, Australia: Author.

Department of Education, Science and Technology (2001) *National Report on Schooling in Australia*. Canberra, Australia: Author.

Durgunoglu, A. Y. and Verhoeven, L. (eds) (1998) *Literacy Development in a Multicultural Context*. Mahwah, NJ: Lawrence Erlbaum Associates.

Evans, B. A. and Hornberger, N. H. (2005) No Child Left Behind: repealing and unpeeling federal language education policy in the United States. *Language Policy*, 4, 87–106.

Fine, B. (2001) *Social Capital Versus Social Theory*. London: Routledge.

Graff, H. A. (1979) *The Literacy Myth*. New York: Academic Press.

Graham: (2005) *Hypercapitalism*. New York: Peter Lang.

Kaplan, R. and Baldauf, R. (eds) (2003) *Language and Language in Education planning in the Pacific Basin*. Dordrecht, Netherlands: Kluwer.

Kellner, D. (1995) *Media Culture*. London: Routledge.

Larson, J. (ed.) (2001) *Literacy as Snake Oil*. New York: Peter Lang.

Lucas, S. (1999) *Tracking Inequality*. New York: Teachers College Press.

Luke, A. (1996) Genres of power: literacy education and the production of capital. In R. Hasan and G. Williams (eds), *Literacy in Society*. London: Longman, 308–38.

Luke, A. (1997) The material effects of the word: apologies, stolen children and public discourse. *Discourse*, 18, 343–68.

Luke, A. (2005) Evidence-based state literacy policy: a critical alternative. In N. Bascia, A. Cumming, A. Datnow, K. Leithwood and D. Livingstone (eds), *International Handbook of Educational Policy*. Dordrecht, Netherlands: Springer, 661–77.

Luke, A. and Luke, C. (2001) Adolescence lost/childhood regained: on early intervention and the emergence of the techno-subject. *Journal of Early Childhood Literacy*, 1, 145–80.

Luke, A., Freebody: and Land, R. (2000) *Literate Futures: Report of the Literacy Review for Queensland State Schools*. Brisbane, Australia: Education Queensland. Also available from the Queensland Government website: http://education.qld.gov.au/curriculum/learning/literate-futures

Luke, A., Land, R., Kolatsis, A., Christie, and Noblett, G. (2002) *Standard Australian English and Language for Queensland Aboriginal and Torres Strait Islander Students*. Brisbane, Australia: Queensland Indigenous Education Consultative Body.

Luke, A., Land, R., Matters, G., Land, R., Herschell, Barrett, R. et al. (1999) *New Basics Technical Papers*. Brisbane, Australia: Education Queensland. Also available from the Queensland Government website: http://education.qld.gov.au/corporate/newbasics

Luke, A., Woods, A., Land, R., Bahr, N. and McFarland, M. (2002) *Accountability: Inclusive Assessment, Monitoring and Reporting*. Brisbane, Australia: Queensland Indigenous Education Consultative Body.

Malcolm, I., Haig, Y., Konigsberg:, Rochecouste, J., Collard, G., Hill, A. et al. (1999) *Toward More User-friendly Education for Speakers of Aboriginal English*. Perth: Education Department of Western Australia.

Marks, G. N. and Ainley, J. (1997) *Reading Comprehension and Numeracy Among Junior Secondary School Students in Australia*. Melbourne, Victoria: Australian Council for Educational Research.

Matters, G. (2004) *Summary of the New Basics research findings*. Retrieved from http://education.qld.gov.au/corporate/newbasics/html/library.html

McNaughton, S. (2002) *Meeting of Minds*. Wellington, New Zealand: Learning Media.

National Institute of Child Health and Human Development (2000) *Report of the National Reading Panel* (NIH Publication No. 00–4769). Washington, DC: US Government Printing Office.

Newmann, F. and Associates. (1996) *Authentic Assessment*. San Francisco: Jossey-Bass.

Pearson, N. (2006) The gammon economy. *The Australian*, May 2, 11.

Street, B. V. (1984) *Literacy in Theory and Practice*. Cambridge, UK: Cambridge University Press.

Vasquez, V. (2004) *Negotiating Critical Literacies with Young Children*. Mahwah, NJ: Lawrence Erlbaum Associates.

Weis, L., McCarthy, C. and Dimitriadis, G. (eds) (2006) *Ideology, Curriculum and the New Sociology of Education*. New York: Routledge.

Postscript

James Collins

I shall begin by thanking the editors of this volume for the invitation to reflect upon and engage with the work of Pierre Bourdieu and the many interesting articles which comprise this collection. I will be able to treat neither to the extent they deserve. Instead, what follows says some general things about Bourdieu's work and this collection of articles, staying within what I take to be familiar terrain. It then turns to less noticed themes which are present in much of Bourdieu's work on education, and on social inheritance more generally, and which have relevance for how we think about literacy, schooling, and society.

Bourdieu's oeuvre is justly celebrated for being empirically ambitious—it ranged from studies of Kabyle/Berber tribesmen (1977), to analyses of French higher education (1988) and contemporary culture (1984), to analyses of photography, sport, and religion as fields of culture and arenas of social domination. It was also lauded for its theoretical ambitions—whether in books such as *Reproduction in Education, Culture, and Society* (Bourdieu and Passeron, 1977), *The Logic of Practice* (1990), *Distinction* (1984), or *Language and Symbolic Power* (1991), Bourdieu continually grappled with the problem of constraint and human action, what are variously called "structuration," "reproduction," or "practice theory." It would be sufficient that Bourdieu's reputation rests on his commitments to both substantive empirical work and probing theoretical argument, but there was another aspect, which came into view most clearly in the last decade of his life. He was also a politically principled and outspoken public intellectual. His slim volume, *Acts of Resistance* (1998), is a compilation of speeches and addresses given at trade union gatherings, anti-racist demonstrations, and anti-globalization rallies. His message was the need to resist neoliberal doctrine and social policy, which he saw as the reigning ideology of the current era and the latest program for the enrichment of the rich. The massive collaborative volume, *The Weight of the World* (Bourdieu et al., 1999), is, as the subtitle indicates, an analysis of "social suffering in contemporary society," whether in prisons, among the ranks of the unemployed, immigrants facing social exclusion, or, most pertinently to our concerns, among those who teach and learn and fail and fight in the expanded post-1960s educational systems.

There is in Bourdieu's *oeuvre* not just range and ambition, but also nuance and subtlety. One of his last works, entitled *Masculine Domination* (2001), is an application of the concept of the habitus to an analysis of patriarchal structures and practices. It argues that patriarchy informs not just our institutions and our interactions but the most basic forms of our consciousness; it ends by arguing that women must be more radical, not less, in the struggle for their liberation. It also contains a brief postscript "On domination and love," which is both moving and clear-headed. *Masculine Domination* continues, as Kramsch's contribution to this volume reminds us, Bourdieu's long engagement with the affective: emotion, feeling, suffering. I will return to this later, after taking up more familiar themes.

Key concepts and their applications

Bourdieu's wide-ranging work continually developed an account of three key concepts—those of capital, field, and habitus.

Briefly, his arguments about *capital* were that economic capital (that is, wealth and income), cultural capital (predominantly but not exclusively, amount and kind of education), and social capital (that is, connections in various social arenas) were primary ways in which conditions of social inequality were organized and transmitted. The capital concept has been presented in brief definitional essays (1986) and extensive empirical accounts (Bourdieu, 1984, 1988, 1993; Bourdieu and Passeron, 1997). It has been the object of various critical responses (e.g. Erickson, 1996), and has been the subject of lively debates in literacy research, as discussed at length in Albright's contribution to this volume (Chapter 2). Other contributions, such as those by Curry (Chapter 14) and Goldstein (Chapter 11), illustrate various potentials of the concept. In Curry's analysis of basic English classes for second language learners, the concept of capital guides an analysis of the role of prior education and social class position in differentiating among people who are the same—"immigrant second-language learners"—yet whose strategies for dealing with classrooms, and success in those classrooms, are quite distinct. In Goldstein's contribution, the utility of viewing knowledge of particular languages as linguistic capital is nicely illustrated, but it is in her analysis of the "capital of attentive silence" that we receive what I take to be best of a Bourdieusian legacy: attention not just to forms of hierarchy but also to dilemmas posed by social positions and pathways; an ethnographic alertness to that which is not yet articulated by our concepts (in this case, what is the relation between linguistic capital and silence?) and thus forces a rethinking of both empirical materials and analytic constructs.

Bourdieu's second major concept, *field*, was an effort to think about society not as a fixed or static hierarchy of institutions with, say, the economy determining the political or religious, but rather society as a set of arenas in which actors would compete. Thus he analyzed the political field (1984), the educational field (1988), the religious field (1991), and also the field of sports

(1988) and that of literary production (1993), as arenas in which there were struggles to define what was most important, and thus to gain advantage, as individuals and groups, *by defining what is most valuable*. Consider, for example, the contemporary educational field in the United States, more particularly the field of literacy, in which university-based academic researchers, elected officials, and variously funded think tanks contend to define what is the best literacy pedagogy and to stipulate via state guidelines and funding criteria what is to be taught and measured, what is to be "legitimate literacy" (Allington, 2002; American Federation of Teachers, 1999; Luke, 2004; National Reading Panel, 2000). There are two points relevant here. First, that to enter a field requires capital, in this case the academic and political capital of those who struggle to define the field. Second, as Bourdieu emphasized, fields have their own autonomy, but there is always also a connection with fields of the economy and power, that is, with the distribution of resources. This has been quite clear recently in countries such as the United States, the United Kingdom, Australia, and New Zealand, where the political field has dominated the academic field in the struggle to define "what is literacy?"

Field dynamics and their relevance for language and literacy pedagogy are instructively treated in Uhlmann's contribution to this volume, "The Field of Arabic Instruction in the Zionist State" (Chapter 6). In this study we learn that Arabic language instruction in Israel has official support and is codified in national education policy; in theory it is an official language, like Hebrew. But the policy is bizarrely implemented. Unlike English, another large, contemporary "foreign" language in Israeli schools, Arabic is taught as a dead language, to be read, not spoken; taught by non-native (Jewish Israeli) instructors, often with a minimal command of the language; and it is an elective course which is often omitted from the actual rather than fictive curricula of schools. The reasons have to do both with the internal dynamics of the field of Arabic instruction, "the poverty of Arabic proficiency among teachers—both at university and at school—reproduces itself down the generations. . . . Departments that lack Arabic proficiency produce graduates who lack proficiency" (Uhlmann, Chapter 6) and with a cross-field dynamic of Zionist mobilization, "the state structure and a myriad of semi-official Jewish bodies seek to mobilise and organise Jews" (pp. 197, 198) against Arabs, and in this case, against Arabic instruction. What Uhlmann calls a "public secret" that official policy is ignored and subverted arises from grassroots political mobilization in tandem with state support. It reminds us that "agency" can be ugly: Jewish Israeli hatred and mistreatment of Arabs is not a pretty sight. It instructs us also that we cannot assume, as Bourdieu sometimes argued, that there will necessarily be an homology or structural equivalence between fields (on this last, see Gross, 1993; Haeri, 1997; Woolard, 1985, for studies of multilingual nations in which field-plus-capital interactions do not follow the predicted field integration, in which the "legitimate" language dominates in political, economic, and cultural fields).

In recent years, it is Bourdieu's concept of the *habitus* that has informed much educational research. The concept was Bourdieu's way of understanding agents as socially inculcated, as significantly constrained in their ways and means, and yet as actors who are not automata in a self-perpetuating social machinery. Variously described as "embodied social structure," "embodied history," and "a virtue made of necessity," habitus is conceived as a social legacy which lives on in agents' frameworks of perception and action. It is key to Bourdieu's understanding of practice. Socially conditioned, the habitus is not simply deterministic, for it operates in a practical world which requires improvisation. In various works containing substantial arguments about the construct, such as *Outline of a Theory of Practice* (1977) and *Distinction* (1984), habitus mediates between the global level of objective structures, the differences of resources, and the local level of agents' strategies, that is, what we would call "situated action." In *Distinction*, for example, Bourdieu attributes to the dispositions and embodied classification schemes of habitus the tendency for students from differing class backgrounds to read and misread the academic market in relation to the wider job market. Habitus *qua* socially inculcated disposition is integral to his analysis of downward mobility, a subject I return to below. Bourdieu and Passeron's *Reproduction* had attributed to class habitus the disposition to assume that you are simply expected and entitled to higher education versus the pre-conscious fear that you will probably fail, leading to dropping out and other forms of educational self-exclusion. Those polarized dispositions have much to do with distinctive styles of living, and they result in decisions and acts in the educational arena which are both conditioned and "freely" chosen.

Recent work in anthropology, in particular the psychological anthropology of Holland and contributors (Holland et al., 1998), has emphasized the production and transformation of habitus, seeing it as a fundamental but not finally determinate aspect of the formation of identity and personhood. This more situated, constructivist emphasis is shared with Scollon's (2001) work on practice as the interface of communication, cognition, and identity. The emphasis on the person is found also in the two treatments of habitus in this volume.

The habitus, whether those of class or gender or other principle of social difference, is initially acquired in the home. Pahl's analysis of family literacy practices, "Tracing Habitus in Texts" (Chapter 10), is an innovative attempt to use the habitus concept to think about how practices are embedded or, in her words, "sedimented" in texts. As I understand it, her argument is that texts contain traces of the social interactions that led to their production and which frame their interpretation. This argument is similar to poststructuralist (Derrida, 1976) and linguistic anthropological (Silverstein and Urban, 1996) arguments about text, and I think it is an important step in enabling us to see texts, and literacy, as a process. Focusing upon the production of texts in homes, Pahl offers a refreshingly broad view of texts—including maps, collections of family memorabilia, and the stories which pertain thereto—suggesting how the habitus concept might figure into the analysis of this type of domestic-discursive activity, a form of cultural production which is also a production of person, in the messy, provisional world where, in Williams' (1989) phrase "culture is ordinary."

Rowsell, in "Improvising an Artistic Habitus" (Chapter 12), also follows the direction of Holland and colleagues, emphasizing the interplay between habitus and practices. In particular she examines how for three Canadian art education students, their artistic production is connected to a changing sense of who they are, as evidenced both in the artistic objects they make and in the things they say about those objects. The account strikes me as plausible—peoples' past experiences influence their preoccupations and (artistic) production—and it seems also a sensible way of thinking about identity practices. I wonder, however, how such accounts relate larger art markets and social fields to what Bourdieu called capital, economic, cultural or other. In Bourdieu's study of *The Field of Cultural Production* (1993), he strongly emphasized the role of class background on artistic trajectories, and on the direct and inverse relations between artistic hierarchies and art markets. Rowsell notes this, but it does not figure in her analysis. We do not know where "arts education" fits vis-à-vis the market for art, commercial or "pure," or whether her students' career pathways are typical or aberrant. Such information, it seems to me, would provide useful information on constraints as well as improvisations in the dynamic of habitus-and-practice.

The larger issue, and I will note it only in passing, is that for Bourdieu, capital in its variants, fields, and the "markets" they took form in, and the habitus and its trajectories, were related constructs for understanding social structure and history in practice. I think that we pull the conceptual edifice apart for various reasons—focusing on capital or field because it seems most appropriate to what we are investigating; analyzing habitus on its own allows us to downplay the determinism that was part of Bourdieu's understanding of the social—but in so doing we risk losing the dynamism of his social analysis and theory: the challenge of understanding improvisation *and* constraint. This view is developed in Albright's "Problematics and Generative Possibilities" (Chapter 2), which also argues that the key concepts—capital, habitus, and field—need to be taken together if we wish to realize the full value of a Bourdieusian perspective on literacy, which is to resolutely ground literacy in the social (rather than the pedagogical). Kramsch (Chapter 3) makes a similar argument regarding the neglect of field dynamics.

The limits and costs of schooling and literacy

This concern brings me to a theme, consistently present in Bourdieu's work but somehow often forgotten when this work is taken up in educational research, including research on literacy, which is that schooling, historically based on a separation of education and learning from the exigencies of making a living, is nonetheless inextricably tied to society and culture. In the somewhat clunky phrasing of American status mobility sociology, this has been termed "the limits of schooling." Numerous syntheses of statistical studies examining the contributions of family socioeconomic status, IQ and testable scholastic aptitude, teacher quality, curriculum, and school characteristics (class size, materials, funding levels) have all asked the question: "How much does schooling contribute to life chances?" And the answer, consistently, has been "Not much." In the United States this has been reiterated by research for the past four decades—ranging from the foundational *Coleman Report* (Campbell and Coleman, 1982) through Jencks' *Inequality* (1972), to the more recent debates about "the black-white test score gap" (Jencks and Phillips, 1998; Rothstein, 2004)—all of which report that schooling accounts at most for 10–15 percent of the variation between the socioeconomic positions obtained by persons and the positions predicted most directly by their family background.

Bourdieu phrased this basic social structural constraint on educational possibility in numerous ways; it underpinned his unwavering recognition that society and culture are always present in the pedagogical encounter, however "hidden" or "misrecognized." He stated his view through reminders in *Reproduction* that the limits of pedagogical reform were set not by educationist effort and intention but by the state of class relations. As Bourdieu and Passeron wrote regarding the desire to transform "the literate tradition and social conservation" by curriculum reform: "In short, only a school system serving another system of external functions and, correlatively, another state of the balance of power between the classes, could make such pedagogic action possible" (1977: 127). Bourdieu demonstrated this constraint in *Distinction*, by exhaustively exploring the ways in which social and economic capital channeled academic choices and subsequent job market experiences (see the section on capital "reconversion strategies", pp. 125–68). He did so also, of course, through his wide-ranging research program, developing and applying concepts of capital, field, and habitus in ways that allow us to better explore the interplay of social position, cultural value, and educational practice. That is why his work still speaks to those of us who would understand literacy in "the social" of the twenty-first century.

But for those of us, and here I include myself as well as many contributors to this volume, who are neither inclined to take up nor skilled in handling macrosociological studies of the school–society relation, I would reiterate Bourdieu's repeated injunctions that taking account of such quantitative material is essential to understanding the "social space" and its structure of possibilities. In this regard, it is striking that in Grant and Wong's otherwise valuable and spirited discussion of race, class, and second language education (Chapter 9), all of their proposals for reform are proposals for curriculum and school reform, as if the pedagogic institution by itself established the hierarchy of languages which they wish to transform in the name of a more equitable world. In this light, it is instructive to consult Heller's schematic ("somewhat breathless" is her description) analysis of the concepts of literacy and skill in the contemporary era. It reminds us to attend to wider political economic dynamics that shape what counts as "legitimate language" as well as educated persons. We should also pay heed to Luke's frequent reminders, in his contributions to this book as well as elsewhere (Luke, 2004), that school reforms do not replace the need for broader social struggles, that curriculum improvements cannot substitute for social policy, or as he puts it regarding the Anglophone literacy debates, "you can't eat phonics" (p. 11).

In a recent book, *Class and Schools*, the economist Rothstein (2004) has said this regarding the limits of schooling and literacy or, put otherwise, regarding the significance of material conditions for teaching and learning:

> One of the great impediments to effective policies that might enhance more equal outcomes between children of different social class background is the tendency of educators to think only about school reforms. In reality, however, for lower-class families, low wages for working parents with children, poor health care, inadequate housing, and lack of opportunity for high-quality early childhood, after-school and summer activities are all educational problems. When a parent's earned income falls, or a parent loses a job, there are educational consequences for their children. Educators who are concerned about the educational consequences should not fail to take notice of the economic and social conditions that cause poor school performance. As citizens who are more informed about these matters than most, educators should not hesitate to call attention to the consequences for children's achievement of the social and economic hardships their families suffer.
>
> (p. 130)

Because of the range of his thinking, the systematic nature of his exposition, the painstaking way in which he combined statistical and ethnographic inquiry, and his numerous explorations of the role of power, it is easy to miss Bourdieu's concern with the place of emotion and feeling in human affairs. It is to Kramsch's credit that her "biographical memoir" about Bourdieu reminds us of his abiding interest in the affective, ranging from his initial dissertation topic, "Temporal Structures of Affective Experience," to his formulating the concept of symbolic violence to capture the fact that domination produces "deep personal distress" (Kramsch, Chapter 3).

The Marxist literary and social analyst Raymond Williams was, like Bourdieu, a "scholarship boy," or in French terms, an *oblat miracule*. Also like Bourdieu, he refused the clichés of educational "improvement" and "self-made men," remaining instead always aware of the social divide marked by education in a class-divided society, and that this division went to the very fibers of one's being (what William's termed "structures of feeling" and

Bourdieu "habitus"). In an illuminating essay on the social history of English prose, Williams says of the novelist Thomas Hardy and his work that he was a:

> man caught by his personal history in the general crisis of the relation between education and class. What this crisis comes out as, in real terms, is the relation between intelligence and fellow-feeling, but this relation in the nineteenth and twentieth centuries had to be worked out at a time *when education was consciously used to train members of a class and to divide them from their own passions as surely as from other men* [emphasis added]: the two processes, inevitably, are deeply connected.
>
> (1983: 106)

Education as separation from others and alienation from one's feelings is a recurring theme in those infrequent works that clearly record the costs of becoming educated. These are works, often memoirs, that avoid the clichéd celebration of social "salvation" through schooling and literacy (see Collins and Blot, 2003, Chapter 5, for a fuller discussion). They include Steedman's (1987) *Landscape for a Good Woman*, which describes with unsentimental clarity the difficulties of literate self-understanding for a girl whose life did not fit the models of the English scholarship boys; whose home, headed by a bitter, downwardly mobile mother, did not encourage fantasies of female or class solidarity. They include Gilyard's (1991) *Voices of the Self*, which traces an African-American boy's experience of early desegregation, a trajectory leading from Harlem to Syracuse University, but with a spell in the Ryker's Island jail. It calls for a full-throated linguistic hybridity, a blending of vernacular sources with school-based "literacy sets," but it acknowledges the substantial psychic toll of his pathways to legitimate language. He says of educating contemporary African-American youth, that one should never do them the disrespect of "sell[ing] myths of simple assimilation" (p. 74). Rose's (1989) *Lives on the Boundary* is both a memoir of his own life and education, and a generous proposal for changing assumptions about literacy and curricula in order to welcome immigrant, minority, and working-class students, the traditionally under-prepared, across the educational "boundary." It describes acutely the relation between class and education, as in the following, from the book's introduction:

> There are some things about my early life, I see now, that are reflected in other working-class lives I've encountered: the isolation of neighborhoods, information poverty, the limited means of protecting children from family disaster, the predominance of such disaster, the resilience of imagination, the intellectual curiosity and literate enticements that remain hidden from the schools, the feelings of scholastic inadequacy, *the dislocations that come from crossing educational boundaries.*
>
> (p. 9, emphasis added)

The theme of dislocation is perceptively treated in Bourdieu's (1984) account of "reconversion strategies," that is, how adeptly or awkwardly people use education pathways to jobs in a changing, post-1960s economy. It is particularly shown in his analysis of the consequences of "degree inflation" for working-class students who have persevered in higher education, only to find that lack of social connections and a "feel" for the job market leaves them in positions they thought they had escaped:

> These young people, whose social identity and self-image have been undermined by a social system and an educational system that have fobbed them off with worthless paper, can find no other way of restoring their personal and social integrity than by a total refusal. . . . A whole generation, finding it has been taken for a ride, is inclined to extend to all institutions the mixture of revolt and resentment it feels toward the educational system.
>
> (p. 144)

And even those who achieve upward rather than downward mobility must pay a price. There is currently much academic talk about "borders" as zones of creative exchange. But crossing borders can be an irrevocable act. What Rose calls "dislocations" frequently entail a renunciation of the past. Here is Bourdieu on the cost of an internalized class division:

> Anyone who wants to "succeed in life" must pay for his accession . . . having internalized the class struggle, which is at the very heart of culture, he is condemned to shame, horror, even hatred of the old Adam, his language, his body, and his tastes, and of everything he is bound to, his roots, his family, his peers, sometimes even his mother tongue.
>
> (p. 251)

The historian of literacy, Graff (1987), has remarked that faith in the progressive powers of literacy remains one of the most enduring myths of an otherwise much undermined liberal optimism. We need to disabuse ourselves of the sentimental view that language and knowledge lead along frictionless pathways to social betterment. Literacy and education are always selective, and acquiring competencies in recognized or "legitimate" varieties of language often comes at a cost to oneself and one's origins. Let us call this the cost of schooling. I have dwelt at length on the themes of the "limits" and "costs" of education because education researchers should not accept the self-definition of the institution they study. Schooling and literacy are not about "success for all," they are deeply implicated in the processes of social, cultural, and educational reproduction that Bourdieu and his collaborators help us to better understand. Literacy "in the social" is not a bloodless affair of light seen and salvation accepted, nor is it simply a matter of power and resistance; like language, literacy embeds relations between classes, races, and genders. Those relations shape and engage our passions as well as our thoughts and deeds. Our efforts to understand and represent the worlds of literacy should reflect this Bourdieusian lesson.

References

Allington, R. (ed.) (2002) *Big Brother and the National Reading Curriculum*. Portsmouth, NH: Heinemann.

American Federation of Teachers (1999) *Teaching Reading is Rocket Science*. New York: Author.

Bourdieu, P. (1977) *Outline of a Theory of Practice*. Cambridge, UK: Cambridge University Press.

Bourdieu, P. (1984) *Distinction*. Cambridge, MA: Harvard University Press.

Bourdieu, P. (1988) *Homo Academicus*. Cambridge, UK: Polity Press.

Bourdieu, P. (1990) *The Logic of Practice*. Stanford, CA: Stanford University Press.

Bourdieu, P. (1991) *Language and Symbolic Power*. Cambridge, MA: Harvard University Press.

Bourdieu, P. (1993) *The Field of Cultural Production*. New York: Columbia University Press.

Bourdieu, P. (1998) *Acts of Resistance*. New York: New Press.

Bourdieu, P. (2001) *Masculine Domination*. Stanford, CA: Stanford University Press.

Bourdieu, P. and Passeron, J. (1977) *Reproduction in Education, Society and Culture*. Beverly Hills, CA: Sage.

Bourdieu, P. et al. (1999) *The Weight of the World: Social Suffering in contemporary Society*. Stanford, CA: Stanford University Press.

Campbell, E. and Coleman, J. (1982) Inequalities in educational opportunities in the United States. In E. Bredo and W. Feinberg (eds), *Knowledge and Values in Social and Educational Research*. Philadelphia, PA: Temple University Press, 88–98.

Collins, J. and Blot, R. K. (2003) Literacies and identity formation: American cases. In J. Collins and R. K. Blot (eds), *Literacy and Literacies: Texts, Power, and Identity*. Cambridge, UK: Cambridge University Press, 99–120.

Derrida, J. (1976) *Of Grammatology*. Baltimore, MD: Johns Hopkins University Press.

Erickson, B. (1996) Culture, class, and connections. *American Journal of Sociology*, 102, 217–51.

Gilyard, K. (1991) *Voices of the Self*. Detroit, MI: Wayne State University Press.

Graff, H. (1987) *The Legacies of Literacy*. Bloomington: Indiana University Press.

Gross, J. (1993) The politics of unofficial language use: Walloon in Belgium, Tamazight in Morocco. In J. Collins (ed.), Language, nationalism, and political economy [special issue], *Critique of Anthropology*, 13, 177–208.

Haeri, N. (1997) The reproduction of symbolic capital: language, state and class in Egypt. *Current Anthropology*, 38, 795–816.

Holland, D., Lachicotte, W., Skinner, D. and Cain, C. (1998) *Identity and Agency in Cultural Worlds*. Cambridge, MA: Harvard University Press.

Jencks, C. (1972) *Inequality*. Cambridge, MA: Harvard University Press.

Jencks, C. and M. Phillips (eds) (1998) *The Black-White Test Score Gap*. Washington, DC: Brookings Institute.

Luke, A. (2004) Literacy and educational fundamentalism: an interview with Allan Luke. *English Quarterly*, 36, 12–17.

National Reading Panel (2000) Teaching children to read: an evidence-based assessment of scientific research literature on reading and its implications for reading instruction. Retrieved August 23, 2005 from www.nationalreadingpanel.org

Rose, M. (1989) *Lives on the Boundary*. New York: Penguin.

Rothstein, R. (2004) *Class and Schools*. New York: Teachers College Press.

Scollon, R. (2001) *Mediated Discourse*. New York: Routledge.

Silverstein, M. and Urban, G. (1996) *Natural Histories of Discourse*. Chicago: University of Chicago Press.

Steedman, C. (1987) *Landscape for a Good Woman*. London: Virago Press.

Williams, R. (1983) Notes on English prose: 1780–1950. In *Writing in Society*. London: Verso, 67–118.

Williams, R. (1989) Culture is ordinary. In R. Gale (ed.), *Resources of Hope: Culture, Democracy, Socialism*. London: Verso, 3–18.

Woolard, K. A. (1985) Language variation and cultural hegemony: toward an integration of sociolinguistic and social theory. *American Ethnologist*, 12(4): 738–48.

Index